Constructing Post-Colonial India

The Doon School, a famous boarding school for boys in India, inculcates in its students the notion that to be post-colonial is to be rational, secular, and metropolitan. The School numbers many of India's political, social, and intellectual elite among its former students; its code of conduct for the modern Indian citizen has been extremely influential.

In this detailed and engaging study, Sanjay Srivastava digs deep to find the roots of the ideological construction of post-coloniality in India. The Doon School is the site of his analysis but his work ranges far beyond the School itself. He uses historical sources, ethnographic fieldwork, and perspectives from cultural theory to question the prevailing theoretical positions of post-colonial studies, arguing that post-coloniality is meaningless unless it is located in historical, social, and cultural space.

Sanjay Srivastava trained as a social anthropologist and is presently senior lecturer in the School of Literary and Communication Studies at Deakin University, Melbourne, Australia.

D1614594

Culture and communication in Asia
Edited by David Birch
Deakin University, Australia

Trajectories: Inter-Asia Cultural Studies
Edited by Kuan-Hsing Chen

The Politics of Chinese Language and Culture
The art of reading dragons
Bob Hodge and Kam Louie

Constructing Post-Colonial India

National character and the Doon School

Sanjay Srivastava

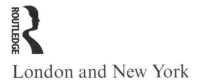

London and New York

First published 1998
by Routledge
11 New Fetter Lane, London EC4P 4EE

Simultaneously published in the USA and Canada
by Routledge
29 West 35th Street, New York, NY 10001

Typeset in Times by RefineCatch Limited, Bungay, Suffolk
Printed and bound in Great Britain by
TJ International Ltd, Padstow, Cornwall

British Library Cataloguing in Publication Data
A catalogue record for this book is available from the British Library

Library of Congress Cataloging in Publication Data
Srivastava, Sanjay
    Constructing Post-Colonial India: National character and the
Doon School / Sanjay Srivastava.
        p.   cm. – (Culture and communication in Asia)
    Includes bibliographical references and index.
    1. India – Civilization – 1947– 2. National characteristics, East
Indian. 3. Doon School. 4. Postcolonialism – India. I. Title.
II. Series.
DS428.2.S77   1998
954.04 – dc21   98–9383
                                 CIP

ISBN 0 415 17855 X (hbk)
ISBN 0 415 17856 8 (pbk)

For my parents, and Radha and Ishana-Rahin

Contents

Figures and tables

Figures

Tables

Series editor's foreword

Critical scholarship in cultural and communication studies world-wide has resulted in an increased awareness of the need to reconsider some of the more traditional research practices and theoretical/analytic domains of arts, humanities and social science disciplines, towards a recognition of the differing imperatives of what critical studies of culture and communication might look like in an Asian context. The demands for research materials, undergraduate textbooks and postgraduate monographs grow and expand with this increased critical awareness, while developments across the world continue to recognise the need to situate work in communication and cultural studies on and in Asia within a more global framework.

This series is designed to contribute to those demands and recognition. It is aimed at looking in detail at cultural and communication studies from critical perspectives which take into account different 'Asian' imperatives. In particular, it focuses on work written by scholars either living in or working on the region, who have specific interests in opening up new agendas for what constitutes critical communication and cultural studies within and about Asia. The overall aims of the series are to present new work, new paradigms, new theoretical positions, and new analytic practices of what might often be traditional and well-established communication and cultural activities and discourses.

The theoretical direction of the series is principally targeted at establishing these new agendas and by critically reflecting upon the appropriateness, or otherwise, of theories and methodologies already well established, or developing, in cultural and communication studies across the world. Having said this, however, the series is not aimed at producing a monolithic blueprint for what constitutes critical cultural and communication studies in or about Asia. Nor is there a specific agenda for what the series might consider to be an appropriate critical cultural and communication studies for Asia.

The series is not, therefore, designed to create an orthodoxy for 'Asian' communication and cultural studies, but to open up new ways of thinking and rethinking contemporary cultural and communication practice and analysis in the arts, humanities, and social sciences. The series is aimed to counter, as much as possible, those essentialising processes of colonialisation, marginalisation, and erasure, which have taken place in the past by the unproblematised imposition of western theory upon cultures, societies, and practices within, and on behalf of, Asia.

Many of the books in this series may not necessarily fit comfortably into traditional disciplines and paradigms of Asian studies of cultural and communication studies, and nor are they intended to. The main aim of the series is for all of its books to argue for a diversification and opening up of existing theoretical positions and specific discourses across a wide range of texts, practices, and cultures. All of the books in the series will be positioned to argue persuasively for the development of studies in culture and communication which are able to frame critical commentary through theoretical and analytic practices informed first and foremost by a concern with Asian cultures and discourse.

The series has as its fundamental premise a position which argues that analysts can no longer operate as neutral, disinterested, observers of some 'reality' which supposedly pre-exists the discourses that they are analysing. To be critical necessarily means to be self-reflexive. In that sense, then, the series is designed to position cultural and communication studies in and about Asia as critical disciplines which require, within their own practices, an approach to developing some sort of praxis that enables the work that we do as analysts to contribute significantly to political, social, and cultural discourses and awareness, at the local, regional, and global levels.

Series editor: David Birch, Deakin University, Australia

Editorial advisers:
Ien Ang, Murdoch University, Australia
Tony Bennett, Griffith University, Australia
Chen Kuan Hsing, National Tsing Hwa University, Taiwan
Jae-Woong Choe, Korea University, Korea
Chua Beng Huat, National University of Singapore, Singapore
Lawrence Grossberg, University of North Carolina, Chapel Hill, USA
Sneja Gunew, University of Victoria, Canada
Annette Hamilton, Macquarie University, Australia
Ariel Heryanto, Universitas Kristen Satya Wacana, Indonesia
Masao Miyoshi, University of California, San Diego, USA
Yoshinobu Ota, University of Kyushu, Japan
Gyanendra Pandey, University of Delhi, India
Ubonrat Siriyuvasak, Chulalongkorn University, Thailand
Panuti Sudjiman, University of Indonesia, Indonesia
Trinh T Minh-ha, University of California, Berkeley, USA
Yao Souchou, Institute of Southeast Asian Studies, Singapore
Robert Young, Wadham College, Oxford, UK

Acknowledgements

This book has been made possible by the advice and friendship of a number of people. I thank the following in Australia: Gillian Cowlishaw, Jeremy Beckett, Tom Ernst, Dale Gietzelt, Peter Hinton, Bruce Kapferer, David MacDougall, Neil Maclean, Jim Masselos, Robin McLachlan, Kim Paul, Viv and Alex Kondos, Alison Leitch, Steve Relf, Michael Roberts, Joy Wallace, and Kerry Zubernich. Parts of this research were funded by the Carlyle Greenwell Bequest. Thanks also to Michael Allen for extraordinary support, and to Dipesh Chakrabarty for kind advice and well-aimed criticism. David Birch's encouragement was an invaluable spur and I thank him for advice on various matters. John Tulloch's input into my work and Marian Tulloch's help in securing time off teaching is also gratefully acknowledged. Finally, I wish to register my gratitude to Kerrie Drew, Janice Lamb, and (especially) Jenny Montgomerie for crucial secretarial assistance.

A sincere word of thanks as well to Elizabeth Gant, Victoria Smith, James Whiting, and Christina Heward-Mills at Routledge for their patience, understanding, and helpfulness in seeing the manuscript to publication. I wish also to thank the two anonymous reviewers who commented on the manuscript.

Without the friendship and support and input of the following people in India, this research would simply have been impossible: Shomie and Feroza Das, Mr A.N. Dar, Mr H.L. Datt, Ela Ghose, Sumit Guha-Thakurta, Becky and Binoo John, S.K. Kandhari, Manju Khan and K.J. Parel, Uma Khan, Krishna Kumar, Piyush Malviya, Ashis Nandy, our extended family of Sheema and Jhampan Mukherji (and Toppa and Munia), Madhusudan, Ashok and Shreya Pandey, Sumer and Meera Singh, and the helpful staff at the National Archives of India, New Delhi.

My parents have been a great source of support for my work and it is my sorrow that my father is no longer here to see the outcome of the effort of the last five years or so.

Our Bathurst family of Helen, Len, and Siobhán have, I need hardly add, contributed in immeasurable ways to this book. Finally, it remains for me to acknowledge the patience, encouragement, and support of Radha Khan, without whom this work would not have seen the light of day for many, many years. She not only relieved me of many of my responsibilities with respect to house-work and caring for our daughter Ishana-Rahin, but also found time to read portions of the manuscript. I thank her for all this and more.

Some of the chapters in this work have appeared in earlier versions in: *Economic and Political Weekly*, *Social Analysis*, *Social Semiotics*, *South Asia*, and *The Australian Journal of Anthropology*.

Introduction: the seductions of capital

Of all the seductions capital could offer post-coloniality, that of a new *cultural* identity was perhaps the most sumptuous. And, with further largesse, the combined enterprise between capital and post-coloniality hummed the incantatory tones of an additional promise: the manufacture of the immortal community, the nation. This book seeks to explore the cultural elaboration in the Indian context of certain cross-cultural phenomena of our time: it is concerned with the minutiae of post-coloniality in general, and the 'nation-building' project in particular. The underlying analytical focus is the manner of articulation of a regime of post-colonial capital with the cultural-politics of post-coloniality.

And, though the focus of this study is an Indian public school ('public', in the contrary British sense of 'private'), my chief interest does not lie in the mechanics of the classroom or in that stream of the sociology of education concerned with innovations in pedagogical methods. My primary intent, above everything else, is to provide an ethnography of Indian modernity. I lay no claims to attempt to 'speak in the "objective" voice of history' (Chatterjee 1986: 52), nor to the 'dispassionate' demeanour of a 'scientific' attitude; for what follows constitutes a *political* engagement with politico-cultural assemblages which challenge us to take sides. The intellectual and ethical inspiration for the spirit of this engagement has come from many sources. It is admirably summarised, however, by Partha Chatterjee's comment that:

> The critical analysis of nationalist thought is also necessarily an interven-
> tion in a political discourse of our own time. ... Thus analysis itself
> becomes politics; interpretation acquires the undertone of a polemic. In
> such circumstances, to pretend to speak in the 'objective' voice of history
> is to dissimulate. By marking our own texts with the signs of battle, we
> [may] go a little further towards a more open and self-aware discourse.
>
> (Chatterjee 1986: 52)

I do not, then, claim this work to be an anthropology, sociology or history of an entire society, but only of a section of that society. The subject matter of this book – post-coloniality, modernity, citizenship – is part of the discourse of a narrow segment of the Indian population and my focus is on that segment; though small in numbers, this segment has played an important role in manufacturing representations of 'India' in the contemporary period. Further, given that to speak of representations is to speak of a contested field of social facts – about the career of truths rather than truth itself – Aijaz Ahmad's recent caveat may serve as an epigraph to the argument of this book. 'To think of the portrait of rulers as a portrait of the country itself', Ahmad says, 'is an error . . . not only of politics . . . but also of the social imagination' (Ahmad 1994: 151).

In 1974, Alfred de Souza, author of an 'intensive sociological study' of Indian public schools, noted that his study was 'the first of its kind' in as much as it attempted to present, 'on the basis of empirical data, a systematic and comprehensive sociological analysis of Indian public schools' (de Souza 1974: 8). De Souza hoped to 'avoid polemical considerations' and concentrate, instead, on 'the central purpose' of his study – which was to 'explain in sociological terms the social and cultural structure of [Indian] public schools as elite institutions of secondary education, and to discuss their relationship with the wider society of which they form a part' (*ibid.*). On several counts, the objects of my own study differ considerably from those that animated de Souza's research. Not least of these is his implied stricture against 'polemical considerations'. For, the institution which is the focus of my study, the Doon School, owes its existence to a vehemence of political manoeuvres on the part of the state, and a ferocity of cultural rhetoric on the part of individuals which make any attempt to skirt the eddies of 'polemical considerations' an intellectually meaningless exercise; that is the task of gracious biographies and pliant histories.

My interest lies in exploring the cultural constructions of a *specific* post-colonised civil society in India: in issues of the image of the 'ideal' citizen for the age of modernity. By implication, then, I am also interested in identities consigned to the margins of the realm of modernity; those cast from the estates of 'progress' and 'rationality'. I understand the term 'civil society' both in the political spirit in which Pateman (1989) speaks of it as that public sphere constituted through patriarchal discourses, and in a sense which is perhaps peculiar to post-colonised societies such as India; for there, the civil is also the metropolitan (versus the provincial), the English-speaking and reading (versus the vernacular world, hence 'post-colonial literature' is both the signifier of post-British rule literature as well as civil society itself), and the religiously neutral or 'secular' (versus the 'fundamentalist'). To comprehend civil society in this manner is to attempt to track the gendered, class- and caste-specific narrative of post-coloniality in India. This book is concerned with analysing the nationalist dialogue – both as theory and practice – of the liberal intelligentsia, and the Doon School as one of the 'salons' for such a dialogue. My use of the term 'intelligentsia' is a culturally delimited one and refers to the milieu of the post-colonised urban space.[1] In my discussion I posit an explicit differentiation between two kinds of intelligentsia: between the discrete worlds, both culturally and linguistically, of the metropolitan, English-speaking groups on the one hand and of the provincial, vernacular-based group on the other. And though my explicit concern is with the discursive universe of the former, the analysis is fundamentally concerned with the implicit interaction between the two worlds.

The Doon School ('the School'/'Doon'), a North Indian public school located in the city of Dehra Dun in Uttar Pradesh, is an important site of construction of the 'modern' Indian citizen. Its historical and political significance lies both in the formidable 'nationalist' credentials of its *dramatis personae* as well as in the eloquence, clarity, and resolution of its dialogue on nationhood. It has served as the palimpsest of a rejuvenated, wilful nationhood, whose anthem was inscribed firmly upon the faded forms of an effete past, forced to yield to the dictates of a vigorous 'new' science of personality. For it is as the lexis of personality – the omnipotence of agency – that the School's charter of 'nation-building' should be understood.

The fieldwork on which this research is based was carried out during 1989–93 and consisted of residence on the campuses of the Doon School, the Mayo College (Ajmer) and the Lawrence School (Sanawar, Himachal Pradesh), and meetings and interviews with a wide cross-section of people connected with these institutions. Further, this work is an attempt to combine ethnographic research with historically and 'textually' orientated analysis. And, though Doon is the primary focus of analysis, the other two schools also figure in the discussion in the book. Doon is a fully residential boys' school and though it revels in the description of an 'all India school', its clientele is largely North Indian. Despite the fact that the School charges a high fee in comparison to private day schools, demand for admissions – favourable throughout its sixty-odd years of existence – continues to grow, and intending parents are advised to 'register' their child at birth for future admission. Boys are admitted at age ten or over in class VI or at eleven or over in class VII and 'are expected to spend six or seven years in School before they pass out after standard XII'.[2] Students are accommodated in different 'Houses', as the hostels are referred to, and the five main Houses are named in honour of some of the School's benefactors.[3] The Indian Public Schools Society (IPSS) formed by the founder of the Doon School, S.R. Das, and conceived by him as a vehicle for establishing a number of public schools in India, administers the School.

Doon is a member of the Indian Public Schools Conference (IPSC), established to represent the interests and define the 'essential character of public schools' (de Souza 1974: 24) in India. In June 1939, the Headmasters of four private North Indian schools met in Simla to discuss, *inter alia*, 'the problems of residential schools, the formation of an association, the inadequate provision for examinations in Indian languages by the Cambridge Syndicate, and a memorandum to be submitted to the Army Indianisation Committee of the Central Legislative Assembly'.[4] The most concrete result of their deliberations, chaired by the then Educational Commissioner with the Government of India, John Sargent, was the formation of the IPSC. The

Conference, whose current membership includes over fifty public schools, was modelled on a similar association of public schools in England.

The leading lights of the IPSC at its formation were the British Head-masters of what were then known as Chiefs' Colleges, established for the sons and wards of princely families (see Chapter 2). The men who established the Conference:

> endeavoured to adapt the good things of British public school life and administration to Indian ways of life and thought and so build up public or residential schools in India with their roots springing from the culture of the country, fertilised by the experiences of residential school life in the UK.
>
> (Handbook 1964)

To qualify as a 'public school', then, a school must be elected a member of the Indian Public Schools Conference. To qualify for membership, it must 'comply with a set of technical criteria relating to the academic freedom of the headmaster, conditions of service of the staff, facilities for games and extracurricular activities, and residential accommodation for a certain proportion of the student body' (de Souza 1974: 2). Among the work conditions for teaching staff which characterise public schools is the facility of free education for their children (so there is a handful of girl students at Doon), and accommodation on campus at a nominal rent. The overwhelming majority of the membership of the IPSC, reflecting the predominance of boys' public schools in India, consists of all-male schools.

British manners, colonial mirrors, and post-colonial dreams

Historically, the public school in its Indian incarnation has been more than just the site of a narrow curriculum for its local proponents: it represented a *novum organum* for the 'total' transformation of a 'people'; a processing sieve to distil and absorb the ethos of a new age, the Age of Reason with its 'ethic' of Rationality. 'Reasoned' and 'rational' existence was, in turn, that which was tuned to the cadence of the regime of capital.

For the British advocates of the colonial public school, however, there were added meanings to these implants in colonial spaces. Along with several other manifestations of the cultural politics of the Empire, the colonial public school functioned as an indicator of the potency, the vigour, and the inventive superiority of an island and a culture separated from its colonies by an oceanic barrier which was both navigable and impregnable according to need. And, just as Englishmen born and reared in the colony could quite often be regarded as inferior to their counterparts nurtured in an English environment, the colonial public schools' efforts at emulating the English ideal proceeded, at best, along an asymptotic curve. Its physical positioning within the complex matrix of a subject environment – subjugated both intellectually and physically – syllogistically ruled out any parity with the prototype. In British eyes these remained the instruments of a labour of civilising which must be carried out, though not with the expectation that it would lead to emulation of the ideal. Rather, the colonial public school would pay homage to the ideal through never quite attaining its standards, never quite replicating its milieu.

To the 'original', mimicry pays the homage of asymptotic effort towards realisation (see Bhabha 1984 for another formulation). It is the praise contained in the perceived debility of a liminal state of being (the valorisation of this state is, of course, part of a discourse of *our* time). And herein lay the appeal of the overseas public school to the British: an imitative culture pays obeisance to the declared original through both the fact of the initial act of imitation as well as through the ceaseless effort at attaining authenticity; the effort is ceaseless because it is unattainable. Public schools in the non-European colonies could, in a perverse sense, be said to have aroused even greater fondness among the British, for these could even less, for crippling reasons of race and climate, hope to impinge on the *beau idéal*.

With the style and the energy becoming of paladins of Empire, its chosen representatives indefatigably reiterated these messages of the immanent superiority of the centre. Thus, early this century the Rhodesia Scholarship Trust provided Montague J. Rendall, Headmaster of the English public school Winchester and a man committed to 'strengthening the spiritual growth of Empire' (Mangan 1986b: 29), with the opportunity of articulating the intellectual and cultural hierarchy which extended from the centre to the peripheries. In 1924 Rendall was funded by the Rhodesia Trust to undertake a tour of the Empire 'to review the method of selection of Rhodesia Scholars' (*ibid.*). The account of the journey unfolds along a centripetal trajectory, each observation reinforcing the irrevocable superiority of the 'mother' civilisation. And, if his evaluation of schools in the 'New World' is anything to go by, his unrecorded view of similar schools in the 'tropical' colonies may be gauged fairly accurately.

Rendall dismissed well-known Canadian schools such as the Upper Canada College, St Andrews, Toronto, and University School, Victoria, as being of low quality. A Tasmanian candidate for the Rhodesia Scholarship was described by him as a 'star of the commerce school', and he concluded his remarks on South African public schools and their students with the words that 'these schools are not meant for Mowgli' (*ibid.*: 32). Similar reservations were voiced at the state of affairs within that most prominent of cultural stepchildren, Australia. 'Culture is a plant of slow growth', Rendall argued, 'and is not easily inculcated (to take an example) in a squatters' son, who came to learn the elements at an Australian school as a new boy of twenty-seven' (*ibid.*).

The homage of the 'not quite' (Bhabha 1984) entities was a well-recognised one, and the state of amorphism was attributed to both colonial public schools and those who studied there. The normalising mission of these schools to the natives was always constrained, it was often noted, by some very real difficulties in the field. References to the approximate nature of the mission can be found in the prologues of 'the little ceremonies of the granting of grace' (Foucault 1979: 179) which were a common feature of public school life in India. In his annual prize-giving address in 1926, the Principal of Mayo College in Rajasthan, a public school founded in 1875 for the education of princes,[5] noted that it was essential 'that the English element in the College should not be overwhelmed by numbers if we are to *approximate* to our ideal of turning out products something only *faintly approximate to the English Public School boy*, in acquirements and character' (*Mayo College Magazine* 1926. Emphasis added).

This was, then, the set of attitudes which formalised the relationship of the public school in England to those in the colonies. It reflected both the intellectual fervour of the age of Darwin and Bentham and the missionary imperatives of an ascendant Christianity. Both of these took on a special significance and inspired particular commitment to the public school project when the theatre of action was in the tropics. For, apart from being charged with the responsibility of acting as agent of transmission of British-Christian establishment culture, the public school in these regions also carried a more onerous responsibility. Its task was also to propagate sentiments of the 'natural' moral and cultural superiority of the ideas of the ruling 'race' among the frequently troublesome elite section of the native population. In India, these ideas of culture, morality, the cult of manliness, and the magical and immutable qualities of heredity, were, in turn, adopted and *adapted* by an indigenous intelligentsia towards its own circuits of power. The Doon School, the pre-eminent institution of its type in India, has played a crucial role in this process.

The national identity project in post-Independence India has largely been formulated and conducted by a relatively small group of political, social, and cultural functionaries. These may be characterised as the ideological heirs of the early nationalists who 'accepted as the basis for their thinking about the future of India many of the formulations of nineteenth century British liberalism' (Embree 1989: 134). Indeed, the spirited condemnation in the recent past by sections of the English-educated intelligentsia of the demolition of the Babri Masjid (mosque) in Ayodhya by certain Hindu organisations should, in addition to other factors, also be seen as a part of the national identity discourse. The 'Hindu fundamentalists' were attacked not merely because they raised the spectre of communal violence but also because they attempted to 'steal' the national identity agenda from its traditional custodians.

The opposition to Hindu militancy by sections of the 'secular' should not be seen simply in terms of the defence of the rights of religious minorities and of religious pluralism in general. For the Indian liberal discourse of 'secularism' is itself circumscribed by (as I will argue in Chapter 4) and permeated with a Hindu world view. The mosque–temple issue can also be understood as a contest on the cultural and ideological terrain between different groups, one defending its inherited dominant role in the national identity project against the other's encroachments upon it. To critique Enlightenment-inspired perspectives on the fundamentalists who are always 'out there' ('we' are always progressive) is not, however, the same thing as playing into the hands of religious bigotry as it far too often seems to be asserted (Chakrabarty 1995).

The Indian public school has been an indispensable adjunct to Indian liberalism, embodying and refining the philosophical grounds of its discourse. It is the central argument of this book that the construction of the urban post-colonial Indian identity owes a considerable debt, intellectually and philosophically, to one of the most comprehensively adapted of all British institutions in India – the public school; and that this identity has remained remarkably unfragmented across widely differing political positions (of the liberal–conservative and left–right kind), united through an abiding commitment to a modernist paradigm of being on the part of the intelligentsia of various shades. And further, that schools such as Doon have contributed to this, producing several generations of a post-Independence middle-class steeped in the boys'-own tales of the all-conquering, modernist, male hero, astride the white steed of Development Theory, the guardian of free-market, and the bridge-builder between a progressive West and a recalcitrantly regressive India. It is appropriate to note here, however, that my discussion treats the Doon School as prototypic, and one of the several sites of a particular type of citizenship project in India – rather than a singularly all-powerful institution. It is as an important *link* in a modernist discourse of class, gender, and national identity that I focus on Doon.

I must emphasise that I do not speak of a national identity project which sustains the interest of the majority of the population; my discussion is concerned, rather, with a section of the population for whom it is a consciously articulated concern, and one which has many avenues of public dialogue and dissemination. This public dialogue also seeks to establish a monopoly of the representation of 'citizenship' in the cultural loam of the post-colonised nation state. However, necessary as the analysis of colonial and post-colonial political and cultural ideas is to the study of contemporary Indian society (e.g. Viswanathan 1989), one is struck by the relative lack of critical attention paid to post-colonial *institutional sites* where such ideas find a conducive location for practical elaboration. The public school in India is one such site. To speak of actual sites (and not just metaphoric ones, though of course, 'actual sites' also have metaphoric dimensions) is also to attempt to move the debate away from a temporal regime towards an attention to the politics of 'the production of space' (Lefebvre 1994). The neglect of space as a 'historico-political problem' (Foucault 1980: 149) in western scholarship, has come under increasing scrutiny, and this book, while it does not purport to be anything like the history of spaces Foucault suggests still 'remains to be written' (*ibid.*), is an attempt to engage the idea of spatialised analysis.

Ideologies need spaces to anchor their abstractions in order to ground the fleeting figures of speech in an artefactual configuration that is then made to speak the self-referential language of proof and permanence. 'What would remain of a religious ideology – the Judaeo-Christian one, say –', Lefebvre asks, 'if it were not based on places and their names: church, confessional, altar, sanctuary, tabernacle? What would remain of the Church if there were no churches?' (Lefebvre 1994: 44).

Nation and citizen: the dynamics of personality

The functioning of institutions can only meaningfully be understood as part of a wider system of symbolic activity and language where the articulation of their goals in the pragmatic vocabulary of every-day existence ('schools educate') and in the sacred language of transcendent goals ('for the good of society') both masks and unmasks the elaboration and consolidation of historically constituted positions and aspirations. It is this historical constitution of a cultural identity, and its political moorings, which is the focus of this study. I have already noted that my interest is not in the pedagogical practice *per se*, but rather in the post-colonised cultural terrain of which public schools in India are a part; the Doon School is the window which affords a view of the cultural politics of the post-colonised state, a daguerreotypic representation of its 'twists and turns, the suppressed possibilities, the contradictions still unresolved' (Chatterjee 1986: 22). An important site of post-colonised liberalism and contemporaneous with the Indian nation state the Doon School is a précis of the larger treatise of post-coloniality.

Michael Young admonishes sociologists for forgetting that 'education is not a product like cars and bread, but a selection and organisation from the available knowledge at a particular time which involves conscious or unconscious choices' (Young 1971: 24). It should also be said, however, that the cultural analysis of an education system in the post-colonial situation must be willing to 'leave school' and explore the annals of the nation state itself, and that the 'citizenship issue' here is of a different order from that encountered in colonising societies. For in the post-colonised situation the figure of the citizen is, in the first instance, a figure of *cultural* import, and only later the anthropomorphic reification of legality and order; that is, the constitutional subject. This is a consequence of the specificity of historical experience: for the 'national question [in post-colonial societies] is ... historically fused with a colonial question. ... The assertion of national identity was, therefore, a form of the struggle against colonial exploitation' (Chatterjee 1986: 18).

In the Indian context, the citizen is a figure suspended in the wash of the nationalist skirmishes with the colonising power and the subsequent conversion of the nationalist project into post-colonial agendas of power and domination. In this, it bears the marks of a tension peculiar to post-colonised societies. For the nationalist struggle for an independent nation speaks the language of inclusiveness: all the members of the national entity are regarded as equals as citizens. Hence, at this point, 'the nationalist's claim is that . . . backwardness . . . is not a character which is historically immutable: it can be transformed by the nation acting *collectively*' (Chatterjee 1986: 50–1. Emphasis added). However, the struggle against the colonial power is waged on two fronts: direct political challenge to colonial authority, and the challenge to the *self* – to the 'native' – to 'improve', to become 'modern' so as to 'rightfully' claim his (*sic*) position as a free person, the citizen of a sovereign nation state.

It is through this second movement – dealing with the perceived problems of the native personality – that the citizen figure becomes embroiled in the cultural elaboration of post-colonised structures of power. For whereas the anti-colonial struggle requires the enlistment of mass support for its success, the emergence of the nation state leads to very specific ideas about who is and who is not part of the post-colonial civil society: women, 'tribals', and 'provincial' populations, among others, come to form the 'masses', who must be nurtured in the ways of public modern life before being allowed to join – or influence – the serious business of civil life. It is here that 'citizen' operates as a cultural category towards the delimitation of groups that have access to the largesse of the state and those who do not qualify. Now citizenship becomes the definition of exclusivity, and power becomes a function of 'cultural capital' (Bourdieu 1986), understood in both gendered and non-gendered ways. Also, the citizenship debate, guided by intellectual exertions of the liberal intelligentsia devoted to the production of the discourses of modernity, takes its place in the matrices of class and gender. It is a modest analysis of these discourses concerned with the cultural requirements of access to the privileges of the state that is the object of this book. For class relations 'which are not already cultural relations', as Connell puts it, 'are as mythical as the bunyip, and an equally bad basis for theory' (Connell 1980: 41).

The Indian discourse of the nation state operates simultaneously, then, on two mutually reinforcing levels: on the level of the *political* concerns of the state and that of the *cultural* preoccupations of the nation. The notion of 'membership' to a delimited sphere of civil society for a specified group, is itself a cultural one. It is elaborated through an 'assemblage' (Deleuze and Guattari 1986) which consists of the qualifications for membership to the civil society. Here, my argument also draws from Gandhi's criticism of the constitutive features of 'modern' existence. Gandhi's philosophical critique of modernity targeted several features of bourgeois existence, and, in addition to feminist critiques, it is his inventory of civil life that I take to be constitutive of post-colonised representations of the civil society. Gandhi's political and moral philosophy (if it is possible to separate one from the other) was in the nature of:

> a fundamental critique of the entire edifice of bourgeois society: its con-
> tinually expanding and prosperous economic life, based on individual

property, the social division of labour and the impersonal laws of the market . . . its political institutions based on a dual notion of sovereignty in which the people in theory rule themselves, but are only allowed to do so through the medium of their representatives whose actions have to be ratified only once in so many years; its spirit of innovation, adventure and scientific progress; its rationalisation of philosophy and ethics and secularisation of art and education.

(Chatterjee 1986: 90)

The cultural aspects of the post-colonised situation are intertwined with questions of membership of the civil society of modernity Gandhi spoke of. This membership issue – its symbolic and other constructions – constitutes the focus of analysis of this book.

There exist a considerable number of approaches to the study of the schooling process. These range from symbolic-interactionist (de Souza 1974; Thapan 1991) to those inspired by Marxist theory (Willis 1977; Bourdieu and Passeron 1977), and still others which combine a class perspective with a feminist one and seek to analyse economic as well as gender oppression (Connell *et al.* 1982). In this study – which is not so much about schooling but rather an ethnography of post-colonial modernity – I wish to make a case for positioning the Indian public school in a context which takes account of the uniqueness of post-colonised engagements with issues of citizenship and national identity based on the specificity of historical experience. The vectors of domination, dissent, and conflict in post-colonised societies can seldom be discussed under such convenient headings as 'class' and 'false consciousness', travelling as they do over a social reality made complex by the inescapable binds of the colonial experience. In such an environment the ideographs of difference and the cartographies of congeniality are etched with the potent hues of language (English versus the vernaculars) and 'race'; and in terms of arguments regarding 'rationality' and 'irrationality', the 'primitives' versus the 'civilised', the 'secular' fending off the 'fundamentalist', the tasks of modernity, and the urgency of a national identity. Class becomes merely one of the variables to be analysed and not an inevitable category to be fitted, as Chatterjee's critique of theorising on nationalism points out, 'to certain universal and inescapable sociological constraints of the modern age' (Chatterjee 1986: 22).

It is true that economic class is an observable fact in India and just as correct that the analysis of class dynamics must form an important part of research into educational issues. However, I would like to suggest that studies within the field of education which have as their point of focus the reproduction of the class structure through the elaboration of a 'dominant culture' pedagogy will, for the post-colonial situation, tend to conceal as much as they reveal; and the assumptions on which they are based are more likely to be true of non-colonised (post-colonial) rather than post-colonised societies. Perhaps the most important of these assumptions is the one which concerns the dyadic nature of the relationship between the oppressed and the oppressor, between domination and dissent, and between exploitation and resistance. The dominant and the dominated, in other words, are clearly identified, and, further, just as clearly seen to have conflicting interests with respect to each other.

One of the most acclaimed expositions of the so-called reproduction approach in education theory is Paul Willis's *Learning to Labour*. Since its publication in 1977 the book's conclusions have been disputed only in as much as one may dispute the tendency – as also apparent in the writings of Bourdieu – to exaggerate 'a good insight' (Connell 1980: 188).

Willis investigates the reproduction of the structure of inequality through the schooling system in industrial societies, which is both the central argument as well as the object of inquiry in the reproduction approach, by positing, both implicitly and explicitly, an every-day world of disjunctive cognition: there is 'us' and there is 'them'. The little battles for personal dignity, the ground gained and the strongholds relinquished, and what, following Gramsci, we may call the larger war of position, are then fought across this class divide. I am not, of course, suggesting the absence of differences and discontinuities between the cultural and social ethos of different classes in post-colonised societies. This would be clearly absurd. What I would like to suggest, however, is that in the process of the invention and reinvention of cultural forms through which society is institutionalised – gains its system of meanings – there emerges the emotionally potent and historically specific third figure of the 'citizen'. And that it is through this anthropomorphic reification of the civil society that we seek to mediate structural contradictions that may exist between groups.

The dialogue of citizenship speaks of the need to address the 'shortcomings' of personality. Here, the discourse of class difference and economic exploitation is reconstituted into differences based on 'absences' and 'lacks' and the need for specific institutions which will alleviate these shortfalls of character. The Doon School, I will argue, has conducted its national identity and citizenship dialogue through such a 'science' of personality which has emphasised the need to develop the secular, rational, metropolitan citizen, and the depredations of the opposite personality-type upon the health of the civil society. The conflict becomes one between the 'modern' type of personality – the light of the nation state – and the 'backward' psyche, forever ready to undermine its integrity. In the enterprise of 'nation-building', then, social analysis – incorporating, *inter alia*, class and gender issues – becomes an 'unpatriotic' rubric, undermining the doctrine of citizenship through interrogating the national attitude. In this book I would like to explore the *cultural* terrain on which the Indian dialogue of citizenship is carried out, rather than begin with a model of research which takes class analysis as the most appropriate one for a study on 'elite schools'.

From a post-colonised perspective, there are other difficulties as well in analysing seeming class institutions such as Indian public schools within the strict framework of class analysis. If we understand a class as 'a set of individuals who have "similar" relations with the means of production . . . and who are such that they have no "contradictions" among themselves' (Rudra 1989: 142) then class analysis (as the *sole* method of problematising society) offers a limited understanding of a school such as Doon which functions quite comfortably, as I discuss in the book, in the embrace of conflicting ideological interests. My discussion seeks to understand the process through which a wide range of seemingly conflicting positions in the discursive formation of the post-colonised nation state become imbricated and produce an agreement – one which is built around the 'truths' of modernity. We find some indication of the attempt to invent a *cultural* space of post-colonised commonality and homogeneity in the 'mature' phase of Nehru's reflections on the national community – during the period in his intellectual career when 'nation' and 'state' became synonymous terms. During this stage for Nehru, 'the world of the concrete, the world of differences, of conflict, of the struggle between classes, of history and politics, now [found] its unity in the life of the state' (Chatterjee 1986: 161), and the Indian nation state became the protector and interpreter of the cultural unity of the modern 'Indian people', defining both modernity and Indianness. The post-colonial period in India, and the period preparatory to it, has been marked by the production of spaces which are both the commodities of capital and processes through which other commodities – such as the idea of an Indian people transcending all differences and conflicts – are produced (Lefebvre 1994).

The Doon School, I will argue in the book, is precisely such a cultural space of 'domesticated difference' such that it brings together in mutual accommodation a range of seemingly opposed interests – both political and cultural, in the broadest sense of the two terms – and prevents these differences from threatening the existent positions of dominance; and that this occurs (to paraphrase Anderson 1986) in the act of stretching the spiritual robe of commonality, woven in the name of the sacred image of the nation and the consecrated figure of the citizen, over a demographic body indelibly marked by the differences and degradations of unimaginable inequality. This aspect of the discussion seeks to point out that in the regime of the bourgeois-liberal intelligentsia it is impossible to clearly mark out the 'system' from its 'critics', and the 'radicals' from the 'reactionaries'; that 'difference' is itself dissipated, and that the Doon School can be recognised as one of the sites of the domestication of such differences.

The epic of the nation and nation-building in the Indian context is congruent with a discourse of personality built out of the specificities of certain experiences and ways of thought generated in the recent period of Indian history. The figurative body of the citizen was, in its earliest incarnation, forged from nationalist aspirations to displace the image of the 'subject' and the 'native'. Since then, the citizen figure has become enmeshed in a subject–object dialectic of a different nature: as part of a project of delineating the *new* 'natives' of the nation state and as an instrument of its cultural and political strategy which seeks to elide the deeper structural contradictions of society. It is the implicit three-way 'dialectic' between the dominant and the dominating classes and the citizen figure, where contradictions and conflicts are sought to be shown up as unnecessary, unimportant, and unpatriotic, which is of interest to me.

This book is an attempt, therefore, to deal with what are commonly referred to as 'elite' Indian schools in terms of the construction of a national identity, the image of the ideal citizen, as I believe this to be an important element in the history of class processes in India. Also, and perhaps more importantly, 'national identity' and 'citizenship' are indispensable rubrics – imbued with the passions and emotions of the freedom struggle – of modern Indian history itself. The alternative when dealing with 'elite' schools is, as indicated above, to analyse them within the reproduction framework and investigate 'how an oppressive and exploitative social system is stabilised' by positing that:

> the production of the right kind of labour-power is increasingly a matter of formal schooling. The school not only teaches basic skills, but also the rules of behaviour and attitudes appropriate for the positions in production the children are destined for, as workers or as agents of capital.
>
> (Connell 1980: 35)

In outlining my preference for a different approach in the study of Indian 'ruling'-class schools I would also like to emphasise that not only do I consider the reproduction approach inadequate in dealing with the Indian situation but also that the idea of reproduction is itself (of cultural forms generally and in education specifically) a somewhat unsatisfactory trope. If we are to recognise that the 'economic' and the 'cultural' are not two separate spheres, and that the cultural is used to reinforce the effectiveness of power relations, then we must account for the cultural specificity of class dynamics through historicising and specifying the 'truths' of culture, rather than proceeding from a pre-given reproduction framework.

It is also not satisfactory to deal with such schools, as a recent study has done, in terms of the ideals and objectives set by the founders of the school and the extent to which these have been realised. Thapan's study of the Rishi Valley School in South India – established according to an educational blueprint provided by the philosopher J. Krishnamurty – is an attempt, she tells us, to 'render the educational institution intelligible sociologically' (Thapan 1991: 1). Thapan sought to establish the social reality of the school along with its pedagogical processes

> by examining the relations between the participants engaged in these processes within an overall sociological framework that takes account of both the structure of the school as an organisation and of the social world of the participants.
>
> (Thapan 1991: jacket)

Thapan considers 'the most significant aspect of school organisation . . . the fundamental dichotomy between the "transcendental" and the "local" orders' (p. 28), where the former refers to Krishnamurty's philosophical guidelines for the functioning of the school and the latter 'constitutes the *actual* schooling process and tends to function independently of the transcendental order' (*ibid.*; emphasis in the original). The book then proceeds to analyse and highlight instances of and reasons for 'the conflict between the transcendental and the local orders' (*ibid.*: 219). With the aid of ample and admirably presented ethnography, Thapan is able to demonstrate that there does indeed exist a conflict between the two 'orders', engendered, *inter alia*, by the demands of 'good' academic results and imperfect commitment on the part of substantial sections of the teacher and student community to the transcendental order.

There are several questions we must ask of a study such as Thapan's. The Rishi Valley School

> may be traced to its beginnings which take us back to 1918, when Dr. Annie Besant, President of the Theosophical Society, formed the Society for the Promotion of National Education. A school was then started at Teynampet in Madras based on the principles of education enunciated by Besant.
>
> (Thapan 1989: 30)

Annie Besant was a prominent, if somewhat quixotic, figure in the early stages of the nationalist movement in India, having formed a Home Rule League in 1915 which, 'At its height in mid-1917 . . . had 27,000 members' (Sarkar 1983:151). The League was mainly supported by 'Tamil Brahmans . . . urban professional groups in the United Provinces . . . younger Gujarati industrialists, traders and lawyers in Bombay city and Gujarat' (*ibid.*). Further, Besant's foray into nationalist politics was one which 'desired to "restore" the lost pride and glory of the Brahmins' (Geetha and Rajadurai 1995: 1768; see also Jaywardena 1995) and return them, once again, to positions of leadership in the life of the nation. It seems somewhat inadequate therefore (though not wrong, of course), to deal with a school whose historical pedigree forms a moment in the life of a very specific type of nationalist activity within such an ahistorical framework as that employed by Thapan.[6] We are entitled also to ask of such a study whether, due to its own unreflexive location within an analytical framework which is oblivious of the cultural, political, and class history of the society in which the school is located, it has actually achieved the task which it set itself, namely 'to examine the relationship between ideology, school and society'. The symbolic-interactionist mode, within which this study is firmly anchored, may well tell us a great deal about what happens within a school, but its results remain of limited interest if the institution cannot also be firmly located within the tangled skein of colonial and post-colonised power and cultural politics. The discourse of 'political Brahmanism' (Geetha and Rajadurai 1995: 1768) espoused by Annie Besant and her associates and their 'discovery' of an ancient golden age of 'Hindu-Sanskritic civilisation' (*ibid*.) are important aspects of the inventions of India during the colonial period – and schools such as the one studied by Thapan need to be investigated as part of the investigation of these discourses; otherwise the late twentieth-century social scientist runs the very real risk of merely reproducing colonial (and post-colonised) discourses of, among others, Brahmanism, patriarchy and orientalism (*cf.* Appadurai 1993a; Chatterjee 1986; Ludden 1993; Mani 1993).

Following Erving Goffman (1976) the concept of 'total institutions' has found considerable favour with social scientists as a tool of analysis for institutions such as boarding schools, prisons, and mental hospitals. Goffman defined a total institution as:

> a place where a large number of like-situated individuals, cut off from the wider society for an appreciable period of time, together lead an enclosed, formally administered round of life.
>
> (Goffman 1976: xiii)

Total institutions, he further suggested, have 'encompassing tendencies', and that the encompassment is most palpably manifest in 'the barrier to social intercourse with the outside world and to departure that is often built right into the physical plant, such as locked doors, high walls, barbed wire' (*ibid.*: 4). Later, the point is made again that the 'inmates . . . have restricted contact with the world outside the walls' (*ibid.*: 7).

Lelyveld's (1978) study of the Muhammadan Anglo-Oriental College (MAO) at Aligarh in North India is a prominent example of the application of Goffman's total institution idea to the analysis of residential educational establishments. For Lelyveld, the College defined itself as a total institution through the ichnography of its presence: the walls surrounding it and the gates, which provided selective passage to the world without and acted as barriers to the realm within. So, Lelyveld suggests:

> The proposed residential framework for the college, rather than the curriculum itself, was what represented a real departure from the existing system of English education in India. What Sayyid Ahmed [the founder] advocated was the creation of a 'total Institution,' where young men would be cut off from ordinary life and raised in highly controlled surroundings.
>
> (Lelyveld 1978: 128)

With the consolidation of British rule in the erstwhile United Provinces (now Uttar Pradesh), the traditional Muslim elite found it increasingly difficult, Lelyveld suggests, to secure 'appropriate' employment through the once well-established avenues of kin alliance and patronage. The Persian

influenced culture of the Mughal court had once provided the liveried
umbrella under which men of 'breeding' instituted a community through
language, music, and poetry; but now the umbrella was gnawed at the edges,
its ambience and delicate hues, which encompassed both a shared culture and
the sharing of power, were slowly made effete with the advance of a more
robust, if more vulgar, system of meanings. It was, however, important to
engage with the new order in order to wrest from it some measure of the
benefits which would, otherwise, accrue exclusively to the Hindus. The establishment of the MAO, according to Lelyveld, was the result of this view:

> in nineteenth century India, the British colonial regime offered new
> incentives for developing social ties that emphasised voluntary participa-
> tion, personal achievement, and non-familial cooperation: hence the
> invention of institutions that would temporarily isolate the young from
> the rest of society in order to prepare them for later life.
>
> (Lelyveld 1978: x)

In the ensuing description of the various aspects of college life, images of a
'world unto itself' occupy a central place. The students, enclosed within the
carefully managed, experimental space of the campus, were to be guided in
every aspect of their existence by the minutiae of an epigraph of discipline
and control dictated by the founders of the College.

Its enthusiastic adoption by Lelyveld and others notwithstanding, I believe
that the total institution idea is not only of limited analytical utility in general, but is also quite inappropriate in the context of educational institutions
which have their origin in the cultural politics of colonialism and post-
coloniality. To label an institution as 'total' is to deny the dynamics of *social*
interaction between the part (the institution) and the whole (the society), the
consideration of which should be regarded as the main object of an inquiry
into the functioning of institutions. The total institution idea, in as much as it
seeks to raise the part to a position of exclusivity, is unsuitable for the purposes of sociological and cultural research in as much as it constitutes a
denial of the understanding that 'the whole is always in some sense superior
and even prior to its parts, which it serves to make effective in the world as
well as to explain and render intelligible to the mind' (Uberoi 1978: 20).[7]

The establishment of an institution (mental hospital, prison, boarding
school) is a statement of societal intent: the walls, the gates, the windows, and
the nooks and crannies are, as it were, constructed from ideological brick
and mortar. The institution lies midstream among the currents and eddies
of contesting political and cultural intents; it is the reification of social
thought. So it is with boarding schools. Hence, in their functioning not only
do these schools maintain an active relationship with the outside world but
also their 'inmates' are actively aware of the 'outside' world to which they
belong and are steadfastly in consonance with its prevailing punctilios. The
institution established under the 'orders' of 'society' cannot but be veined by

the political and cultural catechisms of social thought. The institution is inextricably, though not always obviously, enmeshed within the power relationships which animate that society.

It is not surprising, then, to learn that the MAO did, in fact, engage in an active dialogue with the 'outside' world with which it maintained an ocular distance. The choice of the 'total institution' rubric for the MAO is curious also, as Lelyveld regards as his primary objective the examination of 'the ideological matrix into which the new institution was set, how the founders hoped to make it fit into the total situation of their social relationships and ways of thought' (Lelyveld 1978: 102). Further, there is also the explicit recognition that:

> The founding of the Aligarh College also involved the definition and mobilisation of a constituency. Immersed in a whole new ideology about the history and present status of Indian Muslims, Aligarh was not only a school, it was a political symbol.
>
> (Lelyveld 1978: 103)

Also, the 'political symbol' was in a constant state of innovative flux through conscious interaction with the outside world, a world which was sometimes its cultural paradigm and always its *deus ex machina*:

> Beck [the Principal] always emphasised that cricket could serve to establish bonds between Aligarh and significant groups outside . . . put Aligarh students in an exclusive network.
>
> (Lelyveld 1978: 255–6)

So, the College functioned against the sheer face of an inescapable social situation, and its life was a snapshot in a larger colonial pastiche, 'subject to circumstances of power beyond the college boundaries. That power was ultimately in British hands' (*ibid.*: 269). The label 'total' would only seem to be applicable to the College in a rather limited sense: that it *endeavoured* to a totality of form. It is curious then, that a study which is as historically rooted and methodologically refined (as it is totally engrossing) as Lelyveld's, should yield to the seduction of form over content, which is how the total institution idea may be described.

In several implicit ways, I will suggest in this book that the cultural specificity of Goffman's analysis (his references to the 'norms' of 'civil society' are the most explicit pointers to this) should make us wary of utilising it in an arbitrary manner. So, for example, though the explicit purpose of my discussion of 'surveillance' and 'self-discipline' (Chapter 3) is to dispute the universality of the Foucaulian frameworks, it should also be seen as a disputation of Goffman's conclusions on the matter. Goffman suggests that constant surveillance is part of the process through which total institutions seek to place 'barriers . . . between inmates and the wider world' (p. 14), whereas my argument seeks to point out that in the colonial and post-colonised contexts these processes can be better seen as a complex engagement with the aspirations to modernity and 'civility' on the part of a very specific section of the population. There are some other problems as well with Goffman's model – such as the 'staff–inmate split' (p. 9), and 'impermeability' (p. 119)[8] as defining characteristics of total institutions – which make it unsuitable for deployment in a work that attempts to delineate the historically and culturally specific conditions of non-western modernity. For, as my discussion will seek to demonstrate, the specific contexts of non-western modernity require that we subject all claims of universality of analytical categories to critical scrutiny. This is not to argue for an absolute difference in the human condition, but rather to foreground the complexities engendered by the very different histories of different sections of the human population.

The Doon School, its presence declared by a boundary wall, its students distributed among different Houses or hostels, their conduct and academic training under the strict purview of a disciplinary mosaic, was never intended by its founders to be anything like a 'total institution': its 'inmates' were to be the 'leaders' of the world outside and hence it developed a conscious view of its place within the wider society; a view which was, once again consciously, shared by the School population. The inside–outside distinction inherent in the total institution framework is somewhat difficult to sustain here. The 'outside' was very much within its boundaries. The School was born of a set of intentions and aspirations, the gestation period of which spanned the length and depth of that contentious period of Indian history known as the Bengal Renaissance and which continued to be adapted to different situations in the post-colonised period. It was society, to paraphrase Marx, which spoke through the School, reciting the colloquy of the nation and of the citizen.

To speak of the citizen, of the 'modern' Indian man (and it is a gendered entity, as I will argue later in the book), as Dipesh Chakrabarty has recently pointed out, is to speak of an anthropomorphic narrative born of a fruitful collusion between European imperialism and third-world nationalism (Chakrabarty: 1992). The gift of 'History', as it emerged from the lecture halls of the European university to mingle with the milling crowds in search of a 'collective consciousness', was 'to universalise the nation state as the most desirable form of political community' (Chakrabarty 1992: 19). In turn, the great achievement of imperialism lay not just in establishing material empires, but also in leaving behind the testacy of a much more enduring universe, that of 'historical' existence; a universe where the tautological child of the nation, the citizen, could find sustenance. Third-world nationalists readily adopted this child, incorporating its being into the dialogue of post-coloniality and pronounced all other identities 'non-modern' or even, 'anti-modern'. Modernity, in its various forms, thus became the desideratum of post-colonised existence. One of its most valorised forms was citizenship, which could both serve the interests of dominant positions – the better off as instant citizens –

and be established *publicly* and *legally* within a reasonable time. The written word – the autobiography, the novel, the constitution – and other, ocular, representations, such as the flag, guaranteed for it an unquestionable public existence. In turn, the post-colonised nation state, administered its birth rites by an indigenous class imbued with an awareness of the requirements of modernity, and of citizenship, provided the legal guarantee.

The book is organised around four main issues, three of which are treated as 'qualifications' for citizenship in the cultural sense discussed above. The fourth is concerned with the 'reality' of the civil society itself or, to put it another way, with the strategies involved in inventing a discourse of a 'non-existent' reality. I treat the following as the 'qualifications' for cultural membership of the civil society: 'secularism', 'rationality', and (to coin a somewhat clumsy expression) 'metropolitanism'. Each of these is discussed in separate chapters of the book (though, of course, all three constitute different parts of the same discourse on national identity and citizenship and should therefore be understood with reference to each other). The discussion of the concluding chapter on the 'strategies of the real' (Baudrillard 1988) is concerned to analyse the production of models of 'difference' which seek to separate the 'progressive' from the 'backward', and the 'civilised' from the 'primitive'. These are, I will suggest, strategies towards 'inventions' of difference in the service of existent positions of power.

1   Practical minds, solid builders, and sane opinions

It is from within the celebrations of modernity – in its manifest forms of the nation and the citizen – that the Doon School elaborates its existence. The morning assembly at the School that marks the formal inauguration of the academic day, is, on reflection, a curious affair. For it gathers upon a *shared* temporal and spatial zone all the constituents of the *hierarchical*, academic, order of the school, i.e. Headmaster, senior masters, other teachers, and students of all classes. For that fleeting but recurrent moment in the school's life, heralded by the pealing of the school bell and animated by a vocal harmony – the singing of songs and the chanting of prayers – the School is, in principle, one. The hierarchy of every-day existence on the campus, around which are based the punctilios of daily staff–staff and staff–student interaction, is here, fleetingly, absent. Though the students enter the hall class-wise, with the most junior classes filing in first, inside the hall there are no obvious signs of privilege which distinguish the space occupied by the 'juniors' from that of the 'seniors': the latter, for instance, do not stand near the front of the hall; the senior and junior masters, too, stand together in an undifferentiated manner. The 'image of [the] communion' (Anderson 1986: 15) of the School is fixed, therefore, in a horizontal rather than a vertical plane – everyone sings the same songs, all stand together in the same physical space as well as sharing a temporal space where the actions are simultaneous rather than sequential, or even concurrent.

And what of the songs sung, the prayers chanted, at the morning assembly?

> The original collection of prayers was made by A.E. Foot [Doon's first Headmaster] and his sources were varied, chief among which was R.L. Stevenson's 'Prayers written at Vailima' and 'A Book of Prayers written for use in an Indian College' by J.S. Hoyland.
>
> (*The Doon School Book of Prayers and Songs* n.d.)

The choice of the collection of prayers and songs, one made a decade before the Indian nation state came into existence in 1947, is instructive. Prayer number 6 consists of the following words:

God of all nations, we beseech thee to bring that day nearer when our country shall be truly one, when every barrier shall be broken down, when no man shall work for his own selfish good, when no man shall defraud or oppress neighbour [*sic*], when no man shall reckon his neighbour worse than himself, when none shall be despised or outcast, but all shall be free to work in equal manhood for thee and their country.

(ibid.)

Later, in another prayer from the Hoyland collection, the supplicant beseeches the 'Lord of all nations', to grant that:

in this our nation, there may be none, high or low, whatever his race or caste, who is bound by the shackles of ancient contempt, and barred from his right of free manhood.

(ibid.)

If we combine the image of the assembly as a gathering of different ranks bound through the volitional, albeit ephemeral, surrender of their difference, with the supplications to a god, not of humans, but of 'all nations', then it is possible to see it as a celebration of citizenship: '. . . because, regardless of the actual inequality and exploitation that may prevail in each [community], the nation is always conceived as a deep, horizontal comradeship' (Anderson 1986: 16).[1]

We can also view the assembly, with its unequivocal enlistment of divinity in the cause of an earthly communion – the nation – as a reiteration of its (i.e. the nation's) transcendence and universality. The cultural requirements of citizenship – such as the question of the 'appropriate' personality – are not, as I will later argue, perceived as within the reach of all members of the politically outlined Indian nation. The cultural community of citizens is a discrete set within the larger India. And the task of the School is to establish the guidelines for membership of this community.

It is my argument here that the cultural history of the Doon School is linked to the emergence of a specific post-colonised Indian identity, an 'imagined community' with its own system of cultural meanings; and that this national identity is unique both in the self-conscious elaboration of its world view and the discontinuities it just as self-consciously effects between its milieu and that of the larger society within which it is situated. It is a discontinuity effected, however, through a consciously developed view of the wider society, and not because the School's territory is delimited in the manner Goffman (1971) postulates for his 'total institutions'. I treat the Doon School then as an important site for the production and refinement of a cultural milieu whose main components were/are (middle- and upper-) class and (upper-) caste male identity, the 'scientific temper', 'secularism', and 'metropolitanism'; together, the above constitute an inventory of the cultural desideratum for 'successful' existence in the regime of post-colonial capitalism.

This book, then, seeks to explore the constituents of what Bourdieu and Passeron call 'pedagogic action': the cultural politics of education and educational institutions that carry a resonance far beyond the boundaries of concrete and the circumference of curricula. I mean to employ the term as a useful shorthand to signify the 'centrifugal' tendency of pedagogical practice, that is, to its saturation of the grounds of culture; like the truant school child, education itself escapes the classroom. 'All pedagogic action', Bourdieu and Passeron state, 'is, objectively, symbolic violence insofar as it is the imposition of a cultural arbitrary by an arbitrary power' (Bourdieu and Passeron 1977: 5).

It is 'the imposition of a cultural arbitrary' towards the construction of a very specific idea of the nation state in India that is the object of investigation of this book.[2] This chapter provides an outline of the community which formulated this 'cultural arbitrary'. The founder of the Doon School, S.R. Das, its official history tells us, 'visualised public schools which would be distinctively Indian in their moral and spiritual outlook and yet open to all castes and communities, fostering a sense of comradeship among the students that would transcend social, communal, religious and provincial prejudices' (Singh 1985: 1).[3]

The 'distinctively' Indian national identity that Das sought to formulate was, as considerable recent work (Chakrabarty 1992; Chandra 1994; Chatterjee 1986; Mani 1993; Pandey 1994) has pointed out, one forged out of collusion between colonialist and nationalist thinking. The discussion of this book is both an exploration into a specific site – in its literal and symbolic aspects – of this collusion as well as of Indian post-coloniality itself. The accommodation with colonial rule, which often translated into admiration, is, of course, a recurring feature of early 'patriotic' thought in India. At the Doon School, the earliest traces of the collusive project can be found in the alchemical transformation of the British colonial enterprise into one expressive of a global management enterprise, from which the notoriously inefficient and unorganised natives had much to learn. The move from colonialism as a political process to its portrayal as state-of-the-art scientific management with a 'planetary consciousness' (Pratt 1993: 15) was facilitated through what might be called the epistemology of capitalist realism. As an early (1948) history of the School written mainly by Headmaster Arthur Foot describes, S.R. Das, having sent his own sons 'to be educated at English Public Schools', realised that 'in an English Public School training was given which developed in boys the qualities that enabled them to take the responsibility of officering the services and managing enterprises and administration over a vast area of the world – often many thousands of miles in distance and many weeks in time away from the source of their authority'.[4]

The world in which the Doon School found itself on 27 October 1935 was a world that had nurtured the desire of its birth for several decades in the many scattered recesses of its discursive universe; its coming was, in a manner of speaking, foretold. The society in which it thrives today has given those desires the form of the imperatives of 'modern' citizenship and the School has come to be regarded as the prototype of the civil society itself. The Doon School is a product of, to quote Foucault in another context:

> a multiplicity of often minor processes, of different origin and scattered location, which overlap, repeat or imitate one another, support one another, distinguish themselves from one another according to their domain of application, converge and gradually produce the blueprint of a general method.
>
> (Foucault 1979: 138)

This chapter is concerned with identifying and exploring the social and political world of those through whose exertions the Doon School came into being; it is also concerned to locate these within the wider politics of 'public' affairs and in the broader society of every-day existence.

Public tumult and a private school

'The death of Mr S.R. Das, Law member of the Viceroy's Executive Council', an obituary in a 1928 edition of the *Rangoon Gazette* notes:

> has deprived the Government of India of an extremely able adviser and friend at this juncture. During his practice at the Calcutta Bar Mr Das studiously kept aloof from political activities till the antics of the Swaraj party under his more famous cousin the late Mr C.R. Das forced him to rally sane opinion in that province against intransigent programmes.
>
> He attempted to form a party with a sound programme of solid work. Unfortunately at that period Bengal, running riot with furious political idealism, found no appeal in that programme and the new party was defeated at the polls.

As a man with a practical turn of mind, a 'solid builder', as opposed to his nationalist cousin who 'attempted to build . . . on sand', S.R. Das had made the destruction of the water-hyacinth – 'the ravages caused by which pest . . . are notorious' – an important part of his scheme for the welfare of the people of Bengal. For all his troubles, however, he was ridiculed as the founder of the 'water-hyacinth party'. The memory of S.R. Das may well have met the same ignominious fate that befell his party, for throughout his public life he continued to hold, as an acquaintance charitably put it, 'very conservative opinions with regard to Indian politics'.[5] But S.R. Das escaped the clutches of posthumous anonymity. For although his immediate political aspirations met with little success, his advocacy of the School which, it was hoped, would 'develop in the course of a generation or two as an institution of incalculable value to the future of the educated classes',[6] has secured for him an enduring presence in the annals of the post-colonial nation state.

Satish Ranjan Das was born on 29 February 1872 into a Vaidya family in Dhaka in present-day Bangladesh. He received his primary and secondary education at an English grammar school and later qualified as a barrister at the bar of the Middle Temple. In 1894 he returned to India and became one of the many who took part in 'the growing search for a national Indian identity' (Singh 1985: 11). Inspired by the English public school system, Das was keen to start schools in India on the same pattern; and as part of his 'search for a national Indian identity', he determined to 'establish Indian schools that would promote the ideals of equality and freedom which had inspired him' (*ibid.*). The moving spirit behind the project for an Indian pub-lic school could hardly have imagined – though he was perhaps not com-pletely oblivious of – the encomium which was to surround his endeavours, and ensure for his school a prominent position in the political and cultural life of the independent, 'new', India.[7]

In his own life too, Das performed the various scattered acts of the new man and the modern self: he was an active member of the 'reformist' Brahmo Samaj and, like many of his contemporaries in Bengal, a province which accepted the dictates of post-Enlightenment modernity with particular alacrity, he too kept a diary in which were carefully noted the cultural and political minutiae of a metropolitan existence. We may read Das's diary as autobiography *manqué*, its historical possibilities contained in its comments on the turmoils of its times. Such a reading will also serve as an introduction to the thoughts and opinions of the group of Das's friends who were to take charge of his public school project after his death in 1928. I will deal here with two events of national significance which are mentioned in the diary.

The year 1919 marks the advent of Gandhi's activities in the national movement on an all-India level. It was the enactment of the so-called Rowlatt Act in February of that year that turned Gandhi's attention to the national scene. The protests against the Act inaugurated 'the biggest and the most violent anti-British upsurge which India had seen since 1857' (Sarkar 1983: 189). The Rowlatt Act sought to extend and make permanent civil rights restrictions imposed during the war years through 'a system of special courts and detention without trial for a maximum of two years (even for actions like mere possession of tracts declared to be seditious)' (*ibid.*: 187). The unani-mous opposition from all the non-official Indian members of the Imperial Legislative Council could not, however, prevent its passage in that body. The 'elemental upheaval' – strikes, demonstrations, attacks on symbols of British authority – through which Indian resentment to the Act was articulated in the various cities and towns of the country (it seems largely to have been an urban response), attracted, in turn, a brutal response from the administrative machinery of the state.

The extent of the 'disturbances' and the brutality of the official response were particularly marked in the province of Punjab. On 11 April 1919, following police firing on a crowd and retaliatory attacks on some public buildings, the city of Amritsar was placed under martial law and an army officer, General Dyer, was put in command. The scene was set for one of the most infamous events of the whole of the nationalist period. The carnage at Jallianwalabagh, where on 13 April a crowd – unaware of prohibitions on public gatherings – was fired upon, was to find a prominent place in the nationalist consciousness of sacrifice and martyrdom:

> Official estimates later spoke of 379 killed. . . . Dyer's only regrets before the Hunter Commission were that his ammunition ran out, and that the narrow lanes had prevented his bringing in an armoured car . . . [so as to produce] . . . 'a moral effect'. During the following weeks, Dyer with the full backing of the Lieutenant-Governor went on with his job of 'producing a moral effect' through indiscriminate arrests, torture, special tribunals, public flogging, recruiting lawyers to work on menial jobs as constables . . . and making Indians crawl down *Kucha kauchianwala* lane where a white woman had been insulted.
>
> (Sarkar 1983: 190–1)

The event and official reaction to it caused wide-spread dismay and anger around the country, with Rabindranath Tagore renouncing his knighthood. The poet Hariwansrai Bacchhan, twelve at the time, writes in his autobiography of hearing an eyewitness account of the massacre from a relative and wondering 'how a government meant to look after public welfare could be so oppressive towards it' (Bacchhan [1969] 1993: 125). Finally, the government established a commission of inquiry to investigate the Punjab disturbances. The findings of the Hunter Commission Majority Report, made public on 28 May 1920 and condemned by Gandhi as 'whitewash', absolved the Punjab administration of all blame. On the very same day S.R. Das made the following entry in his diary:

> read . . . Government of India Dispatch in the Hunter Report. Considering all the circumstances I think the despatches are very satisfactory. People will be disappointed but then they expect the Government to feel in the same way as we do over the Punjab incidents, which is asking for too much. On the whole I think the Authorities have said as much as we could expect them to do [*sic*], placing ourselves in their position.[8]

His indifference, indeed antagonism, towards nationalist condemnation of the events in Punjab is not difficult to understand in light of the fact that as early as January 1920 he had been sounded out about the possibility of a position on the Executive Council of the Governor-General.[9]

S.R. Das's engagement with the public life of Bengal, and indeed with that of the rest of the country, intensified considerably in subsequent years. In 1925 he was offered, and accepted, a place on the Governor-General's

Executive Council as Law Member. Das saw in his elevation to high office an opportunity to further his public school project which had, until then, experienced fluctuating fortunes. An earlier effort in 1915 – he had started a school in Calcutta on the premises of the former residence of the first Governor-General – had collapsed after just five years (Singh 1985: 12).

The gathering din of the most momentous upsurge 'since 1857' seems hardly to have unsettled Das as he worked assiduously towards the establishment of the school which, as he once described in a letter to his son, was expected to provide the solution 'of the problem of the nationality of Indians'. The varied rituals of modern sociability did not find this protagonist of 'quiet unostentatious work' wanting: there were meetings of the directors of the Assam-Bengal Petroleum Company, garden parties hosted by the Viceroy and various solicitous Maharajas, Government House balls, treasurership of the Boy Scouts of Bengal and the Lodge of Good Fellowship, shoots in the afternoon 'by the jheel [lake] near the dak-bungalow', and meetings with fellow Brahmos.[10] His was a life of urban pleasance, lived out in the political and cultural interstices of the loyalist universe in the colonial city *par excellence*, Calcutta, and marked by the sagacity of judicious public activity and utterance. That Das's concerns and experiences were almost entirely urban, and that non-urban India punctuated his life as a penumbral Otherness is comically evident from the following entry in his diary:

> [went] to see an animal mela. . . . We walked a part of the way and then rest by ordinary bullock cart. My first experience of a ride in a bullock-cart. It was not very uncomfortable.
>
> (diary entry dated 26 March 1920)

The hectic round of official and social activity in the years following his appointment to the Executive Council also served as a convenient platform for the advocacy of his public school project. In December 1927 he wrote to one of his sons, then studying at Cambridge University, about progress on the matter:

> . . . at the present moment I am frightfully busy collecting some money for my school, which after all is going to be the real, though a very slow solution, of the problem of the nationality of Indians.

The second event of major significance through which we may trace the life and thoughts of Doon's founder occurred in November 1927, around the same time that he was to write to his son in Cambridge that the 'school scheme' was making good progress and that he had been promised 'about 12 lakhs up to now, of which I have collected about 4 lakhs' (letter dated 13 October 1927).[11] This was the establishment of the all-white Simon Commission to inquire into constitutional and political reform, and the *"imperial loyalty + anti-colonial stance"*

unprecedented opposition to it. In country-wide strikes and demonstrations people marched with 'Go Back Simon' banners and in Calcutta, Das's home city, there were 'massive demonstrations . . . [and] . . . simultaneous meetings in all the 32 wards . . . calling for a boycott of British goods' (Sarkar 1983: 265). The tumult found Das engaged in furious lobbying with several prominent politicians; and barely a month after the passing of a resolution by Nehru in favour of 'complete independence', a somewhat disheartened Das wrote to his son that:

> I had also a lot of political work to do on account of this ridiculous boycott of the Simon Commission. I met a number of prominent politicians and argued with them for hours. I think I did some good work but in our un-fortunate country one can never predict an hour beforehand what our politicians will do.
>
> (letter dated 5 Jan. 1928)

S.R. Das died in 1928, 'but his ideas and aspirations illuminated the way for those who took up the task' (Singh 1985: 9) of establishing the school which, Viceroy Willingdon hoped, would 'develop our young citizens with a high sense of honour . . . and discipline, qualities which are absolutely essential to all service in public life'.[12] The coterie that rallied support for the School after Das's death consisted of an influential group of senior bureaucrats (both Indian and European), princes, minor nobility, industrialists, and 'intellectuals'. The list of the financial benefactors (see Appendix 1) of the Indian Public School Society (IPSS) formed by Das with the object of 'founding schools without distinctions of caste, creed or social status' (*DSB*: 1), speaks of a social and political world which secured its sustenance and prosperity through strategic manoeuvres which at times saw it participate in the loyal procedures of the Raj, and at others in the anti-colonial passions of nationalist politics; it was through such deft movements that the School itself was to secure and guarantee its future. In its seemingly contradictory manoeuvres between imperial loyalty and an anti-colonial stance, the metropolitan intelligentsia associated with the School was not, it would seem, in any way unique. For, as Chandra (1994) has pointed out, such contradictory stances also characterised members of the provincial intelligentsia and were quite typical of the attitude of social commentators and journalists such as Bharatendu Harischandra (1850–85) and Vishnu Krishna Chiplunkar (1850–82).

Friends of the School, officials of the empire

When Das passed away, 'the enormous task' of transforming his 'dream' into concrete reality was readily taken up by a group of men prominent in official and Indian princely circles. The names which crop up most often in this connection are those of the Maharaja of Bikaner (who succeeded Das as Chairman of the IPSS), Sir Joseph Bhore (an Indian who was then Railway

Member of the Viceroy's Council), Sir Frank Noyce, Sir George Anderson (then Educational Commissioner with the Government of India), Sir Girija Shankar Bajpai and Sir Akbar Hydari. The social roots of the early Indian bourgeoisie lay, in contrast to its European counterpart, not in industry or trading, but in 'government service or the professions of law, education, journalism or medicine – with which was very often combined some connection with land in the shape of the intermediate tenures which were proliferating in Permanent Settlement Bengal' (Sarkar 1983: 68). Joseph Bhore belonged to this profitable world of the colonial intelligentsia, situated at the junction of strategic complaisance and protean loyalties. For the purposes of tracing the social roots and ethos of the School itself, it is instructive to follow his professional life, which also coincided with the years of nationalist upheaval.

Bhore was born in Nasik, in Western India, the son of Rao Saheb R.G. Bhore – Rao Saheb being one of the many official titles conferred upon Indians for a range of services to the Empire. He received his education at Bishop's High School, Poona, Deccan College, Poona, and University College, London. In 1902 he qualified for the Indian Civil Service (ICS), the apogee of colonial careers. The nature of the system of which Bhore had now become a part was a lively topic of discussion among certain sections of the Indian population. In 1878, the year of Bhore's birth, for instance, there had been a public outcry in Madras over opposition by sections of the European community to the appointment of an Indian as a High Court judge, as this would have led to an Indian drawing the same pay as his British counterpart. The event led to the subsequent founding of the nationalist journal *The Hindu* (Sarkar 1983).

Closer to the period of Bhore's induction into the grid of official power and privilege, there were stirrings too on another front, education. In 1902 – Bhore was twenty-four and had just passed into the ICS – the Indian Universities Commission published its report, embodying reforms which 'implied greater bureaucratisation of university education' (Kumar 1991: 118).

The Universities Bill of 1904 – framed with the object of curtailing student participation in anti-government political activity – was received, as Krishna Kumar points out, with great consternation by the Bengali intelligentsia, and 'the prospect of Bengal's partition provided the broader context in which indignation against sterner government control over university life was expressed' (*ibid.*). The public nature of the resentment over perceived official high-handedness is highlighted in an incident that occurred during one of the many protests against the Bill. These protests were expressed in the vocabulary of a defiant patriotism, resurgent in the face of perceived repression. The incident concerns the issue of a government circular to school and college authorities seeking to prohibit student participation in the Swadeshi movement which sought to oppose Curzon's Bengal partition plan by advocating the boycott of British goods:

[S.C.] Roy [a participant in the nationalist movement and the protagonist of the incident] describes how he and his fellow students violated the instructions issued by their headmaster in line with the government's circular. They chanted *Bande Mataram*[13] and attended a public meeting at the town hall. They were fined and later received an expulsion order issued by their Bengali headmaster. Resentment at this course of events took the form of a student rally in Calcutta where the first 'national' school was planned.

(Kumar 1991: 118–19)

It was during such a period of public upheaval and debate over the nature and consequences of colonialism that Joseph Bhore was setting the course of his future life. He was to chart that course along the clearly inscribed contours of official existence in an era marked by the gathering din of nationalist exertions. That his exalted position as an ICS officer would have engendered a certain political conservatism and very specific notions of 'citizenship' is a truism which, in the context of outlining the early history of the Doon School, needs to be stated. Furthermore, his association with the School as one of its guiding lights, proved to be of great import in enlisting support for it from like-minded sections of the Indian intelligentsia,[14] from feudal and commercial circles, and the government itself. The ICS officer was the very guarantor of those rights, privileges, and legalities of the secure classes – consisting of the groups who provided initial support for the School – which the latter perceived to be under imminent threat from the nationalist movement. Hence, the official impeccability of the following *curriculum vitae* as well as its cosmopolitan resonance in a time not just of political unrest, but of a political awakening on the part of the urban and rural 'lower classes', would have stood its owner, Joseph Bhore, in good stead among the 'educated classes':

Married in 1911, Margaret W. Scott, M.B., Ch. B. M.B.E. Educated at Bishop's High School, Poona, Deccan College, Poona, and University College, London. Entered the Indian Civil Service in 1902. Under-Secretary to the Government of Madras 1910, Dewan [Prime Minister], Cochin State, 1914–19, Deputy Director of Civil Supplies, Madras, 1919, Secretary to the High Commissioner for India 1920; Acting High Commissioner for India in the United Kingdom 1922–23, Secretary to the Government of India in Department of Agriculture and Lands 1924–28, Secretary, Indian Statutory Commission 1928; Member of the Governor-General's Executive Council 1928–35 . . .

(*Who's Who in India, Burma and Ceylon* 1940: 138)

Of the two other Indians mentioned above as part of the group which accepted responsibility for the establishment of the Doon School after 1928, Sir Girija Shankar Bajpai, a Brahmin from Allahabad and thirteen years Bhore's junior, was also an ICS officer. He had received his tertiary education at Muir College, Allahabad, and at Oxford University. The official itinerancy to which his career was subject saw Bajpai traverse not just the familiar routes of the national colonial domain but also the international highways of the imperial enterprise. His was a cosmopolitanism with the added lustre of the experience of the 'true' metropolis:

> Private Secretary to the Rt Hon. V. S. Srinivasa Sastri and Secretary for India at Imperial Conference, 1921 [in London]; and at Conference for Limitation of Armaments, Washington, 1921–22; on deputation to the dominions of Canada, Australia and New Zealand to investigate the Status of Indian residents of those territories, 1922; . . . Private Secretary to the leaders of the Indian Delegations to Geneva, 1929 and 1930; Joint Secretary to British Indian Delegation to the Indian Round Table Conference [London], 1930–31.
>
> > (*Who's Who in India, Burma and Ceylon* 1940: 137)

Sir Akbar Hydari – The Right Honourable Akbar Nawab Hyder Nawaz Jung Bahadur Hydari – who became Secretary of the Committee of Management of the Doon School in 1933, belonged to a section of the Muslim elite in India. Born in 1869 in Cambay in Western India and educated, in part, at Oxford University, Hydari married into the prominent Muslim clan of the Tyabjis, which itself has an enduring connection with the Doon School having sent several of its sons there – the earliest of the entrants having joined barely two years after the School opened in 1935.

Hydari's connections in his professional life ranged from the feudal world of the Nizam of Hyderabad's court to those 'rational' enterprises of colonial capitalism which marked its native practitioners with the redeeming seal of modernity. In 1919, he served as the Acting Director-General of Commerce and Industries, followed in 1920 by a stint as the Accountant-General of Bombay. He also served, during the 1920s, on the board of directors of several industrial corporations and banks. The image of the modern man belonging to a world which could translate the innumerable activities of human existence into the manageable universe of numbers, timetables, and production schedules, was made complete by Hydari's active involvement in that most public and immediate of modernising endeavours, 'native education'. He was, his generous profile in *Who's Who* tells us:

> Chairman, Inter-University Board, 1925; delivered the Punjab Convocation Address, 1925; Fellow of the Bombay, Dacca, Aligarh Muslim and Hyderabad Osmania Universities; conceived and organised the Osmania University, the first university of its kind in India.
>
> > (*Who's Who in India, Burma and Ceylon* 1940: 458)

During his tenure as a senior officer in the Nizam's administration in Hyderabad, Hydari had also taken part in constitutional talks between British and Indian leaders dubbed 'The Round Table Conferences'. In 1930, when both nationalist debate and agitation over a change in the form of governance at the centre and state violence against the 'agitators' were at their peak, Hydari was one of the chief sponsors of the idea of a federal assembly 'with a major section nominated by the princes' (Sarkar 1983: 308). The British were very favourably disposed to this idea, as it would ensure their continuing control over government affairs. Hydari's conservative politics – his open support for the colonial government which, in turn, provided a measure of support for his feudal patrons – occasioned no queries, however, by the School which had openly proclaimed its project of preparing 'citizens' for an 'independent' nation.

Some idea of the social and political world of men such as Bhore, Bajpai, and Hydari, its aesthetic and cultural sense, can be gained from the following views expressed in a conversation I had during 1991 with a former ICS officer. Now in his eighties, K.G.M. joined the Civil Service in the 1930s, having mainly studied in Allahabad. A Kashmiri Brahmin, he is directly related to and a patriarch of the Nehru clan. His two sons studied at a well-known Indian public school in the North Indian state of Himachal Pradesh, and it was as a public school parent as well as a representative member of a certain generation and class of Indian intelligentsia that I had gone to see him. We met at his house in a hill station locality in Himachal Pradesh where he spends the summer months, returning to the plains for the winter season. The huge and impeccably maintained bungalow was adorned both with the memorabilia of a prominent national and international career and the discreet but expensive markers of the cosmopolitan mien.

In early 1950, when his sons were of school age, K.G.M. was posted to Washington as a diplomat. I asked him why he had chosen to send his sons to Lawrence School, the boarding school in the nearby locality of Sanawar.[15] He said:

> My sons were with me in the US and the eldest complained that the academic studies [*sic*] were at a very low standard, that he had already done all this in India. . . . I had heard of a few schools in India, there was Rajkumar College[16] . . . but I didn't want to send them to a Princes college, it would have meant disaster to send a child there . . . private servants, cars, horses . . . and all that. Of course, this was in 1952 and this sort of thing had been considerably reduced [*sic*] . . . but the tradition was still there, and Doon had a very long waiting list for admissions so I sent them to Sanawar.

We can treat the above response as constituting two separate, though related, statements regarding modern, post-colonial, Indian self-hood, as perceived by a member of an intelligentsia which regards its consciousness as synchronous with the moment of post-coloniality; its destiny inscribed in the wider narrative of historical determinism where all populations are transported, sooner or later, from the realm of the 'pre-modern' to that of the modern, from dependency and subjecthood to citizenship and nationhood. The first part of the response, the one regarding his son's comment on American schooling, that 'he had already done all this in India', can be seen as an attempt to establish a dignified presence for a politically recent entity, the Indian nation ('this was in 1952', as K.G.M. specified, barely five years from the formal end of British rule in India), by setting the standard of its academic universe against that of an 'advanced' western nation.

The attempt to locate the new nation within a configuration of characteristics – learning, the intellect, the written word – which speak of the antiquity and the 'authenticity' of that national community, is also an effort to establish the dignity and worth of its intelligentsia, its 'educated classes'. K.G.M.'s particular form of Indianness, which expresses itself in the faultless syntax of progress and the modern, and in the steady, confident voice of the loving citizen-child, next proceeds to distinguish its own specific identity from other cultural selves in the national collectivity. It is this conscious act of setting apart which animates the second part of the response concerning Rajkumar College, and imbues it with a significance beyond the immediacy of its context.

The demarcation occurs at the cultural intersection where the Indian modern, ready to stake its claim in the universal modernity that comes to be translated as citizenship, confronts its perceived antithesis, the feudal order, with which, at other levels, it has forged a mutually beneficial alliance. The feudal order is the antithesis of modern Indianness in the logic of its existence: hereditary elitism; for modernity speaks in the upbraiding tones of individual effort, equality of opportunity. It is the censuring wraith of John Stuart Mill, attempting to transcend rather than confront the dissimulation inherent in its position, which speaks through the discourse of Indian postcoloniality of which K.G.M. is a representative. 'It is desirable', as Mill was to note, 'that in things which primarily concern others, individuality should assert itself. Where, not the person's own character, but the traditions and customs of other people are the rule of conduct, there is wanting one of the principle ingredients of individual and social prosperity' (Mill 1991: 63).

Regarding the erstwhile princes' school Rajkumar College, K.G.M. suggested that it would have been a 'disaster' to have sent his sons there because of an atmosphere which reeked of the decadence of court life. It is also a proclamation, made by several parents I spoke to, of the unmistakable modernity of the class that considered itself charged with the responsibility of ushering the nation into the light of modernity. That the same class in post-Independence India displays characteristics quite similar to those it repudiated – hereditary elitism – is a matter perhaps of only minor irony. For we must remember that while they spoke of modernity and individuality, the founders of the Doon School, mostly belonging to a professions-based intelligentsia, often forged strong and fruitful relationships with feudal interests (see Appendix 1). We need, therefore, to rethink the meaning of modernity, rather than persist with frameworks which posit a sharp division between the 'modern' and the 'pre- (or, anti-) modern'.

This history of Indian modernity and post-coloniality as a collaborative treatise – the traces of which lie buried under the 'joyfulness' of its narrative of progress and 'national' good – can also be found in earlier attempts to constitute modernist subjectivities. In the Foreword to a book on the 'origins' of the turn-of-the-century National Education Movement, Radha Kumud Mookerji speaks of a meeting to consider the implications of the student agitation against the planned partition of Bengal (1905). The meeting, he cheerfully reports, was called by the Landholders' Association of Bengal and 'was a representative Conference of national leaders, of all men of light and leading in the country' (Mukherjee and Mukherjee 1957: x). The Conference resolved that open conflict with the government should be avoided and that 'the boycott of the Calcutta University Examinations be called off by the students concerned' (*ibid.*). However, it also resolved to plan for the education of the expelled students through the establishment of a National Council of Education. The National Education Movement, Mookerji continues, 'received a very good start by the donations announced on the spot by Brajendra Kishore Roy Chowdhury (Zemindar of Gouripur) and Surya Kanta Acharya Chowdhury (Maharaja of Mymensingh)' (*ibid.*). It is in this light – the half-light of the consolidation of a 'national' consciousness – that we should appraise the banishment and disavowal of the 'feudal' from the *tableau vivant* of Indian modernity, since the two are, really, part of the same economy of praxis, expressions of shared commitments, and contiguous emotions.

In the next part of the interview K.G.M. proceeded to provide further elaboration of the world which he and those he considers part of his community, occupy: it is also, of course, a tangential glimpse of those against whom this world must brace itself. I asked him what he thought of the criticism directed at public schools such as Doon:

SS: Among other things, many don't consider the environment at these schools very 'Indian' . . . .

KGM: I don't agree with it at all . . . they give children a modern education and what these people call 'India' or 'Indian' is not modern . . . if they want to go back to the Vedas, they are welcome . . . I don't, I want my country to be a modern country.

SS: What do you mean by 'modern'?

KGM: My conception of a modern country is a rational country, not fundamentalist, where the mind is closed and completely ignorant of what is happening in the world and not interested. . . .

SS: Modernity?

KGM: Modernity is rationalism . . . that's all it is! (*Given that the meeting had been arranged after some difficulty, it seemed best to defer to his pique and change tack.*)

SS: Was your generation more rational than the present one?

KGM: It all depends on the background of the generation . . . the class of people I come from were more rational . . . India was never a rational country.

SS: Which class?

KGM: (*in an exasperated tone of voice*) The upper classes [*sic*], the educated people who have had generations of education . . . and have not been poor, we are not rich . . . we have a tradition of education and at least in my family, of rationalism.

. . . so in the political process in India today people [i.e. politicians] are certainly less rational than they used to be, because those in public life now are much less educated, than they used to be. They are much more traditional, fundamental [*sic*], closed minded, no experience, and proud of their ignorance!

SS: Why has this happened?

KGM: . . . because no honest man can go into public life! (*Pause*) . . . with a few exceptions.

SS: Who are the exceptions?

KGM: That's none of your business! It is not an Anthropologist's business![17]

Those who are 'proud' of their ignorance belong to the larger group, the 'fundamentalists', the narrow-minded, and the 'traditional': the 'masses' that threaten the ordered and 'rational' existence of the nation. There are several issues that are addressed by K.G.M.'s answers to my questions; and their location at that crucial juncture of class, caste, and gender where cultural opinions are made, remade and then presented as 'natural' is unmistakable.

The diatribe against the 'fundamentalists' is also, of course, a comment on and against the tumult of the times when public manifestations of the contemporary religious upsurge in India has made visible, and in that sense empowered, a previously passive class. The mass rallies and *yatras* in support of building a temple where a mosque stands, or against the 'excessive pandering' to 'minority interests', are also insurrectional to the interests of the metropolitan intelligentsia which participates in the politics of cultural representations of national identity. For in the militant visibility of the socio-economic stratum which provides the foot soldiers for these marches and rallies – events of tremendous dislocatory consequence in the urban environment – there lies a threat to the bourgeois-liberal monopoly over the public space, that representational space of culture and national identity whose largely unchallenged guardian it has so far been.

Communalism, or to use its more condemnatory characterisation, fundamentalism, is also a class issue. The pictures, still and moving, which come to us of this or that religious rally, the mammoth crowds responding to their leaders with great ferocity and verve, are also snapshots of the apparent emergence of the subaltern – the slum dweller, the villager, the provincial – as the speaking subject. This subjectivity is, of course, circumscribed and manipulated by the power goals of political and quasi-political groups such as the Bharatiya Janata Party (BJP) and the Vishwa Hindu Parishad (VHP), thereby rendering it more apparent than real. This aspect, however, cannot alter the *perception* of the urban intelligentsia, formed both through individual observation and mass media images, of the linkage between the so-called fundamentalism and the 'lower' classes. Under the banner of the constitutional fiction which defined the Indian state as 'secular',[18] the defence of religious pluralism, through an attack on 'fundamentalism', then elides the presence of both class and (upper) caste aspects of such secularism.[19]

It is this submerged discourse on class and caste, which animates K.G.M.'s comment on those who want to go back 'to the Vedas'. For it is nowhere clear that his stated commitment to the tenets of modernity and rationalism, ambivalently elaborated as these are, is also, on the other hand, a steady engagement with the basic framework of Hinduism itself, or with the bounty reaped by the *upper castes* through their strategic involvement with various levels of the Raj.[20] Indeed, with the disconcerting ingenuousness of a voice which speaks from *within* the experiential matrices of class, caste, and gender power, K.G.M. states quite clearly his idea of those 'classes' which are 'more rational': his family, which has 'a tradition of education and . . . of rationalism', and which is not just 'upper class', but also upper caste.

In this way K.G.M., whom I take to be a representative of the class that provided the intellectual capital for the Doon School, its cultural agenda, its moral and (mostly unstated) political objectives, delineates what could be regarded as a distinct space for a very specific Indian identity. It was the task of producing this identity which was, and continues to be, the stated aim of the Doon School. This identity was explicitly distanced from both the pre-modernism of the feudal past and the 'anti-modernism' of an irrational present. I have already suggested that, in fact, the 'pre-modern' was allied to the Doon project in a very obvious way since a large number of princes and nobles provided financial help to the School; I will later argue that the anti-modern was also co-opted into the being of the School, though in a manner far less obvious and for a purpose far more complex.

By 1934, Doon's management committee had decided that the former campus of the Forest Research Institute (FRI) at Chandbagh in Dehra Dun, would be a suitable site for the new school.[21] The Chandbagh estate then covered approximately 44 acres and the Committee was of the opinion that they 'would be unlikely to obtain a property affording anything like the area and accommodation available at Chandbagh Estate, at anything like the concessional price which the Government are generously prepared to accept. . . . That the value of this offer is increased by the readiness of the Government to lease the land and building for a period of three years at a nominal rent of Rs. 3000 per annum, it being open to the Society then or at any previous time to purchase the Estate and buildings at a cost of Rs 3.5 lakhs [Rs 350,000]' (Singh 1985: 17).[22] The *Times of India* correspondent covering the opening ceremony of the School, presided over by Viceroy Willingdon, noted that the founders of the School 'being shrewd bargainers . . . [had] obtained this valuable property . . . for probably a quarter or even one-fifth of the amount it was originally worth'.[23] Considering the professional intimacy shared by the School's mentors with the government of the day, they need hardly have been 'shrewd bargainers' to obtain the property on the terms they did.[24]

The day of fulfilled dreams

On 27 October 1935, with an 'eminent company' of people for his audience, and with 'all the publicity from the press it could have wished for', Viceroy Willingdon declared the School open. Echoing the sentiments of colonial and nationalist historiography of the time, *The Doon School Book* (hereafter DSB) noted that 'naturally, some of the press comment was sceptical as the history of India contained many episodes of unfulfilled dreams' (*DSB*: 4). 'Fulfilment' – progress, modernity, communal harmony, the 'scientific tem-per', and the 'rational attitude' – under British rule was an important *leitmotif* of late nineteenth- and early twentieth-century nationalist thinking (Chandra 1994; Pandey 1994). In his famous 1884 public lecture on 'How Can India Progress?', the 'father of modern Hindi literature' and social commentator Bhartendu Harishchandra had noted that 'if even under British rule, when we are given every kind of resource and opportunity, we do not progress, it can only be because of our (bad) fate and the wrath of god' (Harishchandra in Pandey 1994: 273). The founders of the Doon School had, then, grasped these opportunities to move towards the realms of progress, and 'on the whole the public [the native intelligentsia? the peasants?] were prepared to wait and see' (*DSB*: 4). At the date of its formal inauguration the School had, in fact, already been functioning for one and a half months, having received its first student on 10 September. That period of its operation sufficiently emboldened the Headmaster, Arthur Foot, recently arrived from England, to observe in his opening day speech that 'our short experience in the Doon School convinces us that the life here is already showing its influence on the boys, and nothing has occurred which has done anything except confirm my deep faith in the future value of the school' (*Times of India*, 28 Oct. 1935 (hereafter TOI)).

A scrutiny of the assemblage which graced the School campus that day provides an instructive picture of the various segments of Indian society involved in the process of forging a contract of modernity and citizenship through the deed which was the School itself. It will also help to place in a wider perspective the notion, quite actively fostered by proponents of the Doon School, that, among other things, 'ignorance' and 'a peculiar interpretation of socialism' have led to there being a substantial body of public opinion which threatens their existence.[25] We have already noted the active involvement of senior ICS officers in the establishment of the School and several of their number, including Sir Girija Shankar Bajpai, then a temporary Member of the Viceroy's Executive Committee, were present for the opening ceremony (*TOI*).

But perhaps the most intriguing presence of all at the inaugural rites of a school which included in its charter of objectives 'the goal of providing the best secular education for Indian children' (Singh 1985: 11) was that of one of the founders and leading lights of the Hindu Mahasabha, Pandit Madan Mohan Malviya. Malviya's involvement in the nationalist movement is too well known to need detailed elaboration here, and I will deal fully with the incongruity of his presence at the opening day ceremony in Chapter 4; this incongruity is particularly piquant when one considers that among the School's several proclamations was one which asserted that 'there was no room' in its 'atmosphere' for 'intolerance of other people's faith' (*DSB*: 14). I will suggest in Chapter 4 that the accommodation of a 'secular' discourse within the framework of a Hindu praxis is a marked peculiarity of the narrative of the nation state articulated at the School.

Malviya's attendance at a gathering of the leading lights of industry, government, non-Hindu religious organisations, 'officers of the Central Public Works Department, leading citizens of Dehra Dun and officers of the Indian Military and Gurkha Regiment' (*TOI*) should not surprise us. For the citizenship compact being sealed at the Doon School involved an almost exhaustive cross-section of the Indian intelligentsia. A figurative graphology of the signatures upon the exordial tract on the desired civil society – the School – would have revealed proclivities from a very wide range of political and cultural positions. And, notwithstanding the antagonism of their public postures, their actual congruence and their implicit congeniality found a fruitful meeting ground in the being of the School. We must remember, after all, that Malviya, a leading figure of the North Indian intelligentsia, not only maintained strong contacts with leading members of the Indian commercial sector (Bayly 1975) but also undertook a 'collection drive . . . among the landed upper castes of the Hindi region in order to provide the Banaras Hindu University with a sound financial footing' (Kumar 1991: 182). The specific nature of Indian modernity on display on the School's opening day – in terms of the various forces which came together to give it life – has continued to persist in more or less unchanged form, its characters and forces continuing to maintain their early influence and vigour in a new globalised environment.

In this way, the School became a protectorate of several vital interests: *laissez-faire* ideologists shared pleasantries with the agents of government intervention; bourgeois aspirations, tuned to and visibly animated by the reformative music of the European Renaissance, established fruitful dialogue with native autocracy; and Hindu communalists advocating a post-colonial nation based on the dogma of scriptural strictures, clasped warmly their Muslim counterparts. Appendix 2, which lists the Foundation Members of the IPSS, provides some idea of the widespread backing for the School in regional, social, and political terms.

The School also came to be located between the complementary poles of 'knowledge and acknowledgment' (Bourdieu 1986: 252) and upon the grounds of a social aestheticism: a visible community of manners and an audible community of speech that constituted and recognised itself through the etiquette of 'civil' life. There are glimpses of this in early school photographs of the annual Founder's Day gatherings. The daguerreotypical representation of a social class and an age, and that of the transformation of positions of power based on the manipulations of the colonial political economy into one of the sublime ethos of social aestheticism and a spiritual communion, are nowhere more apparent than in these images.

This community had its base in colonial jurisprudence and, consequently, in the power of the colonial economy of private property.[26] It was an aestheticism that was, as well, aligned to the very specific idea of individual – 'spiritual' – discipline.

Backwardness in a disciplinary perspective

We may distinguish the idea of the discipline imposed on the outer world of phenomenological existence from that of 'spiritual discipline' by referring to the thought of the nineteenth-century Bengali novelist, Bankimchandra Chattopadhyay. 'Spiritual discipline' refers to the need for the regeneration of the 'inner' self. Bankimchandra's

> blueprint for a programme of national regeneration . . . was evidently concerned with the physical invincibility of the British power in India. In his didactic writings, he speaks of the need for a spiritual discipline, based on the cultivation of all the human faculties, including the physical. The purpose is service to one's country and mankind in a spirit of total detachment. The patriotic monks in [his novel] *Anandmath* are fictional exemplars of this ideal life style. . . . In devising a symbol for [the] militant nationalism of his imagination, Bankim evoked the image of the Motherland, once glorious now reduced to shameful misery. She is identified with the mother goddess worshipped as Sakti i.e. power incarnate, and in his famous hymn to the Mother, *Bande Mataram*, the weapons in her ten arms, her infinite strength and the sharp swords in the hands of her myriad children evoke an image of great power.
>
> (Raychaudhuri 1988: 134)

Hence, early nationalist thought operated with two quite different conceptions of discipline: that which is imposed from without and that generated from 'within'. In both cases the disciplinary enterprise is concerned with regenerating the individual and, *subsequently*, the society; in this, both points of view represented a triumph of a cult of the 'personality', where all transformations are simply a matter of transforming the (male) self. Here, the claims of social action (and analysis) focused on the historically consolidated positions of power are almost completely denied.

The emergence of a disciplinary aesthetics in India should be understood in the context of a colonial milieu where both 'discipline' and 'aesthetics' were denied the indigenous classes that made claims to them. The two examples below provide some idea of what I refer to as disciplinary aesthetics. The first is a description of the European section of the encampment at the extravagant Imperial Assemblage of 1877, organised during the Viceroyalty of Lord Lytton to commemorate the declaration of Victoria as the Empress of India. The observer is Sir Dinkar Rao, Prime Minister of Gwalior state. To fully comprehend the nature and content of British rule in India, and why it will continue to flourish in the foreseeable future, Rao states, 'one need only go up to Flagstaff Tower', from where a panoramic view of the encampment could be had,

> and look down upon this marvellous camp. Let him notice the method, the order, the cleanliness, the discipline, the perfection of the whole organisation and he will recognise at once the epitome of every title to command and govern which one race can possess over others.
>
> (Cohn 1988: 667)

My second example of the discipline which speaks through the organisation of an aesthetic calculus, comes from the autobiography of Bipinchandra Pal. Pal (1858–1932) was active in the public life of Bengal in the late nineteenth and early twentieth centuries, and was a prominent participant in the national movement and a leading light of the Brahmo Samaj.

In 1898, Pal sailed for England to join a two-year course at the Manchester College at Oxford University. Travelling through continental Europe, he disembarked at the French port of Marseilles and travelled overland through France to cross the English Channel at Calais for Dover. His brief journey through the French countryside provided a man of Pal's alert intellect ample opportunity to reflect upon the difference between the land he had left behind and the new world into which he was venturing. He wrote:

> . . . travelling through France, I was struck by the difference between our rural areas and those of Europe. The hand of man was in everything that I saw; there was no rank vegetation, but the whole land by the railway was carefully cultivated. Even the pumpkin of which we take absolutely no care seemed to have been lovingly tended so that every side of the fruit could have the rays of the sun beating on it and painting it with its red colour. The whole countryside was a thing of beauty created by man.
>
> (Pal 1973: 550–1)

The cure for social and economic stasis lay, according to this logic, in *personal* development, which, in turn, often found expression in the grafting of geo-metrical discipline onto the physical arrangements of every-day life; that it was the outer world of carefully arranged domestic furniture, the symmetry of suburban lines imposed upon a temporary settlement, the transformation of natural profusion into herborised order, that most closely reflected, and redeemed, the inner world of a disciplined human existence. These announced the occupants of one society to be not just different from, but also superior to, those of other, less organised societies. The issue of the forms of discipline most becoming the post-colonised nation state has a long discursive pedigree, and I will explore it at some length in Chapter 3.

Untainted harbingers of progressive values

In August 1934, the Indian Public School Society decided that the appointment of a Headmaster for the new school should be made in England, and that 'previous experience in India was not only not necessary but would be a disqualification' (*DSB*: 2). Further, that other Englishmen to be recruited to the staff should also be 'fresh to the country'. In this manner, the School could, perhaps, ensure the service of men untainted by the mores of the society that it hoped to transform. The President of the Board of Education, Lord Halifax, was put in charge of the selection committee based in London, 'in which he was to be associated with the High Commissioner for India, the Headmaster of an English Public School, and a former Educational Commissioner with the Government of India' (*ibid.*).

Away from the distractions of the colony, the committee set to work in earnest on the task of deciding upon the man to head the school where the national identity 'problems' of Indians were to be solved. The successful applicant for the position of Headmaster was Arthur Foot, a science master at Eton and former student of the public school, Winchester College, as well as of Cambridge and Oxford Universities; more than anyone else it is Foot who is regarded as the person most responsible for the School's establishment and success.[27] Upon his arrival in India, the 34-year-old Englishman set about his task with a zeal which was breathtaking both in its sincerity and its presumptuousness. Due to his scant knowledge of the country in which he had been chosen to head a major cultural enterprise, the management committee of the School 'had with great forethought engaged as the Headmaster's Personal Assistant, Captain Sardar Khan, who had retired a year before from the post of Adjutant at the Prince of Wales Royal Indian Military College. . . . [Sardar Khan] . . . was able to steer the Headmaster through the difficulties a new comer to India experienced in matters of etiquette, warning him of the status of his visitors – so often in inverse proportion to the smartness of their clothes – and indicating the right modes of address in the voluminous correspondence' (Singh 1985: 2).

Arthur Foot's reign as Headmaster lasted some thirteen years (1935–48), concluding with his departure for England soon after Indian Independence. In that time he was to lay down the basic framework of school life at Doon – his conception of the civil society, its aesthetic principles, and the rules and ceremonies of its functioning; it is a framework which has found wide dissemination and acceptance in several other schools around the country, its pollen carried, as it were, by the thirty or more Doon staff and old boys who went on to head schools of their own. Discussion and analysis of that framework and its articulation with the community 'outside' forms the major part of the task of this book.

The perception on the part of those associated with Doon School, that it has served, and continues to serve, as a model for other Indian public schools, is particularly strong. This perception itself is part of the larger schematic, visualised by S.R. Das himself. For he had sought the dissemination of the disciplinary and aesthetic minutiae of the post-colonial civil society through a *scattered* network of public schools. And the body founded by Das for the purposes of establishing the Doon School, the Indian Public *Schools* Society, was charged precisely with the duty the plural in its name implies: the setting up of several public schools in India;[28] hundreds of little beacons strategically located in a sea of cultural and political darkness, and beaming out into that darkness messages of democracy, equality, and secularism. 'I would like to believe', H.S., an old boy in his early forties, told me:

> that schools such as Doon . . . are really mother institutions, that they have a social and national role to play which is not simply the education they impart to the students, but in fact the education they impart to the teacher, because teachers from these institutions go out to other institutions across the country and carry whatever they have learnt . . . and in that sense they are mother institutions and I would certainly like to see the [Doon] School play a far more intense role in that.

P.L., an ex-student of Doon, now in his late sixties, voiced the popular perception of Doon as a model for other schools to copy when I sought his opinion of other public schools in India. He had only visited one other public school apart from Doon, he said, but he had heard about the others from various people; for instance, Mayo College:

> a former Chiefs College [that] was later converted [*sic*] into a public school . . . and the person who gave that stamp . . . was my old geography master at Doon, G.,[29] . . . when he went to Mayo College, exactly the same routine which was there at Doon was introduced there, with minor adjustments to suit local conditions. Similarly, some of the others . . . who went to Rajkumar College, the same thing as what they had [*sic*] in Doon School was introduced there. . . .
> M. went as principal to Sardul Public School in Bikaner, and again whatever was in Doon was introduced there. I took a cricket team from

my club in Delhi to Scindia School and I could just see Doon School in Scindia School.[30]

The School constructed the rationale for the necessity of its existence by setting the observable tranquillity of its environment, the great unanimity of opinion which greeted its birth, and the clear utilitarian logic of its discourse, against the pandemic turbulence and the profound disagreements which characterised a colonial society in the throes of the nationalist movement. It embellished that rationale by transcribing the economic and social stasis which characterised such a society with the language of individual pathology; that the 'problems' besetting Indian society could be solved by concentrating on the three elements of individual personality which Arthur Foot had suggested were central to the 'methods and programme' of a public school in his opening day speech: character, intellect, and physique.

The same method of the contrast, where a carefully monitored and lavishly financed institution is set against the general, irrefutable decrepitude and continuing uncertainties of contemporary Indian society, continues to be evoked today by supporters of the School.

Soon after taking over the Headmastership, Foot embarked upon a tour of several cities to meet and goad the 'right' sort of families to send their sons to the new school. Several students from his days as Headmaster recall his 'salesmanship'. I asked R.W., a student at the school from 1937 to 1944, why his parents had sent him to the Doon School. 'I had just come back from England,' he said:

> My father [an army officer sent to England for a training course] had put me in a boarding school there . . . where was a school [in India] which matched all that? . . . And Foot was a magnificent salesman, he grabbed all sorts of people . . . 'Send your son!' My father was a great believer in good education. He [Foot] . . . used to write to people, go and meet people in the holidays . . . get them to be members of the IPSS.

Very soon, however, persuasion from one side gave way to an overwhelming demand for places at the School from the other. M.M., whose son studied at the School in the 1950s, and whose husband served for a period on its Governing Council, describes the situation in the 1950s:

> There was a waiting list [for admissions] . . . and people would send telegrams as soon as their wives were pregnant! And one of them [an old boy] sent three telegrams, but one after the other he had three daughters!

The campus where sons could grow up to be modern citizens of the post-colonial nation state was also, as I have discussed with regard to K.G.M., one which consciously distinguished its unique place in the national collectivity from others within it. One of these Others often employed to do service in outlining the unique position of the School is the 'feudal order'. It is often pointed out by those connected with Doon that the latter was the first real alternative for Indian parents to the residential Chiefs' Colleges, and that there was a ready-made demand for its services because 'progressive' Indians were wary of the 'feudal reputation' of the Chiefs' Colleges. In the next chapter, I provide a socio-historic account of one such 'princely' school, the Mayo College at Ajmer in Rajasthan, in order to place the feudal Other of the Indian 'modern' within a comparative framework.

2   The marble mirage: constructing the Orient

Mayo College, founded in 1875 and located in Ajmer, Rajasthan, owes its name to Richard Bourke, Earl of Mayo and Viceroy of India from 1869 to 1872. Though presently admission to the school is open to all who can pay and it functions much like several other Indian public schools, it was originally established for a very specific clientele. The idea for an exclusive school for the princes of Rajputana was first put forward in 1869 by Colonel Walter, the Political Agent of Bharatpur state,[1] and gained the support of Lord Mayo soon after. Mayo College ('Mayo') was one of the five institutions in India known as Chiefs' Colleges. These were charged with the duty of 'providing for the sons of the ruling classes such an education as will fit them for the discharge of their responsibilities to their subjects'.[2] The other four were Rajkumar College (Rajkot), the Daly College (Indore), Aitchison College (Lahore), and Raipur College (Orissa).

A civilising influence for princes

Mayo is not the oldest of these institutions but was treated by the British as the most important. Hence, between 1887 and 1930 it had been visited by every Viceroy as well as by members of the British royal family, including the Duke and Duchess of Connaught (1887), Queen Mary (1911), and the Prince of Wales in 1922 (*Mayo College Silver Jubilee Souvenir* 1930: 19). These visits often became occasions for elaboration and the celebration of the 'civilising' mission of the West in the East. So, in 1913, Viceroy Hardinge addressed the School on its Annual Day with the following words: 'These Chiefs' Colleges', he said:

> are, to my mind, a civilising and progressive influence in India and at the same time a means of disseminating the breadth of this beautiful land, thanks to the example of the Principals and the Masters employed, all that we of the British race regard as most precious as principles of morality, loyalty and culture.[3]
>
> (*Mayo College Magazine*, Vol. IX No. I, 1913)

The 'work' to be carried out at Mayo College was most often represented as that of bridging the difference between the two cultures, the Oriental and the Occidental. This difference was articulated in several ways. In 1870, a senior government official, while concurring with the opinion that the proposed school should be modelled on Eton, entered the caveat that 'Eton flourishes under traditions and glories which cannot be called up in India', but, he added, 'much which it is in our power to do must be done'.[4] It was Viceroy Curzon, however, who, with characteristic bluntness, articulated the 'difference' which the College was to attempt to bridge. The differences between Mayo College and an English public school could be seen, Curzon said, as a summary of the differences between the East and the West themselves. The English public school system 'in its essence . . . is', he noted, 'contrary to the traditional sentiments of Indian parents of the aristocratic classes, and to the hereditary instincts of Indian parents [in general]' (speech at the Conference on the Chiefs' Colleges, 1902–3).

Curzon wished to highlight a fundamental issue: that of the difference between a society which had evolved an 'enlightened' hierarchy, versus another, mired in a 'despotic' and primitive system of gradations. 'Eton', he suggested, 'is an aristocratic school organised upon a democratic basis', whereas in India this may not be possible. Here:

> You have to deal with a more primitive state of society. . . . That levelling down of class distinctions without detriment to the sentiments of class respect, which is so marked a characteristic of English civilisation, can not be expected ready made in a country like this.
>
> (*ibid.*)

This chapter seeks to explore the cultural and political terrain within which the Mayo College was intended to be situated, in order to provide one of the contexts *against* which the Doon School distinguished its version of modernity and post-coloniality. Among other aspects, I will analyse the physical landscape of the Mayo College, seeking to explore the politico-cultural intent of the architectural style of its main building and the character of the social space that was sought in its ichnography.[5] The choice of a specific style of architecture for Mayo College, and the positioning of the various components of the architecture in the ensemble, represented a conscious effort by the designers to convey certain ideas of culture and politics; it can, in other words, be seen as the spatial expression of an ideological intent: the 'capture' and display of an Otherness that is the past, alongside symbolic markers of a 'robust', progressive culture, proclaiming the dawn of a new age, the future.

Architecture of the past, proclamations of the future

The main building of the College (Figure 2.1), constructed from unpolished white marble, and adorned with numerous canopies, cupolas, arches, eaves, and minarets in what nineteenth-century observers referred to as the Indo-Saracenic style, rises magically, if somewhat incongruously, from amidst its surroundings; it is like a shimmering white mirage in a city itself at the edge of a desert. Its incongruity is compounded by the white marble statue of Lord Mayo, the school's founder, which stands within its shadows, its unwavering gaze fixing the vast distances of what, to him, must have seemed like a secure Empire. And in the middle of this supposed fusion of all the grandness of style which the Orient had to offer, stands a sentinel of British self-perception: the clock-tower.

At first sight merely an incongruous protrusion, the tower, embedded within a concrete representation of what the Orientalists were fond of calling 'The Timeless East', also stands as a potent signifier of the ideological undercurrents which gave birth to the school. For the clock-tower was part of the system of meanings that made up the discrete discursive universe of nineteenth-century Europe; a world which perceived its difference from the ethos of Oriental existence through the intellectual and spiritual elaborations of the European Renaissance and through the mechanisms of the industrial revolution.[6]

Clock-towers built during the Raj can be found in almost all Indian towns which experienced a significant British presence. They are usually located at

Figure 2.1 Mayo College main building.

the administrative centre of the township or at important crossroads. The colonial clock-tower, embedded within the system of cultural and political meanings that defined and animated the Raj, had for long been a part of the mythology and folklore of Britishness. This Britishness was perceived in a like manner by both the colonisers and a large number of Indians who interacted with them. Hence, notwithstanding the Anglo-Indian folklore of the unpunctual native, one of the most persistent themes in (Indian) biographical material of the time is that of the punctual native. The stories are usually a variation on how so-and-so's father/grandfather performed the same routine all his life, regulating his existence to the clock, and 'never once' being late for office. Secular time in these accounts takes on the form of a spiritual calendar, a religious imperative. So, poet Hariwanshrai Bacchhan writing about his father, a clerk in *The Pioneer* newspaper around the turn of the century, notes that the latter would rather forgo breakfast than be late for work and that 'my father would say that in the entire thirty-five years of his working life he was never once late for work' (Bacchhan [1969] 1993: 80); eager 'native' eyes gazed into the time-piece in the hope of finding an altered image, its countenance stretched around the face of the dial, comfortable in the new, 'modern' temporality.

Clock-towers marked, both literally and symbolically, the route the native might take to the realms of modernity; they represented the march of progress, man's (*sic*) control over the natural environment and, ultimately, the management of human destiny itself. Situated in an environment perceived to be characterised by excessive spirituality and other-worldliness, the clock-tower stood as a salient and articulate symbol of the 'rational' West, directing its progressive gaze from various vantage points far above the temporal and spatial anarchy of its surroundings. In a role similar to that attributed by Foucault to the Panopticon, though different from it in what it represented, the clock-tower too was a symbol, an epitome, for a specific society.[7] The major difference between the two symbolic edifices was this: if the Panopticon was the all-seeing eye, the clock-tower was there to be seen and to be attended to. It combined, within its public visage, the functions of both proclamation and directive.

The Mayo College clock-tower could be said to have performed a similar role. It rises majestically above its deliberately ambiguous surroundings, a mixture of architectural expression, and is surmounted by a crown not dissimilar to the one Queen Victoria is often shown wearing in the Empress-and-her-colonies portraits (see e.g. Benson 1987). The symbolic economy of the tower combines, then, the potent image of the crown as a symbol of British power with a representation of British society, the clock; the icon of the secular sovereignty of rational management of human actions is juxtaposed with the metonymical form of divine sovereignty on earth.

If the military garrison stationed in Ajmer represented British political control of the physical territory surrounding the College, then the insertion of the clock-tower into a jumble of diverse architectural styles amounted to a proclamation of the capture of an alien culture; the tower 'controlled' the 'Oriental architecture' surrounding it. At the time of its construction, and before subsequent additions to the main building, three elements combined to give the tower its visible impact: its height, the asymmetrical design of the building itself, such that the tower stood at one end of it, and the profusion of styles in the design of the main building. I mean to suggest, then, that in the symbolic economy of the main building, the profusion ('miscegenation'?) was the Orient, and the unadorned clock-tower its Spartan antithesis.[8] The symbolic intent of the tower drew its authority from the steadily accumulating sentiments on the 'essence' of Britishness; from ideas which linked that essence to the prevalent theories of progress, rationality, and the hierarchy of races.[9]

'Educated' Indian opinion on the essence of Britishness could be found in several contexts, including among the members of the Positivist Society of Calcutta which counted among its number W.C. Bonnerjee who later became President of the Indian National Conference, and the novelist Bankim-chandra Chattopadhyay (Bhattacharya 1974). Bankimchandra provided the following explanation for Europe's 'great success'. It lay, he said, in:

> one particular element of strength in her intellectual tradition – the inductive method based on observation and experiment and the inclination to follow the glimpses of truth revealed to the inspired intellect to their legitimate conclusions. [Bankim cited] . . . as an example the discovery of atmospheric pressure. When the gardeners of Florence found that the column of water in the water pump would rise to a maximum height of 32 feet, Torricelli formulated the hypothesis of atmospheric pressure as an inspired guess. . . . 'A Hindu philosopher in Torricelli's place would have contented himself with simply announcing in an aphoristic sutra that the air had weight. No measure of the quantity of its pressure would have been given; no experiment would have been made with mercury; no Hindu Pascal would have ascended the Himalayas with a barometric column in a hand'.
>
> (Raychaudhuri 1988: 157)

The Mayo College clock-tower drew its authority not just from a well-established European discourse on science and rationality (Seidler 1994; Turner 1996), but also from the Indian internalisation of that ethos. It was one of the several representational adjuncts of the conquest of the realm of the natural – the extraterrestrial movement of the sun and the moon, and those sidereal adjustments beyond human comprehension – by the 'rational', 'scientific' exertions of the European mind; and the fabrication of time embodied perhaps the most potent evocation of this conquest.

In his comprehensive analysis of the cultural politics of colonial architecture, Thomas Metcalf (1989) provides additional insights into the appeal of the Indo-Saracenic style to the British. He suggests that the style was a product of the wider colonial classificatory schema where Indian customs, traditions, and life styles came to be represented in terms of strictly defined religious boundaries: either as Hindu or Muslim. And that, 'by drawing together and then melding forms directly labelled "Hindu" and "Saracenic", the British saw themselves, the self-proclaimed masters of Indian culture, as shaping a harmony the Indians alone, communally divided, could not achieve' (Metcalf 1989: 75). Further, he adds, the choice of an Indic design for an institution meant for princes also sought to establish the legitimacy of colonial rule through linking its authority with that of the 'authentic' rulers who, in turn, were established in *their* authority through the continued employment of the expressive vocabulary of 'ancient' Indian traditions. Acceptance of the Indo-Saracenic style by the princes as 'authentically' Indian was, however, less than wholehearted and when given the choice, they restricted the application of this style to those – public – buildings which served the purpose of 'mediating the encounter with the colonial ruler' (*ibid.*: 137).[10]

Oriental aesthetics and cultural paramountcy

The boarding houses and the playing fields of the Mayo College fan out, as it were, from the main building, which does not itself occupy a geographically central position on the sprawling 250 acre estate of the College. The space it does occupy, however, may once have been of considerable symbolic importance, for the building stands at the junction of two main roads that lead from its two main gates in opposite directions. At the time of its construction, these roads were the chief routes leading to the majority of the princely states of erstwhile Rajputana. For a school that was to be a part of the symbolic medley of British rule, it was appropriate that its presence be announced even at a distance to anyone approaching Ajmer along any of its main roads. Indeed, the clock-tower would have been visible for quite some distance, even before the city came into sight.

The earliest discussions on the architecture of the College concerned the merits of 'Classical' (or 'Grecian') versus Oriental aesthetics, and the task of providing designs for the school building(s) devolved upon the Mayo College Public Works Department (PWD) established in 1871 (Hughes n.d.), and headed by an executive engineer (Metcalf 1989: 69). Initially, both the British and the princes were in favour of a 'European classical' design for the school buildings. However, towards the end of 1871 Lord Mayo changed his earlier stance and ordered instead the drawing up of a 'Hindoo' design (*ibid.*). In preparing the new plan, executive engineer Gordon was asked to seek the advice of the director of the archaeological survey, General Alexander Cunningham, widely regarded for his expertise on matters Indian, and on 'Hindoo architecture' (*ibid.*). After considerable debate and discussion (on, *inter alia*, the 'Hindu-ness' of 'Hindoo' architecture, and the degree to which the mainly Hindu princes would tolerate 'Saracenic' designs), Mayo's successor, Lord Northbrook, turned to Major Mant of the Royal Engineers, who had recently designed a school building at Kolhapur in an 'Indic-style' (*ibid.*: 70–3).

It is in the context of the deliberations upon the most appropriate style for the College buildings, and on the manner of its every-day functioning, that we may explore the nature of the relationship between the British and their princely subjects. An important aspect of the colonial administration of princely states was the so-called 'paramountcy' principle. Paramountcy functioned as a loose and vaguely defined framework of stated and unstated rules and regulations within which the British controlled and influenced the affairs of the states; its very vagueness ensured that all residual powers rested with the imperial power (Rudolph and Rudolph 1984). Mayo College was conceived, it could be suggested, in line with the operation of the paramountcy principle. However, the context in which it functioned may be more accurately termed cultural paramountcy. I use this term in preference to, say, 'hegemony', in order to capture the historical specificity of the Indian experience under colonialism. Recent discussions on Gramsci's methods and concepts have emphasised the importance of being alive to their historical and social specificity. 'It is important to understand', as Sassoon points out, 'that Gramsci develops the concept of Hegemony in his attempt to analyse the state in a specific historical period' (Sassoon 1982: 95). Gramsci invoked hegemony 'to suggest a theoretical basis for a new strategy in *advanced capitalist countries* as well as provide theoretical tools for the building of a socialist state' (*ibid.*: 97, emphasis added).

It is not my intention here to provide a detailed statement on the indiscriminate use of Gramscian concepts, alienated from their original context such that the 'Sardinian, and even the Italian' (Nairn 1982: 162) disappears from view. Rather, I wish to reiterate the importance of explaining events and individuals by their 'position in a particular historical and social structure' (Alastair Davidson quoted in *ibid.*), and thereby to suggest other historically and socially specific ways of conceptualising the Indian situation.[11]

'Cultural paramountcy' has affinity to the concept of paramountcy as employed by the British in the political sphere, and, further, draws upon the connotations of ambiguity and expediency that were the hallmarks of the paramountcy principle in general. It seeks to express the idea of unfettered cultural encroachment upon existing forms by a paramount power through and within an environment marked by the lack of definition of the role of the latter. It operates in the ambiguous space created by the persistent refusal to be pinned down on matters of policy, and a refusal to define what exactly official 'policy' may consist of. And as Rudolph and Rudolph point out, 'vagueness concerning the limits of power is likely to be helpful to those who exercise it' (1984: 4). The interactional arena at Mayo College within which the British exercised their will and the Rajput princes 'saved face' was constructed, then, through the functioning of cultural paramountcy.

The princes found the idea of the College agreeable as the paramountcy of

British power in its functioning was always expressed in an implicit manner. All decisions, such as those regarding the design of the College buildings, were taken after often tortuous cognisance of 'native opinion', and the illusion of a consultative process was never abandoned. In this way, a subjugated 'warrior race', in reality shorn of its 'manliness' – a ruler often owed his position to British sufferance – could continue to maintain the fantasy that it was in fact a respected partner in the administration of the colonial political economy. British rule in Rajputana consisted of a fruitful combination of the threat of force and the invocation of the unwritten charter of co-operation between the brotherhood of 'manly' and 'martial' races (Omissi 1991).[12]

The political use of manliness, where the Rajput, and other 'martial' races, were granted an amorphous equality with the British, was an important aspect of colonial cultural regime. However, the manliness conceded to the Rajputs was qualitatively different from that which the British reserved for themselves. The manliness of the latter was often represented as a combination of physical *and* intellectual prowess, whereas the native manly races were represented as chiefly endowed with characteristics that manifested through physical attributes. For example, in an early edition of the College magazine, Lord Mayo is described as possessing 'great force, both of body and mind. . . . His admirable qualities of mind and body together made up a man who was one of nature's noblemen' (Vol I No. I: April 1905). In the same issue we find a sharply contrasting, almost comical, description of the 'manly' attributes of an erstwhile Rajput ruler of the state of Bundi: '[Suraj Mal] . . . was athletic and dauntless like his father, and possessed the unerring sign of a hero, long arms . . . reaching below the knee' (*ibid.* Both these passages are from an article by an Englishman, Herbert Sherring, master at the school from 1887 to 1911. I will have something to say about politics of his 'Creole' status in Chapter 6[13]).

There were several ways through which the 'martial races' sought to align the manliness attributed to them by the British with that of the colonial masters. One of these consisted of differentiating their own 'character' from other natives whose physical prowess and 'nobility' were also often on display. So, in a magazine article, Bijaya Singh, a student from Dungarpur described the Bhil tribe that lived in his state as possessing 'unequalled' loyalty, and being 'one and all, ready to sacrifice their lives for the sake of their lord and master'. However, he was also to say, 'I regret to say they are not desirable subjects. . . . they are incurably lazy . . . are inveterate poachers [and] . . . are, and have been, from time immemorial professional robbers' (Vol II No. I: February 1906). The Bhil, he concluded, 'is a great hunter, but his methods are generally far from sportsmanlike'. However, it would appear that, in general, the British were uninterested in such claims to difference by one section of the population that they had identified as manly. The Mayo College coat of arms was composed of designs provided by Lockwood Kipling, father of Rudyard, and consists of the various paraphernalia of 'manly' symbols including a rampant lion, a fort, a sword, and a shield. And, curiously – given the above attempt at differentiation – the shield is supported 'on the right [by] a Bhil warrior with string bow and quiver full of arrows, [and] on the left [by] a Rajput armed at all points . . .' (Vol I No. I: April 1906); ultimately, such symbolic positioning seemed to suggest, the manly races are closer to each other as 'type' than to 'us'.[14]

The implicitly differentiated (i.e. between 'our' kind of manliness and 'their' kind) but supposedly shared attribute of manliness was an aspect of cultural paramountcy which illustrates the specificity of the colonial situation in India. And, in the context of Mayo College, co-operation from the feudal elites was achieved through the latter's perception that the 'loss of face' due to their subjection was somehow lessened because of the imprecise definition of the control exercised over them. As an analytical tool, cultural paramountcy can allow for the idea that certain sections of the colonised population existed under a regime of what might be called flexible percep-tions, such that they could, within the given constraints, define themselves as 'subjects-but-equals'. Cultural paramountcy may be used, therefore, to high-light the fact that under a colonial situation different segments of the popula-tion may respond differently to, and be treated differently by, the colonising power.

The ritual of 'consultation' was, as suggested earlier, an important aspect of cultural paramountcy. Hence, though the idea for a public school for princes was originally mooted by the British, the latter were always at pains to emphasise that it was the princes who constituted the guiding lights in its planning and execution.[15] So, during discussions on the possible designs for the College buildings, the Viceroy was advised that the best examples of 'Hindoo' architectural styles which might meet with the princes' approval, were to be found at the locality of Dig (near Agra). In this way, the govern-ment sought to impress upon the princes that their views were considered important, at the same time that it itself defined what these ought to be. So, it was firmly suggested that the most 'appropriate architectural [style] for princely buildings' (Metcalf 1989: 106) was the Indo-Saracenic. And once this view had been put forward, 'no prince was certainly prepared to defy the government by, say, putting up a European styled structure' (*ibid.*). At all times, however, the Viceroy was 'anxious' that 'nothing should be said or done which may give rise to the idea that the Government of India desires to press its own views upon the Chiefs, in opposition to their wishes'.[16] So, it may be possible to add to Metcalf's analysis by suggesting that the princes' acquiescence to British policy was often achieved through the Indian version of a strategy of hegemony, *viz.* cultural paramountcy, a tactic which combined the awareness of force with the dissimulating offer of cultural self-definition.

The strategy through which the princes were made the offer of self-definition would appear to have served an additional purpose: it also con-tributed to British representations of their being and their own ontological universe. The adaptation of the 'ideal' to Indian circumstance could be described, then, as a concession to the will of the princes, and the resultant native forms could be characterised as always *approaching* the European ideal, but never quite emulating it. It is possible to argue, then, that despite its stated objectives, the College did not, in fact, ever reproduce (or aim to reproduce) those conditions of school life supposedly characteristic of the English public school system (*cf.* Metcalf 1989; Mangan 1986b). The 'realities' of the colonial situation, the argument went, necessitated modifications and inhibited emulation.

These modifications encompassed the courses of study[17] as well as several other aspects of school life. And, even during the period in which the curriculum in force was a replica of that at an English public school, it is not at all clear that the British thought that 'they had planted in a tropical soil a foreign seed, which slowly grew into a sturdy miniature of a much larger English plant' (Mangan 1986b: 141). The British view on the nature of the fit between the Mayo College and its English prototype was forcefully summarised by Viceroy Curzon at a 1903 conference in Calcutta, called to discuss 'reforms' to the Chiefs' Colleges. 'In the world of nature', Curzon said, 'a plant cannot suddenly be shifted from some foreign clime, and expected straightaway to flourish in a novel temperature and a strange soil. So it is with the Public School system in India.'[18] And, notwithstanding the replication of Harrovian images in the photographs of the 'Mayo College Cricket XI' (Mangan 1986b), the inculcation of the general 'ethos' of the English public school among Mayo's students appears always to have remained, in the eyes of the British, an extremely incomplete enterprise.

So, through the 1880s, Principal Loch noted with increasing dismay that students continued to commit 'nuisance' in public places despite the erection of urinals, failed to greet masters in any 'regular' manner, refused to rise to their feet when 'a gentleman or visitor approaches', insisted on speaking in vernacular tongues, and resorted to presenting petitions 'soliciting the grant of a holiday'; they also stared at (European) lady visitors, maintained very poor personal hygiene ('I know that Hindus consider bathing not only beneficial but a religious duty'), did not use a handkerchief when blowing their nose, wore 'coloured clothing' to the College, and showed poor commitment to the College as a community by being unpunctual in their return from school holidays.[19] In 1924, one of Loch's successors noted that 'public school traditions which have such immense force in English schools cannot yet be expected to exert the same influence in our institution as they are often not supported by continuity of ideals in home life'.[20]

Hence, many a cherished principle of the (English) public school life, including non-discrimination among students with regard to social standing, was judiciously done away with at Mayo College. Notwithstanding their privileged position within society, most English public schools placed great emphasis on a regime of undifferentiated austerity for all their students; at least in principle, all were meant to be equal. This was expressed in exaggerated, almost caricatured, notions of a Spartan and unostentatious school life, with common dining and dormitory accommodation the most obvious manifestations of this.

At Mayo, the punctilios of cultural paramountcy facilitated the abandonment of the very principles that were regarded by the British as the core of their public school system.[21] And the 'Indian Eton' developed a school culture that was a far cry from that of its supposed prototype, but, rather, was one which suited the needs of a colonial political economy. The princes, it was suggested, would not tolerate dormitory accommodation and common dining as both would violate those principles of secular and religious hierarchy which were facts of their every-day existence. So, neither was insisted upon by any of the College's British Headmasters, and commensality was only raised as a possibility some thirty years after the College's establishment. 'Hardly any Chief speaks of . . . [common messing] . . . without reservations, which suggests to me', one official noted, 'that he lays more stress on the reservations than on the acceptance of the principle. . . . I should be disposed, instead of saying that it is to be encouraged in principle to . . . say that great care should be taken to preserve in all that relates to the taking of food, as well as in other matters, the customs prescribed by caste and religion . . .'.[22] Given this overarching sentiment, the princes lived, dined, and worshipped (a temple and mosque were built for this purpose) in a largely unhindered manner.[23]

'As marking a new era'

In 1871 the Commissioner of Ajmer expressed the view that 'the bungalows for the scholars should be dotted around the compound and not built in a regular row'. 'The Chiefs', he further suggested, may not favour indiscriminate mingling of their wards, though he hoped that they would mix in education and 'in all sorts of manly sports, cricket, boating on the lake, etc.'. The Viceroy concurred with this view and directed that the residences should not be in any fixed line but should be '. . . dotted about as may be thought desirable . . . following the irregular line of the boundary of the grounds'. We may treat such 'irregularity' in design as a metaphor for a policy which in the act of relenting and accommodating Otherness – allowing deviations from the norm – strengthened its hold on the latter.

Native sentiment and 'prejudices' were incorporated into the overall scheme of the College's functioning, for these cultural 'adjustments', in as much as they were seen by the princes as concessions by the British to their wishes, served to dull the edges of the reality of the power relationship between the rulers and the ruled; a false consciousness, we could say, promoted by both sides, with full awareness of its falsity. It also complemented political rule in general: the seeming incorporation of the Rajput value system in the functioning of the College further cemented Rajput loyalty to the British.

There was considerable delay between the decision in 1871 that the site of the old British Residency would be given over for the campus of the new school (Hughes n.d.), and the commencement of construction of school buildings. And, when the College accepted its first pupil,[24] in October 1875, work on the main building had not yet commenced, and classes had to be held in the existing buildings of the old Residency. After much discussion (as we have noted above) on the most appropriate style for the buildings to be put up, approval was given to Major Mant's 'Hindoo-Saracenic' (or Indo-Saracenic) style. By 1877, the year in which work on the main building finally commenced, six boarding houses along with the residences for some of the European staff had been built with funds provided by the government and the princes.

However, before Mant's design could be immortalised in marble it had another hurdle to cross and there were further detailed deliberations, by various committees and (British) officials, on the shape of the clock-tower which was to be an integral part of the building. The chief objection attached to the 'inconsistency' between the design of the tower and that of the rest of the building (Metcalf 1989). Mant stood firm, however, and his design was finally given the go-ahead; as the general construction of the building was itself not of any 'pure style', it seemed pointless, it was noted, to object to the shape of the tower. The situation was, it was suggested, more sanguine than supposed: the tower could, in fact, be seen 'as marking a further transition and the commencement of a new era'.[25] I have already provided an interpretation of the significance of the clock-tower in the cultural and political economy of colonialism and have noted its role as a sort of reverse Panopticon, drawing gazes to itself, rather than gazing out, and thereby asserting authority.[26] Further, I have suggested, the relatively stark, unadorned appearance of the clock-tower, which stands in some contrast to the effusion of styles which characterise the architecture surrounding it, should also be seen as part of the fragmentary procedures of colonial representation of the self and its Others. In this case, the 'self' towered over the Other: controlling, instructing, normalising, cajoling, and, through the very proximity of its presence, reiterating the distance between the colonisers and the colonised that such propinquity, it was frequently asserted, had been divinely constituted to reduce.

Completed in early 1885, the main building was inaugurated on 7 November 1885, by the Viceroy, Lord Dufferin (*Mayo College Jubilee Souvenir* 1930), though, for a considerable period, the task of inculcating the scions of the native ruling families with the values and mores of a 'new era' met with limited success. So, by the opening decades of the twentieth century the matter of poor enrolment figures had become of sufficient concern to be raised by Curzon himself.[27] It was during Curzon's viceroyalty, and with his abundant patronage, that a conference 'to consider the needs of Chiefs' Colleges' was held in Ajmer during March 1904. A resolution was passed to add an extension to the main building that contained all the classrooms and Sir Swinton Jacob was invited to prepare a design for it. Subsequently, several other buildings – mainly boarding houses built by the different princely states for their students – were added to the campus that, in 1930, comprised some 270 acres (*Mayo College Jubilee Souvenir* 1930).

In the following chapters, I utilise specific aspects of the politico-cultural history of Mayo College towards an understanding of the manner in which the Doon School visualised its ethos as a break from, *inter alia*, the 'pre-modern' feudal past. This constitutes the continuing dialogue of modernity that animated K.G.M.'s reasoning in the previous chapter on why it would have been 'disastrous' to send his sons to a Chiefs' College.

The proponents of Doon were concerned to create an environment for their school which was distinct from that which animated the campus of Mayo College in several respects, and the discussion which follows deals with these in the appropriate contexts. As a pointer, however, I will briefly list the three most obvious of these desired 'differences'. The first concerns the 'ambiguity' of 'native' and European interaction as summarised under the conditions of cultural paramountcy. Rather than be seen as part of a realm of wavering opinions and indulgent, 'other-worldly' thought, the philosophical sponsors of Doon unambiguously expressed their desire to be included in the same 'rational' universe as the British; in such a world 'excessive' spirituality and public manifestations of a religious life could not be tolerated. At Mayo, boys can choose to worship at the Hindu temple located on campus – a fact which forms an important part of the comparative discourse of the Doon School when the latter's associates point to the absence of any religious facilities on its grounds.

Second, there is the matter of 'manliness'. Here, once again, the manliness sought and elaborated by Doon was quite different from that which the British attributed to the Rajput princes of Mayo College. Doon aspired to what can be called an intellectual (or epistemological) manliness, aligned to the absorption and practice of the new epistemologies of 'scientific' thinking; it sought to locate itself in the world of the laboratory and to use the method of the positivist experiment as a marker of its manliness. And finally, the School sought to construct its difference through the conscious elaboration – and constant public reiteration – of a milieu where all were to be treated as 'equal': every one ate at the same table, shared dormitory accommodation and, within the School, no concessions were made to the differing social or economic status of the students. This, as I discuss in Chapter 6, came to be expressed in terms of the 'contractual' ethos of the metropolis.

In Chapter 3, I discuss the first of the three 'prerequisites' of citizenship for the post-colonial age as seen through the eyes of the Doon School. This is the principle of 'rationality'.

3   The garden of rational delights

In Fanishwarnath Renu's *Maila Anchal* (1954), a novel about political, social, and sexual turmoil in a rural community in Bihar in the years immediately following independence from British rule, there is the memorable anti-hero figure of Dr Prashant Bannerjee whose politics extend far beyond his rumoured Communist affiliations. Prashant – star pupil of his medical class, and fêted torch-bearer of the light of modern science in the fight against malaria and other diseases – comes to draw the battle lines against the dicta of scientific discourse itself. In post-Independence India – with its iconic citizen the romantic film hero who is also a scientist, or a civil engineer with expertise in dam-building[1] – Dr Bannerjee's recalcitrant turn of inquiry is perceived as a fundamental act of treason against the nascent – but rapidly consolidating – emotions of Indian nationhood. For the doctor now comes to interpret the techno-scientific complex itself as one of the several centres of power whose logic cannot be understood outside a social context whose matrices are class, the functioning of capital, and the consequent control of commodified bodies.

The savage *leit-motif* of Renu's book is the play of commodified bodies and commodified knowledge – scientific knowledge – within the interstitial spaces of a declining feudal order and the new dispensation of capital; his narrative attempts to capture the prolix mechanism through which the old regimes and agents of oppression imperceptibly find their centre in the operative space of the new in a society on the verge of political independence from its colonial masters. How should one understand, the doctor wants to ask, the Hippocratic commitment to saving individual lives in a landscape of every-day social terror? How can the 'national' emotion account for the material circumstance of lives lived on the margins of 'civil' society? So, when one of the editors of the *All India Medical Gazette*, Dr T. Ramaswamy 'M.Sc., D.T.M. (Cal.), Ph.D. (Edin.), F.R.S.J. (Edin.)', writes that 'the entire medical world awaits' Prashant Bannerjee's findings from his research on malaria (in Renu 1954/1984: 158), the latter can only respond with an eye to the social text around him. 'What use a miracle cure?' he asks. 'Is it not better to be struck down by malignant malaria and die a quick death than suffer the drawn out agony of hunger and helplessness?' (*ibid.*: 184).

The doctor wants to interrupt the cornucopian narratives of science and technology with abrasive tales of that 'very miserable kind of capitalism' (Ahmad 1992: 100) that was slowly finding its feet in the corridors of the post-colonial nation state; for him, the 'laboratory' takes on metonymic significance as the production room of the nightmares of 'progress', and as the site on which a national bourgeoisie, rampant in these nightmares, charts the course of 'national welfare' in tandem with the expansionary visions of global capital. Here (as Prashant Bannerjee comes to realise), we are all guinea pigs:

> Laboratory! . . . a gigantic laboratory. The laboratory enclosed within high walls. . . . where scientists work under the auspices of the regime of bayonets of our imperial rulers . . . experiments are being carried out. . . . Red-green rays inspecting the contours of bald heads. . . . And through a fusion of all the energies of death and destruction they are building a bomb, a bomb that can blow us all to pieces . . . atoms are being split . . .! We have been plunged into darkness! A miasmous haze!
>
> (Renu 1954/1984: 326)

The doctor's peculiar angle on things does not go unnoticed, and as part of a concerted drive to round up 'subversive elements' he is placed under house arrest. The reasons for his arrest are not so much unspecified as *unspecifiable*. For what charges should one lay against the perspicacity of epistemological critique? And how can one prepare the charge-sheet against those who have glimpsed the stained under-belly of 'civil' society?

> . . . the children ask . . . 'why have the police come to arrest the doctor? Has he been taking bribes?'
>
> 'Aah . . . it's a very peculiar world [comes the reply]. You just can't trust anyone. This doctor . . . we hear he was sent by the Germans! . . . spying for the German CID. . . . He would make the villagers weak by giving them injections . . . and spread diseases by putting germs disguised as medicines in our drinking water. There is a German party here . . . called the Kommunis I think, he is a member of that party'.
>
> (Renu 1954/1984: 255)

One of the most appealing aspects of Renu's craft is the manner in which he is able to differentiate between science as a specific methodological field, valuable in specific areas of human existence, and *scientism* – the sphere of knowledge, power, control, and homogenisation. Needless to say, his has been a marginalised voice in the history of the discourses that have constituted the Indian nation state. This chapter is an attempt to explore this process of marginalisation as manifested at a very specific institutional site, a site of Indian modernity where a national bourgeoisie has fruitfully married a valorised narrative of science to the world of capital, a marriage which has brought rich rewards for the participants. My objective is also to point to one of the ways in which the insertion of the narrative of science in the epic of post-colonised nationhood has proscribed analyses of the functioning of capital and gender in national life. What follows, then, is a modest ethnography of one of the 'rooms' of Prashant Bannerjee's allegoric laboratory – which is the post-colonial nation state itself – and of the 'scientists' therein. I am also, implicitly, interested in asking the important questions that writers such as Renu had once formulated: is freedom from oppression merely to be judged in terms of the end of formal colonial rule? And, what myths of progress and civility contribute towards the perpetuation of post-colonised regimes of terror and misery?

In this chapter I will suggest that it was precisely that which led to Dr Prashant Bannerjee's downfall[2] – his attempt to position the 'national' within the context of capital – that has led to the prosperity of the Doon School's clientele. For the latter have chosen to utilise this understanding towards developing a 'science of personality' rather than commit themselves, unlike the hapless doctor of Renu's novel, to a praxis of the social. This chapter, then, is about a specific strategy of modernity which is at the heart of the post-colonised 'nation-building' project in India. My discussion does not, however, constitute a condemnation of either modernist projects or the nation state idea *in toto*. In this I follow the critical view-point implicit in Renu's writings, for whom the past was no more a utopia than the future is bound to an iron law of monolithic propensities; the future, Renu might have said, must be negotiated, and political struggle constitutes such negotiation.

The rational native

In October 1990 the Headmaster of the Doon School addressed a special school assembly upon his return from a meeting of the Round Square Conference[3] in Geneva. He spoke to the students on the reasons for German and Swiss 'superiority' over Indians, as had become obvious to him on this, his latest, trip overseas. As the boys and the staff stood in patient silence the Headmaster explained that the German and Swiss 'superiority' (a term not further defined but used, rather, as an omnibus, for a range of unexpressed traits) could be attributed to their 'scientific' attitude to life and second, and as a consequence of the former, their punctuality. The erstwhile physics teacher further suggested that India could only hope to emulate the West by planning for a future tempered by the exactitude of a scientific imagination and the cadenced movement of punctual habits. The Swiss, he concluded, are an advanced people 'because not only are they a scientific people but also because their trains and planes operate strictly according to schedule . . . not like us'.

The ghost of the irrational, unscientific native had pursued the founders of the Doon School with just as much vigour and had occupied their thinking with just as much vehemence as it shadowed the thinking of the Headmaster in 1990. I will suggest here that one of the moulds into which the School sought to cast the 'new' Indian personality was that of the rational, scientific subject. These were attributes specifically denied the latter by the British who had commandeered the nineteenth-century ontological space which conducted its business in vectors of 'objectivity', 'scientificity', and the critical, 'this-worldly' consciousness. The ability to lead a life of the mind was what, so the argument went, set the English apart from their subject races. The Doon School represented both an acceptance of this doctrine and an attempt to overcome it. The efforts of the School's founders were also informed by the philosophical deliberations of the age of capital and the ostensible requirements for participation in its enterprise. As the collective action of a class of men, the establishment of the School also represented the elevation of the individual – the body – as both a 'method' for understanding social predicament and a tool for the amelioration of the 'misfortunes' besetting a colonised society.

The idea of the 'scientific' man as the citizen, imbued with a post-Enlightenment 'rationality' (or, to use Nehru's favourite term, 'the scientific temper'), was one of the corner stones of the so-called Bengal Renaissance and of the various movements – religious, artistic, 'reformist' – which it gave birth to. The Brahmo Samaj – the renaissance artefact *par excellence* – is of special significance in the context of the Doon School. For S.R. Das, the founder of the School, was an active member of the faith which advocated:

> the substitution of a rational faith for the prevailing popular religions of the world, which, [the Samajis] thought, increasingly curtailed the freedom of human beings by enslaving them to mechanical rituals, irrational myths, meaningless superstitions and other worldly beliefs and values.
>
> (Kopf 1979: 1)

And though the School itself came into being some seven years after the death of its founder, it embraced the intellectual legacy – the testacy of the scientific man – of his religion, unequivocally.

The charter of the scientific citizen had many signatories in the Indian political and social milieu of the opening decades of the twentieth century. Of particular interest was its keen reception even in those quarters that actively opposed not just British imperialism, but also the perceived hegemony of western intellectual traditions in the colonies.

Har Dayal (1884–1939) is remembered primarily in the context of the movement called the *Ghadr* ('mutiny') party founded in California in 1913, whose chief objective was the overthrow of British authority in India through revolutionary means. As a busy propagandist for his cause, 'his diatribes – against Christianity, Western law, education, and anything else imported by the Englishman – filled the columns of the nationalist newspapers of the Punjab' (Brown 1976: 4). And in one of his works, he attempted to repudiate

Marx's 'scientific' schema by asserting that, 'society is not an agglomeration of molecules . . . [and that] there is no law of social progress visible anywhere' (*ibid.*: 100).

It was the same Har Dayal, however, who in 1934 was to write in the Preface of one of his books that 'I have tried to indicate and explain some aspects of the message of Rationalism for the young men and women of all countries' (*ibid.*: 245); and on one of the printed postcards announcing a lecture by the 'Hindu revolutionary' in New York were the words 'Noted Oxford and London University Scientific thinker' (*ibid.*: 267).

The achievement of the Doon School lies in the concrete elaboration of the scientific manifesto and its role in the life of the citizen that had found such widely divergent adherents as S.R. Das and Har Dayal. The proponents of the School proceeded to implement this task through developing an analytical scheme where the focus was turned away from the impact of social and historical factors and concentrated, instead, on 'defects' of personality: social and economic stasis as consequence of a lack in the native body and of inadequacies of personality. It was this lack, and these inadequacies – one of which was the absence of the scientific temper – that the School set out to remedy. 'Personality' could now be seen as removed from the grasp of history: timeless, transcendent, and able at any time to be instantly transformed. It is only by situating the dialogue of Doon – the dialogue on 'nation-building', the debates on the Doon man and the new Indian – within the universe of an ahistoricised present animated by the transubstantiative embrace of science and rationality, that we can fully understand the potency of nationalist discourses as commentaries on gender, caste, and class. For the advocacy of such a point of view, that the 'scientific' population is the harbinger of prosperity (in whatever form) and the 'unscientific' and 'irrational' sections are responsible for stasis, establishes a difference, an Otherness, which operates to decentre a view of the entrenched forms of structural oppression.

The importance of the task of preparing 'modern' citizens was articulated at the School from the first day of its existence. In his opening day speech, Headmaster Foot noted that the School would aspire to train students to be 'loyal citizens of a new India, determined to be true to the noblest aspirations of their country' (*The Times of India*, 28 Oct. 1935 (hereafter *TOI*)). Since then, this theme has found extensive elaboration in, among other forums, the articles and discussions of the *Doon School Weekly* (*DSW*). This clarity of vision was, just as unequivocally, elaborated through the lexis of scientific rationality and the rational *personality*. The decentring of history as a mode of social analysis and its replacement with a confessional science of the personality – confessions of individual shortcomings – functioned both to discover and make invisible, to applaud and to banish. The discoveries concerned certain class, caste, and gender-related personality traits that enhanced the ability of certain groups in Indian society to adapt to a 'new' world, their absence making for maladaptiveness in others. This, in turn, was merely a restatement of views contained within the burgeoning field we might designate post-colonial 'scientific philosophy', the most illustrious proponent of which was S. Radhakrishnan (1888–1975) – philosopher-statesman to the nation, and the archetypal *savant* born of a fruitful union between the 'wise' Orient and the 'progressive' Occident.

In his several works Radhakrishnan sought to controvert prevailing views on the 'unscientific' nature of Hindus. Though there existed a body of 'crude beliefs' within Hinduism, he said, the *enlightened* classes of India did not subscribe to them and, in time, these would be 'eradicated' by 'civilisation' (Radhakrishnan 1975: 40). In the mean time, he said, Indian society could only progress through the consolidation of the community of its 'natural elite', which is best able to 'represent the soul of the entire people' (*ibid.*: 66). This may be achieved through adhering to the Hindu view on the superiority of certain groups in society, a perspective which:

> has the support of ancient Greek thought and modern science. The Greeks believed in heredity and actually developed a theory of race betterment by the weeding out of inferior strains and the multiplication of superior ones.
>
> (Radhakrishnan 1975: 72)

The tractable native, the upper-caste male, was poised on the precipice of a new age, willing and able to explore its furthermost possibilities and take part in a world ruled by the scientific imagination, unfettered by the imperatives of 'crude beliefs'. Further, this was facilitated by the very rationality of Hinduism. In a breathtaking act of doctrinal mediation, linking the wisdom of the Book of the Hindus to the liturgy of the *laissez-faire* political economists, Radhakrishnan explains the message of the *Bhagwadgita* in the spirit *and* language of Adam Smith:

> According to the Bhagvadgita, one obtains perfection if one does one's duty in the proper spirit of non-attachment. The cant of the preacher who appeals to us for the deep sea fisher-man on the grounds that they daily risk their lives, that other people may have fish for their breakfasts, ignores the effect of the work on the worker. They go to sea not for us and our breakfasts but for the satisfaction of their being. Our convenience is an accident of their labours. Happily, *the world is so arranged that each man's good turns out to be the good of others*.
>
> (Radhakrishnan 1975: 80, emphasis added)

This discovery that certain Indians did indeed possess the required personality traits for participation in a 'modern' world, was also, of course, an act of making invisible the historical nature of social predicament through explaining the latter as linked to 'defects' of personality; it constructed an anthropomorphic present which obscured the nature of colonial rule, as an external force, and the functioning of power – caste, class, gender – as an internal characteristic of Indian social structure.[4]

The elaboration of the 'scientific attitude' at the School was broadly directed towards two areas that were, sometimes explicitly though often in an implicit manner, seen to constitute the being of the 'modern' citizen. The first was personal discipline. The idea of discipline at the School was, from the very beginning, enunciated within the framework of a very specific ontology: '[this] . . . discipline was not one based on fear, not one that existed by violent repression, but . . . [one] . . . that relied on the development of the boys' own self control' (*DSW*, 31 Oct. 1936). The other realm of scientific scrutiny addressed the issue of the 'rational' attitude towards social and cultural forms. This chapter will deal with the former disciplinary mosaic, and I will take up discussion on the latter issue in Chapter 5.

The ichnography of the scientific estate

Before proceeding to a discussion of the elaboration of the scientific world view and its insertion into the various crevices of school life it will be useful to survey the physical domain which, according to Lord Willingdon's opening day speech, was to provide the setting where young boys would be enabled to 'become useful citizens of their country . . .[having]. . . the chance of developing in conditions which have played a great and precious part in the life of Great Britain' (*TOI*, 28 Oct. 1935).

'In the first instance', Foucault says, 'discipline proceeds from the distribution of individuals in space. To achieve this end, it employs several techniques' (Foucault 1979: 141). One of these, he further suggests, may be referred to as the technique of '*enclosure*': 'the specification of a place heterogeneous to all others and closed in upon itself' (*ibid.*). It is to this materiality of the enclosure of science and discipline, where 'the school building was to be the mechanism for training' (*ibid.*: 172), that I now turn. Of importance to the project of the 'new' national identity at the Doon School was not just the corpus of activity and words which would animate the setting, but also the spatial peculiarities of the setting itself: the precise, utilitarian aesthetics of the architecture, and an appreciation of the history of the site to be occupied as a fragment of the history of 'modern' endeavours.

April in the Doon valley, where the School is situated, is a bearable month. The extreme discomforts of the North Indian summer, though not far off, have not yet arrived, and the surrounding hills display an attractive cover of submontane greenery. It was during such a month of passing weather that Sir Joseph Bhore and Sir Frank Noyce, who had accepted responsibility for S.R. Das's project upon the latter's death in 1928, came to Dehra Dun to inspect a possible site for the school. The year was 1933 and the two were also accompanied on this consecratory journey to give physical shape to a, thus far, imaginative geography of the nationalism project by Sir Girija Shankar Bajpai, then Secretary to the Government of India in the Department of

Education. The site which matched both the resources and sentiments of the Indian Public Schools Society (IPSS) was the former campus of the Forest Research Institute and Forest College (FRI) at Chandbagh. The Chandbagh estate, as it came to be known, was located approximately two kilometres south of the administrative centre of Dehra Dun, a site marked unmistakably by that most visible of all markers of the 'rational' presence of the Occident in the Orient, the clock-tower.

The FRI, established in 1906, was a government body devoted to the identification and classification of plants and forest produce. It was, in this, part of the larger nineteenth-century colonial enterprise of mapping. Along with the various Surveys of India, the Institute formed a part of an exploratory complex, where the unknown of nature and the unfamiliar of culture could, with the exertions of the 'scientific method', be known and captured; it occupied the conjunctional space on the double helix of scientific knowledge and colonial authority. There was an impressive array of experts as well as facilities for their work of the encompassment of the wilderness. Of course, the Institute itself was merely the reification of a historical endeavour whose ambitions were entelechal and whose beginnings stretched back to an era of European history characterised by the most peculiar of epistemological conjunctions. Among the factors which presaged the coming of the nation state in Europe, Anderson tells us, was 'the gradual demotion of the sacred language [Latin] itself' (Anderson 1986: 24), such that by the eighteenth century 'the fall of Latin exemplified a larger process in which the sacred communities integrated by old sacred languages were gradually fragmented, pluralised, and territorialised' (*ibid.*: 25). Now, at the same time, and in connected ways, that the community of the sacred was coming apart at the seams in Europe, another, the scientific, was in the process of consolidating. And the peculiarity of the situation was that both these worlds, with their vastly differing and opposed cosmogonical predilections, expressed their internal unity through the same language, Latin.

In this time of the coming together of the sacred and the scientific in unexpected ways, the year 1735 is of great importance with respect to the FRI and the Doon School. For that year marks the publication of Carl Linné's *The System of Nature*, 'in which the Swedish naturalist laid out a classificatory system designed to categorise all plant forms on the planet, known or unknown to Europeans' (Pratt 1992: 15). The Institute in Dehra Dun was, then, one of the manifestations of the 'planetary consciousness' which was embodied in Linné's original project, one of the many nodes for gathering and transmitting data which contributed to a *Geist* 'marked by an orientation toward interior exploration and the construction of global-scale meaning through the descriptive apparatus of natural history' (*ibid.*). It was to this grid of scientific knowledge – a particular way of viewing, writing, speaking, and classifying – that the FRI belonged as the reification of a discourse which had displaced other, non-European, classificatory systems.

The division of labour at the FRI was between the departments of the

Forest Zoologist, the Forest Botanist, the Forest Economist, the Silvicultur-
ist, the Chemist, the Biologist, and the Entomologist (*DSW*, 8 May 1943).
The lecture theatres combined with a range of laboratories and museums to
function as expository niches in the authoritative geography of an encyclo-
paedic enterprise: there was the Timber Display Hall, the Minor Forest
Products Museum, Chemistry Laboratories, the Photography Laboratory,
the Zoologists' Museum, the Silviculturists' Museum, the Insectary, the
Entomologists' Museum and the Biological Laboratory (*ibid.*). Though the
Institute also functioned to assist forest-based commercial enterprise
(the 'Timber Testing Section'), its place in the field of colonial activities was
one defined by the imperatives of an enterprise which saw as its axes the
methods of the researcher and the ambience of the laboratory; it occupied, in
other words, a space of symbolic potency.

The estate chosen by Noyce and Bhore to be the campus of the future
Doon School was not, however, just an arrangement of buildings for the
dissemination of serious knowledge, it was also a well planted garden. In a
pastiche of the edible, the aesthetic, and the utilitarian, mango and lichee
trees shared the grounds with flowering plants and teak trees. The tennis
courts were 'pleasantly shaded in the evenings by the row of high *Dilinia
indica*', and the appearance of the grounds had been much improved 'by the
rows of champa and *Acrocarpus paxinifolicus*' (*The Doon School Book*: 10
(hereafter *DSB*)). And the garden itself was not viewed by its Indian occupants
as merely a landscape of gratuitous frolic, a grove of non-utilitarian delights,
for such passive identification with the world of nature spoke of a past which
it was precisely the task of the new school to reinterpret and mould to a new
world: 'The Forest Service planted many different shrubs and trees [on the
School campus] and these remain for our enjoyment *and instruction*' (*DSB*: 9,
emphasis added).

The setting spoke of a new dawn, encompassed by the evocative image of
an old dream: the architecture of a new knowledge, scientific knowledge,
embossed upon the undulating canvas of a profusion of nature. However,
though it was a garden with the power to summon a vision of genesis – with
ripening fruits which 'are a perpetual temptation to small boys', and 'a
magnificent tun tree in which nest each year a pair of golden orioles' (*DSB*:
10) – it was a profusion carefully managed, an arboretum. It was entirely
appropriate, then, that the search for a site for the nurture, no, birth, of a new
Indian identity, should find its dénouement in a garden with flowers and
laboratories: the garden of rational delights.

On 27 October 1935, with the 'hot weather' well beyond the horizon, Viceroy Willingdon presided over a ceremony to mark the opening of the School.
On this day of pomp and serious circumstance, attended by 'an eminent
company of people', a canopy had been erected in the shadows of the
School's main building in order to provide cover for the guests. The canopy
was only one part of a celebratory mosaic of ironies and paradoxes which
was to mark that day. The most obvious irony was, of course, that a school

whose intention it was to train a generation of students to be the citizens of a *post*-colonial nation was to be opened by the most important representative of the British crown in India.

A less obvious, and perhaps for that reason, more exquisite, irony was contained in the pedigree of the canopy. Its exalted history also allows us to see it as a metaphor of the School's location within certain political, social, and cultural boundaries: the same canopy had been used earlier at a ceremony to mark the installation of Willingdon as Viceroy (*DSB*: 4). In a period of rising nationalist sentiment, the installation ceremony held special significance in its reiteration of the resolute aim of the colonial government to curb 'subversive' activity. The canopy, its antecedents noted in a straightforward manner by a School chronicle, was gone in a few days, as were the guests. It was a fleeting, if unwitting, reminder of the course upon which the nationalism project of the School was to be charted. A more lasting representation of the image the School sought to build for itself and *its* future Indians was embedded in the very presence of the main school building, a structure in 'mellow red brick' (*DSB*: 4). The contrast between the architectural style of the main building of Mayo College – designed by an Englishman for Indians – and that of Doon's main building is as remarkable as it is worth exploring.

The most enduring impression Doon's main building leaves upon the observer is one of serious intent: an intent to deal with the vagaries of a refractory climate and with the imperatives of creating a working space which would faithfully reflect the *nature* of the work done there. The intent of the design was also to express a certain frugality of style marking a concern with 'direct' thought and action unfettered by the 'flaccid' concerns of diffuse, other worldly thinking. Comparing it with the Mayo College main building can most directly bring out this aspect. The two buildings belong, chronologically, to the same era, the latter being older by approximately twenty years. The difference in style between the buildings can be usefully understood as the process of the creation of very specific spaces. It is here that we must also insert, in the cases of both Mayo and Doon, the identity of those who designed these buildings as well as of those for whom the buildings were designed.

The Mayo College building was designed, as I have discussed earlier, by a British architect (Major Mant of the Royal Engineers), but for a native clientele: 'native' as the Orientalist's analytical and cultural category. The profusion of marble arches, domes, and canopies, a profusion designed by an Englishman, was an act of representation. 'Representation' seeks to convey two distinct processes: the absorption and, ostensibly, critical understanding of that which is to be represented (in this case, the 'essence' of another culture) and, second, the ability faithfully to reproduce it – the antithesis of 'faithfully to reproduce' being 'to mimic'. So, the casting of the Mayo building in an Oriental design, in as much as it was an act of representation within the framework outlined above, was also an act of a display of power and authority: the stylistic excesses of the Orient captured and reproduced by the

representatives of a more rational universe: the style of the building a view
of native life itself – ornate, other-worldly, profuse, dissolute.

The 'mellow red brick' building that occupies the central space of Doon
School, was born of a style whose symbolic intent can be said to be quite
different from its counterpart at Mayo College. It is encompassed within a
geometry of straight, almost severe, lines, unadorned arches, and large rectangular windows (Figures 3.1 and 3.2). It has wide airy corridors, high-
ceilinged rooms, and a small, unobtrusively raised platform on the flat roof
upon which the school bell is mounted: it is a place of work, of serious
endeavour. It is also, in the austerity and the 'rationality' of its visage, an
exercise in self-representation by its original occupants and planners – the
British – of their culture: functional, this-worldly, focused, resolute.

The Indians who chose the erstwhile FRI campus as the site for their future
school did not, of course, design its buildings. The campus was designed and
constructed by the British for both a specific and a general purpose. The
specific purpose was the immediate use to which it was to be put as the
campus of the FRI. The general, more diffuse, nature of the enterprise
belonged to that sphere of the colonial imagination where the European self
was given shape through association with a constellation of objects and activities. The FRI was one of the many ideographs of difference embossed upon
a colonial techno-scientific landscape: such a landscape proclaimed the difference between the 'progressive' ethos of an efflorescent Occident and the
'effete' charter of oriental existence.

Figure 3.1 Doon School main building, front view.

Figure 3.2 Doon School main building corridor, ground floor.

The landscape of masculine lore

Taking on this genealogical heritage, the theme of the physical and 'intellectual' location of the School in the world of resolute 'manly' activity is a recurrent one. However, the School's engagement with ideas of masculinity is not, I suggest, related to the realm of the physical – sports, bodily toughness, and the ability to absorb physical pain. The development of a masculine culture at Doon differed from the corporeal models circulating both among late nineteenth-century Bengali intelligentsia (Rosselli 1980) and on the campuses of British public schools of the same era (Mangan 1986a, 1986b, 1987; Vance 1985). The scene of masculinity into which the School sought to insert its own presence and to be one of its fragments, was one inscribed with the emblems of precise activity and that of the new knowledges of classification and scrutiny. Such a non-corporeal view of manly action is linked to the historical situation of an intelligentsia – the School's supporters – which saw itself characterised (by the English) as 'non-scientific', and embodying, in short, several other 'feminine' traits (Nandy 1983; Sinha 1995).

We may refer to the Doon version of masculinity as 'epistemological masculinity', a notion which seeks to capture the situation of an Indian intelligentsia which sought to present itself as 'modern' (and 'capable' of modernity) through differentiating itself from its Indian Others.[5] This notion of manliness is also in stark contrast to the notions of 'moral manhood' (Mangan 1986b: 147) and 'muscular Christianity' (Mangan 1986a: 139) which animated the English public school in the heyday of Empire. As Mangan points out, for the supporters of the English public school 'moral manhood' came to define the essence of British being, and indeed, explained the glittering successes of Empire. The upper classes saw themselves as a race filled with 'moral and physical steadfastness' (Mangan 1986b: 147) – qualities which had been instilled on the playing fields of the English public school and 'through the spirit of organised games' (*ibid.*). And, armed with this fortifying thought, they now sallied forth to sow the effete, tropical, winds with the manly seeds of a more robust environment.[6]

For the colonised Indian intelligentsia the appeal of such physical forms of manliness held little attraction, and it is the site of knowledge at the School which became the site of gender. Hence the School made a conscious attempt to be identified with 'knowledges' of a certain pedigree. Ludmilla Jordanova suggests that 'the very terms in which knowledge, nature and science are understood are suffused with gender, partly through the tendency, of ancient origin, to personify them, and partly because, as result of personification, we think of the processes by which knowledge is acquired as deeply sexual' (Jordanova 1989: 5). It is important to keep this in mind when reading the passage below from *The Doon School Book*:

> we are very lucky to have with us, and to be able to visit, such interesting places as the Forest Research Institute, the Geodetic and Map

publication branches of the Survey of India and the Indian Military Academy. . . . From them come lecturers to the many different school societies . . . experts to advise us in their special knowledge, and to them we go to watch them at work and to get ideas on what goes on outside our own sphere of life. We are indeed fortunate to have close at hand people who can advise and help us with such diverse problems as to the trees to plant in our grounds, new exercises to introduce into our physical training, the areas in which to find mineral outcrops, how to control pests attacking our vegetables, and a Department to print maps for us.

(*DSB*: 7)

Visitors to the School were also directed towards an appreciation of the specificities of the landscape of which the campus was a part, one removed from the melee and randomness of the world 'outside':

The institution is fortunate in its location. It is well out of town – far from the noise, smells, flies and general confusion of the bazar. It is some distance from the main road . . .

(*TOI*)

The various edificial markings of this landscape – the Archaeological Survey of India, the Vaccine Research Institute at Kasauli in Himachal Pradesh, the Asiatic Society – were more than places where serious men charted the course of useful knowledge, skirting the eddies of colonial cultural politics through firm adherence to the neutral methodology of 'objective' knowledge. They constituted a topography of symbols: symbols of identity and the signifiers of difference between the culture of the rulers and that of the ruled. This particular identity of the 'modern' European self, however, as Nandy (1983) and others (e.g. the writings of Foucault) have suggested, is of recent origin, one whose parentage may be traced to the post-Enlightenment period. Further, the advent of this identity marked the ingress of efforts to erase the marks of the reciprocal relationship between the Occident and the Orient that influenced pre-Enlightenment European perceptions of the Orient. It was through such a rupture, where the rupture was the logos of colonialism, that a different Occidental identity came to be consolidated.

The institutions of 'research' and 'survey' were part of the colonial epigraph, inscribed through both action and words, on the nature of the distinction between the 'races' of the Orient and the Occident. They helped to chisel a distinct space of the Occidental identity from where memories of a pre-Enlightenment intercourse had been purged: western man (*sic*), through his association with the apparent instrumentalities of the reasoning mind – the Survey, the Institute – was proffered as the living embodiment of all the supposed precision of method and the clarity of objectives these institutions contained. In turn, this 'new self-definition' (Nandy 1983: 71) of European identity was linked to Cartesian 'instrumental rationalism or means–end

rationalism' (Turner 1996: 10; see also Seidler 1994) which provided the justi-
fication for the 'truth' of colonial rule. There is a glimpse of the dictate of the
new personality type and the recalcitrance of a critical European perspective
on colonialism that produced unwilling subjects in George Orwell's reflections on his time as a police officer in Burma during the 1920s. On confronting a wild elephant, Orwell realised that he 'did not in the least' want to shoot
the aberrant animal but that his performative role as a European could not
accommodate inaction: for 'a *sahib* has got to act like a *sahib*; he has got to
appear resolute, to know his own mind and do definite things' (Orwell 1978:
29–30).

Colonial scientific institutions represented this world of practical, 'resolute' activity, where men knew their mind or risked 'losing' it. The ordered
world of 'scientific' inquiry, with its visible accoutrements – the hospital, the
Survey, the Research Institute – was proffered as the essence of Occidental
Weltgeist: the spirit which pervaded both its ontological and metaphysical
musings. It was as such that the ascendant indigenous class that was to establish Doon School as the site for the resolution of the 'problem' of Indianness,
adopted this 'spirit'.

Rational individuals and the industrial group

The School's earliest connection with the realms of rationality may be traced
to the tenets of its founder's religious creed, the Brahmo Samaj, which had its
hey-day in the late nineteenth century. The Samaj itself was the confident
child of the so-called Bengal Renaissance, 'inferior no doubt to its Italian
prototype, but still allegedly constituting a transition from medieval to modern India under British rule' (Sarkar 1985: vi). The Brahmos, as Kopf has
suggested in a largely hagiographic account of the movement, 'not only
appropriated [western] science and reason in a very special and positive way,
but also deified them' (Kopf 1979: 44). There were several ways in which
the 'deification of science, humanity, and reason' (*ibid.*: 42) was expressed in
the lives of the faithful; while some found that the scientific principles could
most fruitfully be applied to the realm of spiritual speculation, others combined their Brahmo religiosity with outstanding careers as professional
scientists.[7]

Notwithstanding the uncritical generality of Kopf's account – in particular
his suggestions regarding the continuing importance of Brahmo values for
Indian modernity – it also contains important clues to the modernising vision
of Doon's early proponents. Hence, an important part of this vision was the
close association many Brahmos formed with the world of commerce and
industry. In this way they forged a fruitful partnership between 'useful' and
'productive' work – which had an important place in the Brahmo pantheon
of scientism – and the world of colonial capitalist and comprador activity.
Notwithstanding this, however, some of the most prominent Brahmos, in
ironic contrast to their public outpourings of sympathy for the 'downtrodden'

and their predilection for 'useful' work, were products of, and continued to maintain during their lifetime, remarkably feudal life styles.[8]

S.R. Das belonged to this social and cultural milieu and turned to it for both intellectual inspiration and financial support for founding his school. His diaries indicate his intimate association both with the world of commerce – supposedly fired by the rationality of the free trade doctrine and the modern impulses of the market place – and with an assorted collection of feudal elements whose very existence the bourgeois-liberal free trader was expected to undermine. Apart from regular participation in corporate board meetings, Das was also actively involved in the share market and held shares in some thirty-six different companies.

The philosophy of the market – of industrial society – can be seen as one entwined with the ontology of the scientific gaze: redeeming science which would rescue the native from the primitivism of the barter economy and introduce him to the anonymous, 'neutral', and precisely accountable world of the modern market. By the opening decades of the nineteenth century, science as a way of thinking about and organising human existence, possessed a long and respectable history in European thought. In 1621 Francis Bacon published his *Novum Organum* in which he expounded the 'dream-method of a positivist' (Bajaj 1988: 25), whereby understanding could proceed 'by a true scale of successive steps, without breach and interruption, from particular to lesser axioms, thence to the intermediate (rising one above the other), and lastly to the most general' (*ibid.*); and Thomas Hobbes's outline for 'science as society' was there for all to see in his *Leviathan* (Viswanathan 1988).

The forging of a connection between the 'scientific attitude' and 'members of an industrial group' – the latter term belonging to Alfred Marshall – came somewhat later. And one of the most ardent, and eloquent, advocates of the idea was Marshall himself.[9] 'Normal' action, Marshall asserted, 'is taken to be that which may be expected, under certain conditions, from the members of an industrial group' (Marshall 1938: vii). For Marshall, 'economic evolution' implied a movement towards the industrialised state. This was a movement away from 'savagery' – a condition where humans exist 'under the dominion of custom and impulse; scarcely ever striking out new lines for themselves; never forecasting the distant future, . . . governed by the fancy of the moment' (*ibid.*) – to industrial life; the analysis of this latter, rational state was quite obviously then, a scientific activity itself. The continued reiteration by economists that their subject is a 'science', and indeed its increasing epistemological alignment with the 'proper' science of physics and the exact world of mathematics owe something to this view.

In the Indian context, this simultaneously established a strong link between the national identity project and the imperatives of capital: the 'reasonable' and 'rational' were those aligned to the sphere of capitalist existence. We might, in this context, recall the *laissez-faire* naturalism imposed by Radhakrishnan on the 'way things are' through his assertion that 'happily, the world is so arranged that each man's good turns out to be the good of others' (1975: 80).

The Cartesian logic which assayed modern subjectivity through the looking-glass of instrumental rationalism – preparing the grounds of post-colonial nationalism – was reflected on several surfaces in the colonial sphere. The Indian Industrial Commission of 1916 was established to investigate the functioning and future needs of the industrial sector. It conducted detailed interviews with both industrialists and those regarded as having expert knowledge of the area (bureaucrats, scientists, etc.). In the following comment to the Commission, James Currie of Currie and Company, Delhi, makes the unequivocal connection between the endeavours of the scientist and that of the industrialist that characterised thinking on 'rational human culture' (Turner 1996: 13):

> I am of the opinion that there should be established an Imperial Research Institution, the laboratory of which should be equipped with the best brains that the Empire can produce. . . . There should also be attached to it an actuary and a staff of qualified auditors.[10]

Indeed, S.R. Das's first act towards the establishment of his school carried the imprimatur of this secular magisterium: he registered the IPSS, Doon's administrative body (but also intended for the establishment of other public schools), under the Indian Companies Act of 1860. It was upon such a landscape, anointed with the chrism of the age of science, that the School's disciplinary mechanism was, and continues to be, elaborated.

The disciplined citizen

At the heart of science lies the act of experiment: the calibrated movements of its 'apparatus', the never-ending quest of separating 'truth' from falsehood, its ordinal imperative the immurement of unmanageable multiplicities within the structures of tables and graphs; the post-colonial project of citizenship at Doon School was intimately connected with the idea of the production of the scientific man as a conscious act of the experimental method. That children as young as eleven would, after a period of residence at the School lasting from five to six years, emerge as transformed beings, carrying with them into the wider world, the nation, the methods and habits of scientific thinking and rational action.

The School was to be the scientific, clinical space where, through transformations effected in the individual personality, the perceived social and economic stasis of a colonised society could be ameliorated. Through the postulate of 'a total fit between the needs of a good society and the needs of modern science' (Nandy 1988a: 1), the School could identify its task, in consonance with a large body of 'educated' and influential opinion, as one inspired by the punctilios of the laboratory and by the precise etiquette of the scientific technique; in this way, further, both the every-day life and the long-term plan of the School could be presented as an 'experiment': and the scientific experiment, in turn, would deliver the scientific, rational man. It can be suggested that in emphasising both the development of 'character' and the 'rationalisation' of society as the unfinished business of post-coloniality, the Doon model of masculinity oscillated between Kantian ('inner light of reason') and Durkheimian ('the collective mind') world views (Seidler 1994); and that such oscillation is another peculiarity of colonised and post-colonised situations.

The classical age in Europe, Foucault tells us, 'discovered the body as the object and target of power . . . the body that is manipulated, shaped, trained, which obeys, responds, becomes skilful and increases its forces' (Foucault 1979: 136). At the core of the 'great book of Man-the-Machine', he continues, 'reigns the notion of "docility", which joins the analysable body to the manipulable body. A body is docile that may be subjected, used, transformed and improved' (*ibid.*). On one level, the 'discovery' and reification of the body at the Doon School may be perceived to be congruent to the process described by Foucault. Consider the fine and precise grid of daily routine: rising bell, exercises, breakfast, assembly, classes, lunch, rest period, sports, extra-curricular activities, bathing time, evening meal, study time, sleeping time. However, as I discuss below, the similarity is confined to the *mechanism* of its elaboration; in another very important way the disciplinary regime within the School differs fundamentally from that outlined by Foucault. This difference is due to the fact that the 'disciplinarians' at the School viewed (and view) it as serving different ends to those formulated, as Foucault further informs us, by men such as Guibert and Bentham who visualised it as saturating the entire social (or, rather, 'national') body.

It is through a very specific regime of techniques of the self embodying experimental acts within a controlled environment, that the School carries out its project of producing the 'scientific', 'rational' citizen; this is a process bound to an interpretation of the 'ills' of Indian society in terms of shortcomings of personality. For six mornings of the week the school bell announces the first public act of the day, 'P.T.' or Physical Training. After *Chota Hazri* (tea and bread) boys proceed to the exercise area, the School oval, to take part in a series of co-ordinated exercises:

P.T. was started in 1935 with seventy boys who could easily be divided into two squads and taught by two qualified masters. In 1936 the number increased to 188 boys and help had to be taken from other masters to take the squads [*sic*] and this lowered the standard of P.T. and discipline. . . . Leaders training classes [consisting of senior boys] . . . were started in 1938 . . . the leaders [being] . . . examined by some officers from the IMA [the Indian Military Academy, also in Dehra Dun]. These leaders prove very useful in training other boys and in maintaining good discipline. . . . On two days a week the P.T. leaders' class of about thirty-six boys is conducted by the P.T. master. The class is made up to include, firstly all boys who have taken the School Certificate, and all those who are likely to leave before the following year even if they have not taken School Certificate. This ensures that no boy will leave the School in the ordinary course without this essential part of his training.

(*DSB*: 34–6)

The passage above depicts a scene from life at the Doon School in 1948. The public spectacle of the callisthenics – the 'disciplinary polyphony of exercises' (Foucault 1979: 159) – inscribes both the spatial and temporal aspects of the School with the unmistakable gloss of a drama of the industrial age; gradation, combination, precision, ordinality, the testing of skills, accolades for the artful, opprobrium for the unskilled, the cadence of the laboratory and the relentless order, to avoid waste, of the industrial production system:

> In September new boys are taken for elementary training in separate small squads of 6 to 8, with specially selected leaders who have to be endowed with great patience. After a month the new boys have a passing-out test in the presence of the Headmaster, the master in charge of P.T. and the two senior boy leaders. Those considered fit are allowed to join the ordinary classes, and usually 7 or 8 are relegated to a further period of elementary training.
>
> (*DSB*: 35)

In the intervening fifty years since the above description, the minutiae of the School's corporeal calendar has changed very little and even in the most senior classes some form of physical activity is mandatory. The School's Headmaster during the period of this research, himself educated at Doon, was unequivocal regarding the importance of both solo and team games for learning 'social behaviour', as he put it.

As in 1948, P.T. leaders are still trained from among the senior boys and examined by the School's resident P.T. instructor. When presented for examination, the boys perform their routine in white vests, white trousers, and white canvas shoes: a compressed image – contained in the mechanics and visibility of their hued actions – which carries the resonance of both laboratorial and industrial activity. The 'tests' – unlike the P.T. itself which takes place early morning – are held during class hours. During term time the School plays host to a constant stream of visitors, especially parents, who can be seen wandering about exploring the campus. For such visitors, public activities such as the leaders' test constitute fleeting fragments in the life of the School, fragments towards an entelechy of 'modern' life which animates the campus and whose punctilios the School imparts to its wards.

S.M. lives in the North Indian city of Lucknow. A Brahmin by caste, he is a relatively prosperous businessman and owns cold-storage warehouses used for storing agricultural produce. At the time of our meeting in 1991, his youngest son was a student at the Doon School while the eldest had spent a short time there some years ago, having been forced to leave due to bad health. S.M. is a regular visitor to Doon and described how 'some of the teachers there have become good friends, like younger brothers'. When visiting the School, he said, he usually stayed with one of the masters whom he had got to know well. During our conversation, he alternated between biographical vignettes from his own life and his views on the Doon School. He narrated how he had studied psychology at university, working later at the Planning Commission as a 'social researcher'. He described in detail the 'methodology' of research he had undertaken while employed at the Commission, his conversations peppered with terms such as 'random samples', 'exogenous factors', and 'multivariate surveys'.

I asked S.M. why, when Lucknow itself contained several reputable day-schools, he had sent his sons to Doon. He began with telling me about the early school days of his daughters, now in their late teens:

> I noticed a lack of discipline in my children when they were staying at home. I will tell you about one incident: my daughter was woken up early one morning to go to school ... but she didn't get up when she should have. And when she did get up it was getting late for school [*sic*] so she didn't even go to the toilet – I repeat [said in a tone of considerable consternation] – didn't even go to the toilet! So for three years I put them in [names a private girls' school in Lucknow] ... in their hostel. They improved immediately.
>
> So, I personally surveyed three public schools [for his son] – Mayo, Sanawar, and Doon. I was greatly impressed by Doon. The [then] Headmaster was from a business background ... and he had greatly impressed me with his management style. I was greatly impressed with the discipline at the School. Every one gets up when they must; this is the difference ... between one sort of people and another ...

The difference between the disciplinary regime of the Doon School and that of the world outside as Arthur Foot, Doon's first Headmaster, saw it, can be gleaned from the following sentiments addressed to a special Founders Day Assembly in 1936: 'During his speech the Headmaster said that the idea of discipline was constantly' in his mind, but that:

> the discipline they were building up was not one based on fear, not one that existed by violent repression, but a discipline that relied on the development of the boys' own self-control and that depended on their cooperation. ... and when they grew up he hoped that ... [they] ... would be able to look straight and unflinchingly at the highest in the land, confident in the power they possessed in having accomplished the primary goal of education – self-discipline and control of a trained body and mind and spirit.

(*DSW*, 31 Oct. 1936)

Distant observations and telescopic knowledge: the self through the other

The passage above constitutes one of the fragments from the tract of the School's narrative of Otherness – concerned with establishing the difference between the Doon Indian, the citizen of tomorrow, and those 'out there' – which was elaborated at the School from its earliest days. This Otherness is established through the framework of a space–time dimension which we may, following Mikhail Bakhtin, call a chronotope. The chronotope in its basic sense is 'a way of understanding experience; it is a specific form-shaping ideology for understanding the nature of events and actions' (Morson and Emerson 1990: 36). The name chronotope, Bakhtin says, is given 'to the intrinsic connectedness of temporal and spatial relationships that are artistically expressed in literature' (Bakhtin 1990: 84). Notwithstanding its initial use in the field of literature, the concept of the chronotope is of wider applicability as a means of expressing ideas about the nature of time and space in specific contexts and what they tell us about the social and historical nature of the 'action' therein; each chronotope is a field of action, and constructs its meaning in specific ways, within which 'spatial and temporal indicators are fused into one carefully thought-out, concrete whole. Time, as it were, thickens, takes on flesh, becomes artistically visible; likewise, space becomes charged and responsive to the movements of time, plot and history' (*ibid.*).

So, at Doon the specific characterisation of space and the specific arrangement of time also establish a particular chronotope, the chronotope of the scientific, rational man. But this chronotope, located in a play of unilinear, disciplinary time and a utilitarian, laboratorial space, is itself counterpoised to contrary spaces and contrary times.

The School established the contrary time–space realm through the act of the scientific gaze, 'critical' observation, which *its* population – counted, graded, homogenised, controlled – could train upon the teeming multiplicities outside: where this exteriority is both geographical and cultural. The scattered acts of colonial episteme and praxis – introduced, refined, and reiterated by the British through their own scientific complex – the Surveys, the Royal Societies – now passed on to play a role in the elaboration of an internal colonialism. The School became a vantage point – itself a scientific and rational space through the very specific characterisation of its time–space realm, from where 'other' populations could be observed; and through this act of observation a 'difference' could be established.

The following passages from *The Doon School Book* are important for two reasons: first, they establish the process of observation referred to above, and, second, they situate this process in the 'neutral' space of scientific inquiry; a space embedded within an industrial hieroglyphic of decimals, percentages and within the language of a 'scientific Geography'. The passages are an embellishment to the overall discourse of the School concerned with the construction of its techno-scientific image.

The account begins by providing an epigraph to the act of observation: any discussion on the teaching of geography at the School, we are told, 'would not be complete without a mention of the special advantages of Dehra Dun as a centre in which to teach Geography':

> In Dehra Dun itself are the Forest Research Institute and branches of the Survey of India, both of which are regularly visited, with very valuable results, and from both of which speakers come to address the boys on their special subjects.
>
> (*DSB*: 23)

And then, the School as the experimental, utilitarian space, whereby to occupy it is to simultaneously observe the outside world, the observation itself dictated by every-day existence at the School which unfolds in the play of the several epistemes of 'modern', rational existence; every-day lives in constant cognisance of the imperatives of the scientific ethos, enunciated through a consciousness which is, *inter alia*, histological and anthropological in its being:

> for the study and teaching of Geography the Doon School itself has exceptional facilities. The old Forest College planted a number of interesting trees from different parts of the world; the problem of irrigation can be studied on a small scale within the grounds; boys, masters and servants come from all parts of India and outside.
>
> (*DSB*: 23)

From this vantage point then, a look-out on the techno-scientific age, one may observe the surroundings, the sightings informed by the various epistemologies of this age. A critical reconnoitre will find much of interest in the Doon valley, and

> the caves in its hills, the way its rivers disappear and reappear in their beds, the bizarre structure of the Siwaliks, all may rouse interest in its physical build.
>   . . . we can . . .[also]. . . compare the differences between life in the mountains and life in the plains. In the Eastern Doon only .5 per cent of the cultivated area is given up to millets, whereas in the hill district . . . millets cover 20.6 per cent. .3 per cent only is given up to sugar in the hill district as against 15 per cent in the Eastern Doon.[11]
>
> (*DSB*: 23)

But the enterprise of the clinical eye is not just concerned with measuring, specifying, and sorting the physical landscape as part of the scientific enterprise; the endeavour may also be extended to include 'Human Geography'. Of interest are the identities of those presented as constituting the material of this 'Human Geography': villagers and 'hillmen', the Other India. By weaving the human element into the narrative of scientific observation, the animate and the inanimate become part of the same analysable landscape and the objects of, because different from, the scientific enterprise:

> The Doon [valley] is rich in material for the study of what is called Human Geography. People from the plains, from Garhwal, Nepal and Tibet frequent it, and it is possible to see with one's own eye the different ways people brought up in different conditions, dress and behave.
>   . . . The clothes, the houses and the physique of the hillmen are different from the valley dwellers and the wide differences between a village like Deoprayag and one like Tunwala[12] must strike the observant eye, and rouse a desire to know the causes in those who are curious.
>
> (*DSB*: 23)

The 'desire to know' – to observe the Other – was positioned within a method, and a spirit, of clinical examination, removed from the intimacy of empathy and aligned with the idea of distant observation. The ideal of 'distant observation' which is both minute ('scrutiny') and, simultaneously, removed from the influence of the observer ('objectivity') is a scientific ideal *par excellence*, for only such a method (and it is always a 'method', any other term smacks of imprecision and randomness) leads to the 'cardinal tenet', as Jordanova calls it, of scientific thinking. The passages quoted above are infused with the spirit of this tenet, that of systematic generalisation:

> it is a cardinal tenet of natural philosophical, scientific and medical thinking that it searches for a high degree of generality. The vast majority of writings on sex differences and sexuality were rooted in the search for lawlike statements, which displayed male and female as natural facts.
>
> (Jordanova 1989: 8)

In the process of 'distant observation' of the 'natural' life which could be found in the vicinity of the School, a difference was established between the observer and the observed; the observer looked out from the place infused with the spirit of science onto a scene – random, unassorted, a 'natural' landscape – which became the object of the scientific method. The Other was different – inferior – by virtue of a lack of science and, connected with this, a lack of masculinity.

The dictionary defines 'museum' as follows: 'A room or building for the preservation or exhibition of objects illustrating antiquities, art, natural science etc.'.[13] But, of course, museums are much more than this. They are also repositories for collections 'which embody hierarchies of value, exclusions, [and] rule-governed territories of the self' (Clifford 1993: 52). And though the collection of objects in a modern museum expresses an aspect of wider power relations between populations and societies, it is invariably true that 'these historical relations of power in the work of acquisition are occulted. The *making* of meaning in museum classification and display is mystified as adequate *representation*' (*ibid.*: 54; emphasis in the original). In general, the museum idea simultaneously establishes the notions of evolutionary time (with the 'present' being the most evolved), a primitive space (which is on view in the present in (museum) buildings designed exclusively for that purpose, such that the 'modern' present and the 'primitive' past are brought into sharp focus through contiguous location and are clearly distinguishable), and that of scientific observation of the above time–space dimension. Museums are, then, necessary requirements for societies with a conscious view of their place in a 'modern' world, part of a 'rational' ethos, and the museum collection at Doon in its early days embodied all these ideas. It elaborated upon the 'Human Geography' within which 'hillmen' and 'valley dwellers' became a part of the observable natural landscape. The Naturalists' Society, whose main object was 'nature study' and for which purpose it organised 'frequent expeditions in the neighbourhood', was in charge of the museum. The majority of the exhibited items were acquired, *DSB* notes, 'from the salvaged exhibits of the museum at Quetta after the earthquake of 1935'. And the items exhibited?

> . . . a collection of stuffed birds, animals, butterflies and birds' eggs and a collection of armoury and of models and dresses of Baluchistan tribes.
>
> (*DSB*: 34)

The museum of Other things – where 'stuffed birds' and 'dresses of Baluchistan tribes' constitute a single objectified complex – is the world outside the cultural boundaries of the School. The peculiarities of this other world are explored at the School in different, distant, ways: students take part in 'colourful' pageants illustrating the 'diversity' of Indian culture, dressed as 'tribals' and 'hillmen', singing and playing music which are described as simple, 'but with a purity which we have lost'; earnest teenagers take part in 'village work' so as to 'help those who are, essentially, not able to deal with the complexities of the modern world'; and the Nature Society encourages its members to organise 'exhibitions' for the Founders Day where 'simple' ways of living can be faithfully reproduced.

In an important sense, the difference between the School's and its contrary populations is established through an essentialised view of the different capacities for discipline among the Indian population, and it is to this theme that I return in the following section.

The forms of discipline

I have suggested earlier that my concern with the term 'discipline' is both similar to and quite different from that which engages Foucault. Hence, there is a mechanical similarity between the process through which a disciplinary regime is sought to be established at the Doon School and the one discussed by Foucault. In principle, at least, every single fragment of school life is supervised: it exists, in the various memos and orders of regulation, as a system of mathematical calculation; time spent and spaces occupied – who will do what, when and where – are the objects of ceaseless supervision and constant discussion. The supervision – and the scrutiny – exists apart from the conscious acts of its overseers: it accompanies the students during their waking hours and sleeps with them – in as much as when they must sleep, with whom (no one), where and for how long, constitutes a part of the disciplinary regime of the School. Discipline becomes the unconscious, the tangible intangible, and the object of a fetishisation that seeks to hallow the territory of the School, both physical and cultural, and distinguish it from others (other schools, other people).

The realm of the disciplinary at the School is open-ended, and nothing exists beyond it or above it, it is co-terminus with existence within its walls as well as, at least for the students, beyond it: on days when they are allowed to go out of the School, to the cinema or the shops, they are expected to follow a clearly laid out set of rules as to which parts of the city they may visit and the time by which they must return to the School. As well, on their day of 'outing' they must wear the school uniform. The following description of the disciplinary grid into which a new student is inserted upon his arrival at the School, is worthy I think, of equal honour with the best of examples that Foucault provides from the vast annals of French history he opens for inspection. Though the description comes from the early years of the School's existence, it provides a broadly accurate picture of the situation as I found it during research in 1990–1:

> In a boy's early years we try and establish in him habits of punctuality, attention to obligations and honesty. Shortcomings are noticed and recorded in two main ways. In each school period a list is brought around and a boy is marked as late if either he has not arrived absolutely on time, or has forgotten to bring his book, homework, pencil, or other article [*sic*] that he knows is needed for this lesson.
>
> These original entries are marked up by a clerk on a complete school list, by the date of each entry. The Headmaster sees this list daily and sends for the boys who have frequent entries. He is probably quicker to send for a boy for whom unpunctuality has been a besetting sin in the past.[14]

(*DSB*: 14)

So, in a most obvious sense, the School does indeed seem to function within a matrix where:

> The meticulousness of the regulations, the fussiness of the inspections,

the supervision of the smallest fragment of life and of the body . . .
[provide]. . . a laicized content, an economic or technical rationality for
the mystical calculus of the infinitesimal and the infinite.

(Foucault 1979: 141)

However, discipline at Doon School, despite its enmeshment in and elaboration through a play of rules and exhortations which seem contiguous with
those excavated by Foucault, is *not* substantially akin to the latter's conception of it; it is not the discipline which Guibert, speaking in late eighteenth-
century France, was to say 'must be made national' (*ibid.*: 69). For the
conception of the disciplinary regime at the School is one bound up with
the establishment and articulation of the difference between the scientific
and the rational and the unscientific and the irrational; between those fit to
don the mantle of post-colonial civility and those not so endowed. The specificity of the colonial encounter provides us with a very specific economy of
discipline, one that is quite different from the regime the European patriarchs
insisted should become a generalised condition of existence.

'You must have noticed', one of the teachers explained to me when I asked
him about the system of discipline and punishment at the School, 'that we do
not rely on coercive punishment, whereby discipline is maintained through a
constant threat from above . . . that it comes from outside, that someone has
to always watch over and the boys can see that someone is indeed watching
over their heads'. I have suggested above that this scheme of discipline at the
School is in the nature of a saturation of the field of its survey. In its functioning it unfolds through a system of mutual supervisions and surveillances: 'the
responsibility for the School's functioning in an orderly manner', as one of
the masters put it, '. . . well oiled . . . is really distributed up and down the line
. . . not just the teachers . . . even the students, for instance, take part in seeing
to it that the School, and that includes the teacher body, functions properly'.[15]
Importantly, however, it is in the public articulation of the nature of this
discipline that the difference from the Foucauldian perspective arises. For at
the point when supervision is transformed into transcendent self-discipline –
when the 'mystique of the everyday is joined with the discipline of the minute'
(*ibid.*: 140) – it is also represented as the characteristic of a very specific and
limited section of the population.

Attendance in class, punctuality or lack of it, 'industry', and non-
compliance with rules, are monitored at the School through a system of
culpatory accountancy involving the issuing of red and yellow cards depend-
ing on the seriousness of the breach. Red cards are usually issued to boys who
are deemed 'idle' or show a marked lack of 'industry' in their work.[16] Yellow
cards are issued for serious offences connected with repeated breaches of
School discipline. The issuing of the cards is not, however, linked to corporal
punishment – that is, at least officially, forbidden.[17]

It was clear from my conversations with students at the School that many
had an acute awareness of the disciplinary mechanism that dictated their

existence. This was especially true of boys who came from metropolitan cities and whose families may be characterised under the clumsy rubric of 'western-ised'; the liberties allowed them by their parents seemed to be in sharp contrast to the prohibitions placed on them by the School. Now, given that a good number of parents associated with the School see themselves as 'liberal' and anti-authoritarian in the context of child rearing, a useful way of under-standing their acquiescence to the rigorous disciplinary regime of the School is through the symbolic import of the idea of self-discipline propagated by the School. Their acquiescence in this regard also provides us with a key to understanding the difference between the disciplinary idea that Foucault speaks of, and the one that exists at the Doon School in particular and in a post-colonised context in general. For the form of discipline which is repre-sented as animating the functioning of daily life at Doon – self-discipline – is also represented as a regimen of the body which establishes the difference between the 'modern' and the 'primitive'; and that between the scientific and its antithesis.

Self-discipline is the characteristic of the 'modern' citizen – 'others' may only function within a concatenation of imposed forces and restraints. So, whereas Foucault may say that the technique of discipline refined and per-fected in the barracks and the classroom slowly and silently breached these walls and mingled with the daily pursuits of the general population, 'elaborat-ing procedures for the individual and *collective* coercion of bodies' (*ibid.*: 169), in the case of Doon we may say something different; that the 'Doon discipline' is, in fact, *not* meant to coincide with the discipline that is 'required' by the general population. Otherwise, the Doon School – and the ontology it represents – runs the risk of losing its Other which provides it with a point of reference. For it is through a very specific understanding of discipline that one of the images of the difference between the Doon citizen and its Other is maintained.

The discourse on self-discipline has been present in various forms in several strands of twentieth-century Indian thought. The most common context for these was the colonial encounter and the process of evaluation and re-evaluation of Indian 'shortcomings'. Many thinkers, including Swami Vivekananda and Sister Nivedita – who spoke of the need to make Indian women 'efficient' (Sister Nivedita 1923: 57) – wrote around this issue. It is Gandhi's formulation, however, which best provides an understanding of how the Doon take on self-discipline serves to establish a difference between the population of the School and Other populations. With Gandhi, self-discipline – which 'involved mastering all the senses, especially sexuality' (Parekh 1989: 177) – was a means to an end, it being his ardent desire that the self-discipline he strove for should also be attained by the general population. Indeed, it is the most desirable form of regulation, Gandhi suggested, and must be embraced by all, because *all* are capable of it: 'in this much needed work all who will can take an equal share' (Iyer 1987: 227). His political vision and strategy were intimately connected to this ideal. Hence, since 'outward freedom' from colonial rule was dependent upon the achievement of 'inward freedom' (*ibid.*), or self-discipline, the attainment of the latter by the majority was crucial to the over-all struggle against British rule.

The view at the Doon School was, and continues to be, as I have suggested, quite different. The *leit-motif* of the School's discourse on self-discipline is that the possibility of its attainment and exercise rests with a small section of the population; that section whose responsibility it is to 'produce' citizens. This view was implicit in the ex-ICS officer K.G.M.'s comment, encountered in Chapter 1 in the context of a discussion on 'modernity' and 'rationality': 'modernity is rationalism', he had said, concluding that 'the class of people I come from were [/are] more rational. . . . India was never a rational country . . . we have a tradition . . . in my family . . . of rationalism' (see p. 34). At the Doon School this argument is further extended towards the task of establishing the difference between the milieu of the School and the 'masses' through the suggestion that it is the denizens of the former who are more capable of self-discipline; the 'unscientific' are more responsive to a system of impositions.

However, notwithstanding the specificities of the colonial (and post-colonial) situation with regard to any discussion on discipline and power, it is possible to utilise a very generalised Foucauldian perspective. In *The History of Sexuality* (vol. I) Foucault suggests that the early history of European sexuality is bound up with the attempts of the European bourgeoisie to define its own identity: 'the bourgeoisie began by considering that its own sex was something important, a fragile treasure, a secret that had to be discovered at all costs' (Foucault 1990: 120–1); the deployment of the techniques of sexuality by the bourgeoisie, Foucault says, should be seen 'as the self-affirmation of one class rather than the enslavement of another' (*ibid.*: 123). It is in this sense that one might speak of the deployment of the discourse of self-discipline in the context of the Indian bourgeoisie: that, historically, it has functioned as the discourse of self-affirmation, rather than as a tool for forging a homogeneous national community where *every one* has learnt the science of self-regulation.

The period of my research on the School coincided with the public disturbances associated with the Mandal Report on reservations in jobs and educational institutions for the Scheduled and the 'Backward' castes. The streets and other public spaces of several North Indian cities witnessed large-scale demonstrations by upper caste youth against moves by the central government to act upon the Commission's recommendations to increase reservations. During my stay at the School the Mandal issue was a continuing source of discussion among the senior students and the staff. The objects of discussion were both the demonstrators – upper caste like the Doon students but perceived to be of a different 'cultural' background – and those against whom the demonstrations were aimed, the Scheduled and Backward castes.

The most common epithet directed towards both the above groups was that they were 'essentially irrational'. What do they understand, one of the students said to me, 'about organised thinking, they just react on an impulse'. When asked what he meant by 'organised thinking', the student responded that 'it has something to do with . . . being scientific . . . you know, thinking things through, not simply jumping into something'. This is why, he continued, 'these people need to be controlled, essentially, they need to be told that enough is enough'. Antagonisms based on class were translated into the language of the 'backwardness of mind' and the inability to grasp the minutiae of 'technology'. It was often suggested to me that the violence and 'fundamentalism' to be witnessed 'on the streets' were due to the 'unscientific' attitudes held by the population at large, and that a 'rational' attitude implied 'orderly' conduct.

'Respect for the law' was an aspect of self-discipline, and 'the sort of person who comes out of a school such as this, because rational action has been so deeply ingrained in him, does not need any overt form of control'. Arthur Foot, of course, was quite clear about this. He 'felt that self-control was a concomitant [*sic*] to being a responsible and productive citizen and warned the boys against the danger of allowing their tempers to get the better of them' (*DSB*: 60). During my stay at the School some of the opinions expressed by the boys in this matter were much more forthright: 'we don't want people with spears running this country', one of the students said to me.

Intimate observations: the adult-child

The School's population can be divided into two very distinct, openly acknowledged, groups which we may refer to as its 'official' and 'unofficial' populations. The former consists of the students and a segment of the teaching staff,[18] and the latter of the so-called subordinate staff. The subordinate staff category designates a certain section of the School's employees consisting of, *inter alia*, cooks, cleaners, gardeners, and office attendants. The subordinate staff provide the School's official population with its most immediate referent of the Other that exists beyond its walls. 'From the earliest days', *DSB* says, 'the school has sought to instil in boys the desire to serve the community' (p. 63). A sense of '*noblesse oblige*', as the same account quite unselfconsciously calls it, was intended to be put into practice through activities organised under the Labour Quota System first organised in 1939. The Adult Education Society ('Teaching the servants or organising their games') and the Dehat Sabha ('visiting Tunwala'), operated under the Labour Quota System. Service to the poor and less fortunate, however, was not allowed to get in the way of considerable comforts to the self. The following menu was ordered by Jack Gibson, then Housemaster at the School, for the boys of his house for an end of term dinner in 1939 (or 'Golden Night', as it is called at the School): tomato soup, fish and mustard sauce, samosas, roast goose and apple sauce, peas and potatoes, chicken curry and *pullau*, cheese souffle, *pakoris*, Christmas pudding with whipped cream and fruit (Sing 1985: 65).

The Labour Quota System now functions under a different nomenclature: Socially Useful Productive Work (SUPW). The latter itself has now become a formal part of the curriculum of the Secondary Board of Central Education in India, a fact often pointed out at the School as further proof of its contribution to the national education system. As a metaphor for an endeavour of modernity which combines both the imperatives of *noblesse oblige* and the purposeful utilitarianism of 'scientific' activity, the words 'Socially Useful Productive Work' seem especially apt: the image of service to society embedded in the lexical metaphors of the industrial world.

The 'servants' and the 'villagers' are the living metaphors of a pre-modernity (and 'anti-modernity') with which the School, along with other voices in the national-public arena, has conducted its dialogue on 'nation-building'. This is, of course, the discourse of personality, where the problem of backwardness is the problem of effecting a scientific transformation in the body and mind of the 'native'.

Under the Child and Adult Education Scheme of the SUPW at Doon, instruction is provided on matters of 'general hygiene and manual labour' to members of the subordinate staff and their families. And it is within the impulse of this pastoral scientism that we may locate the following paragraph from an article in an early edition of the *School Weekly*, with its concern with the passage from antiquity to modernity:

> His Excellency the Governor of the United Provinces . . . visited the School on the morning of Saturday October 15th.
>
> After visiting some of the classes and the library, His Excellency went to the Adult School. Mr. Ashraf explained to him the work that the Adult Education Society was attempting among the School servants, and demonstrated the use of the sand-trays, charts, diagrams and other devices that have been planned by Sahebzada Saiduzzafar for use in the Adult School.
>
> (*DSW*, 29 Oct. 1938)

The view that familiarity with the calculative ethos of the market economy is a prerequisite for 'normal' (Marshall 1938) behaviour – where 'normal' does service for 'logical', 'rational', and 'consistent' – is influential in constructions of the 'primitive' at the Doon School. The conception of the free market as part of the *logos* of the 'civilised' was, of course, eloquently and succinctly put forward by Radhakrishnan (1975).

'The servants of the School and their children', a member of the staff wrote in a special edition of the *School Weekly* published upon the death of the School's first Headmaster, 'were also very dear to Arthur Foot, and he was constantly thinking how to help them in their way of thinking [*sic*], in their manner of living, and in their general attitude towards life' (*DSW*, 6 Oct. 1968). The servants of the School incurred, it seems, frequent debts from money-lenders and one of the ways in which Arthur Foot expressed his concern for 'their way of thinking . . . and their manner of living' was to attempt to 'teach' them better money management; their journey from the realm of the pre-modern to the modern was not yet complete, and they often floundered in its commercial and ordinal complexities. These were, of course, the characteristics of the anti-modern personality that became the task of Indian post-coloniality and modernity to both contain and eradicate. If at times the lessons prove to be somewhat harsh, then this, as Foot seems to imply below, is the prerogative of the modernised sections, and the only redemption of the pre-modern:

> In the early days . . . the Hospital Sweeper Banwari was found to have a big debt – about Rs 150/-. Captain Saheb and I decided to teach the moneylender a lesson. We therefore told Banwari to pay nothing but to go to prison. We would keep his job open, and in the mean time allow his son to work instead. He knew that as the law stood, the creditor had to pay enough to support the debtor in prison (Rs 8/- per month) and spend Rs 40/- on his clothes, and after six months the debt would be cancelled.
>
> Banwari therefore ended up free of debt, with, also an extra allowance during his time away from home as his son had drawn his wages. As this story got around the bazaar it discouraged moneylenders from getting our employees into their clutches.[19]

The aspect of the above which concerns me is the treatment of the 'servants' on a par with the children at the School: the process of the 'discovery' of childhood to which the formal schooling system contributed handsomely (Ariès 1973) seems to have been extended at the Doon School to classify as childish those adults who did not display an aptitude for 'modern' life. A lack of self-discipline and an unfamiliarity with monetised existence: these are the marks of the 'unscientific', and also those of the child. And 'it was recognised that the child was not ready for life, and that he had to be subjected to a special treatment, a sort of quarantine, before he was allowed to join the adults' (Ariès 1973: 412). 'We hope', the secretary of the Adult Education Society wrote in 1952:

> to have a whole-time trained teacher soon for a more thorough execution of our schemes, we want to start regular P.T. for servants to smarten them up and give them a better feeling for the gift of physical fitness. And we want to build the Panchayat Ghar ['village parliament'] building anew – a building which would be not merely a pleasant meeting place but which would possess significant form architecturally, wherein it might be possible to realise again the whole man, unfractured in his methods of thinking and feeling.
>
> (*DSW*, 4 June 1952)

The passage from the primitive stage to that of the civilised is also, here, the passage from infancy to adulthood. This is, perhaps, most clearly reflected, as above, in the nature of the discourse within which the existence of the unofficial population is acknowledged. It is the lexical universe of the parent and the child. Social work activities, for example, centre on acts of teaching: general education and hygiene. Leisure activities, such as servants' sports days are 'organised' for them by the School's students and staff, and sections of the subordinate staff are described as 'loyal' while others are 'easily led'. Indeed, the perception of the subordinate staff itself of its place in the 'family' of the School seems clear: 'I have committed a mistake', one of its members wrote to the Headmaster in 1986, accounting for his involvement in a strike at the School, 'so please pardon me. I hope you will forgive me. I have a firm belief in you and hope you will forgive me as you would a child.'[20]

The contrast between the realm and the processes of the School and those of the cultural world that differs from it was also sometimes formulated with reference to the group which has the initial responsibility for the child: early in the School's history the Indian family itself became a metaphor for 'native failings'. The 'other' Indians, characterised by lack of a 'sense of personal responsibility' and used to functioning in an environment of 'instruction' rather than 'organisation', are the products of the peculiar ethos of the native family. Though the passage below on Indian family life is taken from a book written by an Englishman, Headmaster Arthur Foot, the glowing Preface to the same was provided by an Indian, Akbar Hydari, then Chairman of the Board of Governors of the Doon School. 'We believe', *The Doon School Book* stated, 'that character-training is more a matter of organisation than instruction' and that:

> The emphasis [at the School] has always been on the needs of individual boys, and on giving them a sense of personal responsibility. Boys who have been, apparently, well brought up at home, behave well and work well to please their parents, or in order to please their school-masters. This is not a sound foundation for conduct. They must behave well and work well to satisfy their own self-respect and sense of personal responsibility. Often it is boys who have a good record of regular work or conduct who slip up when they have started more difficult work. They are so anxious to achieve a good result that they will use dishonest means. When they are found out they are so anxious about what their parents will think that they will lie most brazenly.[21]
>
> (*DSB*: 12)

The 'unprocessed' child, straight from the bosom of the family, and the 'irrational' Indian, mired in an 'unscientific' ethos and forever a child, share a cultural territory in the discourse of the School. As a consequence of the above-mentioned strike by the subordinate staff, the latter were required to sign a memorandum agreeing to observe certain rules and conditions laid down and drafted by the School authorities as a condition for employment at the School. The memorandum, draconian in its scope, reads like a primer of the chastened child: the strikers become truant, undisciplined children, and the memorandum an expiatory document. The new work-conditions contained in it frame the strikers as suffering from the 'vices' of children:

> We will do the work assigned to each of us honestly and conscientiously and will be punctual at all times.

> . . . [we will not allow] . . . any outsiders (non-employees) to enter the campus at any time to guide or misguide us.

At the time of the strike (1986), RW, himself an old boy, was Headmaster at the School. 'The servants', he told me later, recalling the event in the manner of a concerned patriarch, 'are a problem':

> they just demand things, they get drunk, beat up some one's wife . . . when they were on strike [and had been taken away to jail] . . . I told them that they had been misled . . .

The disciplinary regime at the School ('self-discipline'), formulated in a space of science and rationality, serves to distinguish it and its cultural and intellectual world from the realm of Other populations. These latter function under the mechanism of a 'primitive' supervisory principle: force and coercion. The Doon disciplinary model establishes the difference between it and its antithetical populations, and the former regime is not the one which 'must be made national'. For the contrary disciplinary regime is the one based on coercion, and this 'primitive' discipline is reserved for (and required by) the 'unscientific' and therefore the 'feminine', and, of course, for the childish.

In Chapter 4, I analyse the ideal of 'secularism' as elaborated at the Doon School as part of the larger narrative of citizenship in the post-colonial nation state. It constitutes an indispensable aspect of the overall treatise on post-coloniality, and of the liberal discourse of the nation state which the School both contributes to and draws from.

4   Secularism, the citizen, and Hindu contextualism

In the previous chapter I suggested that the insights generated by Foucault's work on the technique of enclosure might be of uncertain analytical value in thinking about non-European contexts. The discussion in this chapter will attempt to reinforce that conclusion. For this chapter too is about how the enclosure may have differentiating rather than homogenising effects. The discussion attempts to analyse that discourse of Indian modernity that seeks to differentiate the 'secular-modern' citizenry from its 'communal-backward' antithesis. A modification to Foucault's profound insights into the functioning of disciplinary regimes is in order – one which research specifically engaged with colonial and post-colonised issues might be able to offer. The issue of religion and how to deal with the multiplicity of religious voices which characterises Indian society has had a prominent and continuing life in the discourse of the Doon School from its earliest days. It was most often manifested in the question of whether the School curriculum should include religious instruction and whether it should arrange for (or encourage) religious worship. The search for the 'correct' religious attitude, and indeed the problematic of faith – interpreted primarily in terms of its perceived movement from the private to the public sphere – was (and continues to be) part of a wider, national, dialogue on the post-colonial 'modern' mind.

The School's participation in this dialogue was an acutely conscious activity, formulated in the nature of a duty to come to terms with, so as to keep at bay, what was perceived to be an overbearing fact of Indian existence which threatened the society's passage from archaism to modernity. In English-speaking (and writing) circles in India, the realm of religion has increasingly come to be accompanied by a gloss on what is seen as its polar opposite, secularism. 'Secularism', adopted by the urban intelligentsia as modernity's most potent signifier, also enjoys a lasting presence in the public eye through its early ensconcement at a site of considerable symbolic potency; for it appears in the opening – and much quoted – paragraph of the Indian constitution, the legal apotheosis of post-colonial citizenship. The discussion of this chapter will be interwoven with contemporary examples from Indian life (primarily Hindi literature) which provide alternative ways of formulating the issue of identity in a multi-cultural society.

The modern spirit: destroying communal prejudices

The issue of religion and its role in the life of the modern mind was usually formulated at the School in terms of the supposedly destructive forces which strained within the harness of religious belief, and which were a constant threat to the peace and well being of the desirable civil society for which the School was meant to serve as the prototype. And hence, the thinking went, the School itself was best served by domesticating the beast through its banishment from the public life of its members. An information sheet makes the point as follows:

> Boys from all parts of the country, from all castes and religions mix together and lose their regional or religious identity because the School deliberately plays down these differences by
> a common uniform
> the same food
> the same facilities
> irrespective of the background of the student.
> (*Innovative Leadership Provided by the Doon School* c. 1985)

'Region' and 'religion' were antithetical to the oneness of the nation, the achievement of which was considered the most urgent task of the era of post-coloniality, and all symbols of *communal* existence were to be excoriated from the daily schedule of the modern citizen; all acts which secured his loyalty to the *nation*, and which transcended the fractiousness of *communities*, were to be encouraged. These acts and rituals of every-day, national, life were, in turn, to be grafted on to the new public memory which would *re-imagine*[1] a united India, ready to take its place in the international community of respect and nationhood:

> Since its inception the School adopted strictly non-denominational prayers and hymns and does not serve beef and pork. In fact the School adopted 'Jana Gana Mana'[[2]] as its School song in 1935 well before it became the National Anthem in 1947.
> (*Innovative Leadership Provided by the Doon School* c. 1985)

The image of the nation and its grand outline provided a 'natural' contrast to the minutiae of regional and religious emotions – to 'local' passions, in other words. And its unifying cartography could only be inscribed upon their vanquished forms:

> The objects of the Society [The IPSS] are:-
> (1) To establish Schools in India. . .
> to develop a spirit of Indian nationality by destroying all social, communal, religious or provincial prejudices among the students and fostering a spirit of comradeship among them.[3]

So, the 'spirit of Indian nationality', as codified in the inaugural charter of a School which received significant support and encouragement from some of the most important nationalist figures of the time, was seen to evolve in the act of suppression: the nation transcends the particularities of its citizens, their 'primitive' loyalties to immediate environments; and its unity could only be guaranteed through the suppression of these loyalties. Commenting on the changing patois of the students, the *Doon School Book* (*DSB*) notes that 'the change from hybrid Hindustani to hybrid English is not a sign of increased anglicization, but rather of a break down of provincial cliques of which there were some signs in the early days of the school' (p. 20).[4] The danger to the nation lay in the whimsy of the majority of the population which continued to be under the sway of religious and regional emotions which obstructed the 'true' nationalism which transcended these factors (Nehru 1960). This view on the irrationality of the masses, which refused to transcend their commitments to the lesser gods of region and religion, had also found early currency at the Doon School. Many of Doon's ex-students keep in touch with the School through the pages of the weekly magazine and the following is from a 1945 edition of the *Weekly*, written by an 18-year-old ex-student, then studying at the prestigious St Stephen's College in Delhi. India, the author states:

> is still in the Communal or Tribal stage, the latter taking the form of Provincialism. We have yet to attain our nationalism, and no nation, united by bonds of love, born of a common part and common aspirations for the future, can be denied its independence for long. In fact, Independence is a corollary to Nationalism, although we persist in Communalism although it is a negation of Nationalism. By tradition and upbringing the Indian can only think in terms of his class, community and province. In his opposition to a foreigner he may occasionally think and feel like an Indian, but at all other times his narrower claims predominate in his sequence of loyalties.
>
> ('The Political Regeneration of India should be Preceded by her Social Emancipation', *DSW*, 27 Oct. 1945)[5]

Eternal vigilance, in the shape of the 'modern' type of patriot, his loyalty pledged to an abstract transcendent entity, the Indian nation, instead of the concrete, base, environment of his immediate familiarity, was the only answer. But what are the characteristics of the 'modern' mind?

> The modern mind, that is to say the better type of the modern mind, is practical and pragmatic, ethical and social, altruistic and humanitarian. It is governed by a practical idealism for social betterment. The ideals which move it represent the spirit of the age, the Zeitgeist, the *yugadharma*. It has discarded to a large extent the philosophical approach of the ancients, the search for ultimate reality, as well as the devotionalism

and the mysticism of the medieval period. Humanity is its god, and social service its religion.

(Nehru 1960: 406)

The 'this-worldliness' characterisation of the modern citizen has always been an important component of the School's dialogical universe and, along with a general disquiet regarding 'excessive' western materialism,[6] there was the parallel perception that the Indian was still too much of the 'other' world. 'The Indian', a contributor to the *School Weekly* suggested, 'would do well to forget his books and his examinations more often and to spend more time in practical activities with his fellows' (*DSW*, 17 March 1945); and of course, S.R. Das's obituary had described his 'mentality', we may recall, as that of a 'solid builder', rather than someone who 'attempted to build . . . on sand'.

These discussions at the School contain two parallel concerns. The first relates to the construction of a civil society, a new India: the community of law and order, of individual discipline and public morality, 'humanism and the scientific spirit', of 'empirical facts' and 'empirically verifiable truths', the society which has banished 'fruitless speculation' from its realms in favour of practical activity. The second concern speaks of membership of this society: of those who qualify and those who constitute a threat to its well being. An important threat to the nation, an important strand of nationalist thinking of the 1920s and 1930s asserted, lay in the religious 'prejudices' and loyalties of the 'masses', in the primordiality of the latter's thought processes (Pandey 1994: 235).

The early decades of this century, the period during which S.R. Das was busy mobilising moral and financial support for his school, witnessed a growing awareness among the urban intelligentsia of the 'Hindu–Muslim' problem. So, instances of conflict between Hindus and Muslims which might earlier have been regarded as essentially 'of little consequence in the context of the immediate political agenda' (Pandey 1994: 232), were increasingly perceived as highlighting 'dangers arising from community based mobilisation' (*ibid.*: 234). During such a period, marked by the growing consciousness of the 'communal problem' among influential sections of the urban population, the appeal of a school which would be part of 'all those works which are necessary to build up our people into a nation',[7] may well have been expected to contain an obvious logic.

Of the several acts of reification of the national community and its concrete, geographical image during the period, perhaps none was as powerful as its superimposition on a national atlas of violence and disorder. In the Congress Committee Report of 1931, for example, the nation was translated as something more than just a collection of towns and provinces: it was brought 'alive' by the flesh and blood of its, otherwise, abstract populations, which, in turn, threatened to overwhelm the dreams of the 'educated' classes for a united India. The Report compiled a 'casual list of riots' to 'give some idea of the proportions the problem has assumed during the last decade' (quoted in Pandey 1994: 234) and provided an account of communal conflict which encompassed all four geographical directions.

The threat posed by 'religious prejudices' to the unity of the post-colonised nation – which if not checked would only serve to reinforce colonial arguments about the impossibility of keeping together a united India without the firm guiding hand of the Raj – became a regular part of the thinking at the School. It often found a place in the Headmaster's talks at the School assembly, visiting guests – presidents, prime ministers, army chiefs, and others – praised the evident 'secularism' which informed the School's func- tioning, and the public was sternly informed by the School that 'in our organ- isation we insure that there is nothing which could give rise to a separation on communal lines' (*DSB*: 14). The possibility of Doon participating in anything like the Bombay Pentangular Tournament (based on 'communal' considerations) was described as 'unthinkable'; 'nor would communal con- siderations occur to anyone, either boys or masters, in the appointment of prefects or the election of Secretaries' (*ibid.*).

For many who were at the Doon School in the opening decades of its existence, and who were later to play important roles in the public life of the nation as part of the post-colonial intelligentsia – journalists, editors, novel- ists, social scientists, cultural functionaries of the state – secularism became a personal creed. S.W., now himself the Headmaster of a well-known North Indian public school, joined Doon in 1947 as a 12-year-old. In 1942 his father, an army officer, had been transferred to the front in the Middle East, and decided to send his son to Doon on reading 'an advertisement inserted by [Headmaster] Foot'. As a Headmaster, S.W. is now himself required to make decisions about extra-curricular activities at his school. I asked him why he thought that during his student days at Doon, a conscious decision had been taken to inculcate a strictly non-religious atmosphere in the public life of the School. Because, he said:

> you see all around in India today (*sic*) . . . when has religion been a unifying force . . . [it is]. . . always divisive. It [the promotion of a secular environment] was consciously done. I am not willing to have a temple at my school . . . I'm clear about that.

Contemporary events in India have only served, in S.W.'s view, to emphasise the wisdom of the policy on religion followed at Doon. To highlight the success of this policy and the indelible impact it had on students, he recounted his experience upon first going to university. The world outside was vastly different from what he had experienced within the boundaries of the School, and

> The first shock that I got was when I filled up my [college] form and it asked for my caste . . . I didn't know! Most people know it . . . when I

used to stay at my grand-parents [i.e. before he joined Doon] I used to know about *ekadasi, navaratri, shraddh* . . . all this became totally unknown. There was no discussion of caste at all [at Doon].

The difference between the society which exists within the School walls – the prototype for the desirable national community – and the 'other' communities animated by narrow prejudices and 'backward' interests is here addressed through the agency of the caste system. In this view, 'most people' know which caste they belong to, but our Doon School education has taught us to rise above this narrowness of vision. The educational goals of the Doon School, as Viceroy Willingdon put it in 1935, were to be commended 'to all those who are interested in India's youth and the problems and difficulties which confront it' (*Times of India*, 28 Oct. 1935 (hereafter *TOI*)). The School, he added, would be the 'miniature' world where the boys would be trained in the virtues of 'self-denial, leadership, argument, association, in fact all the various aptitudes and forbearances that will be demanded of you later in life' (*TOI*).

'Secularism' forms an important part of the Doon self-identity. It is discussed in public talks, in private conversation, and finds a prominent place, as we have seen above, in the official literature of the School about the nature and objectives of the institution. This apparent lack of a religious atmosphere at Doon was described to me by an English visitor to the School as the feature which most obviously set it apart from its English counterparts. D.H., a master at Haileybury College near London, had come to Doon School for a year as part of an exchange programme. His observations on Doon are of particular interest, for they reflect how 'outsiders' perceive the School's ideologies. Whereas Doon School appeared 'to make a virtue out of being . . . very secular', D.H. observed, at most English public schools religious worship was, more often than not, enshrined in the school constitution: 'a part of what the school is all about'. So, for him it was:

- odd coming here where . . . the Assembly, which makes room for five minutes of meditation . . . is the only form of religious life the School appears to have. [There is] . . . no religious instruction and, surprisingly, no teaching of comparative religion.

Further, it appeared to D.H. that the official attitude at the School towards religion amounted to something more than a lack of encouragement: it was almost in the nature of an imperative. [8]

No place for a modern man: the contagion of the native family

'Our religious outlook', *DSB* notes, 'is focussed in the daily School Assembly' (p. 13). It then goes on to emphasise the non-sectarian nature of this 'religious outlook', and, characterising it as the embodiment of a universal rather than a 'local' emotion, it is simultaneously presented as a private pursuit. This is, of course, in keeping with official School policy. The 'fundamental' religious idea manifested in the Assembly, *DSB* says,

> is a simple one; that in each human being there is an element of divine nature and *it is the responsibility of each person to nurture and develop it in himself* and to recognise it in others. We do not arrange any doctrinal teaching for separate religions.[9]
>
> (*DSB*: 13, emphasis added)

The attempt to 'privatise' religion is also part of discussions that posit a separation between the influences of home and school life. Here, home life becomes a metaphor for the world outside where religion is a public affair, marked by the passions of excessive zeal and resisted by some through 'the revolt against the old orthodoxy'. In either case, the School was to suggest, *its* role was to divert manifestations of public engagement with religious issues into private channels, into individual contemplation:

> Many boys in their home training have a background of doctrinal teaching, and this may provide additional force to the ideas with which they will be surrounded in school. On the other hand many boys have no such training, and in their homes there is a revolt against the old orthodoxy. Such boys find that the ideas in the school prayers provide a practical clothing for the inherent religious instincts that are the property of all humanity.
>
> (*DSB*: 13)

There was to be, then, a sharp break between the school environment and that at home, for many children arrived from a domestic milieu permeated by explicit engagement with religious issues and attitudes. The School must teach them to confine these to the recesses of private thought: it would not discourage the private pursuit of faith, but as a community it was not to be animated by the tenets of any one particular religion. Hence, an 'inferior' public religiosity became linked to Indian home life, and both called out for reform.

The labour that surrounded the task of securing a 'clean break' from the home environment of the students carries a strong resonance of medico-administrative discourses that marked colonial engagements with 'tropical' hygiene and pandemic pestilence such as the plague (see, e.g. Arnold 1993). Recounting the episode of the arrival of the very first group of students in 1935, *DSB* noted the elaborate arrangements that had been made to receive the boys:

> Trains only reach Dehra Dun in the early morning and only leave in the evening, and parents had been warned in advance that they must hand

over their children at the station and then keep away from them until the afternoon, when they would be welcome for tea.

(DSB: 3)

And when the parents joined their newly enrolled sons for afternoon tea, the latter were already part of another world, their mien a proclamation of the rational cartography of existence and thought to which they now owed allegiance:

> The boys' measurements had been received in advance, and the school clothes were ready for them. In the afternoon when the parents arrived, they found their boys all playing games in their school clothes. . . . The boys had already been examined and put into their classes, and the full programme was to start with P.T. the next day.
>
> *(DSB*: 3–4)

The railways in India have for long been an important element of the discourse on disease and contagion, for the boon of mobility that this form of travel was supposed to have granted the natives was also seen to carry the threat of broadcasting contagion over a wider area. By converting an otherwise 'static' population into a 'mobile' one, the thinking went, the railways became a carrier of an altogether different magnitude. The mode of thought which saw the coming of the railways as the peasant-made-mobile continues to have currency; 'the railways', one recent commentator has noted, 'were of special significance to the peasant though he was no traveller' (Verghese 1976: 106).[10] The connection between the colonial discourse on disease and the railways, and the Doon School discourse on Indian home life – manifested in the School's version of the 'arrival scene' (Pratt 1986: 35) depicted above – is best epitomised by what colonial government files called 'Mela prohibitions'. This referred to the power of district and other authorities to prohibit railway travel to or through certain areas upon reports that a region 'is visited by a severe outbreak of dangerous epidemic'.[11] These powers were often invoked on pilgrim and *mela* (fair and festival) routes.

The task of effecting a surgical break between the boy's home and school environment formulated by the Indian intelligentsia connected to the Doon School speaks the same language as that of the colonial disease narrative. For contagion comes in different forms in the colony and need not be expressed only through corporeal signs. And it became the post-colonial task to identify and deal with the varieties of native afflictions. The native family came to be identified as one of the several sites of contagion, and the proponents of the Doon School were swift in their efforts to isolate their young charges – the citizens-to-be – from any possible (or any further) infection. It need hardly be laboured that in such discussions 'family' acts as a code for 'women' and their influence upon the 'manly' character of the civil society; to their (improper) actions and influences is linked the honour of the nation. So, as van der Veer points out, 'nationalist discourse on the nation and the state in South Asia depends, to a large extent, on religious discourse and ritual practice concerning the relation between men and women in the family' (1994: 104); and, further, that the thread which sutures 'national honour' and the family is the 'proper' conduct of women (Das 1996: 55–83; see also Uberoi 1995).[12]

'The nationalist resolution of the women's question' was achieved, it has recently been suggested, through a principle of 'selection' such that modernity was sought to be made 'consistent with the nationalist project' (Chatterjee 1993a: 240; 1993b). Chatterjee goes on to suggest that the nationalist project engaged with all-conquering western regimes of knowledge through the adoption of a series of binaries: the material and the spiritual, and the outer and the inner, which were ultimately transformed into the division between the home and the world (Chatterjee 1993a: 238–9 *passim*). 'The world', nationalist thinking suggested, 'was where the European power had challenged the non-European peoples and . . . had subjugated them. But it had failed to colonise the inner, essential, identity of the East which lay in its distinctive and superior, spiritual culture' (*ibid.*). The home, then, became part of the 'inner' world of 'eastern' life, its 'spiritual essence' (*ibid.*) which needed to be shielded from western encroachments. If 'home' was the sacred domain of Indianness which was to be kept 'pure' at all costs, and if, 'through the identification of social roles by gender' (*ibid.*), women belonged at home, then 'our' women must not be allowed to fall prey to western ways. Home, women, and 'tradition' become synonymous concepts in this argument, all three in need of protection against westernisation which must be the lot of men, the creatures of the external world. 'This was the central principle by which', Chatterjee says, 'nationalism resolved the women's question in terms of its own historical project' (*ibid.*: 243).

Chatterjee's formulation of the debate is a highly persuasive one and yet it seems to fit oddly with the home-versus-the-world discourse I have outlined in the context of the Doon School. For in the latter case, 'home' becomes a place not so much to be cherished, shielded, and nurtured as the site of an essential Indianness, but rather one that must be exposed as the site of Indian shortcomings. This disclosure would serve to reinforce the positive aspects of the new site, the Doon School, where the 'problem of the nationality of Indians', as S.R. Das put it, was to be solved. Hence, we can say that there existed a variety of nationalist points of view on the home–world dichotomy, and while one of these may have pleaded for the 'preservation' of 'home' (and hence of the Indian essence), another was just as vehemently asserting the atavism of the Indian home and the dire need to quarantine citizens-in-the-making from its baneful influences.

There is an interesting parallel here between the discourse of the founders of the Doon School, and colonial thought which culminated in the establishment of public schools in various hill stations during the Raj. This overlap between the two regimes of thought can be illustrated by reference to the Lawrence School, in the hill locality of Sanawar in Himachal Pradesh.

Ideas regarding 'Englishness' and those surrounding the 'essential' qualities of the 'English race' had developed, as Mangan (1986) suggests, within the contexts of class and gender: the rational, honest, and enlightened Englishman was a product of the moral and cultural environment which the English *upper classes* inhabited. The essential qualities of the English race were not part of an open inheritance, to be claimed by *any one* of English descent. It is in this context that public schools established in Indian hill stations by the British are of analytical importance. For these schools were envisaged as crucial sites where 'Englishness' could be imparted, in a 'difficult' environment where it constantly risked 'dilution', to those English children who could not be sent to England for their education. Of course, the 'problem' (of shoring up Englishness) was seen to be particularly acute in the case of the English working class, a group whose 'natural' proclivities towards self-debasement would only be enhanced by the peculiar fecundity of a tropical climate; in such trying circumstances, one must do what one can.

The Lawrence School was founded in 1847 by the Anglo-Irish administrator, Sir Henry Lawrence. Its object was to:

> provide for the orphans and children of [European] soldiers serving or having served in India an Asylum from the debilitating effects of a tropical climate and the demoralising influence of barrack-life; wherein they may obtain the benefits of a bracing climate, a healthy moral atmosphere and a plain, useful and above all religious education.[13]

The English presence in India was a hierarchised presence, divided between the English *mind* and the English *body*. The English upper class constituted the mind and its 'lower' classes supplied the bodies for the functioning of the empire. This implicit dichotomy informed much of the social narrative by the English about the English in India. The aim of the Lawrence Asylum, the above source points out, 'is to awaken the [children of the 'other' ranks] into something like life', such that 'they are no longer mere lumps of inert sluggishness'. Further, the Asylum had altered the essentially corporeal existence of its lower-class wards: 'Their minds have been aroused from their *natural* state of indolence and stagnation; . . . habits of attention and thoughtfulness have visibly begun to supersede the listlessness and ennui of dormant spirits . . .' (*ibid.*, emphasis added). Through its geographical location and curriculum,[14] then, the founders of the Lawrence School sought to address the colonial fear of losing Englishness – a concern particularly keenly felt in the case of the 'naturally' wayward lower classes; 'inert sluggishness' was the inevitable consequence of unchecked exposure to the cultural and climatic aspects of the tropics (see, e.g. Cohn 1983: 88–111).

It could be said that the foundation of the Doon School marks an interesting development of this colonial fear for the soul of the European in India: the Doon School was established to check the 'Indianisation' of Indians which might come about through 'excessive' participation in the activity which came most 'naturally' to Indians, public religious expression. Colonial historiography had, after all, established the 'truth' and distinctiveness of Indian society as that connected with 'religious bigotry and conflict between people of different religious persuasions' (Pandey 1994: 23; see also Inden 1992); Doon's Indian supporters, who saw themselves as nationalists – with Nehru counting himself as one of its patrons – elaborated upon and institutionalised this truth and the School became one of the many sites of post-coloniality where it was converted into practice. The 'paradox' of the complicities between colonial and nationalist thought, that Pandey (1994) speaks of in his study of the career of the truth of the 'inherent' religiosity and 'communalism' of Indians, is quite plain to see in the history of the thought that gave birth to the Doon School. What it is important to remember is that this complicity is not just of historical interest; rather, the complicity between colonial and post-colonial regimes of thought continues to flourish through the proliferation of the Doon model of education which produces the overwhelming majority of the intelligentsia with public voice.[15]

Important aspects of this regime of thought are the reductionism and objectivism that deny the complexity of community life in their attempt to produce a 'national' template. Practice, however, is always recalcitrant towards any effort to theorise it as bounded or set in concrete. This fluidity of community life – though I am not suggesting a utopia of Hindu–Muslim harmony[16]– is well illustrated by the autobiography (1969/1993) of the Hindi language writer Hariwanshrai Bacchhan (b. 1907). The excision of this aspect of Indian existence from the nationalist discourse (the Doon model, as it were) which spoke of the dangers of public expression of religious attitudes is particularly glaring when one considers their contemporaneity.

Bacchhan's narration of events in the life of the community of his childhood, a community with a mixed population of Hindus and Muslims, is notable for its vehement refusal to reduce the life of the community to that of its rulers (or the state). So, while he unequivocally denounces instances of destruction of Hindu temples by Muslim rulers and the construction of mosques in their place (1969/1993: 42), there is no sense in which his descriptions of every-day life present a picture of a Muslim 'threat' to Hindus in general. This was my community, Bacchhan seems to say, its past impinged on by the whimsy of rulers, but its life not reducible to that of the history of the latter.

It was from his mother, Bacchhan recalls, that he received his first lesson in the Urdu alphabet (*ibid.*: 76). It is poignant that in a milieu where the figure of the mother/woman was an important cultural icon as the transmitter of one's 'own' culture – and 'tradition' (Chatterjee 1989; Mani 1989) – Bacchhan's version of Indian culture unselfconsciously eschews any notion of allegiance to a single religion. Cultural and social overlap[17] is a leading motif as well in his anecdote about his family's participation in the annual *Moharram* procession. A Muslim woman from the neighbourhood had advised Bacchhan's mother that dressing up the boy as a disciple of Imam

Hussain ('*Imam Sahib ka fakir*') on the occasion of *Moharram* would keep him from harm and secure divine blessing (*ibid.*: 88–9). His mother followed this practice, Bacchhan says, for several years and on each *Moharram*, 'dressed in white pyjamas and a green mourning sash', he would visit all the houses in the *mohulla* (neighbourhood) to beg for alms in the name of the 'Imam sahib'. The money would buy sweetcorn for the horse which led the *Moharram* procession, and after he had finished feeding it the young Bacchhan would be given the leftovers to be consumed as sanctified offering (*prasad*, as he refers to it). This custom, he says, was discontinued after a clash between Hindu and Muslims when 'the dates for *Moharram* and *Dussehra* coincided' (*ibid.*: 89).

The history of 'Hindu–Muslim riots' is a complex one and part of the story of this history may be enmeshed in colonialist representations of Indian society itself. 'The communal riot narrative' (Pandey 1994: 62) of colonialist historiography was an important adjunct both to the process of generating knowledge about the colonised society and to the argument which justified colonial rule (by referring to the 'naturally' fractious tendencies of the natives). This narrative ranged

> freely through time and space, unfettered by either. In it, all riots [were] the same – simply the reflexive actions of an irrational people ('fanatic' and 'clannish' Julahas/Muslims, riot prone Ahirs and Rajputs, 'the whole Hindu (or Muslim) population' that rises blindly when a religious building is attacked, or such an attack is beaten back, 'criminal classes' who take advantage of this; and so on).
>
> (Pandey 1994: 62)

It was precisely this narrative which circumscribed, and determined, the attitude towards religion at the Doon School. Just as English children had to be removed from the debilitating influence of the Indian environment – both cultural and climatic – Indian children, or at least those who were to be the future of the 'modern' nation, also needed to be saved from one of the most deleterious influences of Indian culture: irrational, uncontrollable religiosity. And it is in this context that we need to think about the masculine contract, which has produced post-colonial civil society in India.

In the European case, it has been suggested, 'the stories of the origins of the civil society can be found in the classical social contract theories of the seventeenth and eighteenth centuries' (Pateman 1980: 33). There is, Pateman says, a ' silence' in these narratives 'about the part of the story which reveals that the social contract is a fraternal pact that constitutes civil society as a patriarchal or masculine order' (*ibid.*: 37). The secular discourse in India, in as much as it is part of the larger biographical epic of the post-colonial civil society – 'nation-building' – is also, then, a story of the 'fraternal contract'.

The 'silent story' of patriarchy that Pateman's work seeks to disturb has its corollary in India in the narrative of the Doon School. For the School was part of the process of the establishment of the dichotomised realms of the Indian 'home', and its antithesis: the 'rational', public world of institutions such as itself. The resolution of 'the problem of the nationality of Indians' could only come about, then, through handing over future citizens to the care of men (or fathers) and away from the pernicious environment whose chief guardians are women. Men would look after the well being of the civil-society-to-come through their own institutions which in turn would reflect civil society itself. This patriarchal compact, forged at the altar of modernity, nationhood, and class, attracted participants who otherwise would seem to have very little in common. For the School has always enjoyed considerable support from a very wide cross-section of political, religious, and other positions.

The economy of contrasts: a *tableau vivant* of secularism

Perhaps the most public elaboration of the School's steadfast policy of secu-larism is contained in the conduct of the morning assembly. Like all rituals the assembly is open to several interpretations, and in Chapter 1 I treated the assembly as a ceremony of nationhood. My guiding strategy here is the observation that 'rituals are an attempt to create and maintain a particular culture, a particular set of assumptions by which experience is controlled' (Douglas 1970: 128). The assembly is also a dramatisation of the ethic of secularism and, like rituals in general, it not merely expresses but also modifies and formulates experience (Douglas 1970). The transformation of the elements which make up its context – 'objects, actions, symbols, and identities' (Kapferer 1979/1984: 3) – has the effect of focusing attention by 'framing' (Douglas 1970: 64), with the participants quite aware of and able to articulate the changes wrought upon them.

The school day is heralded by the ringing of a bell at 6.15 a.m. at each 'House' (as the hostels are referred to), a task performed by a member of the subordinate staff. The bell rings again fifteen minutes later and at 6.40 a.m. the boys have a light breakfast (or *Chota Hazri*) consisting of buttered slices of bread and tea. 'P.T.' (Physical Training) follows this at 7 a.m. for half of the School while the other half attends '1st school' (first period of the day). The lessons are of forty-five minutes duration and at the end of the first period the second half of the School attends P.T. while the first half has its first lesson of the day in the classroom. Breakfast is at 8.45 a.m. and after breakfast, at 9.30 a.m., there is assembly.

The temporal context of the assembly is inaugurated, I suggest, at the beginning of the breakfast session and ends with the filing out of the boys and masters from the assembly hall for the remaining classes of the day. Its spatial context is the *entire* school campus, and not just the assembly hall.

The dining hall during breakfast (and indeed, during all other meals) is the scene of a great deal of frivolity and good-natured banter across tables.

Seating is on a House-wise basis and masters attached to the various Houses (as Housemasters, tutors, etc.) usually occupy positions at the head of the table. Breakfast consists of porridge, eggs, toast, butter, jam, and tea. The menu is slightly different for vegetarians. My most enduring impression of mornings in the dining hall is one of uninterrupted din: boys shouting across tables and bartering with and for desired food items; eating competitions, loud, uninhibited laughter, the sound of steel plates falling to the ground, the scraping of wooden chairs on the concrete floor, the occasional commands by senior masters to 'quieten down', and the vigorous bell ringing by the head boy or a prefect to gain some silence for official announcements. Generally, there is no attempt by the teachers, or others in position of authority, to have the boys eat breakfast in an 'orderly' manner. This is in stark contrast to the situation at, for instance, the Mayo College. At the latter, there is an atmosphere of enforced silence and the monitors are prone to sudden bursts of shouting out warnings when the noise level is deemed to have exceeded a predetermined norm.

The school bell, located at the top of the main building, rings at 9.20 a.m. to announce preparations for the assembly. By this time most of the boys have emerged from the dining hall and are wandering around the corridors. Some sit in the library, talking loudly, flipping through books and newspapers. The bell peals rhythmically, with an insistent ecclesiastical tone and with each tug of the attached rope the bell platform shudders mildly with age. Slowly the boys emerge from the library and the corridors and begin to form queues on the gravel road that leads to the assembly hall. The queues are arranged class-wise and extend from underneath the Headmaster's office, in the front portion of the main building, to the assembly hall entrance, a distance of some 100 feet.

With the resolute resonance of the bell as background, the students forming the queues are goaded occasionally by prefects. The disorder of the dining hall and the mêlée of the corridors soon give way, however, to a disciplined environment, and the boys walk quietly into the hall. The Headmaster, attired in a black academic gown, and accompanied by the other masters, walks into the hall behind the students, and while the teachers arrange themselves in an uneven line near the entrance, he proceeds to the front and mounts the podium to commence proceedings. Inside the building the boys stand divided into two halves, each facing the other, and the Headmaster makes his way to the front through the passage in the middle. There, upon a stage, he joins boys from the School's Indian orchestra. The assembly begins with a prayer read by the Headmaster from a collection[18] largely put together by Arthur Foot. At the conclusion of the reading, the gathering joins in intoning 'Amen'.

The next stage is the singing of songs. The Headmaster announces the song for the day and, to the accompaniment of the orchestra, the entire gathering joins in the singing. Among the songs is the national anthem,[19] as well as other hymns by Tagore, Guru Nanak, the founder of the Sikh faith, and the poet Iqbal. Perhaps the most fervent singing comes from some of the older teachers whose intonations are matched, in its own way, by the curious cacophony of the Indian orchestra on stage. The conclusion of the singing marks the time reserved for official announcements by the Headmaster (changes in the daily routine, academic and sporting awards, the appointment of new prefects, etc.). Students who have done well in some field have their achievements recognised by a slow hand-clap as they walk to the front of the hall to be individually congratulated by the Headmaster. When the latter indicates an end to the assembly, the teachers are first to leave, followed by the Headmaster and the students, and classes resume. This, broadly, is the form and content of the morning assembly at the Doon School.

What is the 'religious life' expressed through the form, content, and performance of the assembly? The context of the assembly is established, I suggest, through an economy of *contrasts*, such that a new relationship is established between the elements of the ritual, a relationship whose meaning derives from the broad context of 'civil' post-colonial existence. During the performance of the assembly-as-ritual its contrasting elements establish a secular (or 'multi-religious') ambience. The configuration of its elements as well as the media through which the assembly is conducted – religious words, music, singing, 'official' words – serve to conjure a liminality of experience where evocations from contrasting religious worlds compete for the participants' attention; and through that competition emerges an experiential moment which by belonging to all the contrasting elements, belongs to none.

In its form the assembly has the potential of being interpreted as either a Hindu or a Christian ritual: the time of prayer is announced by the ringing of bells, the 'worshippers' are gathered in an enclosed space, and singing and music accompany the enactment of the ritual. However, it is through the performance – the ringing of the school bell, the single-file entry into the hall, the geometrical organisation of space occupied by the students within it – that an ambiguity is introduced in the symbols of meaning which animate the assembly. In other words, taken individually, the elements which constitute the morning ritual of assembly at Doon School may lend themselves to specific religious interpretations; however, it is their combination – a combination of contrasts – that gives birth to an altered context, that of secularism. Hence, notwithstanding the problematic nature of terms such as 'consistency' and a 'higher level', Kapferer's suggestion that ritual processes seek to resolve 'contradiction and inconsistency [leading] to the re-establishment of consistency within a new form, which might be organised at a higher level than the contexts previously organised into the rite' (Kapferer 1979: 5) is a valuable one.

The peculiarity of an Indian 'secular' ceremony which includes no references to Islam is, of course, too obvious to labour, and the history of Doon School offers no obvious clues to how this might have come about. However, one can speculate on this in light of a specific historical context of the School. It may be important also to place the religious issue at Doon within the matrix of a much older conflict between the Judaeo-Christian and the Islamic worlds. The School's earliest Headmasters, and several teachers, were chosen in England and came from English public schools which were (and still are) organised explicitly around Christian values; Christian religious life was both their rationale and funding source (Gathorne-Hardy 1978; Mangan 1986a, 1986b). This, of course, forms the basis of the comments of the visiting English public school teacher DH who found it odd that a public school based on the English model should, apparently, be so areligious in its orientation. One may speculate, therefore, that part of the reason for the exclusion of Muslim prayers from the assembly prayer book may be linked to the religious convictions of many of the early Doon staff and to the long history of the conflict between the Judaeo-Christian and the Islamic worlds; this, of course, has been copiously commented upon by several scholars (Said 1978; Kapferer 1988: esp.127–32). But, of course, this can only be a small part of the explanation since there were many Indians, some of them prominent Muslims, who were active participants in the School's functioning from its earliest days.

I have suggested that 'assembly time' and its temporal universe 'opens' at breakfast, rather than at the start of the assembly itself. This stance accepts the association of time with heterogeneity as suggested by Bergson, such that 'in space things exist separately from and alongside each other; in time they interpenetrate and are never completely independent' (Lacey 1989: 22); Bergson had also suggested that any single experience is influenced by all earlier experiences. Now, there are two things to be considered here: first, that the assembly is attributed a 'religious' significance, an aspect which is both formally stressed ('Our religious outlook is focused in the daily School Assembly'), and may be observed in the conduct of the assembly itself. And, second, in the Indian context food, both through its presence and absence, is an important part of the religious experience. It is in the following sense then, that 'breakfast' serves both to inaugurate the experience of the assembly as well as to introduce the first of several conflicting elements which keep the ritual from being exclusively identified with *one* specific religion; Hindu morning worship – at least of the upper castes from which the School almost exclusively draws its clientele – is, traditionally, undertaken on an empty stomach and hence, the assembly is excluded from being identified as a Hindu ritual. The suggestion that assembly time be seen as commencing at the start of breakfast time indicates my belief that this is part of the conscious effort by the School authorities towards creating a context where one of the most public expressions of school life can be presented as free from any particular religious influence.

Noise, as Michael Roberts has recently pointed out, is intimately connected with Hindu and Buddhist forms of worship. The beating of drums, loud talk, the pell-mell of gathering bodies, all form part of the preliminaries to the act of worship itself, and carry on during the ceremonials. And indeed, the general disorder and noise in the period between the end of breakfast and the commencement of queuing for assembly at Doon is quite evocative of the

Hindu pre-worship activity where ' music and noise' give off a 'religious flavour' (Roberts 1990: 243).

But the 'pure perception'[20] of the mêlée which speaks of a very distinct religious environment is replaced, before it can establish itself as memory, by the imagery of a different world altogether; the disorder of the corridors quickly gives way to the single-file discipline of the assembly queue. The process of the assembly changes garb again and now resembles nothing so much as the filing in of a church congregation for morning mass: '. . . the emphasis on silence as a mark of respectful worship was ingrained in the Islamic world as much as Judaeo-Christian civilisation' (*ibid.*).

It is as if there is a series of flickering images upon a crowded screen, chasing each other to the edge of the canvas, leaving behind not the *impact* of their presence but a memory of it; this in turn is reconstituted into a larger presence such that the whole is larger than the sum of its parts. Out of the several flickering images there emerges one meta-image that transcends, even negates, the impact of its individual parts. The several images which constitute the morning assembly carry very specific religious undertones and evoke the punctilios of concrete religious worlds – usually Hindu and Christian and, sometimes, though rarely, Muslim. The transformation of these discrete parts into one continuous narrative occurs in the process of the performance of the ritual, where 'assembly time' and 'assembly space' appropriate and negate the specific religious nature of these several events such that the participants are left with the memory of 'secular time'.

The thickness of time and space: the chronotope of secularism

In as much as the ritual of the assembly is elaborated within a temporal and spatial dimension, we may see it as a specific chronotope in the overall narrative of the School, which, as I have suggested, is the narrative of post-colonial citizenship. The '*technical, abstract connection between space and time*' (Bakhtin 1990: 100, emphasis in the original), that is an attribute of the adventure chronotope, and the fusing together of time and space that is intrinsic to the chronotope of the road (*ibid.*: 243–4), also find play in the assembly chronotope. Most importantly, the chronotope idea also allows us to position the ritual of morning assembly in a social and historical context: Bakhtin's elaboration of the chronotope is, after all, subtitled 'Notes towards a Historical Poetics'. This enables us to locate the assembly in the 'larger political arena in which the performance takes place' (van der Veer 1994: 82); this 'arena' in the present context is the discursive universe of the nation state itself.

At any time, then, 'action' at the Doon School unfolds through a multiplicity of chronotopes that constitute its narrative of self-representation, which itself belongs to a genre of public discourse we may designate the civil society genre. Some of the chronotopes on offer are those of the rational/scientific man, the chronotope of the metropolitan man, and that of the liberal-bourgeois democrat. The assembly, in my discussion here, presents us with the chronotope of the secular man. The chronotope of the secular man is constituted through an intertwining of specific spatial and temporal spaces of performance, through the contrast of moments as they follow each other, and, finally, by their non-interchangeable nature in space. Each moment – or stage – of the assembly is of peculiar and specific importance: each serves to undermine the significance of the other moments. So the chronotope of secularism itself is a result of a series of continuous, circular negations. 'It can be said without qualification', Bakhtin asserts, 'that to them [chronotopes] belong the meaning that shapes narrative' (1990: 250). Similarly, it could be said that the chronotope of secularism does indeed shape the meaning of the dominant narrative of the School, and that the shaping of this narrative itself takes place through a process of dialogue between the multiplicity of chronotopes which circulate in the School's milieu.

In all my discussions on religion at Doon with past and present students and teachers of the School, the assembly was inevitably mentioned. Its chronotopicity – the complex and continuous relationship of time and place which establishes a field for a unique and integral way of understanding experience – was just as inevitably expressed as a consciousness of the secular. The following responses to the question 'Why no religious instruction at the Doon School?' are from students from three different eras:

[B]ecause they wanted it [the School] to appeal to very large section of the people . . . we had a morning assembly which extracted from various . . . [sources] . . . it was universal . . . nothing explicit [*sic*] to any one religion . . . stuff from the Bible, without referring to Christ, from Tagore, Iqbal . . . there was a genuine attempt to bring out what was common in all three. All . . . avoid any specific reference to any one religion.

(S.A. student 1952–8)

[There was a] belief that everything [at Doon School] was very British. . . . They [visitors to the School] were very surprised that we had a very strong Indian music section . . . a lot of prayers [at the assembly] were secular in character. [And] . . . without all this *directly* focusing upon [the students], that is, directed towards making them future post-colonial Indians,[21] I think this sort of thing contributed towards it . . . created an atmosphere . . . and, in retrospect, a large number of Doon School boys have contributed very significantly towards national thought [*sic*].

(H.S. student 1960–5)

The School, as you know, doesn't allow any kind of religious activity on the campus. . . . In fact, we don't even have special food in the dining hall on important [Hindu] festival days. And in the assembly we pray in a very general manner, with prayers and songs from different sources. . . . The assembly really combines many things . . . into something unique.

(A.K. senior student 1990)

The active subjects of the secular chronotope – the students – are positioned in its time–space boundary through evoking a continuity in the temporal dimension of the School's being: the past, the present, and the future become inextricably linked such that the consciousness of the past ('secularism') is seen to hold those of the present and the future in an iron grip. The secular consciousness of the School, defined and elaborated in its past, comes to be presented as timeless as it moves to occupy the spaces of the present and is projected onto the future. The following quotes are taken from interviews with two old boys. The first response comes from a non-Hindu senior corporate executive who was a student at the School during the 1960s. I asked if he thought the School had ever attempted to promote any specific religious point of view. He said:

> None at all . . . [I] can't recall a single incident in my five or six years at school where I can say that the outcome [*sic*] was basically religious. I was pleasantly unaware of even the fact that a religion like Hinduism had so many variants . . . no one really inquired . . . caste we thought was only a matter of historical fact. . . . That it came from history books. Even [the nearby village of] Tunwala . . . the Harijanness of it was only an intellectual fact. We couldn't relate to it as something you believed in.

The second response is addressed to the question of whether there *should* be religious instruction at a school such as Doon. The respondent, a prominent journalist, was a student in the late 1950s. He wasn't 'personally against it':

> . . . but even if you did have it . . . I don't think it would be taken seriously . . . in my time it would have been made fun of, maybe because then a certain kind of atmosphere existed [*sic*] . . . fashions change, maybe the atmosphere has changed . . . but I am not aware that parents, or others, want religious instruction.

Doon men became favourably marked, forever, as secular men and as 'citizens', their concerns for the future of the post-colonial civil society frequently echoed in the public arena. The following letter to a national newspaper was written jointly by a group of prominent journalists, two of whom have intimate connection with Doon School, one as a parent and the other as student:

> The shame that India has suffered over events in Ayodhya should remind us of the peril we face: the peril of society being torn asunder by religious bigotry and fanaticism.
>
> ('A Shrine to Secularism', *The Pioneer*, 12 Dec. 1992)

Through the opinions expressed by various people associated with the School in different ways, and through some of the daily activities that punctuate its existence, I have attempted to describe the School's *conscious* engagement with the issue of religion. Further, I have suggested that the School's response is most prominently marked by the *leit-motif* of secularism: the idea that it does not promote any specific religious attitude and that religion is a private, rather than a public, matter; that the nation was, and continues to be, threatened by the dangers of religious passions and sectarian emotions, their venom clogging the moral and political arteries of the civil society, their violence sweeping away its structures. This was the lesson to be learnt from the evidence of recent history and from the tumult of the present: the Doon School boy, the citizen, must, then, be secular.

Comparative geographies, refractory populations

It is not entirely correct to state that no acts of worship that may be clearly identified as belonging to a specific religion are publicly performed on the School campus. There is, in fact, a small temple on the School grounds, which is the focus of daily religious activity. Also, during the months leading up to the Diwali festival there are *Ram-lila* performances which carry on for several weeks late into the night, each night an episodic elaboration of the *Ramayan*. The platform upon which the performance takes place, festooned with streamers and flanked by the paraphernalia of a public announcements system, is located in the vicinity of the temple and could be said to form an extension of it: a 'sacred complex' (Vidyarthi 1961), defined by the contiguity of its features. The presence of this sacred geography within the larger atlas of secularism that is the School, serves, paradoxically, to re-emphasise the School's public stand on religion. However, as I will argue below, there is no real contradiction between the presence of a Hindu temple on the School campus and the School's engagement with the religious sphere.

The temple and the *Ram-lila* performance space are themselves part of a larger complex, a space which, though physically situated within the School grounds is, in several ways, not a part of it. This complex is peopled, literally and figuratively, by the subordinate staff of the School – the cooks, gardeners, office attendants, dining hall waiters, *dhobis* (clothes-washers), sweepers, and other workers responsible for the up-keep of the Chandbagh estate. In a most obvious way – class – the above group is different from the student and the teacher population of the School. Its members live in cramped accommodation – small tin-roof houses joined from end to end – in a clearly demarcated enclave. Their children, unlike those of the teaching and some administrative staff, are not entitled to free education at the School and their conditions of employment and access to campus recreational facilities similarly distinguish them from the former. These are the obvious markers of their Otherness. There also exists, however, a parallel, partially submerged narrative of their difference, the narrative through which the School illuminates and animates its conception of citizenship.

The space on which the temple and the *Ram-lila* stage are situated is contiguous with the houses for the subordinate staff as well as a building known as the *Panchayat Ghar*. A *Panchayat* is, literally, a village assembly (of men) with cultural and legal say over community matters. In the romantic terminology of nineteenth-century British historiography, it was the 'village parliament'. At the Doon School, the *Panchayat Ghar* was described in an early School publication as the 'Common Room for Servants' (*DSB*: 71). In the mid-1940s the building was used by the Adult Education Society of the School to hold classes for 'servants of the School'. The Society also used it as a venue for 'occasional talks, Cinema Films, Lantern Slides, [and] Ceremonial gatherings' (*ibid.*). The physical location of this unambiguously Hindu sacred complex, then, is very much within a figurative and literal space clearly identifiable as part of a universe which although situated within the School does not belong to it; the subordinate staff are allowed their world but this world is not one in which the 'legitimate' members of the School community participate. It is a world that serves to highlight the divergent ethos of the School, the prototype of the civil society and the progenitor of the citizen.

There is another important marker along the route to producing the 'uncivil' world of the subordinate staff. This refers to the juxtaposition of the term *Panchayat* with the activities of the members of the subordinate staff. The notion of the *Panchayat* is linked closely to the career of colonial historiography in producing an image of India as 'a civilisation that is, in the eyes of the Asian Studies specialist, truly rural in nature' (Inden 1992: 131). 'For many of the earlier orientalists' the discourse of 'village India' provided a contemporary vision of the village organisations of the early Aryan populations of Europe. India was in the present, they fondly reported, what Europe had once been, 'the ancient Aryan village still survived there' (*ibid.*: 132). Around this theme there accumulated an influential body of knowledge which laid down the discursive parameters for subsequent scholarly work on Indian society. Indian village society came to be interpreted through its own enduring lexicon, an interpretation whose faithful reproduction over the decades owes substantially to the seductions of essentialist thought and to the firm connection between objectifying knowledge and the empowerment of the observing subject. In this thinking, 'Indian civilisation' was nothing but the essence of the characteristics of the Indian village: stable and unchanging, 'organically'/mechanically rather than volitionally active, 'a self-contained world of solidarities and reciprocities' (*ibid.*: 131–61), homogeneous and communally co-operative.

For the British, the Indian village became a powerful metaphor for the difference between an Oriental passive subjectivity and its antithesis, Occidental dynamism, as manifested in the various aspects of 'European civilisation' and, indeed, in the ceaseless change which was the supposed legacy of colonial rule.[22] Representations of a 'timeless' civilisation in present-day advertisements and travel literature can be traced, then, to the far more esoteric deliberations on the 'essence' of Indian society carried out in the epistemological embrace of colonial knowledge regimes. What they share in common is the enduring labour of distantiation and objectification.

It is this contextually specific history of the *Panchayat Ghar* as the 'village council' that affords an understanding of its deployment in the setting of the School. For we have here the elaboration of a post-colonised orientalism, its strategies an adaptation of earlier forms, and its objects drawn from realms banished from the orbit of *fin de siècle* capitalism, from those unable to meet the cultural prescriptions of Indian modernity. The members of the subordinate staff at the Doon School have become the contemporary carriers of the old essentialising burden, their being constructed as passive, unchanging, homogeneous, simple, and childlike. And, just as 'Indian' once acted as the complex site of a eulogy for 'British', the subordinate staff category is part of the history through which the modernising urban middle class in India has sought to define its own identity. The strategy has been to dissimulate: to present oneself as part of a contractual world which is driven by 'rational deliberation and decision-taking' (*ibid.*: 159) rather than the 'lower' order existence which is still hostage to the primordiality of family, caste, and religious allegiances.

It is important to point out here that the above discussion is not primarily concerned with trying to explain why the teaching staff and students do not worship at the temple or participate in any substantial way in the activities connected with the *Ram-lila*. Such a concern would, I think, be of limited interest, and could be dealt with by referring to the class and caste differentials between the two sections of the School's population. My objective, however, is to point to the existence of the sacred complex within an avowedly secular geography as an important constituent in the narrative of citizenship at the School. The subordinate staff who occupy that specific niche within the School that I have referred to as the sacred complex, serve, I suggest, as the local referent of the wider community 'out there' which does not qualify for citizenship.

During the post-partition turmoil of 1947 the relative serenity of Dehra Dun was violently disrupted and the violence and terror which swept across large tracts of North India during this time of private dislocation and public mêlée were also experienced in some measure in this otherwise quiet city. At the time, there were frequent reports of impending or actual violence between Hindus and Muslims from the surrounding areas.[23] Among the occupants of the School's campus, who seem to have been left largely and quite remarkably unharmed by the surrounding disturbances, the events elicited concerns of very specific nature. The first was connected to the impending loss in student numbers as many of the School's Muslim students were expected to leave for the newly created state of Pakistan (as indeed they did).[24] The second concern had to do with the possible effect of the events outside upon the 'servants', the subordinate staff, of the School. *Weekly* editions of the time noted that fears were held that the communal violence outside might find an echo among the subordinate staff population of the School, containing as it did members of both Muslim and Hindu communities.

However, the turbulence skirted the School's boundaries and the 'refractory' segment of the School's population[25] went about its business unaffected by the surrounding events. School reports of the time express both relief and a degree of disbelief that no acts of violence had been reported among its subordinate staff. In a post-1947 edition of the *Weekly*, special mention was made of the fact that the 'servants and other menials' had been left quite untouched by the 'troubles'. There is, however, no discussion of the susceptibilities of other members of the School to the 'irrationalities' influenced by religious passion. If one is to look for evidence within the School for the supposed proclivities of the 'menial' group in question, a rather contrary scenario presents itself. As a member of the teaching staff pointed out to me, the above-mentioned *Ram-lila* performances were for many years organised jointly by Hindus and Muslims belonging to the subordinate staff group.

As mentioned in the introductory chapter, the period of fieldwork on which this research is based coincided with the series of public disturbances in North India connected with the Babri Masjid/Ram-Janm Bhoomi issue at Ayodhya. There were reports of occasional violence in the business districts of Dehra Dun, and rumours of this mosque or that temple being desecrated criss-crossed the town sporadically. Gangs of sloganeering young men roamed the streets in support of the demolition of the mosque alleged to be built upon the razed remains of a temple. For brief periods during the day shopping crowds would jostle with the rumours and the anonymous prophecies of the impending mêlée, and then the streets would be empty, shops with downed shutters paying obeisance to the whispers of the day.

The routine of the School during these days of fraction of public life remained remarkably unruptured and classes and games were held according to schedule. At times I was informed that help from the nearby army cantonment had been promised should the campus be under any threat. There was, however, a perceived threat to School security from within its boundaries: some members of the teaching staff suggested that we could soon witness a 'volatile' situation develop among the Hindus and Muslims of the subordinate staff. Recent media coverage had brought graphic images of bloodied Hindu demonstrators in Ayodhya being bludgeoned into temporary submission by the police and para-military forces, and dining hall conversation at the School among some of the senior boys centred on the similarities between the agitators and the subordinate staff. There were two distinct aspects of the reaction of the students to the images of commotion and truculence that pervaded the media and which pervaded the public space of urban existence, disrupting its daily routine.

The first of these concerned the event itself, i.e., the moral, political, and ethical aspects of the seemingly inter-religious dispute, and its implications for the life of the nation, while the second was connected with the identities of those seen to be involved in the violence of the streets, the willing subjects of media coverage. There seemed to be no recognition, however, of the 'event' as a *social* fact, and its field of action – screaming mobs clambering upon walls, saffron-robed men clashing with police barricades, burnt-out bus shells, peace marches – became a space for engagements of an entirely different type. I repeatedly asked some of the senior students what they thought would be the consequences of the events taking place for religious tolerance in a multi-religious community. Very few cared to engage in conversation on the topic and one of those who did suggested that the 'army would take care of it'.

There was, however, a much stronger response to the *images* of the ferment, a relentless barrage that, at the time, saturated the pages of the popular magazines and newspapers in various shades of vividness. The School library contains an excellent selection of print-media sources that were the most frequently consulted for news and pictures on the disturbances.[26] The aspect of the rallies and demonstrations that provoked the most comment from the students concerned the physical space of their unfolding. There was palpable resentment that the rational-industrial landscape of the national capital – the buildings housing the bureaucracy, the streets of tar, corporate offices – had, as it were, been occupied by a 'non-industrial' population, albeit fleetingly. The concern seemed to be not so much that religion was being used by the politicians for their own ends, and that the foot-soldiers of these rallies, the 'masses', stood to gain very little from such exhibitions of public fervour for a *Ram rajya*; rather, the main point of the discussions was a barely concealed contempt at the occupation of the perceived industrial, metropolitan space – the space of post-colonial representations of national identity – by a section of population which did not belong there; the boys made fun of the way the demonstrators dressed, the way they spoke: there was an intense pre-occupation with the notion of civilised spaces being under siege from primitives.

Paul Virilio captures well the other side of the dialectic of the contemporary sieges of Delhi, the aspect that most worries the metropolitan bourgeoisie. Writing on 'speed and politics' in a different context, he notes that 'for the proletarian masses from the country or the suburb, the simple fact of penetrating to the heart of Paris, of feeling under their feet its avenues and opulent streets, is a very concrete way of diminishing a real and measurable social and political resistance between the masses and the constructed power of the bourgeois state' (1986: 19). And, for the 'masses' brought into Delhi at the behest of various political and other groupings, the most reasonable course of action did seem to be to treat their visit as a leisure trip. For, wedged between a political system which would treat them as dispensable refuse at the conclusion of the proceedings at hand, and an economic system which has steadily eroded the capacity of all but a few to treat the urban space as a leisure-zone, incidental pleasures such as those afforded by a 'political' visit to the metropolis took on the seductive powers of subversive acts. Meanwhile, Delhi newspapers sneered triumphantly at the political commitment of the 'backward' villager who could more often be found at tourist sites rather than at rallies and demonstrations for which they had, ostensibly, been brought to the city.

If we view the engagement of Doon's students with media images as of the same order as the general engagement with artistic images, then we can usefully speak in this context of the 'blindness to concepts' (Levinas 1989: 132). A 'concept', Levinas says, represents the grasping of the artistic object, and the act of entering into 'a living relationship with a real object . . . of conceiving through action' (*ibid.*). Further, conceptualisation must occur in the face of a situation where the 'image neutralises this real relationship' (*ibid.*), and attempts to interdict conceptualisation. Now, in as much as Levinas speaks of the relationship of the audience to the image, we can say that the Doon attitude to the Ayodhya events – a specific instance of a general stance – is one of 'blindness to concepts': images (of disorder, say) become the dialogue, rather than 'the beginning of a dialogue' (*ibid.*: 131) about the social; images become the beginning and the end of thought.

The subordinate staff of the School are allowed to have their temple and their *Ram-lila* performance because this world is the Otherness that defines the universe of the School. It contains, however, the Otherness of a work of art in the sense suggested above. The 'masses' and their religious rallies become objects of stylistic discussion, and the substantial content of the rally itself – its political and ethical dimensions – is elided. In this way the world of the subordinate staff, the Other world of the School, becomes the local referent of the wider world of 'irrationality'. Why the 'lower classes' do certain things becomes less important than *what* they do, and it is this that establishes difference. It is through the establishment and recognition of multiple spaces in the overall geography of the School – non-substitutable spaces positioned alongside each other – that the difference is grounded.

Secularism and Hindu contextualism

During my stay at the Doon School I gradually became aware of the sharp disjunction between its conscious discourse on secularism – disavowing patronage to any one religious view – and what appeared to be a distinctly Hindu religious atmosphere which pervaded the being of the School. This section seeks to explore this Hindu world of the School that seems to be at odds with the official ideology.

Perhaps the earliest indication of the complexity of the School's engagement with the religious issue was to be seen on the very first day that the School announced its birth to the world: the guest list for its inauguration ceremony in 1935 makes for an extremely curious alignment of people and politico-religious interests. The birth of the School, as I have suggested in the previous chapter, can be seen as the culmination of a process of critical self-evaluation by the 'educated classes' of their shortcomings, one of these being identified as the tendency to divide along religious lines. This tendency was perceived by the western-educated intelligentsia as one of several obstacles that stood in the way of the unity of a post-colonised Indian nation. Such a disposition, the nationalists suggested, only served to underline the stereotypical image of fractious natives incapable of national unity, and of irrational communities irremediably enmeshed in a web of local, parochial loyalties.

The inauguration ceremony of the School on 27 October 1935 was, by all accounts, a day of great expectations. The chief guest Viceroy Willingdon inaugurated not merely a school, but an entelechal project towards which a most remarkable cross-section of the Indian intelligentsia had offered its felicitations and fulsome commitment. In Chapter 1, I noted the oddity – given the School's profession of secularism – of the presence of Madan Mohan Malviya at its inauguration ceremony.[27] And, in light of the School's public proclamations on the issue of religion in the 'new' India, it is pertinent to list some of the high points in the public career of its unarguably eminent guest.

Malviya's most tangible claim to fame lies, of course, in his successful campaign to establish a Hindu University at Banaras. His political strategy lay, it has been remarked, in a combination of 'political moderation and uninhibited Hindu communalism' (Sarkar 1983: 126). He was also one of the founders of the Hindu Mahasabha (1906), the organisation which was to sharpen the communal divide and raise anti-Muslim intransigence to new heights. Both in his individual capacity and through his association with the Mahasabha and other Hindu revivalist movements such as the Arya Samaj, Malviya also championed the cause of a Sanskritised Hindi in the North Indian hinterland. The Hindi movement was intended to take the form of a cultural cause, but its 'anti-Muslim character' (Kumar 1991: 144) was never far from the surface.

Malviya was always keen to extend public assistance to like-minded individuals and organisations devoted to the cause of establishing a Hindu hegemony. Soon after its founding in 1925, the chief organisers of the *Rashtriya Swayamsevak Sangh* (RSS), the organisation devoted to the cause of establishing a Hindu *Rashtra* (nation), drew up plans for its expansion to areas beyond Maharashtra, its initial base. In this connection, three of its workers were sent 'to the Banaras Hindu University as students to start a RSS unit there' (Basu *et al.* 1993: 20–1). Malviya's patronage of the fledgeling organisation was both generous and timely, for his prominent position at the University allowed him the opportunity of providing the 'students with a premise where they could start their RSS office' (*ibid.*).

But Malviya's was not the only vehemently religious presence on that auspicious occasion. We must also note the presence of Chaudhuri Sir Muhammad Zafarulla Khan. A London trained barrister and a member of the Viceroy's Council, Khan had served as Crown Counsel in the Delhi Conspiracy case. In 1931 he had also served, according to the Indian *Who's Who* for 1939–40, as the president of the All India Muslim League.

There are other pointers as well to the persistent disjunction between the official rhetoric of the School and its actual practice signified by the presence of members of the Hindu Mahasabha and the Muslim League at the 1935 opening ceremony. In 1945, for example, one of the members of the Board of Governors of the School was Dr Shyama Prasad Mukherjee, the founder of the Jan Sangh, a political party with a militant Hindu posture and the precursor to the Bharatiya Janata Party (BJP) whose role in the mobilisation of the 'Hindu vote' and in the demolition of the Ayodhya mosque are too well known to warrant further elaboration.

Secularism and the matrix of Hindu aesthetics

The official stand of the School on religion was often queried by some of the parents I met during the course of this research. Some among them suggested that the School should arrange for religious instruction and indeed should have facilities on the campus for worship. These suggestions came almost exclusively from North Indian Hindu parents. And all of them insisted that their opinions were not to be quoted in their name to the Headmaster, and that they were expressing 'private opinions'. The School, of course, publicly and vehemently rejects any ideas that may associate its physical or cultural space with the markings of a specific religion. And yet the campus, I suggest, is unambiguously animated by the consistent elaboration of a public Hindu existence. This is effected through a constellation of symbols and symbolic actions that form a part of the routine life of the School, and those which animate events of special significance.

The School's crest is a long stemmed oil lamp designated the 'lamp of learning'. The most immediate visible impact of the crest is to evoke the specific world of Hindu worship. The significance of oil lamps of various shapes and sizes in the Hindu ritual and cultural world – inaugurating a *Kathakali* performance, the *arati* ceremony during worship, and the symbolism of fire, *agni*, itself – need hardly be laboured (see, e.g Coomaraswamy 1964). I am not suggesting that those associated with the School consciously refer to the School's crest as an emblem drawn from the world of Hindu existence. On the contrary, I wish to point to the absence of such a consciousness. In this manner, one might say, what passes for a multi-religious or anti-religious environment is in fact lodged within a very specific universe, one evocative of the sights and sounds of the Hindu existence.

It is instructive, also, to trace the process of selection of the School crest. The 'lamp of learning' was adopted by the School in November 1937. Leading up to this, however, several other designs had been submitted by students for consideration by the School authorities. All of the ten designs (Figure 4.1) suggested by students, including the one finally chosen, incorporated motifs – or fragments – expressive of a Hindu aesthetic: the lamp, the sun, and the lotus. These motifs, though removed from their original context, i.e. their specific role in Hindu life, nevertheless carry, to return to Bakhtin, 'a certain chronotopic aura', a memory of their time and place: they 'remember' and

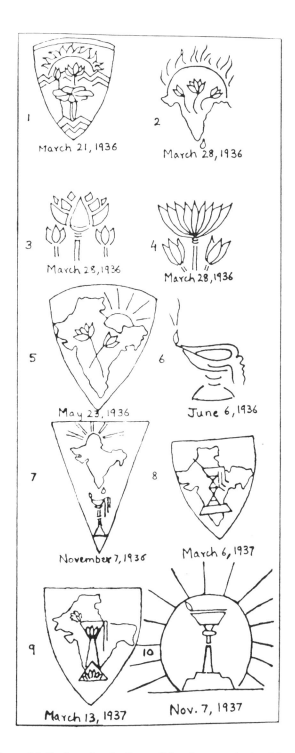

Figure 4.1 Designs for the Doon School crest submitted by students in 1936 (Singh 1985: 70).

resonate their past.[28] It is not surprising, therefore, that the political party with a public manifesto on *Hindutva*, the BJP, uses for its symbol the lotus flower (see also Coomaraswamy 1964).

The elements of the various designs for the crest proposed by the students are important not because they were used *consciously* to emphasise a Hindu identity for the School, but because although they were drawn from a recognisably Hindu context, this fact itself was never recognised. A specific religious context in the absence of the recognition of its specificity, then came to be regarded as areligious.

The Doon School crest is all the more striking for reasons of the simplicity of its design: the central feature is not crowded by a host of other symbolic representations. As a genre, heralds and crests, because of their elaborate and complicated designs, suffer the handicap of fading recall on the part of those who may have once thrived under their aegis. The Doon crest avoids this through speaking clearly and plainly of its presence and is, thereby, easier to commit to memory. What is simultaneously committed to memory, I think, is the implied symmetry between a Hindu world and a 'secular' ethos. These vivid fragments of a Hindu reality seem to undergo a perceptual transformation under the unwavering gaze of the School's secularism policy. In my discussions on the religious 'atmosphere' at the School with students, past and present, none – including those who saw themselves as critical observers of the School's being – thought it worthwhile to comment on the crest. It became part of the prescribed narrative of secularism.

Early accounts of the School sought to give the new institution solidity and substance through associating its brief existence with longer histories and more elaborate evocations of space. These also positioned it within a very specific set of imaginings and traditions. So, representations of the physical landscape within which the School is positioned abound with the myths and legends of the majority community (Figure 4.2). They reverberate, in these accounts, to the coursing of 'holy' rivers and the tones of temple bells. The 'most common way of entering the Doon',[29] *DSB* informs its readers:

is by train arriving at Hardwar in the early morning. The name Hardwar, meaning 'the gate of Vishnu' may remind the traveller of the religious and legendary associations of the Ganges and the Himalayas which bound the Doon to the east and the north.

... The Doon is connected in legend with Shiv and Bhima, Ram and Lakshman, Hanuman, Drunacharaya and the Pandavas. The hill Nagsidh is said to have been the abode of the snake Baman. . . .

[B]ut this is not the place to write a history of the Doon. . . . It is desired only to show that for anyone with a feeling for the past, which it must be one of the aims of education to awake, the Doon is a very suitable site for a school.

(DSB: 5–6)

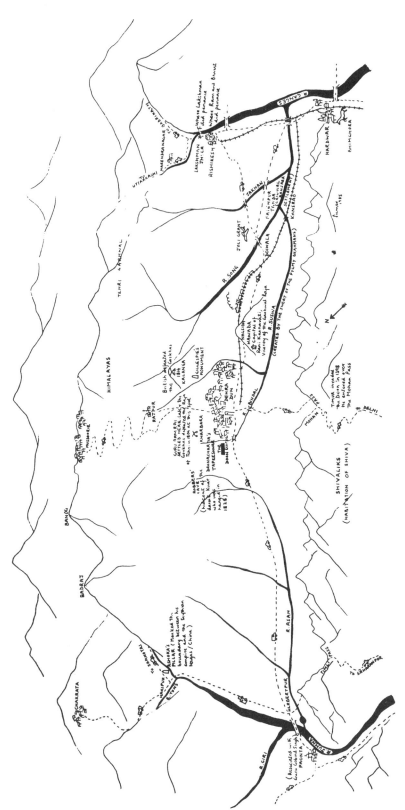

Figure 4.2 Map from the official history of the Doon School, noting places of significance in the region surrounding the School (Singh 1985: 6).

The suitability of the 'site for a school' is established by appeal to a 'legendary' past drawn from the religious tradition of the majority community. There is an ironic, if unintended, parallel between the world of images and associations of a school with its self-professed secular manifesto, and that of the Banaras Hindu University:

> the location of the only 'Hindu' University of the country in the heart of the Hindi region had its obvious symbolic significance. It complemented the process whereby significant geographical symbols, such as the Ganga, the Himalayas and the Vindhyachal, had been appropriated in literary writing to project a hegemonic destiny for the Hindi region.
>
> (Kumar 1991: 129).

DSB also contains references to the non-Hindu associations of the Doon valley and the surrounding areas. But these references are passing and seem to occupy the space of an inert history rather than possessing the living aura of the 'traditions' of which the School sees itself a part. So, we are informed in a single sentence that 'another way of entering the Doon is by road from Saharanpur, the city of the Sufi mystic, Shah Haran Chisti, who lived there in the first half of the fourteenth century' (*DSB*: 6). 'The city of the Sufi mystic' becomes a minor cultural sign-post, of historical interest perhaps, within the grander cultural space, 'rich in legendary and historical associations', where the School is evocatively situated:

> Shortly after crossing the Jumna, the western boundary of the Doon, [the traveller]. . . will pass through Kalsi where he may stop to look at the well preserved Asoka pillar, with its edicts over two thousand years old, proclaiming a morality man has not yet learned to observe.
>
> (*DSB*: 6)[30]

Though the choice of the School crest had been made quite early in the School's life, the search for a motto to accompany it took a little longer. Some of the suggestions put forward at the time are also indicative of the nature of the School's engagement with the religious issue. In 1953, Headmaster John Martyn joined the debate on the School motto in a letter to the *School Weekly* in the following manner:

> Dear Sir,
>
> It is a pity that the Doon School has not yet decided on a motto. It should, I think, be in Sanskrit, and should be something that goes with the lamp. The following have been suggested:
>
> Tejo mayi dhehi
> 'Give light unto me'

A Jyoti reti
'Light is near'

Jyotir me dehi
this means 'Give me light'

Tamaso ma jyotivagamaya
'Lead us from darkness into light'

Appo dipo Bhav (Pali)
'Be a light unto thyself'

Any comments?[31]
(*DSW*, 19 Sept. 1953)

The incorporation of the paraphernalia of the Hindu 'Great Tradition' (Singer 1972) – its calibrated positioning upon the symbolic atlas of the School – at strategic intersections of visibility and permanence, is also apparent in some other, more concrete ways. Immediately below the Headmaster's office, mounted on a pedestal, is a rectangular block of carved rock depicting a scene from Hindu cosmology and a plaque noting its considerable antiquity; girding the School's amphitheatre known as the Rose Bowl are life-size statues of, among others, Mahavir, the founder of Jainism, Buddha, the torch-bearer of 'muscular-Hinduism', Vivekananda, and the poet Tagore; and its external walls are adorned with friezes depicting scenes of music and dance not unlike those found at the caves of Ajanta and Ellora. It is through such a scattered tableau, consisting of piquant depictions of a Hindu antiquity, that the past is employed to represent the history of the post-colonised nation.

There is very little reference in early School publications to contemporaneous currents in educational thinking in India and their articulation with its own pedagogical practice. There is a sense in which existent educational thought is seen to be part of a world which – along with many other aspects of Indian life – needed to be extinguished, or certainly not allowed any further public hearing. School history – meticulously recorded in campus magazines and journals and preserved with the care both nostalgia and a sense of history lend to the process – represents its foundation as an event marking an unequivocal break with the 'parochialism' of traditional Indian thinking on education.

Of the several strands of educational thought that competed for public acceptance early this century, that which coalesced under the rubric of the National Education Movement was particularly prominent. Promoted by a conglomeration of upper caste and feudal interests (Mukherjee and Mukherjee 1957), the aims of the movement were formalised in the manifesto of the National Council on Education (NCE) established in 1906. Krishna Kumar suggests that the NCE's conception of national education 'was grounded in a revivalist perception of culture' (Kumar 1991: 120), and that 'the reading and discussion of ancient Indian texts of religion and literature acquired a central place in the curriculum of national education' (*ibid.*). How ironic then that the following description of the *Andhra Jathieya Kala Sala* at Masulipatnam in Andhra Pradesh established under the auspices of the NCE, should have such resonance with the cultural and symbolic ichnography of the Doon School:

> The very ordering of the scene with its sketches of sweet water and garden ground, its specimen of ancient drawings and statuary, and many a morning opening with recital of Vedic hymns and many a day closing with a lecture or reading of the Epic story or a Bhajan party, helps to create an atmosphere strongly reminiscent of ancient Indian Vidhyalayas.
> (Hanumantha Row, quoted in Kumar 1991: 120)

Hence, following the above discussion, we might say that the cultural project of modernity represented by the Doon School was from the very beginning of its history unproblematically placed within a cultural matrix – of morality, spirituality, and purity – which was clearly Hindu; and that right from the moment of its placement within this configuration, this religious specificity was never recognised.

'Indian culture'

The ease with which the School fixed cultural practices redolent of Hindu existence under the rubric of 'Indian tradition' was also highlighted at a function held at the School during 1991. The occasion was the Round Square International Service (RSIS) Conference, an off-shoot of the Round Square Conference (see Chapter 3). The RSIS was started in 1981 and one of the primary objectives of member schools consists in carrying out 'social service' activities (*Chandbagh IV. A Doon School Miscellany* 1985: 174). Hence, selected students and staff from member schools make yearly 'social service' visits, usually to countries in Asia and Africa. These visits quite neatly combine the philosophies of 'adventure' and 'progress' and one Doon document referred to them as the 'annual village development expedition'. When visiting India, the group works in collaboration with the Indian Public Schools Conference. Part of the objective of the RSIS conference held at the Doon School during November 1991 was to evaluate past activities and to decide on the course of action for the future. The chief guest was the ex-king of Greece, who is also a patron of the organisation.

Approximately twenty schools (Indian and foreign) participated in the conference, with 'The Challenge of Poverty' as its theme. The gathering, from the point of view of the Doon School, was also to serve as a showcase for Indian culture, a forum for the exposition of 'Indian thought'; it was hoped that the foreign visitors would go back with an experience of the 'real' India. One of the special invitees to the conference was Dr Karan Singh, son of the Maharaja of the erstwhile princely state of Jammu and Kashmir, former minister in the Indira Gandhi government, a widely hailed 'philosopher' of religion, and a former student of the Doon School. He was to deliver the keynote address on 'eastern' religious belief.[32] On the day of the speech, the entire student and staff body of the School along with the visitors gathered at the Rose Bowl, the mini amphitheatre which is a common venue for school plays and similar events. A teacher had been asked to prepare a hymn to inaugurate the occasion. At the appointed time a group of boys, accompanied by the master, all attired in white *Kurta-pyjama*, entered the arena of the amphitheatre and, taking their position at the back of the stage, broke into a Sanskrit hymn taken from the Vedas. The inaugural moment of the ceremony was, in this way, stamped indelibly with the aural and ocular pastiche, the totality of which spoke of the 'great tradition' of Hinduism: sonorous Sanskrit sounds, and the singers dressed in white, the colour of purity and abstinence in Hindu belief.

At the conclusion of the singing, Karan Singh was invited to deliver his talk on religion and religious tolerance. The speaker's sartorial elegance – shoes, well-creased trousers, Jodhpuri jacket, and a Gandhi cap of matching colour – conveyed a strong sense of the 'modern' savant.[33] To one side of the stage stood the choir in white, hands folded in front in a gesture of reverence, front centre a burning oil lamp, and in the middle of the stage, preparing to declaim, the speaker. Singh began by informing the audience of the great antiquity and religious significance of the hymn just concluded. He then proceeded to the main body of his exegesis on religious tolerance and 'spirituality' in the contemporary world, devoting almost the entire speech to a description of Hindu cultural and religious practice. An engaging speaker, he received a full round of ovation at the conclusion of his talk.

Later, I spoke to some of the students and staff about the events of the day, and specifically, about the opening segments of the function held at the Rose Bowl. The students perceived no religious significance in the elaboration of the ceremony and neither did its articulation through the vivid lexicon of Hindu symbols and rituals elicit any comment. One of the teachers, however, was more forthcoming. The morning's activities, he suggested, would have 'given the visitors a fairly good glimpse of the high points of Indian culture'.[34]

It is crucial, then, to understand that the process of the ensconcement of the School's official ideology of secularism within the contours of a Hindu system of meanings – one which both echoes and reinforces wider tendencies in Indian metropolitan life – was initiated in its earliest days. And hence, that the choice of its emblems of public presence was one in keeping with this pattern. The representational space of the School – that occupied by the crest, the motto, special ceremonies, the field of visible impact, in other words – is embedded within a very specific but silent configuration of signs. This is a configuration that belongs to a Hindu sacred cache of gestures, colours, and sounds. This silent space envelops, so to say, the presence of the School, saturating the grounds of both its routine and non-routine existence. It also encompasses, and is encompassed by, the public voice of the School, the ethos of secularism. The consequence is, we might say, a Hindu contextualism. It is this 'ethos', I suggest, which the students imbibe during their stay of five to seven years at the School, and it is this that they carry with them into the broader sphere of public life as 'leading' citizens of the nation state.[35]

The location of the secular ethos of the School within a Hindu ambit, as I have suggested above, has, of course, its echoes in various interstices of the national life. Many public figures made 'pilgrimages' to Doon to witness for themselves the decreed site – the laboratory – of the invention of the post-colonial Indian identity, a site anointed and sanctified for the 'great experiment', as Headmaster Foot called it, by a diverse section of the 'educated' classes. One such visitor, President Rajendra Prasad, spoke of its students as the 'torchbearers' of 'the resurrection – the resurrection of that past when the world was so new, so fresh and so wonderful to me. But even more than that [he continued], they are to me the promise of the future' (*DSW*, 28 Oct. 1950). President Rajendra Prasad's Founders Day address at the School in 1950 was full of concern for the 'new' India and the institutions crucial for its progress. And no task was more important in this context, he suggested, than the nurturance and inculcation of a 'truly' Indian culture among the young. Hence, he continued, 'children in such institutions . . .[as Doon, were in need of]. . . spiritual nourishment from the literature of our own country', proceeding to equate this literature with that linked to and animated by the spirit of Hindu thought:

> [I] feel that the Public Schools have not only to adopt Hindi in Hindi-speaking and the language of the people in non-Hindi speaking areas as the medium of instruction, but they also have to give much more importance than they at present do to the History, literature and social patterns of India. This is in any case absolutely necessary for children of schools, for thereby alone they would remain an integral part of the Indian people. I would strongly urge that you should see that your children are fed on Valmiki and Vyasa, Kalidas and Bhavabhuti, Tagore and Gandhi.
> . . .
> I may add that whatever difficulties may exist with regard to the adoption of the language of the people as the medium of instruction there are none in the immediate adoption of Indian literature as the main subject of literary study.
>
> (*DSW*, 28 Oct. 1950)

The almost exclusive identification of 'Indian literature' with, among others, the putative authors of the *Ramayan* and the *Mahabharat*, may well be an extreme example of religious chauvinism; it is, nevertheless, another point along that chain of cultural construction of Indianness that also embraces the Doon School.

Continuities and ruptures

Both Chandra (1994) and Pandey (1994) – the latter more explicitly – have spoken of a break between the nineteenth- and twentieth-century (Hindu) North Indian nationalist consciousness. Nineteenth-century public figures such as Bhartendu Harishchandra and Bishan Narayan Dar, they argue, conceived the nation as both based on 'common interests of all Indians' (Pandey 1994: 231) *and* consisting of 'discrete communities, each with its own priorities and interests [such that] India was "Hindu" + "Muslim" + "Sikh" + "Christian", etc.' (*ibid.*). However, by the 1920s nationalist wisdom had come around to viewing the emerging nation as consisting of the citizen who had forsaken all the parochial ('little') loyalties in favour of a grand pledge to the nation. And, as Pandey further suggests, it was this second phase that saw the emergence of communalism as we understand it today.

Notwithstanding the overlap in some of their subject matter and arguments, the unifying theme of Chandra's book would seem to be quite different. The main thrust of his discussion is concerned with analysing the pattern of 'ambivalence' which for him characterised the 'psychological make-up' (1994: 126) of nineteenth-century North Indian Hindu intelligentsia. The contradictoriness that marked the response of the above group to issues such as child-marriage, widow-marriage, and the place of Muslims in Indian society, was a result, Chandra suggests, of two factors. First, it reflected the compressed nature of the changes foisted upon Indian society due to colonial rule. And second, it constituted 'an attempt to construct a Hindu ideology which would not be subject to attacks from the viewpoint of European Enlightenment or Christian ethic. This could be linked to a past that appeared as wise and enlightened in its original impulses, these being corrupted by the pressure of alien [Muslim] invasion' (*ibid.*: 130).

The most appropriate socio-political context for the Doon School lies somewhere between the discursive territories outlined by Pandey and Chandra. For while it may seem obvious that the Doon School scores a neat fit within the second phase of nationalist thinking marked by the advent of the 'purely national' subject 'beyond the religious communities, beyond caste' (Pandey 1994: 239), it is Chandra's view-point on 'ambivalence' which really completes my argument.[36] For otherwise it may be tempting to argue that the presence of members of both the Hindu Mahasabha and the Muslim League on the occasion of the Doon's inauguration ceremony is really a demonstration of the School's commitment to secularism. If we view it however as a combination of a 'second phase' secularist-nationalist project circumscribed by an implicit ambivalence towards the Muslim presence in India, then we may be able to fully understand the location of this project as one of 'Hindu contextualism'. The nationalist resolution of the religious question – at least at the Doon School – lay, in other words, in the establishment of a supra-context which was Hindu, and within this context of hierarchised encompassment, circulated/circulates a discourse of multi-religiosity and secularism.

The first and second phase nationalism, not that they were homogeneous and consistent bodies of thought, have combined to produce a context which cannot be understood exclusively through a realist epistemology which confines itself to the analysis of 'real' structures (e.g. Hindu organisations) and discrete boundaries between the fundamentalists 'over there' and the progressives 'over here'. The presence of Madan Mohan Malviya and Muhammad Zafarulla Khan at the Doon School can be understood, then, as part of the process of creation of Hindu contextualism: the secular twentieth-century (Hindu) intelligentsia giving expression to its multi-religious beliefs within a larger constructed context of Hinduism (see also van der Veer 1994). I have attempted in this chapter to analyse the many ways in which the Doon School has constructed this wider Hindu context – from the iconography of the campus to official accounts of the surrounding sacred geography – and has contributed to a larger national project which is still in train. The 'ambivalence' of the early nationalists gave way not just to the adoption of the secular citizen-subject as the *beau idéal* of modernity, it also evolved into an acceptance of Hindu contexts as multi-religious; and this happened not because of a conspiracy among Hindu nationalists but, rather, due to the structuralist and literalist (or realist) perspectives which developed out of liberal nationalist discourses and the historiography which has traced its career.

There are two prime characteristics of this realist position. The first of these is its preoccupation with centralised structures and organisations, and the second is its implicit positing of a sharp divide between the fundamentalists ('over there') and the secularists ('over here'). I am not suggesting, of course, that research into institutions and organisations is unimportant, but only that such 'centralised' history can, at best, give us a history of the functioning of publicly articulated ideologies; at worst, it may convince us that once we are able to, say, get rid of the Hindu Mahasabha we get rid of Hindu bigotry. It tells us very little, in other words, about the conditions of possibility of the existence of centralised forms of organisations such as the Hindu Mahasabha and the persistence of their ideologies. An understanding of these conditions of possibility involves the investigation of all those invisible (or silent) practices 'on the ground' which support the large-scale organisations. And further, these conditions of possibility emerge out of the practices of a far wider cross-section of society than a realist epistemology is able to account for.[37] I have argued in this chapter that an important basis upon which the public bigotry of Hindu organisations is premised is the development of Hindu contextualism and the manner in which this context has been made to pass as multi-religious.[38]

In a recent publication, Basu *et al.* (1993) have provided an important institutional account of the Hindu right, through focusing on two of the major organisations involved in the propagation of *Hindutva* in recent times – the Rashtriya Swayamsevak Sangh (RSS) and the Vishwa Hindu Parishad

(VHP). Crucial as this publication is to the larger project of combating Hindu bigotry, it nevertheless seems to share considerable ground with the realist secular perspective that, as I have indicated, cannot capture the Hindu contextualism which is part of the Doon (and Indian) secular landscape. Also, in implicitly positing a clearly identifiable support base for these organisations in certain sections of the Indian population (and not others), it reproduces an argument about 'them' and 'us' which is itself part of the mainstream (Doon) discourse of secularism.

In light of my discussion of the Hindu context of Doon School secularism, what is of particular concern in the above publication is the Othering of the support base for the RSS and the VHP. The supporters are almost exclusively identified with the small-town, provincial, non-professional (and, one might say, non-English educated) milieu. 'The games-cum-physical culture aspect of the [RSS strategy] have a major appeal', the authors state, 'particularly in the overcrowded lower middle class living areas in the city or small-town neighbourhoods' (1993: 35); and that 'as training proceeds, RSS recruits acquire a new sense of corporate identity. This is often desperately desired among traders, shopkeepers, clerks, and petty professionals' (*ibid.*). Further, their case study of the town of Khurja in Uttar Pradesh, the site of recent communal disturbances, provided

> an almost claustrophobic sense of a small-town Hindu trade-cum-professional milieu where any alternative culture seems, quite simply, non-existent: the young men move from communal-minded families to schools and colleges full of RSS teachers, and RSS *shakhas* provide practically the only other source of recreation, leisure-time socialisation, and intellectual training.
>
> (Basu *et al.* 1993: 36)

The elements of the realist position I have outlined above seem to be present in full measure in the extracts quoted here: there is the association of the support for Hindu bigotry with certain structures (the RSS, the VHP), and there is the identification of Hindu bigots as 'them', i.e. the lower middle class, the non-professionals, the small-town petty bourgeoisie, etc. 'Academic refutations' (by 'us'?) of the Hindu right's revisionist history of the Indian past

> have gone on, but myths persist and proliferate providing a simplistic, hand-me-down history to the lay person. Modern secular historiography, still composed mainly in English, has a very limited reach in a subcontinent marked by mass illiteracy, generally poor and dated textbooks, and now by the attempt of the VHP and the BJP to dominate oral culture through the audio-visual media.
>
> (Basu *et al.* 1993: 3)

As my discussion of Hindu contextualism at the Doon School has indicated, to speak of a secular intelligentsia which has access to English language 'secular historiography' and is, therefore, less likely to imagine the national community in Hindu hues is a simplistic – realist – understanding of the production of discourses. The lack of access to English language secular historiography no more inclines the provincial resident to religious intolerance (does progressive vernacular literature such as that of Fanishwarnath Renu not count as educational and liberating?), than the lack of institutional affiliation on the part of the metropolitan intelligentsia frees it from a 'communal' imagination. And, in the context of the discussion of the previous chapter, the *lack* of emphasis on the 'games-cum-physical culture aspect' – which latter the authors consider to be particularly attractive in 'the overcrowded lower middle class area' – does not seem to warrant the conclusion of a more 'secular' attitude. The various sites of Indian secularism have for some time now been circumscribed by a Hindu contextualism, and 'secular' institutions such as the Doon School (and it *has* served as a model for several other schools), applauded for spreading the gospel of the nation at the cost of narrower affiliations, have played a considerable role in producing an intelligentsia which perceives Hindu contexts as synonymous with a multi-religious one.

As I write these lines, I have in front of me a recent copy of the journal *Economic and Political Weekly* which contains an advertisement inserted by a major government undertaking, the Unit Trust of India, and in which the central motif is a Kalash which forms an important part of many Hindu ceremonies. Post-Independence popular cinema which has sought to 'imagine' (or invent) India also provides several illustrations of Hindu contextualism. In *New Delhi* (1956), actor-singer Kishor Kumar plays the citizen-subject in search of a new India where the 'primordial' loyalties so abhorrent to second-phase nationalists will have no place in every-day life. *New* Delhi, the metropolis, is of course the (new) nation *manqué*. The story unfolds through tracking the efforts of a Punjabi migrant to New Delhi, 'Mr Anand' (as the Kishor Kumar character 'castelessly' introduces himself), in finding rental accommodation in the metropolis. The journey from the province to the metropolis as a journey to the realms of modernity is a recurring *leit-motif* of recent Indian cultural productions, and I will return to it in Chapter 6 in my discussion of the metropolis as a metaphor in contemporary Indian life. After many refusals Anand discovers – much to his chagrin – that even in this 'modern' city potential landlords will only let to their regional or caste brethren. Disillusioned, he secures accommodation from a Tamil house-owner through posing as a 'Madrasi'.

However all is not lost, and the young demonstrate the fatuity of the parochial loyalties of the older generation: Anand falls in love with his landlord's daughter, and his own sister is charmed by a Bengali artist (whose father had earlier rejected Anand as a potential tenant). Parental objection, however, leads to dire consequences with Anand's sweetheart attempting suicide and his sister being betrothed to a Punjabi boy whose family threatens to humiliate the bride's father through making exorbitant dowry demands during the marriage ceremony. Through the intervention of an 'enlightened' older man, however, Anand's beloved, Janaki, is saved and the 'unsuitable' Bengali suitor comes to Anand's father's rescue through offering his family heirlooms to satisfy the greedy marriage party. In a flash the utter foolishness of elevating the *biradari* (the regional community, in this case) over the nation is apparent to all and the film concludes with the Punjabi Anand being wedded to the Tamilian Janaki, and his sister marrying the Bengali artist. A definitive 'national' closure is effected through a cohabitational dénouement of the 'problem of the nationality of Indians': the nation is the co-mingling of the blood – and reproductive fluids – of its various people.

And yet, in all this euphoria of a 'people' coming together and a nation forming through their abrogation of parochial loyalties, there is an omission which is startling for its audacity: there is no representation anywhere in the film that suggests that the nation has any place for Muslims or any other denominations. The problem of primordial loyalties is represented purely as a Hindu problem, and therefore, Hindu Punjabis, Hindu 'Madrasis', and Hindu Bengalis, achieve its resolution. Of course, this is not to suggest that the film is explicitly anti-Muslim (or anti any other religious group); rather, I want to point to the Hindu contextualism that is at work here in the construction of the nation.

There is a need, however, to pay critical attention to the formulation of Hindu contextualism. For it is not at all clear from other contemporaneous sources of artistic endeavour that representations of the national subject were constituted in a manner similar to that adopted in Hindi films. Mid-twentieth-century Hindi literature, for example, makes a decisive break from the constricting embrace of the anti-Muslim thematics of turn-of-the-century works. So, whereas the leadership of Mahavirprasad Dwivedi (1864–1937) ushered in an era of literary production with a heightened and somewhat uncompromising belief in the superiority of mainstream Hinduism (Gaeffke 1978: 17), by the mid-1920s the influence of the *Chayavaad* school had already begun to open up the boundaries of the expression of personal experience and subjectivity in a multi-cultural society. What is important is not so much the subject matter of the *Chayavaad* poets, but rather their engagement with a notion of individuality which breached the limits of permissible (religious) experience and grappled with more fluid, sometimes evanescent forms of human experience where the divine took the form of a 'mysterious lover' (*ibid.*: 33).

The continuities between the abstract space of experience opened up by the *Chayavaadins* and later writings on Indian society which deal with notions of identity, home, and being-in-the-world are reflected in the complexity of a sentience which constantly criss-crosses between alternative ways of being, and struggles against the delimitations of being 'this' or 'that'. There are numerous examples in mid- to late twentieth-century Hindi literature of attempts to resist the statist tendency to confine subjectivity to the categories of the census, the imperatives of bureaucratic practice, and the strictures of constitutional law. So although Fanishwarnath Renu in his novel *Maila Anchal*, writes of the post-Independence turmoil in a largely Hindu community (1954/1984), it is chiefly to introduce complexity into his characterisation (and hence implicitly to write against the 'simple villager' stereotype), rather than as an act of Hindu exclusivism. And the struggle to formulate an alternative to a preordained religious and secular identity is also present in *Ghummakkad Shashtra*, the work of that eclectic thinker, Rahul Sankrityayan (1948/1994). For, *ghummakkadi* (aimless wandering/loafing) is the metaphoric expression of an existential ideal: identity as the constant displacement of the self such that disappearance (or self-abnegation) becomes as coveted as appearance; and where the possibilities of non-monetised interactions are counterpoised to the imperatives of property – of self-definition through possessive individualism.

I have referred above to the poet Bacchhan's description of his childhood which embraced the praxis of more than one religious context, reflections which are quite unconscious in their recounting of the multi-contextual nature of being. However, the struggle with the dictates of governmentality in the age of the individual is even more sharply etched in a beautiful and complex novel on the nature of home, belonging, longing, and the ruthlessness of the project of border-construction which follows in the wake of moments of 'national awakening'; moments when being and subjecthood come under the purview of a dictate which seeks to substitute the connection between people as the basis of human culture with an enforced longing for a land and a territory.

Badiuzzaman's *Chanko Ki Wapasi* (1975/1985), an exploration of the meaning of subjectivity in the age of nationhood, covers the period of the partition, and is based in the city of Gaya in Bihar. Chanko, the son of a tailor, is a childhood acquaintance of the narrator, a man of lower middle-class background whose friendship with the former gradually dissolves through the corrosive effect of class and the ceaseless efforts of his petty bureaucrat father to maintain the facade of being *sharif* (a gentleman). Pakistan has just come into being, and Muslims, including Chanko's and the narrator's families, are being asked to give their 'option' for either staying in India or going to Pakistan. Many leave, convinced that the territory of Pakistan is where Muslims 'naturally' belong and that once there they will indeed find the peace and happiness that comes from being at 'home'. Chanko too leaves, hoping to find a better living than has hitherto been his lot.

The turmoil which both preceded and followed the partition is the material through which Badiuzzaman explores questions of identity, difference, and the shock of the discovery that 'home' is the site of memory and tactility, and that territory is a cruel parody of the promise of paradise and the dream of stability. However, not every one is convinced by the politico-administrative dictate to delimit identity to Hindu or Muslim, Indian or Pakistani. The

Hindu Ramdhani is the local barber who performs ritual services for both the Muslims and the Hindus of the locality on the occasions of *Moharram* and *Mundan* (tonsuring ceremony) respectively. Then one day a group of Hindus threaten him with dire consequences should he continue to be part of the religious life of both communities: 'this will no longer do' (Badiuzzaman 1975/1985: 24), they tell him. Stunned by the audacity of the order to make such stark choices when his daily life is marked by a more graduated awareness of the differences between the self and another, the barber can only ponder his fate through the syncretic cognisance which is his heritage:

> Ramdhani was in a spin. Had his ancestors not bequeathed him all these various tasks? How could he neglect some and not the others? What would people say? And it was not merely a matter of what others might think, it would be a sin [*paap*]. Would he not be cursed [*shraap*] by the Imam Sahib [whose martyrdom the occasion commemorates] if he didn't participate [in Moharram]?
>
> (Badiuzzaman 1975/1985: 24).

And woven in between all this is the story of Chanko, who, tricked into going to Pakistan by his employer, is now bewildered by the citizenship rules of the Indian state which prohibit his return home. 'Chanko's return' is the desperate longing for the connection between humans, summarily banished by the laws of citizenship and the discourse of territorial allegiance. Chanko is the mocking twin of the narrator who as a civil servant in independent India has the task of informing him that he cannot return, that he must surrender the sense of belonging to a community and readjust his allegiance to favour territory. Chanko's return is illusory, since it involves the movement from one way of thinking – the statist, which Badiuzzaman's ironic mode of writing powerfully explores – to another that is largely in tatters. But dictates do not necessarily overwhelm the recalcitrance of other memories. On seeing Chanko's distress, Ramdhani, by now doubled over with age but with spirits unflagging, calls out to him: 'Stay here Chanko. There is no need to go anywhere else. Just build a house here' (1975/1985: 158). But innocence and belief, no matter how strong, are no match for the powers of a statism whose relentless energy enforces new rules of association, blind to the potential of extant ones, its gaze turned away from the signs of dissent which it interprets as the childishness of 'backward' populations. Chanko can never return.

I have discussed Badiuzzaman's novel at some length in order to indicate that Hindu contextualism is not the only text which has constituted Indian reality during the twentieth century, and to note that there have been competing interpretations of subjectivity in Indian society. What has increasingly transpired, however, is the hegemony of Hindu contextualism, and the marginalisation of a more complex, overlapping reality. One could of course multiply the examples of Hindu contextualism already cited: from official ceremonies which involve breaking a coconut, to Hindu swastika signs which are unofficially inscribed upon construction sites of public buildings during foundation-laying ceremonies. These are only examples of the wider Hindu contextualism of which we (the secular 'us') are all a part, and in the establishment of which 'we' have all played a role. The public expression of religious beliefs is *not* at issue, but rather the process of misrecognition of the religious milieu of one section of the Indian population as synonymous with that of every other. The transition has been from the first phase nationalist thought, with its ideology of India as discrete communities, to one where those who have wished to install a secular subject in its place have paid scant attention to the larger context in which the citizen-subject has been nurtured. In the process, this has led to a reductionism where Hindu life ways have come to stand for all possible ways of being. This unwitting convergence between the world of the 'secularists' and the aims of the 'fundamentalists' is ironic indeed.

We might say that *our* training ground – where *we* have been taught that 'Hindu' (ceremony, prayer, whatever) means 'secular' – has been the various 'secular' institutions where we have been educated. The success of this training has been our inability to think in non-literal ways about contexts, and the tendency to reduce ideology to institutional affiliations, and continuously to reproduce a discourse of distancing where the violence of bigotry has its roots elsewhere and where the 'fundamentalists' are always 'over there'.

In this chapter I have attempted to deal with the issue of religion in the life of the citizen-under-preparation. I have suggested that the Doon School may be seen as one of the construction sites of the post-colonised national identity, and that the issue of religion was, and is, seen as one of its control and harness: secularism as a prerequisite for 'modern' citizenship. By extension, those who are regarded as 'non-citizens' are the ones who do not possess this trait of 'character', this embellishment of education.

I have, also, implicitly, tried to suggest that a certain form of Indian selfhood, which I have referred to as 'modern', is inextricably entangled with the idea of citizenship; and that those forms of subjectivity which are perceived to lack the 'prerequisites' of citizenship are to be regarded, essentially, as 'children of a lesser god'. This, of course, implies the elevation of the nation state 'to the status of the end of all history' (Pandey 1991: 559). In such a situation, 'threats' to the nation state become matters of disqualification for the 'grant' of citizenship. I have suggested, however, that notwithstanding the official proclamations of a secular manifesto for the School, sharp disjunctions exist at the site of practice: that the 'secular', public, voice of the School is ensconced within a silent space of Hindu symbols and rituals, and that, in this manner, the Indian liberal-bourgeois discourse, of which the School is an important part, speaks unselfconsciously through the vocabulary of majority opinion and with the gestures of that majority's cultural and religious universe.

In Chapter 5 I return to the discussion initiated in Chapter 3 on the construction of time and space at the School as that of 'rationality'. The discussion is supplemented with a concern with the specific class, caste, and regional representation at the Doon School, and with an attempt to locate Doon in a specific history of the functioning of capital in North India.

5 The management of water: capitalism, class, and science

The autobiography of the nationalist Bipinchandra Pal (1858–1932) – memories of 'my own infancy, boyhood and youth' (Pal 1973: iii) – is a fascinating historical document, replete with the observations of an eminent figure of Bengali public life on important events and processes of his times; his intimate association with the latter adds, of course, to the value of the document. It can also be read as the intellectual history of what could be called the metropolitan and the provincial secure classes – intelligentsia in the broadest possible sense of the term. Of particular interest for the discussion of this chapter are glimpses of the attitudes held by sections of the metropolitan intelligentsia, in this case the Bengali, towards the Punjabi 'educated classes'.[1] These attitudes constitute an important part of the historical context in which the Doon School may be situated. The role of the School as one of the sites of nurturance of a 'provincial-metropolitan' intelligentsia[2] can be seen in sharper relief against the background of the judgements embodied in these attitudes.

Vigorous bodies and simple minds: a metropolitan verdict

Among the several social reform movements that proliferated during the nineteenth century in India, the Arya Samaj, based on the teachings of Swami Dayanand Saraswati, is of particular, and lasting, significance. Dayanand's invocation of Vedic infallibility – 'similar to the doctrine of infallibility . . . among Christians and Muslims' (Pal 1973: 455) – provided the liturgical foundation of his movement. Primarily, the Samaj sought to revivify a 'fallen' society through the task of forming 'a sound, active and decisive character in . . . students' (Pandit 1974: 193) – a task perceived to be neglected by other educational systems. The conjunctional site of the Arya Samaj discourses of a Hinduised past and present, of the centrality of the male citizen, of the male sexual regimen, and of national greatness through the development of 'personality' and 'character' was the Gurukul educational movement. The first of the Gurukuls was established in 1902 'in the Kangadi valley [Haridwar] on the banks of the river Ganges' (*ibid.*: 211) and manifested a dissatisfaction within the Samaj with its own earlier educational work which was seen to be taking on a 'foreign' character. It was aimed to stem this through the propagation of the Gurukul movement – of 'ancient' and Vedic origin – within which 'the students were called *Brhamacharis* on the pattern of the Ancient Gurukulas' (*ibid.*: 210).

Arya Samajis strongly emphasise that the founder of their creed held views which have been validated by 'scientific' method: 'Swamiji [touched] upon what can be some of the vital aspects of and components of early childhood education which the modern child psychologists and educationists have priced highly' (*ibid.*: 156). So, while on the one hand the Samaj is/was represented as countering the 'degenerate' effects of westernisation (and of missionary activity), on the other, the ultimate validation of its philosophy rested upon the touchstone of a western knowledge regime; this, of course, is the double bind of colonial cultural practice, of 'wanting and not wanting a relation' (Metcalfe 1988: 197).

The Arya Samaj operated, it has been suggested, 'within the parameters of the given social structure', attempting to 'reform only those features which they thought acted as obstacles in the way of the economic and social advancement of the educated elite' (Kishwar 1986: 151–2). The movement found its most receptive audience, and achieved its greatest proselytising success, in the province of Punjab, a region where the endeavours of the other major nineteenth-century religious movement, the Brahmo Samaj, seemed to have struck particularly barren ground. A discussion of this issue – the unequal success enjoyed by the two movements in Punjab – is the central concern of a chapter in Pal's autobiography: entitled 'Swami Dayanand and the Arya Samaj', the chapter can also be read as an evaluation of the 'Punjabi mind' by its Bengali counterpart.

Anchored within a discourse of despair and condescension, Pal's narration of the congregational conquest of Punjab by the Arya Samaj opens with an account of the political atmosphere in which the 'rising generation of English-educated Punjabees' (1973: 448) found themselves in the closing decades of nineteenth century. The discussion on the political proclivities of 'young Punjab' is inaugurated through an overview of what was then the Oriental University at Lahore; in the ensuing discussion, the Oriental University becomes a metaphor of the difference between the political life of the young educated Punjabi, and that in which the educated Bengali youth was, supposedly, nurtured. The inspiration for the Oriental University, Pal notes:

> came very largely from a body of Punjab officials, who recognised the danger to British rule which the Universities like Calcutta offered. They wanted to protect the rising generation of the Punjabees from the influences of modern European thought and culture that had found an efficient instrument in the system of education promoted by the Calcutta University. . . . The Punjab officials did not like the spirit of freedom and self-assertion bred in the new generation of Bengalees brought up under

the influence of the Calcutta University. . . . This was the psychology really of that reactionary educational policy which found its most open and organised expression in the new Oriental University at Lahore.

(Pal 1973: 448–9)

The object behind the establishment of the University at Lahore, Pal continues, 'was openly political. The officials did not want a second Bengal in the Punjab, and they thought that they would be able to stem the tide of modern ideas by encouraging medieval Sanskrit and Arabic learning' (*ibid.*). And, as far as Pal – the man 'acknowledged to be a maker of modern Bengal and India'[3] – could see, the efforts of the Punjab officials had met with great success. However, though 'modern European culture' did eventually manage to find a foothold at the Oriental University, the 'rationalism' which subsequently developed there was of a fundamentally different order to that which had emerged at Calcutta:

In Bengal the movement which it ['English education'] called into being was a movement of pure rationalism. The logic of the teachings in the University and the schools worked unhampered by any prepossessions.

(Pal 1973: 450)

The purer form of rationalism which coursed through the lecture rooms of Bengal and the 'prepossessions' which hampered its efflorescence in Punjab marked the two regions, in Pal's account, with the distinguishing features of two very different intellectual worlds; the political and intellectual attainments of the late nineteenth-century Punjabi intelligentsia, though once suffused with a certain promise, were seen to possess 'nothing more than the discrete charm of a second-order simulacra' (Baudrillard 1988:166). The failure of the Brahmo Samaj – a creed inspired by 'the ideals of rationalism and freedom' – among the educated Punjabis, was, then, a measure of the 'backwardness' of the latter. The more sophisticated 'Bengali mind', nurtured upon a diet of the 'prevailing European rationalism and scepticism', had found in the liturgical and intellectual complexities of the Brahmo Samaj a doctrine to match its genius. The Punjabis, on the other hand, were unschooled both in the realm of Great Tradition learning and the scientific ethos of a new age, and hence were ideal material for the exegetical ambitions of a 'simple' religious movement such as the Arya Samaj. Hence one of the reasons why 'Swami Dayanand's message found little or no response from the Bengalee Hindu community' was

that the new generation of educated Bengalees were fairly acquainted with Sanskrit literature and the Vedic exegesis of Pandit Dayananda failed therefore to make an impression on them which it subsequently did on the Punjabee mind, that was less familiar with Sanskrit. Dayananda's law of interpretation was very simple, and like all simple explanations of complex problems it did not satisfy the more critical Bengalee mind.

(Pal 1973: 456)

Pal's analysis of the situation in Punjab *vis-à-vis* the differing situation of the two Samajs progresses, as it were, through a physiognomic evaluation of the Punjabi 'mind', its base character revealed through its eager acceptance of the imperatives of the Arya Samaj. The identification of the peculiarities of the Punjabi mind was not difficult to come by: 'It did not take me long,' Pal says, 'when I came in personal contact with the Arya Samaj movement in Lahore, to find out all these things' (1973: 457). The Punjabi mind was more open to the ideas of the Arya Samaj due to its own 'helpless position' – a euphemism, perhaps, for the limited ability for intellectual retort – against the 'attacks of Christian and Muslim propaganda'. The absorption of Arya Samaj propaganda by the Punjabis was facilitated, Pal seems to suggest, through a fortuitous coincidence of the tendencies of the Punjabi mind and the epistemological proclivities of its new faith: narrowness of vision, simplicity of reason, a spirit of intolerance, and a keenness towards violence. Pal's narrative is deftly interwoven with the theme of the intrinsic distinction between the 'gentle', subtle, but more complex nature of the Bengali mind and the 'robust', crude, and simplistic inclinations of its Punjabi counterpart.

Thus, 'the keen humiliation' experienced by 'the new generation of Hindus in the Punjab . . . in their inability to meet the attacks of Muslims and Christian propagandists', was alleviated, he suggests, through the 'violent attack' mounted by Dayanand 'on Christian and Muslim propaganda' (*ibid.*). Through such sinewy *modus operandi*, the Arya Samaj was able to 'feed the pride of race of the Punjabee Hindu'. The term 'pride of race' is, of course, an indispensable part of the descriptive vocabulary with which a more 'complex' society seeks both to describe and categorise a 'lesser race': it comes from the same lexical universe as, and is the mirror twin of that other term of the collision of cultures, the Noble Savage (White 1992). The well-intentioned young men of the Arya Samaj, Pal concludes with a flourish animated by the momentum of stereotypic formulations, were fired by 'narrow patriotic aspirations' which, in turn, have 'always carried with [them] a spirit of intolerance' (Pal 1973: 464–5).

The subalterns of capital and the acolytes of science

Provincial men and metropolitan desires

The Punjabi world which Bipinchandra Pal purports to describe is the world to which middle-class men such as Prakash Tandon belonged. Tandon was the author of the autobiographical *Punjabi Century 1857–1947*, and later the first Indian Chairman of Unilever's Indian subsidiary.[4] Born in the opening decade of the twentieth century, Tandon's immediate locality of birth can serve as a piquant spatio-temporal metaphor for the age which fuelled the very specific visions of future for his generation and class, and for the aspirations with which this future was inscribed. He was born, as it were, in the very geography of a human industrial enterprise engaged in the conquest of nature. If the manner of our birth is completely arbitrary, then sometimes this arbitrariness presents us with the most beguiling metaphors.

Tandon's father, of the generation which 'founded the new Punjabi middle class and added some modern values to the old Punjabi character' (Tandon 1968: 35), was an engineer with the irrigation department of the Punjab government, engaged in the construction and maintenance of the irrigation canals which were then beginning to criss-cross the Punjabi countryside like a thousand electric eels. The development of the nine canal colonies marked the 'process of agricultural colonisation commenced [by the British] in the western Punjab from 1885' (Ali 1988: 8). The breathtaking immensity of this particular colonial project of agricultural extraction – breathtaking too in the complexity of its social consequences – can be gauged from the fact that between 1885 and 1947 the area affected by canal irrigation in Punjab swelled from three to fourteen million acres (*ibid.*: 11–12). The colonies were in the swathe of a new industrial prowess, bringing with it material prosperity for a select few, and, through a slew of policies on land grants, hardening the lines of existing social and economic division in the Punjab region.

It was in one of these canal colonies that Prakash Tandon was born, 'one of the most distinguished members of the new generation', which, the Preface to his autobiography informs us, led India into its 'new, managerial world of industrialisation and State Capitalism'. How apt the locale of birth of the post-colonial male 'destined' to take the Faustian plunge into modernity's whirl (Berman 1988), a locale bristling with all the images and equipped with all the accoutrements of a new regime:

> As the canal system was first started and for many years run by the officers of the Corps of Indian Engineers, its organisation was based on military lines. Our colony was the Headquarters of a division which extended about fifty miles on either side along the main canal and included its lateral distribution channels which carried the water to the fields. The whole division was connected by its own telegraph, and later by a telephone system as well, which also connected with our neighbouring divisions.
>
> All along the canal men were also posted at such key points as at falls in the canals and at the junctions where the smaller channels left the main line. They were on round-the-clock duty to take readings every few hours which they telegraphed to father's office. All day long and till late in the evening, and sometimes even in the middle of the night, these telegrams would keep coming in. . . . Run on a strict regimen of constant

communication and speedy action, our colony was on duty the whole time and always in a state of alert.

(Tandon 1968: 41–2)

Tandon's parents belonged to one of the earliest generations of Punjabis for whom the creed of the Arya Samaj became an internalised reality. Some measure of the increasing influence of the Samaj in Punjab can be gained by reference to the extent and nature of its public activities in that province. As early as 1885, when Tandon senior would have been around ten or eleven years of age, the Arya Samaj was not only advocating but also carrying out well-publicised widow marriage ceremonies as part of its reform agenda. One of the journals of the movement, the *Arya Patrika*, reported in September of that year that 'another widow marriage has been celebrated under the auspices of the Umritsar Arya Samaj', and that, 'this is the second widow marriage which has taken place at Amritsar through the efforts of the local Arya Samaj' (Kishwar 1986: 170). By the closing decades of the nineteenth century, then, the movement which came in for such opprobrious appraisal by Pal had grown considerable roots among a large section of the Punjabi intelligentsia.

The attractions of Dayanand's teachings for a certain section of the Punjabi population, according to Tandon, were several:

To our new professional class it provided a Western social reorientation combined with simple Vedic belief and ritual. Its opposition to orthodoxy and idol worship, and its revival of Vedic ritual in modern form, without temple and priest, made a direct appeal to the Punjabi intelligentsia.

(Tandon 1968: 33)

Along with several others of their class and cultural background, the Tandons took wholeheartedly to the tenets of their new religion, and often attended a *mandir* 'which did not look like a temple, but more like a lecture hall with a pleasant open courtyard and a garden' (*ibid.*: 33). A professional class, the administrative and technical preceptors of an incipient industrial order, which marked its progress through the deep furrows of the irrigation canals and the measured distances of the railway track, was in the process of defining its presence. The impact of this presence was magnified through the diasporic nature of its settlement. This was the class which, it seems, awaited the founding of the Doon School, to overwhelm its dormitories and its 'waiting lists' with the bodies and names of its sons and wards.

Of course, the Doon register of students in its early days did not exclusively consist of boys from Punjab; students from the erstwhile United Provinces, Bengal, Bombay, and Madras also made up the numbers. However, by far the largest representation came from North India, and of these, the single largest recognisable group was of Punjabi origin, if not residence. The point I wish to make is that the School facilitated the rise of a section of the North Indian intelligentsia into national ('metropolitan') prominence, a section whose members had traditionally played only a limited role in the political and cultural economy of the state. This 'rise' was consolidated in the years following Indian Independence.

The North Indian intelligentsia which patronised the Doon School, and which was the object of Bipinchandra Pal's upbraiding narrative on the Arya Samaj, emerged from that juncture where colonial capitalism met an industrial science of the frontier. And the Punjabi intelligentsia's experience of the prowess of the 'new sciences' was, compared with its Bengali counterpart, of a much more 'hands-on' nature. For they were, mostly, men like Prakash Tandon's father who, as Tandon recorded in the second volume of his autobiography, 'after high school . . . sat for the entrance examination of the new engineering college of Roorkee, the earliest of its kind in Asia, where they taught the new science of engineering for building canals, dams, roads, and railways' (Tandon 1980: x). This was a class enmeshed in the momentum of a transformative enterprise where, with every extra cusec of water which found its mechanical way to a distant field and with every extra kilometre of rail and road which traversed new territory, the potency of the 'new science' was manifest.

The 1880s marked a decisive change in the policy of the colonial government towards the agricultural sector in Punjab. It undertook specific measures directly linked to raising agricultural productivity which it hoped would 'increase land revenue and export income' (Fox 1985: 53). The government invested – with capital raised in England with promises of high return which were fulfilled in the course of time – in an impressive network of irrigation canals:

> Starting in the mid-1880s with two small irrigation works along the Sutlej River and continuing with the large, lower Chenab River project in 1890, which watered the new Lyallpur District, the irrigation canals moved steadily westwards until the Nili Bar, finished in 1926, inundated the Multan District. By the 1920s over 10 million acres of formerly desert lands, most of which had been the hitherto uninhabited and worthless property of the Raj, had been irrigated under state capitalism.
>
> (Fox 1985: 53)

Of course in reality, the areas designated 'uninhabited' did in fact contain local populations, and they were 'worthless' only in terms of the colonial economy. The uninhabited nature of a territory was established through a legal fiction that was all too common to the colonising process (the doctrine of *terra nullius*, in the Australian context, for example). Until the advent of agricultural colonisation in Punjab, vast tracts were in fact the domains of semi-nomadic pastoralists collectively referred to as *Junglis*. The process of land colonisation was effected through a denial of proprietary rights to these populations, and the government 'instead asserted its own ownership over land' (Ali 1988: 18). The territory, rescued from the impress of the 'wilderness' of the *Junglis*, was now ready for more 'worthwhile' use through its inclusion in the project of establishing canal colonies. Here, superimposed upon the natural landscape, was an elaborate and impressive montage of modernity, administered by its specially trained cadre of industrial and technical specialists: engineers, 'colonising officers',[5] and forest officers; the whirring of canal devices, measuring and delivering precise quantities of an imprecise fluid[6] and the salient architecture of railway stations. The following lines of a Punjabi ballad, purportedly sung by 'a blind poet' in honour of Captain Popham Young, Colonising Officer of the Chenab Canal Colony, capture well the visible process of transformation of the natural landscape at the turn of the century; even the blind sang of the glories of the progress that only the sighted could actually behold:

. . . There at Wazirabad

Where the whirlpools churn,
A weir has been made and the river dammed,
Young Sahib has peopled the land.

Hard by run the trains,
Whereon those who pay may travel,
Telegraph wires have been extended,
Babus came and occupied the stations,
Praise to thy power, O God,
Young Sahib, etc.

The English have measured the whole land,
Here a Patwari, there a Patwari,
Zilladars galore and mighty Munshis,
To them has been given the authority,
Water where they will they give,
Young Sahib, etc.[7]

It was from this industrial milieu that Doon drew its earliest clients: 'Lawyers, Doctors, engineers, civil servants, forest officers, teachers; they came from villages and small towns and spread all over the Punjab' (Tandon 1980: x). Now, while the ground for the ideological inclination towards techno-capitalism may have been prepared by the specific spatio-temporal dimension of the canal colonies, certain other factors within the province led increasing numbers of the urban, upper caste intelligentsia to seek an education for their children which matched, both in content and style, that which was available to the children of the metropolitan intelligentsia of cities such as Calcutta.

One of these was the Land Alienation Act of 1900 which aimed to prevent non-agriculturists from buying up large tracts of land in the countryside 'as they came into the market' (Puri 1985: 73). The Act, Fox suggests, targeted the urban lower-middle class by 'first dividing the Punjab's population into putative agricultural and non-agricultural tribes (castes), the former mainly rural, and the latter mainly urban, and then restricting the freedom of the nonagriculturists to purchase land or hold mortgages on it' (1985: 165). With respect to the 'non-agricultural tribes', the Act would seem to have had two main consequences. The first was

> to serve notice on the urban castes, mostly the educated, professional and commercial classes to cut the Gordian knot and sever relations with their landlord and *Sahukar* [money lender] village past, and come to the cities to seek new opportunities and venture on new enterprise.
>
> (Puri 1985: 75–5)

This process, among others, provided the numbers which swelled the ranks of the urban middle classes in the larger towns and cities of Punjab. The existing 'urban castes' – Khatri, Bania, and Arora – were gradually joined by their counterparts from the countryside. In the opening decades of Doon's existence and for several years thereafter, it was precisely these three castes which were most numerously represented in the student population of the School.

The second consequence was the creation of a market for government land and the inflationary impact on the price of this land. Merchant capital, prohibited by the Act from carrying out land transactions directly with the cultivator, now flocked to government land auctions – sending the price of irrigated land spiralling (Fox 1985: 56). In one canal colony 'a tract sold four years before the Land Alienation Act brought an average price of Rs 50 per acre, whereas one sold four years after the Act earned the government an average of Rs 266 per acre' (*ibid.*). A consequence of this was the consolidation of an urban population with an accumulation of valuable property: wealth with which to finance the education of their children at schools such as Doon. 'The unanticipated consequences' of the colonial government's action, as Fox puts it, 'were true to the spirit of colonialism . . . in that the British did well for themselves by doing some little good for others' (*ibid.*).

To return to Bipinchandra Pal's description of the Punjabi intelligentsia: the Punjabi middle class now had the financial capital but not the cultural capital; this is, of course, the kernel of Pal's discussion. In this instance, however, we must position 'cultural capital' within the dialectics not merely of a class situation, as Bourdieu seeks to do, but also within the dynamics of the *history* of the formation of cultural class in India. The analytical trope that links Pal's observations with the life world of Prakash Tandon is cultural capital.

Shopping for culture: the exchange of capital

We cannot account, Bourdieu suggests, 'for the structure and functioning of the social world', without wresting from economic theory its attempted hegemony of 'capital': 'we must reintroduce capital in all its forms and not solely in the one form recognised by economic theory' (1986: 243). Cultural capital, then, is one of the 'three fundamental guises' in which capital can present itself, the other two being economic capital and social capital.[8] Together, they form the constituents of a 'general science of the economy of practices' (*ibid.*: 242). This 'general science' must grapple with that universe of practices which, though connected to the 'economic', cannot be reduced to it, and cannot be analysed through the limited tools of economic theory; for capital is gathered and distributed, Bourdieu says, through 'a whole labour of dissimulation' (*ibid.*: 243).

For an incipient North Indian intelligentsia the Doon School provided the site of a cultural pedagogy, a place where the cultural capital of the colonial metropolis (Calcutta, Bombay . . .) was made available to the 'educated classes' of the hinterland. In this way, the School provided a specular mechanism – different to missionary educational endeavours – in which was reflected and refined the cultural capital of the metropolis. This transubstantiative enterprise had as its concern not just classes but the journey of classes from a cultural map of the province to that of the metropolis; the School was both the journey and the means of passage through which a provincial intelligentsia took its first step towards becoming 'metropolitan'.

As I have noted above, the metropolitan intelligentsia also sent its sons to the Doon School. However, it is important to understand that for most of these families Doon was an *option*: earlier, their children had studied in England or had had access to suitable schools in one of the presidency cities; the establishment of the Doon School did not lead to a drastic change in the opportunities available to them in terms of acquiring cultural and social capital. Bengali, Maharashtrian, and Tamil (almost exclusively upper caste) names may be found in the School lists, but these are significant for the relative infrequency of their appearance. It was chiefly the rising provincial intelligentsia which flocked to the new school, and it is to the sons of this group, and the succeeding generations of those who studied at Doon, that we may apply the term provincial-metropolitans. I mean to employ this appellation as one of contrast, for concurrently there existed other types of provincial intelligentsia. The most obvious of these was the category we may call, somewhat clumsily, the provincial non-metropolitans. This cultural group had as its hub the cities and the Universities of Allahabad and Banaras, among others. Krishna Kumar's (1991) discussion of the formation of the cultural identity of this group is illuminating for its focus on the specificities of the cultural process which delineated it from the group which patronised the Doon School. The shaping of 'a collective identity in the Gangetic-Vindhya region', he suggests, 'was intertwined with the character that Hindi acquired in the process of serving as a symbol of political mobilisation' (1991: 145). This 'collective identity' was fashioned out of a 'Hindi-Hindu' milieu which centred around the Universities of Allahabad and Banaras in the erstwhile United Provinces (UP). The gradual but determined Sanskritisation of Hindi, purging it of its Urdu heritage, was, Kumar also suggests, a part of this process.

The 'educated elements' in the Hindi region, which formed the nucleus of the 'quest for self-identity' (*ibid.*), as an intelligentsia built the accoutrements of their journey out of cultural and religious material which differed sharply from that which found favour among the future patrons of the Doon School. And the difference concerns not just aspects of class. The cultural cause of the UP intelligentsia was marked strongly by the strident tone of a religious agenda: the primary vehicle for the advancement of this agenda came to be a form of Hindi – its vocabulary and idiom revamped for the purpose – from which 'its Urdu heritage was deodorised' (*ibid.*: 142). The result of this linguistic engineering, mainly supported by a narrow band of upper caste literati who also supervised its passage into school-level texts, was both 'a very restricted sphere [of its appreciation and use and] . . . an exacerbation of syntactical complexity and a Sanskritisation of vocabulary' (*ibid.*).

The eyes of Punjab, or at least the section of its intelligentsia I have discussed above, were, so to say, turned towards Bengal. It was on two fronts that the Punjabi intelligentsia desired to emulate their Bengali counterparts: the cultural, and what might be called the politico-economic. The improved career prospects which became available to a section and generation of the Bengali intelligentsia at the turn of the century – whether in the upper echelons of the bureaucracy, in law, or in a limited number of commercial concerns – still seemed beyond the Punjabi grasp. While members of the metropolitan intelligentsia, with their considerably longer history of English language education, could entertain ambitions for their children which steadily moved beyond the clerical and petty bureaucratic stage, the Punjabi canal engineer would still have to satisfy himself with more modest visions. These modest hopes were, however, transformed into a grander future in the political economy of the independent nation, and the Doon School, together with other schools modelled on it, has played a substantial role in this transformation. It was through a process of 'localisation' of the metropolitan cultural capital – and its further elaboration – that the School has participated in the discourse on citizenship and nationalism; and it was participation in this process which propelled a regional intelligentsia into the light, and the benefits, of a metropolitan cultural milieu, and a metropolitan political economy.

By the time the School opened its gates to students in 1935, Prakash Tandon was well past the schooling stage, his life launched upon a successful corporate career. By the 1950s, when the sons of men of Tandon's generation and class reached school-going age, the cultural and social capital that Doon had to offer had become well recognised. It was to Doon, in fact, that Prakash Tandon sent his son for primary and secondary education.

S.W., whom we met in Chapter 4, belongs to Tandon's son's generation. When he joined Doon as a 12-year-old in 1947, his father was an army officer from the (then) undivided Punjab and was representative of the North Indian intelligentsia which, in the main, provided the School with a steady flow of students from the very first day of its establishment. 'My father', S.W. told me, 'had never considered [sending me to] any other school . . . there was no real pressure [then] of getting in [at Doon]. . . the problem would have been, would I get into class six, etc.'[9] He had often been told by his father that Doon was a public school, the type of school where 'other officers from England . . . had been'. We get a sense of the world Prakash Tandon describes in his *Punjabi Century*, the universe which is the object of Bipinchandra Pal's condescension, from the following description S.W. provided of his family background:

> [My father] . . . came from a Punjabi family . . . he was the first one to have got a M.Sc. degree and [had] done well. My mother came from a background of Lawyers and Engineers. . . . they wanted a different type of education for me . . . so there was really no question of putting me in a day school in Amritsar. This is true of most of us . . . [whose] parents were in the civil services.

The possibilities of all action are generated within very specific contexts: specific times and spaces which, as Bakhtin suggests, are to be regarded 'not as "transcendental" but as forms of the most immediate reality' (Morson and Emerson 1990: 367). The class which sent its sons to the Doon School, for 'a different type of education', was, as I have suggested, nurtured in the embrace of an industrial regime where science met its perceived antithesis, nature. At this juncture, the railway and the telegraph tamed the tyranny of distance and filled space and time with the palpable geometry of mechanical effort. Here also, in the canal colonies, science 'domesticated' nature, harnessing its exuberance to counter its arbitrariness: 'The new canals brought water to the land which had always lain fallow because of a scant and uncertain rainfall' (Tandon 1968:176).

Canal colonies were settlements situated within the heart of the transformative industrial enterprise and were part of its mechanical geography. There were also other towns constructed in tandem with the burgeoning technological activity, and as a corollary to it, where a new urban population was beginning to take root. One of these was Sargodha, where Tandon's father was sent on a posting and where the son spent some of his childhood. Like other such settlements, Sargodha was 'made in the image of the Settlement Officers', and proffered a very distinct aura of modernity: it was a stretch of the industrial space and of its measured regime, the suburbia of a new rationality of time and space. The carefully constructed spaces here constituted an observable, experienced reality of a new age, and time – to use Bakhtin's terminology – was of 'real duration': it mattered, it had content, the split second as the emblematic representation of the new, scientific, age was able to eclipse larger, imprecise, durations, as if the latter stood for an altogether different world:

> Methodically planned, Sargodha was so different from the medieval [town of] Gujarat.[10] It was built in a square, bounded by the new canal on one side and by the new railway line that went across the canal at a right angle on another; on the third side it had a belt of gardens, fruit orchards and vegetable patches through which ran a water distributary; and on the fourth there was a mandi [agricultural market], the wholesale produce market next to the railway station. The town was divided into two parts, the city and the mandi on the one side of the railway line, and the civil station on the other. On the outskirts there were three more innovations, the waterworks, a seed farm, and an area set apart for factories. . . .
>   The mandi was a big square with ground floor shops on all sides. . . . Men would pick up a handful of wheat, look at it casually and let it drop through their fingers, as the auctioneer sang the bids in a soft voice . . . four rupees two annas, four rupees two annas, to four rupees three annas. . . . Months' toils, hopes and fears were settled in a few minutes.
>
> (Tandon 1968: 158–9)

It was from this milieu – where ordered space and finite, fractional time entered the life of a class in an intimate, every-day manner – that Doon drew several generations of its clientele. A broad picture of the background of the early students of the School, in terms of region, caste, and father's occupation, can be attempted by sifting through the information contained in *The Dosco Record*, the School directory initially compiled by ex-Headmaster John Martyn and first published in 1979.[11] This attempt should be regarded as tending towards an approximation rather than a precise exercise in small-scale demography since the data upon which it is based are often incomplete. *The Dosco Record* was compiled, quite obviously, with celebratory rather than sociological objectives in mind. However, I have taken as few liberties with the information as possible and, given the *caveat* above, it is possible to observe certain trends in the regional, caste and parents' occupational backgrounds through the early years of the School.

Of the sixty-one students who constituted the very first batch of students in 1935, at least thirty-nine (Hindu students) can be identified as being of North Indian origin (mainly Punjab and the United Provinces). There are three or four others who, going by their surnames, may also fall into this category, but, due to the nature of the information, it is difficult to be absolutely certain. There were eight Muslim students, four of whom gave a North Indian town as their place of residence. Out of the thirty-nine Hindu North Indian students, at least seventeen may be identified as being of Punjabi origin. Once again, I have not included two or three names which, given more information, may also have qualified for this category. The rest were distributed between the UP and the erstwhile states of Rajputana and other parts of India. One of the Muslim students was also from Punjab. The castes most numerously represented, as far as can be deduced from the surnames, were Khatris, Aroras, Banias, Brahmins, and Kayasthas. Within this upper caste milieu, the first three predominate.

The following table gives some idea of the occupational background of the fathers of the students of the first intake.[12]

Table 5.1 Fathers' occupational backgrounds, Doon intake, 1935

Engineer	5
Colonisation Officer	1
Merchant	5
Bureaucracy	13
Legal Profession	6
Doctor	11
Landlord	3
Army	4
Corporate Sector	1
Aristocracy	1
Accountant	1
Total	51

Source: Compiled from *The Dosco Record*, 1987

It is possible to identify the occupational background of forty of the forty-three fathers (thirty-nine Hindu and four Muslim) of North Indian origin. The breakdown is as follows:

Table 5.2 Fathers' occupational backgrounds, Doon intake from North India, 1935

Aristocracy	2
Army	1
Bureaucracy	11
Business	4
Colonisation Officer	1
Engineer	3
Landlord	3
Legal	6
Medical	9
Total	40

Source: Compiled from *The Dosco Record*, 1987

Of the one hundred students who are listed as having been admitted to the School in 1936, fifty-six can be identified as belonging to Punjab, Rajasthan or the UP. Of these fifty-five, twenty-nine came from Punjab. For the North Indian group as a whole for 1936, the two most frequently listed occupational descriptions are the bureaucracy and engineering. The engineers were mostly attached to irrigation works or the railways, some belonging to the Imperial Service of Engineers (ISE); 'my father', Prakash Tandon notes, 'having started low struggled hard till he reached the nirvana of his service, the cadre of the Imperial Service of Engineers' (1968: 31). The caste configuration for 1936 is almost identical to that for 1935. Five years later, in 1941, thirty-nine students were admitted to the School of whom twenty-three can be clearly identified as being of North Indian origin – the children, in terms of the occupational background of the fathers, of the provincial intelligentsia I have referred to earlier.

The picture remains constant as we move through data for the 1940s. For 1947, twenty-four out of the thirty-nine students are identifiably North Indian;[13] for 1948 the figure is forty out of eighty-two. In all of the above years, the cities and towns of Punjab find prominent domiciliary status in the information on the students' backgrounds. The change, as far as the numbers of students coming directly from Punjab is concerned, occurs in the mid-1950s. Though even during this period the overwhelming majority of students are of North Indian origin, there is a marked decline in those who list as their place of residence Punjab proper: Punjabi surnames are now juxtaposed with cities and towns of Uttar Pradesh and other parts of North India. Also, during this period New Delhi, the site of a great post-Independence Punjabi influx, comes to figure prominently as a residential address for students; it is this diasporic movement, of course, which constitutes part of the *mise-en-scène* for Kishor Kumar's 1956 film *New Delhi*. In 1955, out of an intake of sixty-five students, thirty-eight may be identified as North Indian; however, only four list their place of residence as Punjab. The majority of the students with Punjabi caste names now come from more scattered locales. The same trend is discernible for the 1960s as a whole: North Indian domination but with declining numbers from (the Indian) Punjab itself.

Some explanation of the declining frequency of the occurrence of Punjabi towns in the *Record* may lie in the cataclysmic upheavals of the post-partition period. The migration of large numbers of Hindus from West (Pakistani) Punjab to East (Indian) Punjab effectively shifted the School's catchment area; the momentous dislocation of Punjabi (and other) populations which followed the carnage of 1947 in that region in the wake of partition also relocated the Hindu intelligentsia who were Doon's chief patrons. 'Six million Hindus and Sikhs from the West Punjab', as Tandon puts it, 'began to move in one dense mass towards safety, and from the east of the border a similar mass movement was under way in the opposite direction' (*ibid.*: 246).

Two other changes in the School's demographic profile for the decades immediately following Independence need to be noted. During the 1960s and the 1970s the occupational background of the boys' parents changed (in so far as can be determined) in favour of the upper echelons of the professional classes, men whose – often extravagant – perquisites of office were guaranteed by the nation state whose defenders, administrators, and 'organic intellectuals'[14] they had become: army officers, Indian Civil Service and (its successor) Indian Administrative Service officers, and corporate executives. Of those students at the School during the 1960s and 1970s who came from a professional background we can say this: they were no longer the sons of fathers who had 'started low' and then worked themselves up to the 'nirvana' of their service; their parents were members of a class which had, since Independence, acquired both considerable social capital and a firm grip on the levers of the licence-permit raj.[15]

There is considerable debate on the role and importance of the professional and bureaucratic groups in the life of the Indian nation state during the early and middle years of existence, and while this is an inappropriate venue for an extended discussion on the matter, some comment is necessary. My discussion of the 'second generation' Doon parents may be seen as coterminous with that provided by Bardhan (1984) on 'professional' classes in contemporary Indian society. However, while Bardhan suggests that conflicts might arise between the (upper) echelons of the state bureaucracy and the industrial bourgeoisie over the latter's attempt to maintain the system of state protection for domestic industry (the licence-permit raj of the Indian state's central planning regime), I would suggest that the permanent executive of the state has also been a beneficiary of this planning regime. And that in fact, a considerable part of its power and prestige derives from its intimate role in administering the system of rules and regulation which constitute a system of scarcity in the domestic context. And further, that members of this secure class (the groups identified in the previous paragraph) are linked to each other not merely through a common ideology and culture but also through ties of kinship; that there is an endogamous space which unites the secure classes and which includes not merely the professional groups referred to above but also a national intelligentsia in the usual sense of the term: journalists, academic and independent scholars, social workers, urban-based political activists, etc. It is this group – the secure classes – that comes to figure strongly in the second-generation parent category at Doon. The security of the secure classes lay in the interconnection ('social capital') of its members – of both kin and non-kin types – and in its ability to maintain its place in the cultural map of post-colonial modernity, i.e., to represent itself as indispensable in the process of acquiring modernity for a non-modern society.[16]

The second change in the composition of the School concerns the admission of sons of old boys to the School. In 1955 three of Doon's ex-students (from the class of 1936) sent their sons to their *alma mater*. In 1960, this number was nine, twelve in 1965, twenty-three in 1970, twenty in 1975, and twenty-four in 1976. From the early 1980s, however, there seems to be something of a decline in this trend, with just one admission each in the above category for the years 1983, 1985, and 1986. This does not mean, of course, a decline in the School's popularity. In fact, demand for admissions continues to grow unabated – a trend which in no small measure is linked to the emergence of a new clientele at the School during the 1980s.[17] This consists of a class which has had limited representation in the School rolls: small traders and businessmen, whose children are first-generation public school students and whose relevance in the context of the School will be discussed in the concluding chapter of this book.

The measure of things

The School's promise of producing a 'new' personality – one reiterated several times in the speeches at its inaugural function in 1935 – rested on the premise of a specific totality of action and thought which would animate the campus. In this section I seek to draw a connection between the student and parent population of the School (the teachers will be discussed in another context in the next chapter), and the earlier discussion on its 'rational' and 'scientific' universe. The latter, as I have suggested, is one of the fragments of the totality of the modern, post-colonised Indian identity. The identity project at the School was, and continues to be, part of a most comprehensive system of exchange and barter between different sections of the society, where the media of exchange are economic capital, cultural capital, and social capital.

In a letter to his son (then at Cambridge University) written in 1926, S.R. Das noted that to establish 'his' school he would require a sum of Rupees '25 to 30 lakhs'. He also mentioned that he 'was lunching with the Maharaja of Kashmir the other day, and all the Princes were there, including the Jamsaheb ("Ranji") were enthusiastic about it and offered to contribute towards the fund' (letter dated 2 Dec. 1926). In another letter he pondered whether he should accept an offer of land for the school: 'The Nawab of Bhopal is very keen that I should have it [the school] there. He has offered quite a good and suitable piece of ground free and he has offered a permanent endowment of Rs 30,000 a year if I have the school there' (letter dated 13 Nov. 1927)

Eventually, substantial financial donations were received from, among others, the Maharaja of Jammu and Kashmir, the Nizam of Hyderabad, the Maharaja of Jaipur, and the industrialist Sir Dorabjee Tata. There was, however, as should be clear from the preceding discussion, a sharp disjunction between the group which offered financial patronage to the School and the group which actually sent its sons to study there. It is for this reason that I have almost completely avoided the term 'elite' in discussing the circumstances surrounding the School's origins; the School was the cultural product of a process of cultural and political ferment, defined discursively within a framework of an emerging dialogue on modernity and its antithesis, rather than the reification of an established elite ideology.

The Doon School is the cultural corollary of two very distinct though intertwined processes. The first is linked to the process of the formation of a cultural class, enmeshed in the history of regional differences resulting from the differential impact of colonialism. The second process may be seen as part of a Marshallian *Weltanschauung* where the 'industrial group' becomes the repository of 'normal' action and the methods of industry – precision, classification, reduction – become the cornerstone of a general understanding of the world; where science – the sustenance of technology in its every-day application towards a mechanical end – becomes the logic of the every day even in its most generalised functioning. The epistemology of capitalism – with Alfred Marshall as its eloquent expostulator – refracted through the prism of scientific understanding, comes, then, to inform the comprehension of all areas of human existence. Thus, those associated with the School can say that the 'cultural' needs to be placed within the matrices of a mental and social space consciously created out of the mortar of the 'scientific attitude', 'understood as the application of "epistemological" thinking to acquired knowledge' (Lefebvre 1991: 4).

R.W., an ex-student then in his sixties whom we met earlier (p. 89), joined the School in 1937 at the age of ten. His family came from Lahore in the undivided Punjab and he was among the fourth intake of students. After finishing school R.W. obtained a degree in science from a North Indian University and joined a fledgling consumer goods company. He was the Boxwallah of Anglo-Indian vocabulary. He retired from the company after having reached the highest level of management, having, he said, 'built it with four or five others . . . from nine employees to . . . over two thousand when I left. . . . From a turnover of Rs two lakhs per year to Rs 152 crores.'[18]

R.W. left the corporate world to take up the Headmastership of the Doon School. Some of the parents, according to him, were not entirely happy at the choice of a 'non-educationist' for the Headmaster's position: 'a small number said "who is this coming into education . . . what does he know about education?"'. But the objections, as he emphasises, came from a very small number. The majority was happy with the choice of the new Headmaster. R.W.'s own views on his suitability for the position are anchored in a logos animated by, and situated at, the conjunction of 'industrial' activity and 'normal' action: the breadth of rationality and a stretch of the scientific imagination itself. He said:

> I wouldn't have left [the corporate world] if, for example, I had been offered the Headship of Mayo College . . . I came only because of Doon School . . . because I was a boy there and I had been on the Board of Governors since 1966. I was very actively involved in the School [*sic*] . . . I studied the financial reports . . . I helped the School, so, one day, the Board of Governors suggested that I run the School. When some of the parents objected that I didn't know anything about education . . . I answered that the fact that someone has taught in a classroom doesn't make him an educationist . . . [that person] may be totally ignorant of what's happening. . . . I don't claim to be an educationist, I claim to be a manager with common sense. I was equipped to deal with any situation,

having worked in an area connected with being methodical, precise . . . where everything must be accounted for . . . in a precise, clear manner.

When I joined the School I said: 'let us examine everything . . . and continue with things if they make sense . . . otherwise discontinue'. I proved that you don't have to be a so-called, in inverted commas, educationist. . . . I'll give you an example: one day the chemistry master asked me for some funds for the laboratory. I asked him how much and he replied that Rs 2000 would do. I said: 'how can you equip a laboratory with that sort of money?', and asked him how much he needed . . . he said Rs 6000. I said I'll give you Rs 10,000, he couldn't believe his ears . . . but I had done my homework, I knew the budget, the financial situation. So, they [the School] got quick decisions . . . clear, concise instructions and a scientific method of working . . . I had a different professional outlook.

The juncture at which the administrative manifestation of the scientific enterprise – double-entry book-keeping – translated the task of education into its own language and marked it with its own cadence, was one where some of the parents I spoke to themselves stood, and which they spoke of approvingly. S.M., whose son is currently at the School, and whom we met in chapter 3 in connection with his appraisal of the School's disciplinary system (p. 76), was one of those who saw R.W.'s methods as part of the ethos of a different epistemological universe. Disenchanted with the disciplinary aspects of day schools, S.M. said he had 'surveyed' three different residential public schools for his son's education and finally decided on Doon. 'I was greatly impressed', as he put it, 'with R.W.'s management style, he had clear, well-defined ideas . . . that's the difference between S.R. [R.W.'s successor] and R.W., the former is more of an academician [*sic*].'

R.W. retired from the corporate world a prosperous man. During his working life in the corporate sector he had, as is apparent from his long tenure on the Board of Governors of the School, kept in close touch with his *alma mater*. He had also, during that period, bought some land for a house as well as a 'farm'[19] in the Doon valley, and put his two sons through the School. Public school education in India is the most expensive form of primary and secondary education in the country, and between 1947 and 1968 – roughly the period during which R.W. and his sons studied at the School – fees at Doon rose by some 66 per cent (de Souza 1974: 34). R.W.'s own prosperity was planned for by parents of a very specific class, that which I have earlier referred to as the ascendant North Indian intelligentsia. It was predicated upon participation in post-colonial capitalist economy, perceived as pulsating to the rhythm of a *technocratic* beat. Throughout the School's history, a technocracy of opinion – the 'industrial' attitude – found a prominent place in the elaboration of its *Weltanschauung*; a general understanding of the world of human action became irretrievably bound to the imperatives of the 'scientific attitude'. The environment for the nurturance of this attitude was assiduously maintained and the significant social spaces of the School were industriously filled in with conversations and debates of a very specific sort. These spaces, we might say, became Euclidean spaces.

In 1948 there were some nineteen 'societies' at the School. These were meant to 'stimulate a fuller use of leisure, to cater for outside interests, to provide opportunities for discussion and for exploring by-paths that cannot be fully followed up in the classroom' (*Doon School Book* (*DSB*): 51). It was also their purpose, *The Doon School Book* notes, to 'vary the monotony of ordinary routine'. The extraordinary space which the societies sought to offer students, away from the routine of the every day with its practised thoughts and movements, was, however, contiguous to the overall self-imagined space of the School itself; the societies both contributed towards the collective consciousness of the School – in the sense of a coenaesthesis – as well as drawing from it.

Of the nineteen School societies in 1948, eight, in one way or another, were linked to the areas of science and mathematics. The Colloquium was the School's Mathematical Society. Its members were senior students who, at the meetings, 'read . . . papers on a variety of mathematical topics' (*DSB*: 51). The most common areas of discussion by the boys were: '(1) the history of Mathematics, (2) Relativity, (3) Mathematical Paradoxes and Fallacies, (4) Statistical Subjects, (5) Mathematics in relation to Engineering, (6) Astronomy' (*ibid.*). Boys who hoped to take up engineering as a career were encouraged to join the Engineering Society, and those with an interest in photography could become members of the Photography Society which was charged with 'the management of the dark room, and . . .[was]. . . gradually . . . accumulating more equipment' (*ibid.*: 52).

Among its other activities, the Geographical Society looked after weather reporting, a task it had taken over from the Naturalists' Society which, as noted in Chapter 3, undertook 'nature study' and organised 'frequent expeditions' in the Doon valley. Members of the Society also 'read' papers at its meetings. The Museum Society, run by Naturalists, was responsible for looking after the School's collection of 'stuffed birds, animals, butterflies and birds' eggs and a collection of armoury and of models and dresses of Baluchistan tribes' (*ibid.*: 52–3). The Scientific Society was founded in April 1937 and 'industrial chemistry' seems to have held a particular attraction for its members.[20] It organised tours to places of 'industrial' interest such as factories and large industrial complexes in the cities of Lucknow and Kanpur as well as holding an annual 'conversazione . . . at the end of summer term when exhibits and experiments are on view in the Chemistry, Physics and Biology laboratories' (*ibid.*: 54).

The activities of the Scientific Society were not, however, limited to the field of the strictly 'scientific': there was also an attempt to apply the vision of the laboratory to the organisation of every-day life; the endeavour to process the fleeting, seemingly normative, mêlée of every-day existence through a *novum organum* which was scientific thinking itself, and which would lead to a more precise understanding of the abstract and the normative. Among the exhibits at the *conversazione*, there were various kinds of apparatus 'devised to test people's muscular co-ordination, their ability at driving cars and one year the Scientists aspired to measure people's aesthetic tastes' (*ibid.*: 55).

More commonly, meetings of the Scientific Society provided the venue for papers on topics such as the 'Blood System' and 'Modern Lighting' (*Doon School Weekly* (*DSW*), 23 May 1923). In addition, the Fellows of the Scientific Society, with a smaller membership than the former, was organised to give senior students the opportunity to carry out work of 'an advanced nature'. It is tempting to attribute the various societies listed above to an attempt to emulate the mien of an English public school (and a perceived Oxbridge aspect). However, while this is no doubt part of the story, it is only a part, and we need to position the establishment and functioning of these societies as part of the endeavour by a rising Indian middle class to create a very specific space for itself.

The societies continue to function with considerable gusto in the present time. In October 1990 at the School's annual Founders Day, the Chief Guest, the Vice-President of India, was eagerly conducted around the various exhibitions mounted for the purpose; the greater proportion of space was given over to exhibitions dealing with scientific works 'of an advanced nature'. In the Chemistry section an elaborate arrangement of glass tubes, beakers, and Bunsen burners produced an ethereal display of chemical phenomena – a litmus conversion here, a sulphatic reaction there – much to the gratification of the appreciative audience made up of visiting parents and boys' relatives. The Physics section provided mechanical delights of its own and, just as in the Chemistry section, visitors were asked to participate in the experiments which formed part of the exhibition: 'to sample the force and reality of scientific principles at first hand', as one teacher remarked to me. The Biology room also provided immediate experiences of scientific phenomena: here visitors were invited to feel the contours of a chemically preserved human brain and administer electric shocks to earth worms suspended in an electricity conducting liquid. The object of the latter was explained to me in terms of furthering a more precise understanding of the nervous system. The audience could also witness the anatomical functioning of a freshly dissected frog pinned to a table, its heart palpitating to an irregular beat, and its muscles animated by spasms of mechanical energy.

The computer exhibition, a relatively recent addition to the Founders Day displays, also drew large and interested crowds. The two young teachers in charge of the display, one a physics master and the other an American university student on a short teaching assignment at the School, found an eager audience for their explanations of computer technology. With the accumulating perception of the importance of computers in daily life, and especially as to how knowledge of such technology might enhance future career prospects, this exhibition is bound to gain in interest. I provide the following extracts from an article on the Founders Day Science Exhibition for 1966 to emphasise the sense of continuity of the 'scientific tradition' at the school:

> Most of the onlookers did not quite grasp what was meant by benzoic acid sublime, but they gazed with surprise at the window of artificial snow on a very warm day; and so the chemistry department continued to wonder its visitors [*sic*]. . . . The lab was a bustle of chemical activity, but to us in school this was all familiar. . . .
>
> [In the biology department]. . . experiments to show the growth of plants under different soil conditions attracted visitors. . . .
>
> The wavelength theory was effectively shown in the ripple tank [at the physics exhibition]. Visitors lingered around the impressive aero-modelling displays while the wireless room with radio and inter-com sets caught the attention. A visit here was very refreshing; it fully showed some genuine scientific activity by boys in the Science Club and the labs.
>
> (*DSW*, 22 Oct. 1966)

The intellectual agenda of the post-colonised self at Doon had been set from the earliest days of the School's establishment. The arrangement of the time–space field at the School, what, following Bakhtin, I have called its various chronotopes, has contributed to very specific representations of this self. The chronotope of the scientific attitude or rationality – expressing 'the intrinsic connectedness of [certain] temporal and spatial relationships' (Bakhtin 1990: 84) – is a field of meaning constructed out of a specific time–space zone at the School. The spatial aspect – discussed at some length in the previous chapters – is linked to the very location of the School's campus in the history of scientific endeavours, to its former life as the Forest Research Institute and the continued elaboration of the 'scientific' theme within the School. The temporal aspect is expressed both through the every-day arrangement of time – the minute-by-minute accounting of the school day – and the passage of time between the day a boy enters the School and the day he finally leaves. 'Daily time' is fractional time: divided into discrete segments where a sequential order of the segments is prefigured. This is also, of course, the procedure of 'rational' activity, the method of science: the elaboration of the mechanical principle in time.

The total time spent at the School by a student is similarly perceived as fractional and segmented, though on a much larger scale. 'School-life' time, as we may call it, 'thickens' in its passage, 'takes on flesh, becomes . . . visible' (*ibid.*). This 'thickening' and this 'visibility' of the school time of each individual student, as both it and he begin their simultaneous journeys through the various stages of school life, become amenable to precise measurement; they too express an idea of science.

School time changes its objects, and it is this change which becomes measurable. The idea of the change that the time spent at School engendered in the students was expressed in several ways. One of these was the supposed change that a student underwent in terms of his attitude towards leisure. Here, the Other of School time was 'pre-school' time. The passage below expresses the idea of the qualitative difference between the student as he was at the beginning of his school life and his altered state at the end of his 'journey' at the School:

> On half holidays, and Sundays the three places [the music and the art schools and the workshop] are open to all boys. . . .[However]. . . only such boys avail themselves of the opportunities offered in the school as have realised the urge within them to express . . .[the]. . . instinctive enjoyment of beauty and a desire to conquer difficulties, and to shape out of hard wood and metal, objects that are both useful, and pleasing to the eye. There are many who have not yet learnt to use their leisure – whose idea of spending their spare time is either to play rounders or idly turn the pages of a picture magazine and suck chewing gum – but it takes time to form an interest when one's pre-school days have been spent unoccupied by any satisfying and engrossing activity.
>
> We feel [however] that with years the tastes of the boys have matured. . .
>
> (*DSB*: 45–50)

My use of the term 'journey' in the context of the School is also meant to emphasise the temporal dimension, which is perceived as transforming those who embark upon journeys The chronotope of the road is another in the inventory of chronotopes described by Bakhtin in his analysis of the novel:

> The chronotope of the road is both a point of new departures and a place for events to find their denouement. Time, as it were, fuses together with space and flows in it (forming the road); this is the source of the rich metaphorical expansion on the image of the road as a course: 'the course of a life,' 'to set a new course,' 'the course of history' and so on; varied and multi-levelled are the ways in which road is turned into a metaphor, but its fundamental pivot is the flow of time.
>
> (Bakhtin 1990: 243–4)

The Intelligence Test was one of the ways in which the effects of the passage of time at School were measured. In this way, *this* time, represented as accessible to the speculum of the scientific method, became a part of it; school time also became scientific time through both its measurability and its transformative capacity: after their passage through a sequential series of segmented time periods – the School calendar – the boys emerge transformed from one kind of being, as it were, to another; chronometry and psychometry combined towards a phenomenology of mappable subjectivity.

On 29 March 1943, the *Doon School Weekly* published results of 'Matrix' tests designed to measure the intelligence of the students – divided into age, religious, caste, and regional categories. Percentiles were provided under the headings 'Superior intellectual ability', 'Above average', 'Average', 'Below average', and 'Underdeveloped'. The students were further categorised according to whether they were 'Moslems', 'Brahmins', 'Kshatriyas', or 'other Hindu Castes', and according to the professional background of fathers and their region of origin. Headmaster Foot elaborated on the results as follows:

> The percentile gives the percentage of scores in the grade given and lower grades i.e. 79% of all the scores are in grade II or lower. Thus a high percentile means a larger percentage of scores below a certain standard.
>
> The variations in the percentile of boys of different regions are small and not at all significant. It appears, however, that *many new boys* have a very low score, and after a year in the school the number of low scores is much reduced, though owing to age, they have not yet reached the normal number of high scores.
>
> (emphasis added)

In the following issue of the *Weekly*, the Headmaster offered his concluding remarks on the tests. 'In the column for professions', he said

> it appears that the children of people in the services and learned professions have smaller numbers in the lower grades, but towards the top the difference is less marked. This suggests that these parents pay more attention to the . . .[pre-school]. . . training of their children, *but that the training of a good school tends to bring the others upto the same standard* and that the people in the services . . . [do not] . . . have a hereditary monopoly of brains.
>
> (emphasis added)

A.K. was a senior student at the School during my stay there in 1990. Active in the Drama Society as well as an organiser for the Doon School branch of Amnesty International, he was one of my regular acquaintances on campus. He was one of a group of senior students at the School with whom I interacted on a relatively friendly basis. He referred to me by my first name and would often drop into my room for a 'chat'. I had been given accommodation in the same House as A.K. and hence our interactions were quite frequent.

As A.K. was in the final year of his life at the School, a life he felt was profoundly shaped by the School, our conversations often turned to how he felt he had changed during this period. One of his frequent refrains on this issue was how the School had helped to settle the 'confusion' he experienced when thinking about 'the world'. 'During my first few years at Doon', he would say, 'I was really confused.' But slowly, the measured cadence of life at the campus had changed him into a person 'who is able to sort out . . . issues

. . . and come to clear conclusions'. He often stated his belief that every single year at the School had had an accumulating effect on his personality and intellect, that the passage of each major temporal segment of his life at the School – the academic year – could be measured in the steady transformation of his being. He believed, he said, that 'very definite things' happened to every one who 'went through' the School. He didn't think, he would say, that from one year to the next a boy at the School 'remained the same'; time at School was not circular and hence unquantifiable in terms of changes in the boys, but rather it moved in a straight line, 'thickening' along its course, becoming quantifiable in the units of 'intelligence' or 'ability'.

The Doon School and the city of Dehra Dun complement each other in the most beguiling series of characteristics. However (and this can only be put forward as a speculative hypothesis) perhaps the parallelism is not just a matter of fortuity and may have its roots in conscious design. For the chosen site for an institution designed to prepare 'modern', 'scientific' citizens was located in a city which was already host to an evocative geography of modernity, the material manifestations of an episteme which, since the European Enlightenment, had come to establish great sway over the indigenous intelligentsia of colonised societies such as India.

As I have indicated earlier, it was at Dehra Dun that the offices of the Survey of India were located. In one of its preceding incarnations as the Great Trigonometrical Survey of India, it had, '. . . come into its own in 1830 under Lieutenant Colonel Sir George Everest . . . [and had]. . . fixed with great accuracy the longitude and latitude of a large number of places' (Kochar 1991:1928). It was also from Dehra Dun that the altitude of Mount Everest was computed. Like the School, which had found accommodation at the former premises of the Forest Research Institute 'laid out like a park for purposes of administration, lectures [and] scientific experimentation' (*Times of India*, 28 Oct. 1935 (hereafter *TOI*)), the city too was situated within a politico-scientific matrix. It was here also that in 1878 the Survey of India carried out its first experiments in 'solar photography' – the photographs 'sent to England for analysis' (Kochar 1991:1930). The relationship between the School and the various 'scientific' establishments located in the city, including the Military College, was an active one, a process through which it conjoined its 'ethos' to their episteme. Membership of this episteme also became a matter of concern for a provincial intelligentsia – Doon's clientele – striving for metropolitan status. In turn, this episteme came to inform views within the School on a large range of topics, not the least of which concerned the matter of 'Indian culture'; or, perhaps more accurately, on the issue of its delimitation and 'control'.

A.K.B. was the Head of the music department at the Doon School for ten years in the late 1970s. A former performance artiste himself he joined the School, he said, because he was also interested in teaching and 'making young people aware of Indian culture'.[21] Despite the fact that from its earliest days the School has had a strong emphasis on 'the arts' – both performing and fine – A.K.B. conceded that none of the School's alumni had gone on to professional careers as musicians. A handful have, however, achieved prominence as painters and sculptors. V.S., perhaps the most prominent among the younger generation of painters in India, is one of these. He suggested to me that though the foundations of his skill may have been laid during his school years, the latter had not influenced his choice of career. On the contrary, he said, 'when I told people that I wanted to become a painter and wanted to go to an art school, they were quite aghast and suggested that if I was interested in drawing I should take up draughtsmanship, and pursue art as a hobby'. The cultural sphere at the School seems always to have existed within a zone defined by, what might be called, the imperatives of rational activity. The School has always had both outstanding facilities for the teaching of performance and fine arts and extremely qualified personnel to provide instruction. The first art master at Doon was Shantiniketan-trained Sudhir Khastgir, who achieved considerable national fame as an artist and, at the invitation of the state government of Uttar Pradesh, became Principal of the Government Arts College at Lucknow in 1956. 'There was little doubt', the introduction to a booklet on his life and work points out, 'that the parents and the guardians of students of Doon School had immense regard for the art master of their son and knew how liberating was his influence over the children.'[22]

But this 'liberating' influence itself was incarcerated within very strict boundaries of a technocratic regime at the School, a regime which drew from the 'urge to modernity' at the national level during the School's early years, and contributed to it, through the prominence of its students – journalists, academics, and others – in its 'mature' phase. The every-day manifestation of this incarceration lies in the portrayal of 'culture' as a set of practices removed from the practice of 'rational' existence and hence marginal to it. Modernity suffered the 'artistic' as an expression of the 'irrational' that needed to be controlled as part of the citizenship project in the age of the post-colonial nation state.

The attitude of the students at the School towards subjects such as painting and music is one of both bemusement and condescension. For the majority, classes in the music and art departments constitute a 'soft' option. The association of these subjects with aspects of femininity is a frequent response in discussions about them; with the sure momentum of a self-fulfilling stereotype, painting and music classes at the School tend to attract a high proportion of the girl students (i.e. the daughters of Doon teachers). Also, music and art teachers tend to have a limited say in the general running of the School, their activities confined to their immediate domain and in the organisation of choral performances or art exhibitions for specific events such as Founders Day. The place of 'culture' in the life of the School in its early days seems to have been quite similar to that which it has now. I asked R.W. his opinion of some of the Indian teachers at the school when he was a student there from 1937 to 1944. Specifically, I enquired about three early teachers, one a philosophy graduate from Oxford, and two others – art and music teachers respectively – trained at Tagore's Shantiniketan. R.W. confined his comments to the music teacher: ah, yes, he said 'Shirodhkar was Shantiniketan trained, trained by Tagore . . . a fine singer . . . but we didn't have much time for Shirodhkars . . .'.

Debates and discussions in the various School publications spoke of the necessity of saturating the grounds of culture with the ether of science, and the importance of rupturing its opaque fabric with the sharp instrument of 'method' such that the abstract and the wildly luxuriant (the Orient itself) became comprehensible: 'the conjunction', as Baudrillard might say, 'of desire and value, of desire and capital . . . of desire and the law' (Baudrillard 1988:176). In a chapter of *The Doon School Book* entitled 'Arts, Crafts, Music and Drama', the following descriptions of the work at the 'workshop' are offered:

> [Here]. . . the boys can try their hands at making anything . . . even a piece of delicate scientific apparatus . . . but the boys were not content with making mere wall-pegs and ink stands out of *Cedurus deodara* or even *Pinus excelsea*; nothing short of beautifully finished writing bureaux or china cabinets of *Cedera toona* or *Dulbergia sissoo* would satisfy them.
>
>   . . . the patient, practical scientists availed themselves of the various machines that had been installed as years passed, in making apparatus for the science laboratories, or for making exhibits for the annual science exhibition.
>
> (*DSB*: 47)

Of interest in the above passage is not merely the statement of the ends to which the boys are seen to put their artistic endeavours, but also the positioning of the latter in a descriptive complex marked by the scientific authority of the 'sacred language' – once sacred in the religious sense and now in the service of science – of the new episteme; each kind of wood is given its botanical name, as if in an act of inscribing the cultural with the spirit of the scientific.

The prescriptions of the scientific attitude carry the imperatives of an ineluctable momentum towards a pruning of the 'unmanageable', and the precise ordering of the diffuse; modernity as the urge to systematise 'luxuriance' and reduce heterogeneity. It was as if with a felicitous sense of occasion that, in the very year of Indian political independence, 1947, the Headmaster-designate of the Doon School, John Martyn, chose to share his views on the most appropriate cultural accoutrements for a 'modern' nation; that, in other words, which befitted the needs of a progressive attitude, through which the post-colonised nation might take its place among other 'rational' communities of the world. With extraordinary confidence – almost a religious zeal with its own cosmological consciousness – Martyn declared in a *Weekly* article that 'Indian culture seems to me to be vast, unwieldy and diffuse' (*DSW*, 31 May 1947). Further, it seemed to him that it was precisely due to this 'diffuseness' that 'it [Indian culture] has less impact on [life] today and therefore less value in practice'. The needs of 'today' and the imperatives of 'practice' dictated, according to the first post-Independence Headmaster of the school which had caught the imagination of the rising intelligentsia of the country, a 'reorganisation' of the cultural arena to be inhabited by citizens of the nation whose arrival was, now, imminent.

First, Martyn provided a diagnostic exegesis touching upon several aspects of the problem: 'When one looks back to the [Indian] past', he said, 'one's gaze becomes lost in the vastness and obscurity of ages whose history is not yet fully known':

> This is not a demerit but it is a disadvantage. Culturally, Europe looks back to a single city, Athens, whose life and thought still shines for us with amazing clarity. . . . [there is also a wider familiarity with] Roman authors in Europe today than there is in India with ancient Indian litera-ture mainly because the former falls within a more manageable compass. . . . in comparison Indian scriptures are much less compact. . . . It is symptomatic that India should have produced the longest epic in history.
> (*DSW*, 31 May 1947)

European music, Martyn suggested, is also marked by a compactness and precision which makes its absorption into the general milieu a much easier task than is the case with Indian music:

> The history of European music is largely the history of not many more than a dozen great composers. Knowing something about them as most people do they can use them as landmarks in their study of music. There appear to be no comparable landmarks in Indian music.
> (*DSW*, 31 May 1947)

And what of the history of European public aesthetics, the account of its achievements in the field of architecture? It too exists, Martyn suggests, in a space of ordered sequences and through a finite narrative, along with a '. . . more coherent and a well known history of its development from classical to Gothic and back to classical motives again' (*ibid.*).

That an 'educated man' must have knowledge of the arts is, he continued, an indispensable part of civilised existence. The task must be to reduce the cultural in the Indian context to 'manageable' dimensions by subjecting it to the scrutiny of the scientific mind and pruning its excrescence. 'This problem of Indian culture', he concluded, 'concerns us in the Doon School; it con-cerns all those of us who are connected with education': 'It [Indian culture] needs to be edited, clipped, trimmed, reduced to manageable proportions.'[23]

There were other contributions as well to the School's discourse on the various routes, as it were, to the realms of science. The debate over the adoption of Roman scripts for Hindi also echoed the sentiments of scientific necessity. 'The adoption of the Roman script', one contributor to the *Weekly* wrote, 'would be the most practical and convenient way of incorporating scientific formulae and technical terms in our language.' Citing Turkey as an example, the author concluded that 'They have adopted the Roman script and this has enabled them to advance very much more scientifically . . . than they would have done otherwise' (*DSW*, 9 Mar. 1946).

The un-mysterious East

A crucial difference between the 'classic' English public school and its Indian counterpart – often regarded as a simple imitation of the former – is that the latter contained at its core, right from the moment of its inception, an essentially technocratic ethos. It is not, I think, a crude generalisation to suggest, as others have, that notwithstanding the broader framework of 'scientism' which foreshadowed discourses of British identity (as discussed e.g. by Mangan 1987), the heart of the English public school system was, essentially, non-technocratic (Mangan 1986a 1986b; Vance 1985).[24] This difference between the two systems of education points to one of the specificities of the post-colonised condition. Historically, the difference – technocratic versus non-technocratic – can be explored by situating the focus of analysis at that juncture where the aspirations of an indigenous, and incipient, educated class collided with the restrictive levee of a colonial cultural and political economy; its continued sway may be attributed to the ideological and material momentum of the nation state launched in the waters of 'rational' existence.

The four largest categories of parents which provided students for the School, as discussed earlier, were, respectively, bureaucrats, doctors, lawyers, and engineers. In fact, these four categories between them accounted for approximately 60 per cent of the student intake. The representation of these occupations on the School's rolls has remained constant through the decades. Through the figures on the background of parents provided earlier, I wished to point to those 'mundane' crevices of indigenous colonial existence that provided the nurturing space for a particular national identity. In light of my discussion on religion at the School, I would like to suggest that this identity itself was constructed in the vivid, abstract, colours drawn from a 'spiritual' past and a utopian, scientific future.

The national identity under discussion here was constructed, I suggest, not to be a *transcendent* identity – as nationhood and nationality are usually discussed – irreducible to any concrete manifestations of specific practice. On the contrary, this was a national identity that is marked by a willingness to be deconstructed, to lay bare its heart and offer its 'essence' for observation. For this is a national identity of redemption: it constructed a certain category of the native population as certain types of human beings in *opposition* to the prevailing generalisation of the native character and spirit by the British. It posited as its heart a 'rational', technocratic spirit. Hence in the every-day unfolding of its being at the School it makes its moorings quite explicit, its core quite apparent: it is a redemptive core, reinterpreting upper caste Indian identity and constructing it as no different from the *Homo scientificus* of the 'progressive' regions of the world, but still, Indian.

It also reinterprets, in the process, the nature of the state itself, the ideological laboratory of the intelligentsia under discussion. The School served and continues to serve as a *tableau vivant* where this experiment could be observed and applauded. Perhaps one of the most striking instances of this experiment is the Doon School orchestra that accompanies the singing of songs and prayers at morning assembly. The orchestra is made up entirely of Indian instruments. As an attempt to mediate between the harmonic and the melodic styles of music, the orchestra is also an attempt to mediate between two worlds: through this visible metaphor the 'scientific' world of western harmony is encompassed by the 'spiritual' world of the eastern melody.

For the School's identity project to claim that nationalism and national identities have a mysterious, undefinable core, would have been far too much akin to that very image of the entirely Other worldly native which was the dominant trope of colonial discourse on Oriental societies; the School saw as its most important task the undermining of this very perspective, and to offer an alternative image of Indianness. It was, then, not surprising that the most ardent disciples of such a nationalism should have been a class which had managed to secure employment in those very areas anointed with the approving gaze of the rational-scientific spirit. The engineers, accountants, bureaucrats, chemists and others who formed the nucleus of the group most strongly represented at the School were not just men involved in any activity: they were involved in *useful*, *practical* activity and translated the aura of their profession as rational men of this world to the task of reconstructing the image of the 'native' himself.

I have suggested earlier that the colonial techno-scientific landscape created by the British through the topography of research institutions and scientific surveys was also a tool of self-representation. Here, the physical activities of the men who worked in these organisations – their steely vision charged by both a precision and a clarity of method – was gradually transformed into a living metaphor for western subjectivity itself. The outer world of human activity came to represent the inner world of human existence. The necessity of co-opting this world into the framework of a new national identity was not an unfamiliar project for a certain class of Indians. For, employed as they were in professions imbued with the imperatives of both capitalism and a new scientific age – to order, to count, to classify, to account for, and to operate on the natural world with the instruments and methods of science – they already considered themselves a part of the privileged world of scientific and utilitarian thought and harbingers of a new identity, an identity free of the shackles of the native stereotype.

In the discussion above, I have tried to point to what I perceive to be an indispensable aspect of the Indian national identity under discussion. I am not, of course, suggesting that this is the only national identity in circulation in India; there are other ways of thinking 'Indian' – each variously influenced by such factors as socio-economic conditions, the urban–rural divide, and regional cultural differences. What I am suggesting, however, is that the national identity project at the Doon School is one which has and continues to have considerable influence within a wide cross-section of people. An important aspect of its appeal lies in the nature of the symbols employed in the performance of school life that establishes a distinct aura of modernity. These, I have suggested, should be seen not just as mimicry but as a conscious mixing of the 'Oriental' with the 'Occidental'. And finally, that this national identity project has been organised around a technocratic and utilitarian mould. My implied objective has also been to link the construction of this new Indian identity, couched in the vocabulary of Rationality and Spiritualism, to the aspirations of power and authority emanating from the ascendant, 'mundane' classes.

I will conclude the discussion of this chapter with an extract from a letter by S.R. Das, written over seventy years ago, to his son in England. In the letter he talks of his visit to the Indian-owned Tata Iron and Steel Works in the North Indian city of Jamshedpur. In the following few words Doon's founder provided a tantalising glimpse of the ethos which came to occupy the heart of the national identity project at the Doon School:

> . . . there are fine young Indians there particularly Bengalee, employed in and about the Works. Employed as Engineers, Chemists, etc . . .
>
> (letter dated 13 Jan. 1927)

The missive is anchored in the images of a post-colonial cosmos of the nation state: an industrial landscape ('Works') occupied and administered by *men* of science – the 'fine young Indians', note the elision of class identity – and the entire landscape itself expressed as part of the ichnography of the city. Jamshedpur, the industrial city established by the industrial dynasty of the Tatas, is an apt spatial metaphor – and all specific spaces have their unique temporal dimensions as well – for the realm which Das, and later his School, came to construct as the realm of the post-colonised citizen. He also returns us to the exploration of space with which this chapter began, and the canal colony, the Doon School, and the industrial city are forcefully joined as contiguous spaces.

It is to images of the city, and of the metropolitan man, that I turn in Chapter 6 in order to examine the remaining fragment – as far as the discussion of this book is concerned – of the post-colonised identity which Doon School saw itself charged with the task of nurturing.

6 The order of men: sentiments of the metropolis, settlements of civil society

There is by now an elaborate – though largely unanalysed – history of representations of the metropolis in Indian life. As the complex site of modernist sanguinity, of Gandhian cautionary tales regarding the pitfalls of modernity, and as the ambiguous *mise-en-scène* of Hindi films – both threatening and alluring – the metropolis as image has constituted an important aspect of representations of the Indian post-coloniality and nationhood. And, when its presence is not *directly* figured in these texts, it attends the narrative as the improving efforts of the city-educated son come home to the village, the cynical glance of the allopath upon the wiles of the 'traditional' healer, as the 'fast' urbanised young women visiting the countryside, and as the national highway in films and novels which, every villager knows, leads to the urban beyond; like *waitaal*, the poltergeist from the North Indian children's folk tale whose cunning keeps the hapless king Vikramditya in his unremitting service, the metropolis foreshadows post-colonial subjectivity as spectre, morality tale, and an allegory of possibilities.

Perhaps the most enduring presence of the metropolis as an idea occurs in the corpus of Hindi films made in the decades immediately following political freedom from colonial rule in 1947. In films such as *Shri 420* (1955, Raj Kapur), *New Delhi* (1956, Mohan Segal), *Sujata* (1959, Bimal Roy) and *Anuradha* (1960, Hrishikesh Mukherjee), the struggle over meaning and being in a post-colonial society takes place in a context where the metropolis is always a wilful presence; so, whereas it is the decadence of the urban milieu which structures Raj Kapur's *Shri 420*, the other three films are paeans to the liberating and progressive sway of a masculine modernity which is the influence of the city. Here the city is a *novum organum*: it magically transforms – through the work of the logical medical man, and the rational university graduate – the life of ignorance, superstition, and venality which marked the cinematic village.

In these films, the aura of the metropolis manifests itself through a new language of cinematic space, one where striation and secularisation become important expressive principles. *New Delhi*, which we have had occasion to discuss earlier, is a good example of the manifestation of the striated spatial sensibility of the post-Independence film. Through its opening shots, as the camera looks out from a car being driven along an urban boulevard, it establishes the sense of the modern nation (which the hero hopes to discover in the matrix of the city, New Delhi) as a measured grid of roads, traffic lights, and footpaths. And indeed, like Nevsky Prospect in nineteenth-century Russian literature (Berman 1988), the streets of the newly planned post-colonial city also provide the spatial ambience of the film; the camera and the hero, and with them the audience, move along these wide thoroughfares which meet at calculated angles, a progression marked by the various symbols of a visible modernity of city planning. We are in the realm of planned space, at a juncture where state intervention and a geometrical sensibility of modernity produce a peculiarly post-colonial nationalist aesthetics.[1]

The specular mode of filmic representation that seeks to express the aura of the city is linked, on the other hand, to the penetrative capacities of the modern male body. In *Sujata* and *Anuradha*, for example, it is the male 'improver' who is set down in – or rather travels out to – the countryside. Here, the male body, imbued with the transformative powers of the metropolis – his 'natural' habitat – sets about unsettling the preconceptions of non-urban milieux, mortifying habits of millennia with the prod of the new; what is on display, of course, is the supposed transformative power of individualism (a metropolitan virtue, as the films narrate it) against the stultifying impact of (non-urban) communal life. The male body is a projectile, clearing the way for a national space and effacing the embarrassment of backward spaces (and 'mentalities') with searing speed and unstoppable forward – always 'forward' – momentum.

Sometimes – as in *Anuradha* – during this work of the penetration of the province with the masculine method of the urban milieu, the hero faces obstructions to his rational enterprise and his relentlessness in the service of modernity is interrupted by the unreasonableness of feminine demands; Anuradha, the wife in the eponymous film, is increasingly agitated that her doctor husband's preoccupation with serums and diseases leaves him no time for her company. A former singing star, who had given up her own career to follow the idealistic doctor to a small village, she now begins to question his neglect towards her. Appropriately, the imbroglio achieves its denouement through the pronouncements of a 'renowned' doctor visiting from the city that Anuradha's husband's work is of foundational importance to the nascent nation state; and that her role is to provide the adequate succour so that her husband's work may continue unabated. Here, it is possible to read the figure of the wife as the passive femininity of the province itself such that Anuradha (= art = province = feminine) must suppress her subjectivity for the important work of science and rationality (= husband = the metropolis); the woman is, once again, 'tradition', who must be kept 'pure' from modernity but must not, concurrently, stand in the way of its implementation.

In this chapter I link these issues to a discussion of the image of the nation fashioned at the Doon School. I will argue that the image of the nation at Doon is inextricably enmeshed in pageants of the city: the metropolis as the

fulfilled dream of modernity. And that metropolis here is not merely a conglomeration of specific spatial practices, 'which embraces production and
reproduction' (Lefebvre 1994: 32–3), i.e. physical and material flows – but
also a configuration of 'social inventions . . . that seek to generate new
meanings of possibilities for social practices' (Harvey 1989a: 261).

Roads, rubble, and sites of modernity

As epigraph to the discussion, I want to present an abridged version of a
Hindi short story by Mithileshwar (1993), in which the construction of a
pucca road through a village comes to represent, in a synecdochical manner,
the luscious promises of general well being, the anticipation of the comforts
and the good life of the metropolis, and the cornucopia of modernity. In his
pithy rendering of the fate of the 'non-modern' in its encounters with the
cunning of modernity, Mithileshwar writes a chapter on the cultural politics
of metaphors in the realm of the post-colonised nation state; and through a wry
turn of historical and sociological sensitivity, he extends the Bakhtinian idea
of the chronotope of the road in unexpected and original ways. The road, in
Mithileshwar's 'Between dead-end streets' (Bund raston ke beech), is the
mark of the ferocious manoeuvres modernity – in this case, the insurmount-
able absolutism of the Indian nation state implementing 'development' –
practises on 'non-modern' populations.

When the villager Jagesar comes to know of government plans to lay a
bitumen road through his village, he considers his days of misery over. With
alacrity he organises the conversion of a small shed he owns by the side of the
proposed road-site into a tea-stall so as to service the expected flow of traffic.
He borrows heavily for the construction work, happy in the knowledge that in
the coming days he will not only be able to repay the debt but also have a
secure source of continuing income. The road becomes metonymic with well
being, and the village begins to hum with good-natured envy at Jagesar's turn
of fortune.

The new road and the refurbished shop constitute a fragment of the iconography of modernity, and wedged between them lie Jagesar's hopes of
subjecthood, of freedom from the savage constraints of his marginal existence in the village. But then, one day, Jagesar is visited by government officials inquiring after the ownership of the refurbished tea-stall. Why did he
build his house there? they ask him. But this is not a recent construction, he
responds, 'this is my ancestral house'. The building has got to go, Jagesar is
informed, for the road is to be inaugurated soon and there are orders that
there are to be no buildings 10 feet to either side of it. Jagesar pleads
with the officials: 'it has been there since my grandfather's time'; but the
geometry of modernity brooks no interference and the stall is demolished.
Jagesar's future has slipped away, reduced to the rubble of his shop.

The account of this chapter – a story of sorts – concerns the construction
of a narrative of the metropolis – and of modernity – on a wider scale than

that in Mithileshwar's story. It is an account of the grafting of the narrative of the metropolis to that of 'civil' post-colonial existence. I have, in effect, sought to supplement Mithileshwar's story through treating the Doon School as a *tableau vivant* of the metropolis, in an effort towards an exploration of the bond which unites modernity and the functioning of capital; and the manner in which it marginalises those who are seen to fall outside its ken. For this is the 'problem' with people such as Jagesar: in awaiting the largesse of modernity with earnestness, they assume the neutrality of capital.

The objectified province and the metropolitan imaginary

The Doon School discourse on the metropolis is, as I have outlined above, part of a wider dialogue on Indianness. In this dialogue, the metropolis, its concrete presence apart, is also a settlement of the mind: an imagined configuration of desires and comforts, hopes and projections; a specific way of viewing the unfolding of both every-day human life and the more distant future in which these lives may find their destinies. This process of imagining the city is also bound to what might be called the fetishism of the metropolis. It is a fetishism in which the metropolis functions as a sign. This fetishism has as its *deus ex machina* the 'spirit' of the metropolis which transcends its objective reality – the relations of power and exploitation which characterise the contemporary city – and takes on a life of its own.

The fetishism of the post-colonised metropolis is contained both in the unofficial images of the media and the official pronouncements of policy makers. It appears, and lodges itself in public thought during the process of the transformation of the metropolitan idea from the realm of use-value – lived experience – to that of the commodity, the commodity which forms part of the discourse of the post-colonised nation state. It is then that the metropolis becomes 'a very queer thing, abounding in metaphysical subtleties and theological niceties . . . [taking on] an enigmatical character' (Marx 1978: 76). The metropolitan theme in the discursive realm which constitutes the arena of citizenship and nationhood progresses through an effacement of the concrete subject in favour of 'the abstract subject, the cogito of the philosophers' (Lefebvre 1994: 4). The Doon model of the citizen – the metropolitan man – occupies that metropolitan habitat which exists as a fetishised 'philosophico-epistemological notion of space . . . [and where]. . . the mental realm comes to envelop the social and physical ones' (Lefebvre 1994: 5).[2]

The valorisation of the metropolitan milieu in India would seem to be coeval with the formation of a 'national' consciousness. During the period of the nationalist movement in India it was not just an abstract Indian nation which was being 'imagined', but a nation with a very specific metropolitan identity; its inhabited spaces animated by the spirit of a supposed rupture between the 'backward' and the 'progressive', and its inhabitants alive to the necessity and the incontrovertibility of a new temporal regime.

This metropolitan model of national identity was, however, contested at its birth, and through the various stages of its maturation. Paradoxically though, it drew its sustenance from this contestation, and eventually triumphed at the very moment that its opposition – the provincial or the non-metropolitan model – provided the most cogent picture of an alterity. The reasons for this lie in the objectivist and essentialist arguments employed by the critics of the metropolitan model of Indian post-coloniality.

In presenting the case for an alternative model of national life – encompassing, *inter alia*, the education system, a national language, and the methods of the creation and distribution of private and public wealth – this latter perspective also constructed certain typologies of non-metropolitan life. The metropolitan project at the Doon School operates through an engagement with these very typologies as *static* categories, a characterisation made possible through the initial taxonomic act of political 'non-metropolitans' such as Gandhi. Specifically, it was the establishment of a series of binary oppositions between the milieu of the metropolis and that of the non-metropolis – all the emotional and political evocations contained in the debates which presented the symbolic opposition between the mill and *Khadi* cloth – that set the stage for the 'modern' nation state's assault on the 'primitivisms' within it. The point is this: the proponents of the alternative point of view, those who sought to contest the modernist *Weltanschauung* of the state, presented their case in such terms as to reduce its actors to passive caricatures. They presented their protagonists and their life worlds as changeless, their actions to be judged according to some predetermined and static morality and world view. The view of the non-metropolis as a zone of morals and goodness was an objectivism that undermined its own position.

In a different context, Metcalfe speaks of the 'logic [that] underlies the work of all theorists who *analyse* society as they might analyse an organism or thing' (Metcalfe 1988: 13, emphasis in the original). This line of analysis proceeds, he suggests, as if 'workers are merely the bearers of a proletarian essence', and that 'history' can simply be 'read off' in a mechanical manner from these essential qualities. The proponents of the non-metropolis similarly objectified the rural/provincial figure that was meant to provide the alternative model of the post-colonial citizen. Imbued with a static morality and made part of a fixed, absolute world view, he/she came to be constructed more as a caricature of the 'ideal' citizen, rather than as an individual negotiating life between the bounds of structures and the imperatives of agency. If Nehru was the *flâneur* of metropolitan fetishism, then Gandhi,[3] no less, provided the text for the objectification of 'non-metropolitan' India.

For Gandhi, the *Khadi* programme was the blueprint for national regeneration in material and moral as well as spiritual terms. The spinning wheel would provide not merely the mechanics of personal prosperity to pauperised villagers, but also stood for the fabrication of a symbolic web knitting the entire Indian population into the seamless fabric of a moral community. The discussions on the importance of the *Khadi* programme became a platform for comparisons of the metropolitan 'ethos' with that of the 'non-metropolis'.[4]

The All-India Spinners' Association, Gandhi suggested, could be instrumental in providing employment to those villagers who, in the absence of gainful employment in their immediate localities, were forced to migrate to urban centres. He further noted that villagers worked in cities under 'immoral' conditions, and returned to their villages 'bringing with them corruption, drunkenness and disease' (Gandhi 1927a: 108). The villager here is represented as a passive object who becomes 'infected' with the contagion of the metropolis, a contagion which exists as some kind of an essence apart from the social and political life – the exposed injuries of class and capital and the hidden exploitations of caste – in which the inhabitants of the metropolis are embroiled. The corollary of this view was, of course, that the 'non-metropolis' has its own essence, its own spirit.

In the wake of the adoption of the *Khadi* spirit, Gandhi noted, village artisans will find local employment, and 'will then find themselves reinstated in their ancient dignity, as is already happening wherever the spinning wheel has gained a footing' (*ibid.*).

Gandhi was not, of course, the sole contributor to the objectifying metropolis versus non-metropolis discourse. His colleague and fellow nationalist, C. Rajagopalachari asserted that 'the peasants of India . . . are gentle, industrious and good folk', and that their enforced migration to the cities had turned 'such people' into 'victims of vice' with debilitating effects on the 'national programme' (Gandhi 1928: 756).

In this defence of the non-metropolis, it is as if the subjectivity of those who occupy it is effaced from the scene of action and they become merely objects constantly acted upon. Their defence by Gandhi and Rajagopalachari becomes the defence of a timeless essence. This leads, in other areas of discussion, to their transformation into strategic caricatures upon the surface of a montage of the 'pre-modern' that becomes the urgent task of modernity to transform. The sympathisers of the non-metropolis can be seen, in this way, to be complicit in the production of those very ideas about the so-called non-modern world that they wish to dispute.

Objectivism, Bourdieu suggests, subjects practice to a 'fundamental and pernicious alteration', and through 'withdrawing from [the action] in order to observe it from above and from a distance, [it] constitutes practical activity as an *object of observation and analysis, a representation*' (Bourdieu 1977: 2, emphasis in the original). In the Indian situation, the contested terrain of national identity – metropolitan versus non-metropolitan, 'modern' versus the 'pre-modern' – was, paradoxically, queered in favour of the metropolitan/ modern by those very groups who sought to present an alternative to the dicta of the modernists.

The championing of the *Khadi* programme, in itself a fundamental critique of the organisation of civil society and the pauperisation of large sections of the non-metropolitan population, was elaborated through an essentialist moral schema which reduced its constituents to the state of passive observers, the noble primitives. The post-colonised Indian state, administered by the potentates of an intellectual estate with its chiliastic shrines to the 'scientific attitude' and 'progress', found the task of constructing its Other already accomplished; its putative quarry turned out to be a mere shadow of the active subject, instead of the 'ever-baffled and ever-resurgent [agent] of an unmastered history' (E.P. Thompson quoted in Metcalfe 1988: 211).

One of the ways in which we might visualise the relationship between thinkers such as Gandhi and Rajagopalachari and the non-metropolis they sought to represent (i.e., defend) is through reference to the established relationship, increasingly under scrutiny, between anthropologists and 'their' villages. A recent example of the on-going critique of the house that anthropology built is provided by Gupta and Ferguson who note that 'representations of space in the social sciences are remarkably dependent on images of break, rupture, and disjunction' (1992: 6). The social sciences, they suggest, posit 'the distinctiveness of societies, nations and cultures upon a seemingly unproblematic division of space, on the fact that they occupy naturally discontinuous spaces' (*ibid.*). The lack of problematisation within anthropology of a 'spatialized understanding of cultural difference', they further argue, has, notwithstanding 'sensitive' efforts to the contrary, led to a subtle nativisation of the Other and the latter has come to be strait-jacketed through its confinement 'in a separate frame of analysis' (*ibid.*: 14).

In keeping with their professed empathy and concern to give the non-metropolis a voice, we could figuratively refer to Gandhi and Rajagopalachari as its anthropologists. The inherently discrete space assumed in their discussions of *their* villages and the city denies the interconnected nature of the two and, along with it, the possibility of questioning the 'radical separation between the two that [made] the opposition possible in the first place' (*ibid.*). The case *for* the non-metropolis, as presented in Gandhi's dialogue against the city, elides in other words, a more fundamental critique of the particular sensibility of space which characterised the debates on national identity; what was side-stepped was the issue of 'exploring the process of *production* of difference in a world of culturally, socially, and economically interconnected and interdependent spaces' (*ibid.*, emphasis in the original).

In other words, a radical critique of separateness in the Indian case would have concerned itself not with villagers as '"a people," "native"' to the village, but, rather, 'as a historically constituted and de-propertied' category systematically relegated to the [village]' (*ibid.*: 16). Human social experience, as Williams (1975) suggests, cannot simply be broken down into distinct 'singular forms' such as 'town and country'; it consists, on the contrary, of a variety of 'intermediate' and newly consolidated forms of communal and other life. The metropolitan idea elaborated in several diverse ways at the Doon School derives its sustenance from a history of objectification of non-metropolitan entities, which has quite successfully managed to singularise experience. And, paradoxically, those opposed to the pernicious aspects of the Indian modernist project have contributed to this history almost as much as those who championed it.

Post-coloniality and the production of desirable spaces

Reflections in the metropolitan mirror

The city in the post-colonial context is the logos of the erasure which the modern nation state seeks to effect upon its 'primitive' spaces, and upon its equally intemperate 'pre-modern' temporality. The metropolis is not just a category of a simplistic sociology but also an image and the desire of the coming of age of the nation; not merely a physical space, it is also a category of thought.

Jawaharlal Nehru's masculine explorations in *The Discovery of India* – 'it was presumptuous of me to imagine that I could unveil her and find out what she is today and what she was in the long past' (1960: 113) – were part of the discourse which saw the nation state's future as one inextricably enmeshed with the vista of the metropolis. B.G. Verghese, a student at the School from 1936 to 1944, and subsequently of Cambridge University, and who later served as the editor of *The Hindustan Times* and the *Indian Express* newspapers, was another such 'modern' Indian involved in the process of discovering a very specific India. In the mid-1960s, he criss-crossed the country, writing of his travels in a series of newspaper articles. A quintessentially utilitarian modern journey, Verghese's pointed wanderings from this factory to that laboratory were in the nature of a progress report on the post-colonial nation state: he aspired 'to report on economic development and social change after almost fifteen years of planning' (Verghese 1965: vii). En route, the traveller 'rediscovered an immensely exciting country pulsating with life and vigour, a country in which great things are happening and one full of abundant promise' (*ibid.*).

Verghese's sanguine inventory of 'great things' and 'abundant' promises was undertaken with the cache of tools which has also, ostensibly, enabled contemporary historians to uncover the 'unmoving histories' concealed 'beneath the rapidly changing history of governments, wars, and famines' (Foucault 1982: 3). Hence, despite the unsettling turbulence of events on the surface, the Chinese attack in 1962, Nehru's death, 'and the present economic crisis', Verghese suggests that India 'is resurgent'. The tools of his analysis match the inventory outlined by Foucault: 'models of economic growth, quantitative analysis of market movements, accounts of demographic expansion and contraction, the study of climate and its long term changes, the fixing of sociological constants, the description of technological adjustments and of their spread and continuity' (*ibid.*).

The underlying and consistent tendency towards 'progress' that Verghese discovers submerged under the capriciousness of surface events emerges from a survey and valorisation of a very specific landscape: 'The assignment', he says, 'took me to farms, factories, mines, dams, power stations, research establishments, *zila parishads* and cooperative offices, industrial estates, technical institutions, housing developments ... defence establishments, large and small industry, and cooperative enterprises' (Verghese 1965: x). The over-whelming presence of the metropolis is too obvious to be laboured in this enumeration of the topography of 'nation building'. Indeed, the *Geist* of metropolitan existence, Verghese suggests, can even be utilised to transform the 'non-metropolitan' impediments to modernity into the foot-soldiers of a technocratic regime. The 'tribals' of Orissa, he argues, can easily be 'detribal-ised' through 'large residential schools with mechanical workshops' which will enable them 'to participate fully in the industrial civilisation developing around them' (*ibid.*: 110–11).[6]

'City', as Raymond Williams tells us, is derived from *civitas* 'which was in its turn derived from civis (a citizen in the sense of a national)' (1975: 307). The analytical importance of the post-colonised metropolis lies in its role as complementary trope to the 'modern' nation building project; in its role as an abstraction from the urban *contestations* of space and place. This contest-ation – 'the coming together of two complex worlds, interacting in major ways in a division of labour yet distanced and differentiated from one another [in which] the urban poor subsidise the city in terms of services, the provision of casual labour and yet are slated to live out their lives outside the enclosure of the formal city' (Chandoke 1991: 2871) – is the uncomfortable reality of the metropolis. However, in the dialogue of the nation it is the sentiment of the metropolis, its metaphysics, that predominates.

To return to Lefebvre (1991), we might say that in the discourse of the post-colonised nation state the spatial practice of the metropolis ('which embraces production and reproduction') is 'overwhelmed' with the onslaught of representational spaces. These representational spaces constitute the scat-tered canvases for the murals of the nation state in which imagination becomes substantially free from the constraints of experience. As far as nationalist narratives are concerned, the 'inconvenience' of spatial analyses which deal with the metropolis on a different level is that 'they take on spe-cific meanings and these meanings are put into motion and spaces used in a particular way through the agency of class, gender, or other social practices' (Harvey 1989a: 264). A consciousness of the metropolis expressed in the lexicon of the material and physical flows which order its existence, and the antagonisms of class, gender, and ethnicity which vein its social fabric, threatens the 'wholesomeness' of its image, and that of the post-colonial nationhood itself.

Valorisation of the sentiment of the metropolis – celebrations of progress, and 'civilisation' – have not, of course, been confined to the post-colonial context, but in this case they are embroiled within the poignant politics of the representation of the 'modern' self. In other, non-colonial contexts, the city becomes the battleground, both figurative and literal, and the descriptive trope for a different set of meanings and images. So, for Baudelaire, the metropolis – and the modern ethos which makes it what it is – was experi-enced not as a national-social project, the anthropomorphic transmogrifica-tion of a social milieu into the concrete modern citizen, but rather as a strictly personal consciousness. The crowd that occupies the spaces of his metropolis consists of abstract figures, and not the exemplars of the citizen. The 'metropolitan masses' which surged through Baudelaire's pages, as Benjamin pointed out, have no specific identity: 'They do not stand for classes or any sort of collective; rather they are nothing but the amorphous crowds of passers-by, the people in the street' (1985a: 165).[7] Such non-utilitarian pleasures, I would suggest, are scorned by our post-colonial 'nation builders' for whom the metropolis is an *episteme*.

The contractual space of the little republic

Rebellious citizens, civic sensibilities, and lessons in democracy

Perhaps one of the most articulate examples of the conflation of the metropolitan sentiment with the ideal of the post-colonial citizen comes to us from Bipinchandra Pal's autobiography (1973). His journey from the provincial backwaters of his home town of Sylhet to Calcutta, in order to pursue a tertiary education in one of the premier colleges of the colonial metropolis, was also for him a journey to the realm of a new ontology. Pal came to Calcutta in 1874 to join the Presidency College and his recollections of city life as noted in his autobiography written some fifty years later – after his own transformation into the archetypal metropolitan – provide a useful contrast between views of the metropolis in colonial and post-colonised times, and in other (non-colonised) situations.

Upon arrival in Calcutta, the relatively prosperous Pal joined the Sylhet 'mess', one of several such establishments, organised along regional lines, to cater to the eating requirements of (male) students from outside the city. The messes also functioned as centres of social activity where prospective doctors, lawyers, civil servants, and others – the indigenous colonial intelligentsia – made each other's acquaintance and, quite often, formed life-long friendships. Mess membership tended, largely, if not exclusively, to be from the higher castes. It was at the Sylhet mess, Pal says, that he had his first 'taste' of city life: the stark atomism of metropolitan existence versus the communal ethic of the non-metropolis. Whereas in his father's house everybody, 'whether master or servant, had the same kind of food', at his mess – 'for the first time' – he saw that:

> my neighbour had fried eggs which were not served to me. Another gentleman had ghee with his dal, which he did not share with anybody else; and someone had curd which was not given to others.
>
> (Pal 1973: 156)

Located at the intersection of fragmentary existence and non-traditional aspirations, the student messes of Calcutta were metropolitan inventions *par excellence*; and it is the sentiment of the metropolis – as anticipation of the post-colonial nation state – which is expressed in Pal's subsequent portrayal of their functioning:

> The student messes in Calcutta, in my college days, fifty-six years ago, were like small republics and were managed on strictly democratic lines. Everything was decided by the voice of the majority of the members of the mess.
>
> . . . almost in everything that concerned the common life of the mess, the members had a supreme voice. If a seat was vacant applications for it came before the whole 'House', and no one was admitted into the mess unless he was known to or certified by responsible people to be a decent and respectable fellow. . . . Disputes between one member and another were settled by a 'court' of the whole 'House'; and we sat night after night, I remember, in examining these cases; and never was the decision of this 'court' questioned or disobeyed by any member.
>
> We made from time to time laws and regulations for the proper administration of our little republics . . .
>
> (Pal 1973: 157–8)

That the author means to present the 'little republic' as a microcosm of the life of the city itself[8] – different from the ethos of the provincial places of origin of its members – is somewhat clearer in his discussion of the 'compromise' over food between 'the so-called orthodox and the Brahmo and other heterodox members of our republic'. The 'republic', Pal says, passed a rule by unanimous vote 'that no members should bring any food to the house (except, of course, loaves and biscuits that had commenced to be tolerated by the orthodoxy of the Metropolis) which outraged the feelings of Hindu orthodoxy' (*ibid.*: 159). Pal's fond remembrances of the student messes of his youth seem directly linked to his conception of the hopes and desires a modernising society may place in the milieu of the metropolis; the student mess was a metropolitan artefact in the sense that it mirrored the larger milieu of which it was a geographical and cultural subset.

In the city Pal meets individuals actively involved in the process of transforming the *Gemeinschaft* rigidities of native existence into the *Gesellschaft* imperatives of a new age. Among others, there was Babu Pyari Charan Sircar, 'the man who had the greatest influence over forming my mind and character', who had worked tirelessly in the cause of widow remarriage among upper caste Hindus. The influence of the metropolitan milieu was also crucial in transfiguring the intimacy of Pal's mother's death into his own personal passage to a different, public, realm. There is a piquant sense in which the gathering sentiments of the metropolis in the young Calcutta student come to signify the substitution of the biological mother with a new maternal ideal; the corporeal ideal, bound in tradition, is replaced by an abstract entity – the city itself – aligned to 'progress'. The open breach that later eventuated between Pal and his father over the former's rejection of Hindu orthodoxy, first appeared as a crack in the context of his mother's death. For nearly a year after she died Pal reports that he dutifully performed the *shradh* ceremony in strict conformity with Hindu tradition. However, the force of metropolitan influences determined a different course of action and

> Towards the close of the year, and before the day of the first anniversary of my mother's death came I had openly rebelled against the old faith and society, and thus gave it [the *shradh* ceremony] up. That was the first cause of open rupture between father and son.
>
> (Pal 1973: 179)

The metropolis as the expatiatory scene of modernity – the redemptive rupture with a 'primitive' past and the eager union with a 'progressive' future – is also the theme of a series of post-Independence publications entitled the *Bombay Citizenship Series*; the nomenclatural embrace between 'Bombay' and 'citizenship' is worth noting. In one of these publications (Bulsara 1948) the narrative of the metropolis employed in the book slips in and out of a discourse of nationhood with relative ease. We are presented with a meta-vision of the national future determined by the civil society of the metropolis: a homogeneous history to be made by the secure classes of the city in the absence of proper judgement and suitable faculties on the part of the provinces.

Here, the nation–city identification takes a perennially evocative route through a borrowing of the vocabulary of nationalism itself. Bombay is described as the 'mother city' (Bulsara 1948: vii), a template whose manner of life and culture is put forward as the exemplar of nationhood. The 'non-metropolis', in turn, is the palimpsest, the site of a new inscription of identity eagerly attempting to emulate the ways of the 'mother'.

However, the civilisational destiny of the metropolis – as the template for the 'national' – is constrained by the physical presence within its very boundaries of refractory sentiments, which belong to another space:

> . . . merely removing or cleaning up dust bins, refuse sheds and dirt carts from the city will not keep it clean, so long as the people, who create the conditions of filth, *remain in the same primitive mental condition*. Our trouble is not merely physical or external. It is *psychological, social and internal*. We suffer from a preponderance of illiterate populations, which we recruit year by year from our numerous villages. Its mind is still largely rural. It is almost completely undisciplined. . . . we have to instil in this population a sense of civic consciousness, which demands a mind trained to the restraint of co-operative living. Their illiteracy and profusion of dialects is a hindrance in the path of quick progress.
>
> (Bulsara 1948: 19–20, emphasis in the original)

The School's students, especially those who had travelled overseas with their parents, learned to imbibe sentiments of the metropolis from the earliest days of its existence. One of these was an 18-year-old recent graduate of the School who accompanied his diplomat father to the United States in 1942 and recounted the experiences of his journey in an open letter to the *Doon School Weekly* (*DSW*). The letter is in the form of an itinerary of colonial desire, tracing, as it does, the journey,[9] via many secondary ports of call, to the 'true' metropolis; the concrete fruition of an abstract excursion made in thought many times, and in many ways. The moment of encounter with the exemplar proves in every way to be a fulfilment of the abundant promise of the wait:

> We docked at Hoboken, New Jersey. . . . I have some vague, but never the less vivid mental pictures of London and Paris, but New York is in a class by itself. A majestic monument to man's engineering genius. I cannot ever hope to put down in this letter even a small description of New York, or give an idea of the emotions which I felt when I saw this city.
> (*DSW*, 4 April 1942)

But the passage to the metropolis of ineffable emotions was littered with provincial outposts of the global economy, and this traveller, for one, noted their presence with the acuity of a pilgrim bound to the centre of a 'true' civilisation:

> [After Capetown]. . . The next stop was Trinidad. I was particularly looking out for the various landmarks which had been made familiar to me by Mr Gibson's strenuous efforts to instil some geography into our arable heads. . . . I cannot say that I particularly liked Trinidad. It is a dreary place with a lot of rain, tropical vegetation and a whole lot of rum-swilling planters: the most inefficient and oppressive Negro waiters who breathe onions and garlic down your neck, but rather meek and polite Indian taxi drivers (there are quite a number of Indians there). I was certainly glad to get away.
> (*DSW*, 4 April 1942)

There were, it would seem, undesirable provincials and primitives everywhere.

The idea of the Doon School itself as a microcosm of metropolitan existence has been reiterated through the notion of the community of contract: the School's attempt to reproduce one of the aspects of the 'progressive' ethos of the city through the 'arbitrariness' of the constitution of its own community; and this is attempted not just through the absence (in principle) of prohibitions on who may or may not join the community – regarded as an aspect of 'pre-modern' existence – but also the notion of heterogeneity which is a definitional characteristic of modern, metropolitan, life. In the city, Engels was to write in a different context, one may see the 'hundreds of thousands of all classes and all ranks crowding past each other' (Engels quoted in Williams 1975: 215).

The depiction of the metropolis as the space of individualistic existence unfettered by the oppressive demands of custom and tradition which characterise the 'non-metropolis' is one of the most lasting formulations of the creed of modernity, itself an indispensable adjunct of twentieth-century capitalism. The 'essentially intellectualistic character of the mental life of the metropolis', Simmel was to say, is in contrast to 'that of the small town which rests more on feelings and emotional relationships' (1971: 325). It is precisely this move away from 'primitivism' that the Doon School wished to convey through depicting itself as a community of contract rather than one of prescribed association; 'we pride ourselves', a School publication comments, 'in the fact that two boys can sleep in adjacent beds for six years and be friends without even finding out each other's background'. The School as the embodiment of the 'progressive' anonymity of metropolitan space is nowhere made more explicit than here.

The metonymic juxtaposition of the milieu of the School and that of the metropolis – as communities of contract and coincidence – was present, at the very outset, in the Constitution of the Indian Public Schools Society (IPSS), Doon's administering body. Among the objects of the Society listed there is the founding of 'Schools in India . . . without distinction of race or creed or caste or social status' (*Constitution of the Indian Public Schools Society*, 1936/1986). However, if the post-colonised metropolis is to serve as the prototype of the national community, then the heterogeneity which is a characteristic feature of 'modern' existence must also be tempered by the needs of 'co-operative' existence. Another School publication contains the following passage: 'Boys from all parts of the country, from all castes and religions mix together and lose their regional and religious identity because the School deliberately plays down these differences by a common uniform/ the same food/the same facilities.'[10] The heterogeneity of the School's population, which aligns it to the image of the city, is first constituted, and then surrendered – much as the author of the *Bombay Citizenship Series* believed it should be – in favour of constituting an ordered, co-operative, civil society: the ideal metropolis.

The ostensible reproduction of the conditions of 'modern' life within the School's boundaries – the multiplicities of cultural, social, and economic backgrounds – also has its corollary in the field of the 'political': the representation of the School milieu as a training ground for future citizens in the theory and practice of 'democratic' existence. The School Council is an important part of the representational pastiche through which Doon seeks to secure its place in the grand narrative of the post-colonial nation state. Chaired by the Headmaster, the Council is the 'apex student body of the School' (Singh 1985: 62) and meets every month to 'consider all matters which affect the discipline, manners and amenities of life at School' (*ibid.*). The minutes of the Council meetings are published in the *DSW* and student members 'represent' different forms (grades) as well as different areas of school activity.

However, the sentiment of civitas at the School is a differentiating sentiment: it seeks to establish both the future of the nation state as well as the identities of those most 'qualified' to be at its helm. In this sense, all cultural history of India is that of the state (Chakrabarty 1992), and that of those trained in its punctilios: others – 'tribals', 'provincials', women (as I discuss later) – provide the peripheral backdrop to the essential procedures and groups of the nation:

> [The School Council]. . . has a written constitution . . .[and]. . . endorses each year the award of School colours for good citizenship.
>
> The working of the School Council and the freedom allowed to the *Weekly* are, in a sense, training for the wider world, when the boys are expected to be knowledgeable, responsible and active citizens of a democratic country.
>
> (*Doon School Book*: 62–3)

The city-state milieu of the School casts its redemptive spell on many a pilgrim. In the autobiography of ex-student Karan Singh (1942–46), the scion of the erstwhile princely family of Jammu and Kashmir presents the School as the sacred ground of a rite of passage, and the very site of the birth of the modern man. He speaks of his father's decision to send him to Doon, rather than one of the many Chiefs' Colleges (see Chapter 2), as 'imaginative and forward looking' (Singh 1982: 24). His years at Doon made it possible for him, he further notes, 'to make the crucial transition from feudal to democratic life' (*ibid.*).

Of course, the above discourse of the metropolis in Indian life did not go altogether uncontested, and instances of such contestation can be found, for example, in Hindi literature of the recent period. Here, there were critical voices which sought to question fetishism of the metropolis while avoiding the temptation to romanticise – an enduring aspect of so much of modern Indian cultural and political life – the village and its 'traditions'.

I have referred earlier to Renu's novel *Maila Aanchal* (1956) as an example of a powerful and complex critique of post-colonised modernity and particularly of the scientific episteme which attempts to hegemonise the other ways of knowing, reducing the adherents of the latter to marginalised Otherness. The greatness and enduring value of Renu's novel, too often narrowly described as *Aanchalik* or regional and illustrative of local peculiarities and concerns, also lies in his vehement attempt to grasp non-urban subjectivity – cultural, political, gendered, sexual – in all its complexity. This can be seen to be a particularly valuable (not to say radical) project in an era which witnessed the high modernist rhetoric of the Five Year Plans which arrogated all powers of discrimination to the urban inhabitant ('The Planner'), reducing the non-urban component of the national community to an undifferentiated (and unthinking) mass. Another aspect of the latter position can be seen in the attitude of the post-Independence metropolitan intelligentsia in its evaluation of Indian popular culture. In the 1950s realist critique of Indian cinema – pioneered by groups such as the Calcutta Film Society, for example – 'the spectator of the popular film emerges as an immature, indeed infantile, figure, one bereft of the rationalist imperatives required for the Nehru era's project of national construction' (Vasudevan 1995: 308). Renu is the ethnographer of this 'infantile' audience, his ethnography capturing the nuances of rural subjectivity through an attention to the manner in which people manoeuvre between the constraints of structure and the imperatives of agency, rather than be reduced to passivity and befuddlement.

Importantly, Renu's critique of the homogenising tendency of metropolitanism proceeds not through a portrayal of village life as wholesome, honest, pure, and noble, but rather through a political and social contextualisation of the conflicts, tensions, dispersions, and solidarities which characterise non-urban life in a period of consolidating capitalism and advanced rhetoric about nation-building. It is precisely through his refusal simply to rebut the dominant logic of his time that Renu's work achieves its most fundamental success. So, instead of arguing that rural life is not as 'backward' as the metropolitan intelligentsia may suggest (a response which would only pay homage to the original point of view), he, instead, proceeds to question the qualities which the discourse of metropolitanism valorises. What, he asks, are the politics of being more 'rational', of striving for 'progress', and of being unanimous in the task of 'nation-building'? These questions effectively decentre the grounds of the debate and shift the focus of attention (and the analytic vocabulary) to a different level altogether.

The heirs apparent, the minions of destiny, and the vertical invaders

To return to the ethnography at hand, however, evocations of the School's metropolitan sentiment also unfold through the identification of groups at the School which serve as the negative reflection of this sentiment. We have already come across one such section of the School's population, *viz.* the subordinate staff. A section of the teacher population also serves a similar purpose. There are two types of teachers at the School: those who consciously chose to teach at the Doon School, and others who are there due to circumstances quite beyond their control. It is the latter group that constitutes one of the fragments of Otherness against which the official ethos of the School both defines and differentiates itself through an explicit dialectic. I will deal with the former group that is part of the metropolitan milieu of the School first. D.L. was a teacher at the School from 1984 to 1991. Before joining Doon he had been an executive with the Indian subsidiary of an international publishing house in Calcutta. A Master in history from the prestigious St Stephen's College in Delhi, he also studied at Oxford University as a Rhodes Scholar. The avenues of social and economic mobility open to an individual such as D.L. in Indian society would seem to be almost infinite; and yet he made a conscious choice to opt for a career which many Indians would regard as the last resort of the desperate and the unemployable.

The low regard in which the school-teaching profession is held in India is fairly well documented in scholarly literature and needs no detailed elaboration here. 'With the advance of the colonial system of education', Krishna Kumar notes,

> the school curriculum became totally disassociated from the Indian child's every-day reality and milieu. . . . Moreover, the teacher had no say in the selection of knowledge represented in the school curriculum. His low salary and status ensured that he would not exercise any professional autonomy or even have a professional identity.
>
> (Kumar 1991: 14)

The post-Independence situation in India represents a variation on the same theme.[11]

So why does someone like D.L., socially and economically a part of the metropolitan spoils system in India – the 'right' type of education and the 'right' sort of contacts – willingly opt for the life of a school teacher? The reason, I suggest, lies in the existence of an informal 'reservations' system in the public school system in India with respect to the 'best' jobs, i.e. Headmasterships of other, major, public schools. Through this system the top jobs at important public schools circulate among a small group – the culturally metropolitan – on recommendations from others of similar background who have preceded them; and the Headmastership of a prominent public school – the maturation of the investments in metropolitan cultural capital – carries with it the benefits both of an immediate and concrete nature and of more distant and abstract social capital.

The Headmaster of a school such as Doon enjoys a life style which parallels that of a senior public servant or corporate executive: a colonial-style bungalow with extensive and beautifully manicured grounds, a number of 'retainers' for their upkeep, a car, an 'entertainment' allowance, travel allowance, and several other perquisites that make for a life of considerable luxury. These are, of course, in addition to the facility of free education at the School for the Headmaster's children. In his professional life, the incumbent makes the acquaintance of a wide cross-section of parents who are often some of the most influential people in the country – politicians, senior bureaucrats, corporate chiefs, industrialists, officers of the defence forces, university Vice-chancellors,[12] and journalists, to name just a few. We may usefully speak here of the benedictory web of social capital. 'Social capital', as Bourdieu put it,

> is the aggregate of the actual or potential resources which are linked to possession of a durable network of more or less institutionalised

relationships of mutual acquaintance and recognition . . . which provide
each of its members with the backing of the collectively owned capital.

(Bourdieu 1986: 248–9)

That the greatest responsibility for the maintenance and advancement of
an institution which defined post-colonised citizenship in terms of a 'metropolitan' identity should be seen to devolve upon those identified as 'metropolitan' is not, perhaps, surprising. In this manner the metropolitan ethos
continues to be both reproduced and valorised. During 1991, after just seven
years as a schoolmaster, D.L. left Doon School to take up the Headmastership of a well-known public school in South India. By any yardstick, he had
made exceptional progress through the ranks to the new position he now
holds. The majority of the teachers resented this, but also recognised that
'people like D.L. are destined to progress rapidly'.[13]

Of course, not all 'metropolitan' teachers at Doon necessarily go on to
Headships of other public schools. The point is, however, that they form a
distinct sub-stratum of School society. They are regarded by others, the 'provincial' teachers, as enjoying the privileges of those charged with the
responsibility of representing the ethos of the School; as the possessors of
plena potestas agendi et loquendi. They are 'organic intellectuals' in Gramsci's
terms, charged with the duty and authority of propagating a cultural
programme of a national self. The most powerful signifier of the privilege
that this 'metropolitanism' bestows upon its acolytes, as far as the
'non-metropolitans' at the School are concerned, comes in the form of a
dispensation: the relative ability to determine one's own destiny.

K.M., the geography teacher, is from a small town in Kerala. His journey
from his home state to the Doon School is also a narrative of the cultural
economy of the post-colonised nation state. It is an epigrammatic rendition
of the multitude of several such journeys undertaken by many others of
K.M.'s peripheral cultural circumstance, to the cultural nuclei of the nation
state. A 'Gold Medallist' from his home town university, his reasons for
accepting a position at Doon, as explained to me, constitute reflections on the
cultural and economic constraints faced by the group of teachers at Doon I
will refer to as the 'non-metropolitans'; and the explanations were offered to
me simultaneously in tones of resignation and anger which derive from a
perception, no matter how dim, of the double bind of human existence.

In 1979, K.M.'s father, a junior police officer, retired from the Force and,
the following year, died of a heart attack. This forced K.M. into a profession
'which was certainly not my first choice'. But the oppressive compulsions of
economic need form only a part of the story of how men such as K.M. come
to be at Doon: there is also the determining force of cultural capital which
constitutes that quite often insuperable difference between the metropolis and
the province. For the majority of the teachers at the School, teaching was not
a 'first choice'. Almost all members of this group have come from an educational and cultural milieu that has experienced systematic devaluation in

the metropolitan nation-building agenda of the post-colonial state. They have studied in schools where the medium of instruction has either been Hindi or one of the vernacular languages, and have graduated from universities that occupy a similarly enervated space of 'linguistic backwardness'. At Doon, they are the butt of the students' jokes: for the manner in which they dress, for their attempts to rid themselves, much like the young Bipinchandra Pal, of their provincial patois, and for their attempts, taken as parody, to mimic the 'life' of the metropolis.

I do not mean to use 'mimicry' in the exact sense in which Bhabha (1984) speaks of it. The 'mimic-men' role which is the lot of the non-metropolitan teachers at Doon is both prescribed – for metropolitanism needs its Other to authenticate itself – and adopted voluntarily by the non-metropolitans as a strategy of negotiating their position in the School. The mimicry of the Doon School teacher is the metonym of a mortal wound of identity. In private conversations with me these teachers made it clear that in this way they masked their 'real' beings. Where the non-metropolitan is 'forced' to mimic the metropolitan, to measure up to the definition of the 'ideal' and live a 'double' existence, mimicry is the manifestation of the purgatory of identity; 'we have to act like some one else', as K.M. once said to me, adding that the only way for him to be his 'real self' was to go back to his home town and 'get a job there'.[14]

But for most of the teachers of K.M.'s background, the dreams and plans of returning to a place where they are not the constant objects of a 'normalising' gaze (Foucault 1979) turn out to be illusory. As Berger and Mohr say of the yearnings of the 'provincial' migrant worker in metropolitan Europe:

> The final return is mythic. It gives meaning to what might otherwise be meaningless. It is larger than life. It is the stuff of longing and prayers. But it is also mythic in the sense that, as imagined, it never happens. There is no final return.
>
> (Berger and Mohr 1989: 216)

For, despite the strong expressions of outrage at the perceived ignominy of their life at School – 'disrespect' from students and 'metropolitan' colleagues, poor prospects of 'moving up', lack of any voice in the running of the School – very few actually 'return'. In the helpless embrace of a double bind – 'wanting and not wanting a relation' (Metcalfe 1988: 197) – they barter their ignominious present for a more hopeful future.

This future is that of their children – who are entitled to free education at the School – through which they are enabled to join the circuit of the metropolitan cultural capital, the lack of which by their parents has condemned them to their present, strongly perceived, ignominy; Doon School education is beyond the means of men such as K.M. and teaching at the School is the only practical way of acquiring the cultural and social capital of the metropolis for their children. For this reason, the majority of the teachers who have a clear perception of their own 'invisibility' and fundamental marginality as autonomous agents at the School do not, in fact, leave once they have 'qualified for a pension'. Their concern to ensure for their children a foothold in the cultural world of the metropolis was constantly reiterated in my conversations with some of the older teachers at the School.

To use a phrase John Berger (1965) employs to describe Picasso – the European provincial who conquered Paris – these children are the 'vertical invaders' who arrive at the cultural metropolis through the 'trap door' of the School. And for this ontological leap, their parents must pay through bartering their own present.

The children of the (non-metropolitan) Doon teachers move 'up' into the circuit of the metropolis through the 'trap door' of the School, but like Picasso, they too remain conscious of being vertical invaders. They share this consciousness with another group at the School also constituted as its non-metropolitan Other: the scholarship students ('the Scholars') funded by the central government.[15] The scholarships are means tested, the ceiling on parents' income in 1992 being Rs 25,000 per annum;[16] for the same year the annual fees for the School amounted to some Rs 20,000. The awards are made on a competitive basis through a series of tests.

The visibility of the Scholars' separation from the various aspects of school life is particularly marked: they tend to congregate with other Scholars, have very few friends from among the category of 'metropolitan' students, and are the frequent objects of their humour. That the Scholars form a distinct community within the School is recognised by both their teachers and their parents. The former speak of the 'adjustment problems' these students face at the School and the delicate, often overwhelming, nature of the mediation they must effect between the two very different environments of their home and the School. There is about them the eternal heaviness of lives lived in two distinct but unconnected worlds, where to pledge commitment to the 'modern' world of the School would mean abandoning, or at least substantially abandoning, the affective ties of family. These students mostly avoided any open criticism of the School in their conversations with me although there were certain occasions on which they expressed the alienation the School milieu imposed on them. Their parents, however, were less inhibited in discussing the situation faced by their sons at School, constantly characterising their children as 'outsiders' in the Doon School milieu.

At the time of this research, M.K.'s 13-year-old son was a scholarship student at the Doon School. A retired railway clerk in his early sixties M.K. and his family live in a modest house in one of the newly developed outlying 'colonies' of the rapidly expanding city of Lucknow. I had obtained his address through the School and located his house after considerable difficulty due to the somewhat arbitrary numbering system in a locality which, going by the state of the public facilities, seemed to have an extremely modest position in the ranking of the local municipality's priorities; dirt roads darted in and out from behind half-constructed houses, narrowing and widening at random, and lamp posts, mostly without bulbs and with red streaks of rust careering down their sides, arranged at will – symbolising the asymptotic fulfilment of a municipal intent. M.K. had not been expecting me and when I told him that I had come from the Doon School and was 'researching its history' he said that he felt 'very appreciative' that 'even' people like him were 'being consulted'. We spoke mostly in Hindustani.

'Before we moved to this house after my retirement', M.K. told me, 'six of us, four children and my wife and myself, all lived in one room. . . . that is all I could afford. . . . and now my son studies at the Doon School . . .'. In response to my questions about how his son was faring in the environment of the Doon School, M.K. fetched a recent letter from his son and proceeded, with palpable pride, to read its contents to me. In the fading light of late evening he carefully read out the missive from his son reporting on the recent earthquake which had devastated certain parts of North India and the tremors of which had also been felt in Dehra Dun. 'You see', he looked up, 'he is learning some vital new skills . . . writing like this . . . to do well . . . I am very grateful to the School.'

The letter, written in English, began with the words 'Respected abba, Salamwalekum', and M.K. noted with satisfaction that his son 'had not forgotten his roots'. I commented that his son seemed to have adjusted quite well to his new environment and that this was at variance with the experience of several other scholarship students. Before responding to this, M.K. sought to establish my own position *vis-à-vis* the School: Was I also a teacher there? Would any part of our conversation be reported back to the Headmaster? There was genuine concern on his part that any critical comments regarding the School may find their way back there, jeopardising his son's position. He seemed unconvinced by my argument that his son was on a government scholarship and hence his position at the School was quite secure; the faintest possibility of the barring of that golden 'trap door' through which his son had slipped, and through which the light of a superior future could be glimpsed, was unbearable.

Eventually, however, he became less guarded in his comments on the School. His son quite often felt very 'isolated' there, M.K. said, not just because of his modest economic background compared with the others, but also 'because the other boys think that he is backward . . .'. What did he mean by 'backward' I asked; oh, he said 'that our mentality is not progressive . . . my son is quite religious . . . his English is not very good . . . that sort of thing'. On inquiring as to how often he visited the School, M.K. replied that he hardly ever went there, as he felt 'intimidated'. And his son? His son was not intimidated any more, he said, but he always felt 'like an outsider'.

It is in this sense that I wish to compare the teachers' children and the 'Scholars' to Berger's portrayal of Picasso as a 'vertical invader'. Each remains 'conscious of being a vertical invader, always [subjecting] what he has seen around him to a comparison with what he brought with him from his own country, from the past' (Berger 1965: 41). This consciousness is manifested in the conciliation which both the above groups must effect in order to come to terms with an environment which, while making of them objects of jest, also holds the only possibility of a future more prosperous than that which was the lot of their parents; their affections for the School, unlike their metropolitan counterparts, are guarded, and they speak of it as a staging point, rather than as 'home'. They live out their school lives – playing, eating, and studying – in tightly knit congregations of their own, speaking, sometimes, of parents too intimidated to be regular visitors. This private consciousness of Otherness is voiced warily in public, lest its articulation obstruct their passage to the new shores of 'citizenship'.

But for the non-metropolitan teachers of the School – their children launched upon new lives – life must be lived in the debris of 'backwardness' and 'unsuitability'. It is of them that S.S., a Doon ex-student and now himself a public school Headmaster, speaks when he says that schools such as Doon are 'no longer getting good teachers . . . . these are people who have ended up here after having tried everything else . . . quite second rate people'.

If Picasso's ascent into the European metropolis is the image appropriate to a section of the student population at the School then the situation of individuals such as K.M. may be compared to the case of Herbert Sherring, applicant to the position of Headmaster at the Mayo College in Ajmer in 1907.[17] This was a position reserved for Europeans, and government files indicate that Sherring, an Englishman born in India, was denied the position, because he carried the taint of having been born in the colonies. His was a 'lack' for 'having been brought up in this country'. The distance in time which separates Sherring from K.M. does not, I think, invalidate the comparison; my intention is to point to those 'counterintuitive imaginings that must be grasped when history is said to be remade, and a rupture is too easily declared because of the intuition of freedom that a merely political independence brings for a certain class' (Chakravorty-Spivak 1989: 274).

In the context of the Doon School and its citizenship project, men and women such as K.M. are the post-colonial Creoles: those who travel 'up' to the 'metropolis' in the hope of a brighter future, but who must then spend their lives there irreparably marked by the cultural and social 'affliction' of 'having been brought up in this country'.

Recently, there has been scathing criticism of the 'decline in prestige' experienced by 'memory' during 'modern' times (Casey 1987). 'The fact is', Casey says, 'that we have forgotten what memory is and what it can mean; and we make matters worse by repressing the fact of our own oblivion. No wonder Yates can claim that "we moderns have no memory at all"' (1987: 2). Yet it is precisely through a process of 'active forgetfulness' (Nietschze 1983) – a practice Casey disparages as inducing a state of 'half-reality' – that the 'non-metropolitans' of the Doon School come to terms with the overwhelming burden of their invidious place in the School community.

'Active forgetfulness' is a corollary to the situation of the double bind.

Many of the older 'non-metropolitan' teachers at the School, now in their fifties, have spent almost their entire working lives at the School, but still do not share the rapport the 'metropolitan' teachers have with both the students and the power structure of the School. Yet their talk of the School – memories of their early days, dialogues about the present – is animated by an almost unbridled enthusiasm. 'Forgetfulness' in this context is the negotiation and a vehement appropriation of a space of dignity; it is the creation of a forgetful memory through which dignity is salvaged by discarding the experience of pain lest it become overwhelming.

Gendered localities

I will conclude this chapter by returning to the image of the School as a microcosmic representation of the metropolitan milieu and to my earlier discussion of the connection between the metropolitan 'sentiment' and sentiments of the civil society.

I have argued that the citizenship project at the Doon School is one whose philosophical underpinnings lie in the ethos of metropolitan and technocratic existence and that those who are seen to belong to different milieux become the Other of this project. The contractual foundation of 'modern', metropolitan existence stands in direct contrast to the milieu of the 'small town and rural existence ... rooted in the steady equilibrium of unbroken custom' (Simmel 1971: 325). The most salient characteristics of the metropolitan ethos are 'punctuality, calculability, and exactness, which are required by the complications and extensiveness of metropolitan life' (*ibid.*: 328). 'Cities', Simmel suggested, 'are above all the seat of the most advanced economic division of labour. It [the city] is a unit ... which is receptive to a highly diversified plurality of achievements' (*ibid.*: 325). Contract provides the means through which the diverse elements of the metropolis interact, 'free' from the 'trivialities and prejudices that bind the small town person'.

The image of the contractual settlement is also central to the School. Prior to its establishment, the School would like to claim, Indian educational institutions functioned within the 'sensory-mental phase of small town and rural existence' (*ibid.*), resulting, as Doon's official history puts it:

> in a variety of institutions ... which reflected the social environment in which they existed. There were Hindu tols and Muslim madarasas, both of which imparted learning in their respective religious traditions. There were [also] the newer Christian mission schools. ...
>
> The System established at these and other institutions did not seek to educate their students for the challenges of the future. Instead they maintained the status quo, instilling in their students all the taboos and conventions of a rigidly structured society.
>
> (Singh 1985: 9)[18]

This, then, is 'the mental life' of the non-metropolis, resting 'on feelings and emotional relationships. These latter [in turn] are rooted in the unconscious levels of the mind and develop most readily in the steady equilibrium of unbroken custom' (Simmel 1971: 325). 'Lasting impressions', Simmel says, 'the slightness in their differences, the habituated regularity of their course and contrasts between them' characterise the life of the 'non-metropolis'. The Doon School, on the other hand, is marked by the unmistakable signs of metropolitan life: diversity of population; wilful arbitrariness in the selection of this population; lack of barriers to entry; the intrinsic 'punctuality, calculability, and exactness' of its daily routine; the prolific elaboration of the acts of that daily routine. Within it we find a 'rapid telescoping of changing images . . . and the unexpectedness of violent stimuli . . . [a] psychological condition [created] . . . with . . . the tempo and multiplicity of economic, occupational and social life' (*ibid.*). The School reproduces the conditions of the metropolis through a metonymy of content: gathered here are 'children of all castes, creeds, religion and colour, without distinction' (Singh 1985: 19).

The metropolitan imaginary finds play at the School, then, through both abstract and concrete acts that attempt to mime the metropolis. The abstract elements may be grouped under the rubric of 'school ethos' the reiteration of the idea of the 'free' flow of people and knowledge within the School's domain, for instance. The materiality of metropolitan life is represented through the scattered tableaux of archetypal metropolitan spaces: the library (with its extended opening hours) and the Rose Bowl amphitheatre for the gratification of 'civilised' senses, the utilitarian red-brick presence of the School's main building (once a laboratory), the dormitory accommodation with its 'anti-status' (i.e., 'anti-primitive') connotations, and the School Council as a manifestation of the contractual-democratic existence.

The School's metropolitan imaginary is also constructed through an articulation of its 'negatives' and a conscious strategy of delineation. The 'non-metropolis' at the School – the non-metropolitan teachers, the scholarship boys, and the subordinate staff – is confined to the borderlands of School life. These define the School's metropolitan consciousness through being confined to the margins of its existence. The technique of 'bordering' is, of course, intrinsic to defining the centre.

In as much as the discourse of the modern metropolis represents it as the concrete form of the contractual civil society, it is also, in the sense the latter is discussed by Pateman (1980), a settlement of contemporary patriarchy. It is founded on the rejection of the paternal forms of non-metropolitan existence, while absorbing and 'simultaneously [transforming] conjugal, masculine patriarchal right' (*ibid.*: 37). We may say, extending Pateman, that if post-colonised metropolitan life, through the notion of the social contract which provides its philosophical underpinning, represents the 'overthrow' of the rule of the father, then the ' "natural foundation" [of the metropolis] has been brought into being through the fraternal social contract' (*ibid.*: 43) – the rule of sons and brothers.[19]

It is in this sense that the project of citizenship at the School lies deeply lodged in the interstices of a patriarchal logic and a masculine order. The logic of masculinity at the School inheres not so much in the emphasis on physical activity, adherence to which on the part of the students is erratic at best, but in the very metonymy of the metropolitan presence within the campus; it is the metropolitan *Geist* which saturates the being of the School, which simultaneously and unequivocally defines the citizen as a male subject. In this way the sentiments of the metropolis speak of the settlements of the civil society as gendered localities. The gendering of the post-colonised nation was, as Veena Das has pointed out, an important element in the earliest processes of its constitution. Hence, in the aftermath of the violence of the partition 'the task of flushing out Muslim women from Hindu or Sikh homes was constructed as duty by which Hindu men would regain purity, while the task of bringing back Hindu women from Pakistan was seen in terms of the honour of the new nation' (Das 1996: 75).

It is here that the multiple strands of my discussion converge. Manifestations of masculinity at the School are not primarily expressed through techniques of the corporeal self; rather, they are elaborated through alignments with 'new' knowledges and 'new' forms of community, the idea of the contract. It is these that articulate the imaginings of a specific national community through the vocabulary of difference. This specific form of post-coloniality inscribes its territory against its various Others: so not for it the masculinity of brute strength, for that belongs to the realm of one of its 'primitive' pasts – the feudal nobility which patronised the Mayo College at Ajmer. Its realm lies in the flux of 'pragmatic' actions and 'scientific' thoughts, contractual existence and the 'equality principle', for these signify a masculinity which sets it against the identities of the 'natives within'. This process of differentiation – of outlining a masculinity marked by the conspicuous absence of the body from the scene of robustness – is also the articulation of an insistent dialogue on the functioning of capital; it outlines both the 'requirements' of life under the regime of capital and the marginal fate of those who are seen to fall outside its ken.

7 Conclusion: 'post-coloniality', national identity, globalisation, and the simulacra of the real

This chapter is an attempt to situate the preceding discussion in the context of certain contemporary theoretical positions in order to argue for a post-colonised perspective which pays heed to the cultural and political specificities of the contemporary *fin de siècle*. There are two 'framing' positions I want to invoke for the present discussion. The first of these comes from Aijaz Ahmad. 'Very affluent people may come to believe', Ahmad says 'that they have broken free of imperialism through acts of reading, writing, lecturing, and so forth' (1992: 11). For the populations of the 'backward zones of capital', he continues, 'all relationships with imperialism pass through their own nation states, and there is simply no way of breaking out of that imperial dominance without struggling for different kinds of national projects and for a revolutionary restructuring of one's own nation state' (*ibid.*: 11).

I read Ahmad's work as a forceful plea for the foregrounding of the complex forms of asymmetries which characterise post-colonised human existence around the globe; asymmetries which simply cannot be comprehended through the abstract vocabulary which has come to be an indispensable part of the deconstructivist turn in the social sciences. Somewhere in all the copious canon of the 'post-colonial' oeuvre, Ahmad suggests, we need to speak of the functioning of capital, and the functioning of the post-colonised nation state within its ambit, neither of which can be simply wished away through epistemological refinements, or through well-meaning exhortations to 'think ourselves beyond the nation' (Appadurai 1993b: 411). The problem for a large proportion of humanity is that the nation state is still too much with us, both as oppressor and protector (though a miserable protector it has usually turned out to be).

The somewhat simplistic tendency to essentialise the state through attributing to it an 'inherent "logic" of repression', is, as Frankel has suggested, 'both misleading and politically dangerous' (Frankel 1983: 17). For this only serves to make abstract the historically and culturally specific conditions of possibility of different state forms and their functioning. Hence, my use of the term post-colonised is an attempt to foreground the specificities of the erstwhile colonised non-western societies. 'Post-colonial' has come to be used with such – 'joyful' – abandon as to leach it of any

post-colonised"
coloniser √ *post-colonial*.
post colonial

analytical worth, and there is a case for arguing that 'post-colonial' Australia (Turner 1994), for example, ought to be discussed differently from, say, post-colonised India.[1]

My second frame of reference for this discussion comes from Dipesh Chakrabarty's attempt to steer an intellectual course between Marxism and its post-structuralist critics; between 'intellectual criticisms of historicism' and a post-colonial (in my sense above) 'attachment to Marx's thought ... [that goes) back to the question of European imperialism which cannot be separated from the problem of Indian modernity' (Chakrabarty 1993a: 422). In the wake of the post-structuralist intervention, however, Chakrabarty says, engagements with Marxist thought cannot simply be in terms of seeking a preordained fit for the Indian body-politic in the ready-made garment of European history. In an age of multinational behemoths, a critical discourse from a 'third-world' perspective must work (to use Stuart Hall's wonderful phrase) 'within shouting distance of Marxism' (1992: 279). However, as Chakrabarty puts it (employing the uncannily similar metaphor of vocality), 'a postcolonial reading of Marx would have to ask if his categories can be made to speak to what we have learnt from the philosophers of "difference" about responsibility to the "plurality" of the world' (1993a: 423).[2]

I want to combine the positions taken by Ahmad and Chakrabarty towards a study of the articulation of a global form ('post-coloniality' as ontology) with a local, historically and culturally specific formation which has been the object of my discussion, *viz.* the Indian nation state. I use the word 'formation' to indicate that I am referring to a *set* of factors: the material as well as the ideological manifestations of the nation state, its buildings and bureaucracies as well as the discourse which surrounds these symbols. At another level, it is also my intention to reiterate the importance of the study of national forms in the social sciences. This is, of course, becoming an increasingly unfashionable suggestion to make in the era of the 'new' social sciences, with their focus on 'postnational social formations' (Appadurai 1993b: 420).

'The journey from the space of the ex-colony ... to the space of the post-colony', Appadurai has recently written, 'is a journey that takes us into the heart of whiteness. It moves us, that is, to America, a *postnational* space' (1993b: 241, emphasis added). Post-national spaces, post-national formations, a post-modern world where the characteristic subjectivity inheres in the 'ontological homelessness' of the diasporic individual, a post-colonial world where the idea of 'relations of travel' is the primary configuring trope, and where the study of 'relations of dwelling' (Clifford 1992) has suffered crushing intellectual demise; these are the dominant themes of our (metropolitan) time. The intellectual currency these 'topics of discourse' (White 1992) enjoy, however, is, I want to suggest, also part of a curiously universalising tendency which marks the efforts of the theorists of post-colonial/post-modern/ 'global' culture. There are two levels at which this occurs. The first is at the level of analysis of the action 'on the ground': 'there is now a world culture, but we had better make sure we understand what this means' (Hannerz 1993: 237); and, 'the role of intellectual practices is to identify the current crisis of the nation and, in identifying it, to provide part of the apparatus of recognition for postnational social forms' (Appadurai 1993b: 411).

Now, the 'complex environment in which diasporic ideas and intellectuals meet in a variety of special settings ... to generate, reformulate and recirculate cultural forms that are fundamentally postnational and diasporic' (*ibid.*: 426) is, without doubt, an important area of study of late twentieth-century human existence.[3] What is of concern, however, is the manner in which insights generated from the study of a particular set of circumstances ('migrancy'; the experiences of first-generation Asian-Americans; the 'diasporic' intellectual writing from an imagined space which lies in the 'homeland' left behind; the culture of the new class of international professionals, etc.) are sought to be presented as *the* defining experience of our time; for all people – migrants or otherwise – and for all cultures, North American or otherwise. The 'diasporic' identity has come to pass as a representative identity for late twentieth-century human existence; it is enough that 'everyone has relatives working abroad' (*ibid.*: 423). Apart from the ambit claim made on behalf of 'everyone', the assumption that if 'everyone' (a Nigerian living in Nigeria, an Indian resident in India) has relatives 'abroad' (i.e. in America) then this, somehow, implies a complete transformation – and not just a widening – of 'everyone's' sense of being is itself questionable. Notwithstanding that for those 'left behind', the Green-card relative is an object of considerable envy as well as a reference point for future action, it seems somewhat sweeping to suggest that the cultural and historically generated – local – experiences of that specific 'non-abroad' space are either jettisoned or substantially overwhelmed by the vicarious experience of life in America. I think writers such as Appadurai exaggerate a good insight. For even in these itinerant times the vast majority of the world's population do not take part in the kind of transcontinental movements Appadurai has in mind, and it seems of continuing importance to conceptualise globalisation also from the perspective of non-metropolitan societies.

It is no doubt true that one of the ways in which the migrant populations of the United States nurture and preserve memories of the 'home-country' is through participation in their respective 'delocalised *transnation*, which retains a special ideological link to a putative place of origin but is otherwise a thoroughly diasporic collectivity' (*ibid.*: 424).[4] However, does it really follow from this that 'the nationalist genie, never perfectly contained in the bottle of the territorial state, is now itself diasporic' (*ibid.*: 413)? It is one thing for a 'postcolonial intellectual', caught in the very real dilemmas of transcontinental existences (both material and emotional) – and such existence is led in the ambit of the nation state rather than under the aegis of 'postnational social formations' – to ask 'does patriotism have a future?' (*ibid.*: 412); it is quite another to suppose that (a) this question will even make sense to 'everyone' and that it does not spring primarily from the specific circumstances generated by the 'diasporic' experience; and, (b) that the conditions of possibility of such questioning – the context of Appadurai's discussion is, really, the experience of migrant life in North America[5] – define the analytical framework for *all* debates on nationalism and nation states. We have here a complete inversion of the now discredited anthropological dream of the strictly bounded culture that could only be understood from 'within'.

The intellectual challenge of Appadurai's work – how to theorise aspects of the contemporary *fin de siècle* – is undeniable,[6] twinned as it is with the proposition that 'the [discursive] sphere of the postcolony' needs to be extended 'beyond the geographical spaces of the ex-colonial world' (*ibid.*: 412). And further, who can argue with the proposition that our allegiance (or 'patriotism', in the context of Appadurai's discussion) need not be to some monolithic entity called the state, and that allegiance to other sorts of 'causes' – women's organisations, traditional forms of medicine, etc. – needs also to be cherished and nurtured? The regrettable imperiousness of Appadurai's stance lies in the attempt subsequently to read life in the ex-colonies in terms of the insights on life in the post-colony that is America (or, for that matter, the post-colony that consists of the routes taken by immigrants and refugees, and the entrepôts of the transnational managerial cadres).

This attempt to utilise a 'global' framework as the master-narrative for 'national' discussions produces some rather curious observations in Appadurai's work. The 1992 urban riots in India in the wake of the so-called Mandal Report (which, to over-simplify, favoured greater positive discrimination in favour of certain 'lower' castes) form the background of one of these. How astonishing that anyone with a scholarly interest in India should find it 'astonishing ... that anyone would die or kill' for entitlements associated with being the member of an 'other backward caste' (OBC) (*ibid.*: 415). However, a magisterial history-of-the-world kind of framework makes such astonishment entirely feasible. For then, the OBC category becomes merely one of the 'terminological distinctions of the Indian census and its specialised protocols and schedules' (*ibid.*) and it does seem quite remarkable that 'terminological distinctions' and the 'technical needs of censuses' (*ibid.*) could occasion such carnage.

But the Mandal riots were not simply about how the nation state's 'preoccupation with the control, classification, and surveillance' (*ibid.*) can 'draw groups into quasi-racial identifications and fears' (*ibid.*). And it is altogether too romantic to suggest that 'previously fluid, negotiable' ethnic identities are now at each other's throats as a result of the classificatory acts of the state; the Mandal riots were also about issues of power (the threat to the hegemony of the upper castes), about class (the majority of the rioters and those killed were lower-middle class or upper and lower caste youth), about metropolitan versus provincial systems of education in India (those who felt most threatened by the Mandal recommendations were the provincial upper castes whose chief form of secure employment has been with the government), and about the fact that the lower castes have been at the receiving end of inter-caste violence in India for a very long time; that is, the Mandal violence has a specific history. Very little of this can be captured through a framework whose exclusive impetus comes from the preoccupation with global flows and where the issue of the Mandal Report and the OBCs becomes merely one of the links in the chain of violent eruptions around the world; a global ethno-racial expository chain whose other links are, *inter alia*, the violent episodes associated with 'the Serbs and the Moluccans, Khmer and Latvians, German and Jews' (*ibid.*).[7] Neither can the Mandal episode be understood in some general manner which has to do with the universal nature of nation states.

The second of the two levels at which the universalising tendency referred to above manifests itself, is through certain prescriptions of method which are current in the rapidly consolidating field of cultural studies. I will restrict myself to brief comments on an introductory piece on cultural studies edited by Grossberg, Nelson and Treichler (1992). In a telling comment, Morris notes that 'the formation of intellectuals in English-speaking countries produces the peculiar assumption that Europeans talking about their own countries without including any parameters can be forgiven for their Eurocentrism because the knowledge they produce is automatically useful and interesting to people all over the world' (1992a: 53–4). This is a particularly apt epigraph for the article by Grossberg *et al.* The gloss on an anti-discipline whose ascendancy is charted in the essay makes such vast claims for cultural studies (or for the particular version espoused here, although the piece does read like a manifesto), that one is left craving for those realms of irony and self-reflexivity where contemporary cultural studies is supposedly most at home.

The essay in question begins by stating that 'the field of cultural studies is experiencing . . . an unprecedented international boom' (Grossberg *et al.* 1992: 1) and, some ten pages later, further informs us that 'one purpose of the book is to present cultural studies as a genuinely international phenomenon and to help people compare and contrast the work being done in different countries' (*ibid.*: 11). And yet, not one of the forty-odd contributors to the volume can be identified as living and working outside North America, Europe, and Australia. Lest this be dismissed as a positivist correlation between location and intellectual concern (though 'location' in its several senses ought to be an important part of the formation of intellectual and political concern), it is instructive to look at the subject matter of the contributions. On this count, the conclusion is substantially similar: there are two articles (one by Bhabha and one by Mani) which can be said to be concerned with non-metropolitan issues; the rest of Asia and Africa don't even get a look in. The incorporation of distinct cultural spaces with specific histories into an *epistemological space*, such that, say, Nigerian reality can be read off from certain methodological prescriptions, has, of course, become the dominant tendency in certain strands of post-modernist thinking. 'The conceptual annihilation of the postcolonial condition is actually necessary', as During puts it, 'to any argument which attempts to show that "we" now live in postmodernity' (1987: 33).

There are two assumptions implicit in both the Appadurai and Grossberg articles – those of objective existence and homogeneity: that there now exists a generalised 'post-modern world', open to the verification of the senses, and that 'post-colonialism' is (like its predecessor, colonialism) a homogeneous space of experience defined by 'style' and a certain 'joyfulness' (to use a term During employs in a caustic mode). The former leads some thinkers to suggest that we should (*now*) 'think ourselves beyond the nation' (Appadurai 1993b: 411); the latter allows others to elide issues of structure within post-colonised societies such that the post-colonial space becomes purely an aesthetic category, rather than one marked by various forms of social practice. The predominant mode of exposition of this stylistic sense of post-coloniality has been, of course, the field of 'post-colonial literature'.[8]

The discussion presented in this book has sought to suggest that neither of the two assumptions above is satisfactory for understanding life in the 'post-colony' that is India. First, because generalised announcements of the death of the nation state idea ignore its particularised persistence; and because one cannot wish the nation away, one must continue to confront it. Second, 'post-colonialism as style' has become an important part of the Indian metro-politan public culture's fabrication of primitive and progressive spaces of the post-colonial nation state. This tendency, exemplified in the ritual denigrations of vernacular literature and 'provincial' ways,[9] emerges out of the tendency to think in essences, rather than about the history of post-colonised modernity and capital which has left some with no choice but to act in violent and 'primitive' ways.

This chapter is an attempt to investigate the nature of the claims that speak of the existence of fundamentally discrete segments of Indian society, each animated by a separate public morality and a distinct private ethos. These are the claims which address the issues of the roots of order and disorder, of progress and backwardness, and of the lightness of contract versus the weight of custom; of separate realities, and discontinuities in the patterns of behaviour. I would also like to suggest, contra Appadurai, that the study of *post-colonised national* forms – rather than 'post-national social forms' – should be an integral part of scholarship on countries such as India. These schools, research and survey institutes, etc. are the sites of production of post-coloniality as a strategy of differentiation between 'progressive' and 'backward' populations, and the ideologies of the nation state are, in fact, quite unambiguously present in the ethos of some of Appadurai's 'post-national social formations' such as non-governmental organisations (NGOs).

One of the most prominent forms of NGO in India is the village-level development agency, and one of the most prominent of these, whose work I am familiar with having spent extended periods of time on its campus, is the Social Work and Research Centre (SWRC) in Rajasthan. The SWRC was established by an ex-student of the Doon School, and like Doon, though at a different level entirely, borrows from a statist ideology of 'nation-building'. Hence, an important part of SWRC's 'night-school' curriculum, meant for working village children, is concerned with instructions on proper voting procedure and other aspects of the parliamentary system of government.[10] In general, if one means to suggest that 'post-national social formations' contest the ideology of the nation state, then the inclusion of NGOs (of whatever form) in this category is a wildly optimistic, not to say inaccurate, exercise. It is in this context – that of post-colonised social formations – that I borrow from Jean Baudrillard's concept of the 'strategy of the real'.

The real

'To dissimulate', Baudrillard says, 'is to feign not to have what one has. To simulate is to feign to have what one hasn't' (Baudrillard 1988: 167). The realm of 'order', and 'proper functioning' in the regime of capital is what I will, following Baudrillard, call the 'real'; it is the state of affairs that capital would like us to believe is the norm in its realms. However, order, legality, etc. are constantly confronted by an oneiric swirl of events, constantly nibbling at its fragile edges: an intolerable situation for power and order, which must be remedied through the rejuvenating 'strategy of the real'. Hence, the fundamental urgency of the task of 'production and reproduction of the real' (*ibid.*: 180). The preceding chapters have outlined the several constituents of Indian modernity and in the present chapter I am concerned to draw together the various threads of the argument in order to outline the functioning of Indian modernity as a differentiating strategy. Strategies are produced at specific sites and the Doon School can be treated as the terrain of production of a post-colonised modernity – an Indian 'real' .

This task – the alchemical endeavour towards the resuscitation of a 'reality' which constitutes the blueprint of the post-colonised civil society and within whose circumference order may ply its trade – has, in the Indian case, involved a number of seemingly antagonistic forces. The transmogrification of public difference into private mutualism as a characteristic of Indian post-coloniality which, in effect, renders 'difference' impotent and domesticates its refractory possibilities, is also a topic of concern in this chapter. In the present discussion I mean to employ the term 'the post-colonised real' to refer to both an image as well as a process. In the discourse of the nation state, the real is that which is counterpoised against the disorder, the religious 'fundamentalism', the violence, the 'primitivism', and the 'backwardness' of the 'masses': it is the ordered, enlightened realm of the civil society which, precisely because, I suggest, it can be no where found, must be generated 'by models of a real without origin or reality' (*ibid.*: 166).

I do not regard this discussion, however, as 'part of the monolithic attitudes towards the issue of nationalism – shifting rapidly from unconditional celebration to contemptuous dismissal' (Ahmad 1992: 41); rather, I offer this critique as homage to the life and work of the socialist writer and activist Fanishwarnath Renu for whom the important question was 'what kind of community?', and 'for whom?'. For, without denying the colonial damage, imperial attitudes could be Indian as much as British. Renu's was a selective evaluation of modernity which exhorted us to analyse the post-colonised space as the realm of practices structured by the distribution of economic, political, and cultural power, rather than a condition to be either accepted or rejected monolithically.

The Doon School as an enclosed space with its own strictly regulated regime of time, morality, personal discipline, and public thought – the web of its regulatory fabric, in other words – is such a model of the real. There are, however, certain differences between the manner in which the School functions as a simulacrum of the post-colonised real and that proposed by Baudrillard in his more generalised discussion on the topic. His 'Disneyland imaginary' will serve to illustrate the point.

'Disneyland', Baudrillard says, 'is a perfect model of all the entangled orders of simulation' (1988: 171). The pastiche of phantasmagorical ideation and dream-like reality which is 'supposed' to be Disneyland's drawcard, he says, is not, in fact, what brings in the crowds: 'what draws the crowds is undoubtedly much more the social microcosm, the miniaturised and religious revelling in real America, in its delights and drawbacks' (*ibid.*, emphasis in the original). However, Baudrillard continues, the microcosmic flamboyance of the fantasy town's depictive energy which presents its audiences with an idealised version of a far from ideal reality – America without the warts – 'conceals something else':

> Disneyland is there to conceal the fact that it is the 'real' country, all of 'real' America, which *is* Disneyland (just as prisons are there to conceal the fact that it is the social in its entirety, in its banal omnipresence, which is carceral). Disneyland is presented as imaginary in order to make us believe that the rest is real, when in fact all of Los Angeles and the America surrounding it are no longer real, but of the order of the hyperreal and of simulation.
>
> (Baudrillard 1988: 172, emphasis in the original)

In Baudrillard's analysis, Disneyland operates as an 'inner' expiatory imago which, through the exaggerated drama of its operations, implies the presence of an 'outer' world which is its opposite:

> It [Disneyland] is meant to be an infantile world, in order to make us believe that the adults are elsewhere, in the 'real' world, and to conceal the fact that real childishness is everywhere, particularly among those adults who go there to act the child in order to foster illusion of their childishness.
>
> (Baudrillard 1988: 172)

The functioning of the Doon School as one of the elements of the simulacra of the real in contemporary Indian society – the world of 'post-colonial literature' to which I will return later, is another – unfolds in a different direction however. Within the geographical boundaries of the School are enacted measured scenes from the life of the civil society intended to show that 'uncivilised' existence is *elsewhere*: the 'secular' morning assembly, student interaction which emulates life in the contractual space of the metropolis which does not inquire after the caste of its citizens, and the constant effort to establish the 'scientific temper' as the defining ethic of the post-colonised nation state. These are elements missing from the life of the 'elsewhere' populations. And, as I have noted in earlier chapters, the School's pronouncements of these aspects of its life are pointed and explicit.

The caprice of 'ignorant' populations, their acts of public disorder, and the unaccountability of their 'regressive' impulses: these belong to refractory realms elsewhere; to a place with 'an element of magic about it, an uncritical credulousness, a reliance on the supernatural' (Nehru 1960: 163). The School and its population exist apart from these ways. And, further, they exist in silent but active communion with a larger but scattered community – of the 'civilised' post-colonials – which constitutes the community of the real. The Doon School is one of the elements of the strategy of the real which manufactures a discourse of difference on behalf of the nation state: that there exist civil spaces where the 'essential' nature of the nation state is both revealed and constantly under siege from forces of unreason. The School is Baudrillard's Disneyland reversed ('all sense exists here'), and the attempt here is towards an application of Baudrillard's political intent, rather than a perfect fit between his theory and my ethnography.

The terrain of this real is animated by those meticulous canons of 'modern' existence where the dogmas of atavistic custom have given way to the rationality of the social contract. The scattered community – shored up in fragmented spaces such as the Doon School, English-language newspaper offices, and post-colonial literature reading formations – most commonly gains its sense of collectivity through the written word; like anguished missives to fellow believers whose faith is in the process of being trampled by barbarous heathens, English-language magazines and newspapers carry reports of attempts on the life of the civil community and the 'body politic'; these are communiques from the front-line, describing the real under siege from its enemies. The word comes to constitute the world of the real: readers are joined together in a silent, horrified, embrace, against the savagery of their times, and within the 'civilised' sanctuary of the cognitive spaces of their habitus.[11]

Let me now reiterate the problematic of this chapter. The discourse of the post-colonised nation state speaks of a realm of order, rationality, efficiency, secularism, etc., with which it seeks to characterise its own present and future; and this discourse is disseminated through several sites of the civil society. The Doon School is one such site – a microcosm of the wider civility of the nation state operating according to the etiquette of 'civilised' existence. But the dissemination of this dialogue, I am suggesting, operates in the manner of a 'precession of models' (Baudrillard 1988). For neither at the level of the nation state, in terms of its actions that is, nor at that of its modular elaborations, the level of the School, do we actually find such a reality in operation. There are simply models of models, and maps of maps, and the only reality is that of the articulation of the discourse itself. And because the 'civil-system' comprehends this, the need to generate models of reality is absolutely essential. It must manufacture the mirrors in which to reflect its own non-existent image. And further, in this context, several types of organisations Appadurai refers to as 'post-national formations', assigning to them an anti-national disposition, function, in fact, as the bearers of the ideology of the nation state. The manner in which this ideology is disseminated has undergone transformation and scattering, not obliteration.

So the post-colonised nation state in India is based not just on imagination and on immense powers of coercion, but also upon, as it were, tiny playhouses constantly improvising dialogues on 'order', 'merit', secularism, rationality, etc.; little stages dotted all over the country, together forming the theatre which is the nation state itself. There is, I am suggesting here, a necessity for such a discursive universe because though it means to *reflect* the reality of the nature of the contemporary nation state, it is actually involved in the process of *manufacturing* it; it must manufacture it because it can no where actually be found, and for it to be common knowledge that the nation state is not, for example, secular or based on some neutral and 'modern' principle of merit is to put the 'reality' principle – and the interests of the chief beneficiaries of the largesse of the Indian nation state – in mortal danger. The Indian nation state is also figured through what could be called the 'primitive-civilised' imaginary. The 'primitive' is that which, either explicitly or implicitly, challenges the conflation of all existence into that of the nation state. The 'primitive' then also challenges the functioning of capital and the power vested in the most powerful of its supporting discourses: the techno-scientific enterprise of modernity. So, the simulacra of the real are crucial as circulating signifiers, constantly bolstering a reality that, in fact, is one which gets established in discourse.

Two specific occurrences of our time have helped particularly to bring into sharp focus the premonitions of the impending 'death' of the real. These are the opposition to the recommendations of the so-called Mandal Report by the upper castes, and the outbreak of Hindu barbarity over the Babri Masjid-Ramjanm Bhoomi affair at Ayodhya. Both events, in constituting important sites of delimitation of the real and the permanent from the 'aberrant' and the ephemeral, also signal the importance of the principle of 'death' (or 'near-death', we should say) for the continued health of 'a reality principle in distress' (*ibid.*: 173).

Media coverage of these two events should be seen as part of a mode of social analysis of civil society that is characterised by a teleological vehemence to locate savagery and 'aberrations' elsewhere. 'Mandal' and 'Babri' are also located in that redemptive space of liberal social science which exults in emblematic representations of its Others, their uninterrupted supply its succour. It requires their presence in order to further exhibit its own delimited territory.

The real as the territory of 'excellence' and 'merit'

Opposition to the Mandal Commission's recommendations on increased reservations in jobs for socially disadvantaged castes was as swift as it was unequivocal. Journalists, academics, and a bevy of media commentators spoke of the impending decline of 'merit' and 'efficiency' in the 'reserved' sectors, and of a new 'heightened' awareness of an aspect of Indian life which was, supposedly, fading into the background pursued by the avenging light of modern existence. And, as scores of agitated upper caste youth (mostly male) took to the streets to protest against the 'deleterious' effects of a reservations policy, others expressed their disgust in more tragic forms, setting themselves alight in a series of imitative self-immolations. Indian sociologists who had earlier expounded the importance of caste expeditiously discovered class (*viz.* their advocacy of an 'economic criterion' for reservations), and the central government faltered in its resolve to implement the recommendations of the Commission. The National Front, which had championed the cause of reservations, lost government at the next polls and the Congress party was returned to power with a substantial majority. It, in turn, referred the whole issue to the apex court of the country, the Supreme Court, for a legal opinion.

The account of the Mandal controversy provides the coda to the treatise on civil society: the urge towards 'merit', the striving for efficiency, the principle of 'objective' selection; the very reification of the idea of the social contract itself. It also brings into play that moment of concealment which seeks to evade the experiential brutality that 'capital doesn't give a damn about the idea of the contract which is imputed to it: it is a monstrous unprincipled undertaking, nothing more' (*ibid.*). The meritarian discourse also contributes, of course, to the elision of the fact that not only are there no 'realms' which operate according to some transcendent dictate on order and 'civility' – and that there is a continuity between the violence of the *Lumpenschaft* and that of the *Gesellschaft* – but also that, quite often, the 'disorder' of the former has its roots in the innate savagery of the latter.

In media analyses, the reservations issue was placed firmly in the wider narratives of order and disorder, rationality, custom, and contract: in the pronouncements of the 'civilised' national community, in other words. In December 1992, the Supreme Court declared itself in favour of the Mandal Commission's recommendations, endorsing 'Mandal's concept of caste . . . as the basis of reserving twenty seven per cent of all government jobs for Other Backward Castes' (Pathak 1992).[12] '[I]n the name of social justice', the *India Today* news-magazine noted, the verdict had 'paved the way for massive social confusion' (15 Dec. 1992). The spectre of 'social confusion' which is made to haunt the imagined space of the real – until now ostensibly *financial → cultural capital.*

animated by the cadence of contract and the lightness of the 'progressive' touch – is the specular mechanism employed to demonstrate that 'out there' there exists another world run on different principles.

But there are no other principles, no 'ideal' realm and its antithetical aberrations, and hence no possibility of acts of redemptive excoriation which would rid the social 'body' of cankerous accretions and restore it to 'normality'. For the sake of power's functioning, however, the system requires us to view certain zones of activity as aberrations. It thrives upon the tactic of visions of ruptured landscapes, of discrete realities. In recent years the School has witnessed an important change in the composition of its 'clientele' and this changing scenario provides a glimpse of the 'integrated' nature of the social. And the patronage of the School by this new clientele pays homage to the seamlessness of social practice and to the ineluctable importance of the School's social and cultural capital in the post-colonised condition.

This new clientele of the School consists of small business people, wealthy agriculturists, and other social groups who in India would not be regarded as the 'traditional' public school clientele. In 1991 I met one such parent, S.H., a resident of Calcutta whose main business was the manufacture and supply of school uniforms and who had brought his son to Doon for its admissions test; from his Muslim skull cap to his nylon trousers, S.H. stood out from the 'traditional' type of Doon parent through a differentiating technique of the body Mauss (1973) once spoke of.

I asked him why, when there were a number of 'good' schools in Calcutta itself, he wanted his son to study at Doon. 'It is not so much a matter of good schools', S.H. said, 'I am not greatly concerned with top marks in examinations . . . what I want is that he should understand that . . . in India . . . examination marks are not everything . . . there are other considerations.' These 'other considerations', S.H. elaborated, concern the forging of links which, as he ingenuously put it, 'is how the people here [i.e. those connected with Doon] do so well'. It is in this light that the supposed rupture between the real – the realm based upon the 'logic' of merit, the rule of 'law' – and its aberrant Other, the 'backward' realm marked by the claims of the unmeritorious who secure positions due to 'other' factors, should be seen.

S.H. and several other parents I talked to during the course of research – a shop owner from Meerut, a small-time politician in Luckow – implicitly contest the image of itself the School would like to foster: that it occupies a domain which is discontinuous with the rest of the society, a discontinuity informed by an ethical schema. With the merciless scrutiny of dealers in the currency of capital – financial capital for cultural capital – they strip the nostalgia of the (School's) real of its pretensions to carve out dichotomous domains. In effect they say this: that the way in which the culturally specific world of the School functions is entirely along similar lines to that in which, say, an official system of job reservations might work; that the School is able to equip those with financial resources with the cultural capital to manoeuvre both in the cultural world of Indian modernity and in that of the emergent global system. And hence, they are willing to pay for the right to participate in the gracious unfolding of its bounties.

In fact, quite early in the life of the School, Headmaster Arthur Foot was assiduously at work preparing the ground for the play of social capital, working the soil, as it were, for that fruitful encounter between colonial cultural capital and post-colonised capitalism; his activities in this regard should also be seen as a statement on the nature of the narratives of the real: that these function as constituents of the strategy of the real, that task of producing a likeness – through the photism of working models – of times, spaces, and moralities which can no where be found.

In 1939 Foot undertook a remarkable journey, the aim of which was the consolidation of the nexus between industrial capital and the post-colonised cultural capital the School was in the process of evolving. In that year Foot met the heads of several large private firms and secured a recruitment relationship that endures, in various forms, to this day. Outlining the importance of his 'expedition', Foot noted in the *Doon School Weekly* (*DSW*) that Doon boys should enjoy good prospects with industry 'having developed the same qualities' as those of English public school boys:

> My visits were made to the heads of separate undertakings, such as engineering works, shipping lines, tea estates, jute mills, cement factories, in each of which the parent company owns the major part of the share capital, while independent shareholders hold the rest. . . . In the past the majority of the technical staff, engineers, mill managers, chemists etc. have been Europeans, but for various reasons they are now appointing Indians with technical qualifications instead.
>
> (*DSW*, 11 Feb. 1939)

It is the functioning of the 'democratic' nation state, with its 'free' citizens, as a configuration of networks based on a system of personal knowledge and obligation, which it becomes the task of the strategy of the real to mask. And schools such as Doon are important outposts of this strategy.

The charter of the post-colonised civil society is written in the vocabulary of 'objective' qualifications, 'equality of opportunity' and the 'compensatory principle' which 'seeks to discriminate in favour of groups that had in the past been discriminated against' (Béteille 1981: 23). The real is marked by the 'reasonableness' of these two concepts of 'equality'. The real is 'reasonable' by virtue of the judicious mix of the policies that govern its functioning. Hence, Béteille speaks of the balanced nature of the Indian constitution, a document *par excellence* of the real: 'Both the meritarian and the compensatory principles are to be found among the equality provisions in our Constitution' (*ibid.*).

However Foot's elaboration of the nature of 'qualifications' – an indispensable phoneme of the politico-cultural lexicon through which the notion of the contractual civil society is articulated – which made for success in the post-colonised condition is interesting; if we are to follow his discussion on the matter, they would seem to be somewhat other than the mundane distinction of a university epaulette, or some objective criteria open to all. 'The Imperial Bank of India', Foot reported of his travels, 'has a definite scheme laid down in a prospectus ... for the recruitment of boys.' Boys wishing 'to qualify for a post as an officer', he continued, would have to join the bank as clerks and would be paid a small stipend. However

> While working as a clerk a boy who is of the social class and personality likely to qualify him for future selection as an officer will be under the special notice of the authorities, and will be able to study for the Examination of the Institute of Bankers, which must be passed before reaching a higher grade.
>
> (*DSW*, 11 Feb. 1939)

Further, there were certain other 'qualifications' also required in the new world of 'merit' and 'efficiency'. It was also important, Foot concluded, 'that a boy who aims at achieving success in the administrative side of any business must be able to speak English with a very high degree of accent and fluency' as well as 'correct pronunciation'; and further that 'efficiency in this respect is a sign of self discipline and can be achieved by any boy in the Doon School, if he takes the trouble' (*ibid.*).

'Efficiency' was a matter of a social cosmetic and linked to the task of curing faults of personality. So, the *Doon School Book* (*DSB*) noted that '[Headmaster Foot] takes the responsibility of teaching boys in the lower classes the way to correct common errors in the pronunciation of English, and inculcates simple devices to cure the common faults':

> These faults are really only 5 in number (1) v for w, (2) w for v, (3) d for th in the, and t for th in thing, (4) slurring of ch, dge sounds and terminals, (5) said, head, and allied words pronounced sad, had. He shows how these can be corrected by proper use of the tongue, lips and teeth.
>
> (*DSB*: 21)

Arthur Foot's deft positioning of the desideratum of liberalism – 'efficiency', 'discipline', and, he may well have said, 'merit' – into a discretionary taxonomy of 'social class and personality', seems not, however, to have led to any amount of self-reflexivity on the part of the School's associates. Indeed, almost all the ex-students of the School I met spoke out vehemently against the recommendations of the Mandal Report, describing it as anomalous in a democratic society and against the norms of 'rationality' and 'equality'. In recent years the School has attempted to add to the system of contacts with prospective employers initiated by Foot – and a system of 'apprenticeships' for senior boys, to be undertaken during school holidays, was initiated during the 1980s.

The editorial comments from *India Today* that the Supreme Court's validation of the recommendations of the Mandal Report would lead to 'massive social confusion'[13] typifies the process of sustaining the real. The twin spectres of disorder and 'demerit' function as a deterrence mechanism: involved in the process of the manufacture of the image of orderly realms – of a real whose integrity is threatened by the 'irrationalities' of a system of job reservations. 'Social confusion' is, then, the border between the Indian real and its perceived enemies, and a *cri de coeur* against encroachments upon its territory; the preservation of the real becomes a task for all 'civilised' citizens, for the 'social confusion' which threatens to ride the wake of reservations is the very mark of an 'immature', 'backward' people. The defence of the realm of the real is articulated in terms of a moral duty, and extant positions of power find play as spiritual crusades against barbaric others.

In as much as the School functions as an important adjunct of Indian liberalism – embodying and magnifying all its attitudes: 'modernity', 'rationality', 'secularism' – we must also see it as embodying all its vicious contradictions and all its monstrous hypocrisies. And it is here, in the attempt to circumvent the contradictions and obscure the hypocrisies, that the 'strategy of the real' takes on an urgency all its own; the task of fabricating the real – in the telling and retelling of its myth of order, merit, and efficiency – and of maintaining its cohesiveness has always attracted the support (as I have argued throughout the book) of a very wide cross-section of the Indian intelligentsia.

Romancing the real: the helpfulness of friends and the kindness of enemies

The discursive project of the real unfolds at two distinct levels: on the level of abstraction that allows for the play of a theory of civil society, and on the level of modular representation which makes for a concretionary elaboration of theory. The first strand is most clearly articulated in the annals of the various sciences of society. 'The distinction between societies which assign priority to the group in their classification and those which assign priority to the individual', Béteille suggested in an essay on the 'backward classes', 'corresponds in large measure to the distinction made famous by Henry Maine between societies based on status and those based on contract' (1981: 32). There is a strong case, he goes on to say, for ensuring that 'justice' – in terms of constitutionally enshrined positive discrimination – be rendered to those castes and communities which in the past have suffered the most under the prohibitions of the Brahminical order. However, while conceding the need for the 'compensatory principle' of equity, a strong plea is made for 'individualism' and hence, by implication, for that social realm where the 'new social order' forges its community through the logic of contract:

Justice must be rendered to the castes and communities which have in the past been denied justice; but if we do this without any regard at all for the cost to the individual, instead of moving forward into the new social order promised by the makers of our Constitution, we might move back into the Middle Ages.

(Béteille 1981: 32)

And then, a few pages later, 'social confusion' makes an appearance in one of its several incarnations, here as the atavism of communitarian frenzy and the embrace of parochial passions:

Above all, in the context of Indian society, here and now, we must realize that the alternative to individualism may not be the cherished dream of socialism, but a moral order in which the individual is once again displaced by clan, caste and community.

(Béteille 1981: 44)

This position has strong historical precedence in Indian reformist discourse. Govardhanram Tripathy (1855–1907), the author of the famous nineteenth-century Hindi novel *Sarvaswatichandra*, for example, was a staunch supporter of widow marriage but was happy to see the issue deferred so as not to upset social equilibrium (Chandra 1994: 111) – just as Béteille wants to prevent 'social chaos' which might come about through a too zealous attitude to reform. 'The morality of justice, in the final analysis' Govardhanram was to suggest, 'is neutralised by the need for a social equilibrium' (*ibid.*). It was within these realms of the moral and social order – where individualism could find full potential – that S.R. Das wished to situate his school, inscribing its territory with the techno-cultural hieroglyphics of the civil society; the solution to 'social confusion' lay in the forceful acts of every-day life at school. Das's formulation of the objectives of the Indian Public Schools Society (IPSS), the School's governing body, provides the link with the wider discourse of post-coloniality such as that of Béteille's:

The objects of the Society are:-

... to develop a spirit of Indian nationality by destroying all social, communal, religious or provincial prejudices among the students and fostering a spirit of comradeship among them.

(*Constitution of the Indian Public Schools Society*, 1936/1986)

The second level of the project of the real, the one at which the School enters the picture and also at which the metaphysics of 'post-coloniality' is produced, is concerned with epigrammatic elaborations of the little way-stations of the civil society; at this level attempts are made to forge links between the theories and dreams of civil society and the sites of praxis where these are given concretionary existence. This is where, of course, the School participates in the overall project of the real. For some, the assassination of Rajiv

Gandhi – Prime Minister and former student of the Doon School – provided a singularly apt occasion for its amplification; the tragedy of a sudden, grotesque, death along with the mnemonic and rhetoric of civil society – specifying the personality and training required of its chief actors – combined to produce a potent sense of the evanescence of the real, the impending disintegration of the civil itself.

The following is one example of the media discussion surrounding Rajiv Gandhi's assassination. In the process of establishing the separateness of the system which had produced men such as Gandhi from the society characterised by the 'timelessly churning wheel of vicissitude',[14] it implicitly outlines the specific qualities which delimit institutions of the civil society such as the Doon School. The following obituarial note written by the editor of *India Today* provides a good example of the nature of the linkages sought to be established between the theory of civil society and the various sites of its implementation:

> I was Rajiv Gandhi's classmate in Doon School but I was never his friend. We just knew each other. At school he never drew attention to himself either in the classroom or in the playing fields. In those days it mattered little whose son or grandson you were.
>
> (*India Today*, 15 June 1991)

Here, 'those days' refers not just to the passage of time, but also to the delineation of space such that 'those days' is the 'timeless' space of the School: 'that time' does duty for 'that place' and, through the fantasy of nostalgia and the sieve of memory, the space of the School is transformed into an emotionally experienced reality. Hence, the commutation involved is not merely a celebration of childhood – 'school days' – it is also a statement of the specificities of the environment of the Doon School. The nostalgia for the past combines with the specifications for how 'society' should function. And, because the milieu of the School with regard to the operation of social capital – 'contacts' – belies the rhetoric of 'merit' and 'efficiency' through which it seeks to constitute itself as unique, the strategy of the real becomes imperative in manufacturing a discourse of difference.

The manufacture of what we might call the little discourse of the real, the second level of the overall project, also takes the form of an eristic engagement with the 'enemy', whereupon the triumphant outcome becomes as much a function of the nature of the 'arguments' as of the identity of those presenting them. In this context, it is important to consider the public positions of some of those who have spoken on behalf of the School. The School gains from their advocacy as a 'corollary' to public knowledge of their 'eminence' in various fields; the munificence the comfort of their words brings is particularly substantial where the advocate happens to be a representative of 'mass' interests, having 'proved' his or her credentials in the 'service of the nation' on behalf of its most disadvantaged populations. For here, those who would 'naturally' oppose the School on the grounds of political belief, come to 'rationally' appraise (and appreciate) its value in national life.

The Founders Day celebrations of the Doon School, held during November each year, are an important occasion for the speeches and talks which go towards constituting the discursive domain of civil society: the domain of what, in the opening paragraph of this chapter, I have referred to as domesticated difference. The School is one of several sites (English-language newspapers are another) of civil society where seemingly opposed opinions gather to join into a harmonious whole in praise of the real. In this manner, it serves as an important location for the epistemic elaboration (with all the connotations of boundedness and discrete territories that 'episteme' entails) of a fundamental theme of civil society, that of 'freedoms', here in the form of 'diversity of opinion'; the real exists within a 'healthy' tension of diverse opinions, in the pell-mell of a multi-vocality presented as the condition of modernity itself.

A large number of the invitees to School events are drawn from the political and cultural world of which the School is also a part and one would expect an active association on their part with the School. Their involvement in the discourses of the School, as part of the strategy of the real does not, then, come as a surprise. Hence, School visitors such as Sir Mirza Ismael, a prominent administrator in the princely states of Mysore, Hyderabad, and Jaipur, Sir Akbar Hydari, also an officer of the Hyderabad court, and Prakash Tandon, corporate luminary, were, of course, part of the School's constituency; feudal interests and major industrialists had, after all, provided generous financial support to the IPSS (see Appendix 1). The visitors list, and the unfolding of the strategy of the real, takes on a special significance, however, when we come to those whose public stance was one of seeming opposition to the ideals and objectives of an institution such as Doon.

Since Independence, succeeding governments have reiterated their 'commitment' to an 'equitable' system of education as a matter of public policy. So, if the Report of the Education Commission of 1964 spoke of the 'equalisation of educational opportunity' (Singh 1991: 1606), then the Ramamurthy Report on education (1990), devoted a 'good deal of attention . . . to issues relating to social justice and education and allied matters' (*ibid.*). These public commitments, and their formal expressions as policy, did not, however, inhibit many of the states' most senior functionaries from showering their effusive benediction onto the Doon School. The list of ministers of education of the central government and university Vice-chancellors who have presided over various School ceremonies bears witness to that.[15]

The School also played host to figures whose public activities could be interpreted as dissidence against the 'system'. The careers and commitments of two of them, V.V. Giri and Jayprakash Narayan, and their liaison with the School forces us to reflect upon the nature of dissidence and 'opposition' within the contemporary nation state in India. Giri, who first visited the School in 1958 and was later, when President of the Republic, again invited to preside over the Founders Day ceremonies in 1973, spent his early life as an active trade unionist. A founder member of the Indian Railwaymen's Federation, he also served as president of the Trade Union Congress;[16] and the long and sustained commitment of Jayprakash Narayan to both socialism and Gandhian philosophy hardly needs detailed reference here (see Bhattacharjee 1975).

Visits by men such as Giri and Narayan – delivering homilies at a gathering of students, handing out awards at Founders Day – were meticulously recorded in School publications and play an important part in the construction of the local level discourse of the real; a range of opinion, seemingly antagonistic to it, comes to pay homage to the School and the world to which it belongs.

Among the many building blocks of the real I have earlier mentioned, are the arguments based upon the play of 'natural excellence' and 'merit' that supposedly obtain there. A succinct summary of this view was provided by Vice-president Dr Zakir Hussain in a speech to a gathering of Doon students and masters in 1963. In the public arena, Hussain's image was of a man who 'under the transforming and transmuting spell of Gandhiji's leadership [had] decided to dedicate the best years of [his] life to the cause of national education' (Hussain 1965: 1–2) under the aegis of the National Council for Education. Responding to the 'fervent criticism' of the system of public school education, the official history of the School notes, Hussain 'summed up' the case for these schools in his speech 'with his customary rationality' (Singh 1985: 102). 'Allegiance to democracy, equality and a classless society', Hussain noted, 'sometimes makes people feel jealous of, even impatient with, excellence which is not universally shared. This could happen with reference to your school as it happens to public schools in other places' (*ibid.*).

The real as the domain of the secular

The other event of contemporary importance through which the strategy of the real can be glimpsed is the 'dispute' over the Babri Masjid-Ramjanm Bhoomi site in Ayodhya. I have suggested earlier that what passes for 'secularism' among the members of the School and its visitors is, in fact, strongly circumscribed within a cultural and ritual framework distinctly redolent of Hindu religious life, and that in this way the School has contributed towards producing an intelligentsia – prominent journalists, novelists, and others – which regards its own cultural world, one hemmed in by the symbols of the *majority* culture, as multi-cultural and multi-religious.

In Chapter 4 I noted that the demolition of the historical and religious structure known as Babri Masjid in Ayodhya elicited a large volume of anguished public opinion on the part of the 'secular' intelligentsia. From among the reactions, I reproduced a section of a letter to *The Pioneer* newspaper – written by, among others, associates of Doon – condemning the Hindu agitators. One part of the letter spoke of the 'abyss' at which the nation stood and the need to reaffirm 'India's traditions of religious tolerance and diversity'. In the same edition of the paper is a comment from a journalist questioning the 'moral' right of Prime Minister Narasimha Rao to continue in office in the wake of the demolition. After what the demolishers have done, the journalist concludes,

> they can have little rationale to offer as to why the Kashmir valley should continue to be on the map of India, or why, for that matter, some of the north-eastern States with Christian majority should not break away. The only rationale for these territories to remain within this country is its basic secular ethos which has bound the nation together so far.
>
> (Jha: 1992)

They are to be blamed: this is the discursive realm of the Indian version of a 'two worlds theory', where the liberals forever hold the fort in the name of the nation state against the fascists 'out there'. This is also the place to make the connection between the post-colonial literary formation (its readers and writers) and the two worlds of Indian post-coloniality proffered in these works; for, like the Doon School, Anglo-Indian writing is also a part of the simulacra of the Indian real, manufacturing images of the enemies of the modern nation state. Here, as Chakrabarty notes (citing an instance from Rushdie's *The Satanic Verses*), 'too often it is assumed that the battle lines are clear: it is the values of a modern, liberal and secular outlook confronting those of an anti-modern, dogmatic, blind, illiberal and fundamentalist one' (1993b: 3). But, precisely because the battle lines are not clear, and because those espousing the 'values of a modern, liberal and secular outlook' have for long enjoyed the very anti-modern munificence of extensive state patronage, the strategy of the real must be brought into play to create the illusion of difference.

So, the attack on the Babri Masjid came to be constructed as another manifestation of the difference between the civilised post-colonial identity (the cosmopolitan, 'post-national' reader of *The Satanic Verses* perhaps, in whose world the critical perspectives of Fanishwarnath Renu, Rahul Sankrityayan and Krishna Sobti have no place) and its primitive, provincial, antithesis. The strategy of the real in this instance – as it functioned in newspaper and magazine pages – acted to elide the fact that the mosque was demolished through a coalition of forces which included the 'modernist, Westernised middle class intelligentsia' (Nandy 1990: 98) along with the 'fundamentalists' being denounced.

There are, however, *two* fronts on which the strategy of the real must operate in the present context. On the one hand, it must reiterate that the nation state and its ancillaries such as the Doon School operate in a secular manner, contrary to the ethos of the world of the 'fundamentalists'. And on the other, it must emphasise that there are no connections whatsoever between the 'non-modern' and the 'modern' worlds of the post-colonised nation state. I want here chiefly to concentrate on the latter claim and will address the issue via a controversial essay by Ashis Nandy on a case of *sati* by the young widow Roop Kanwar in Rajasthan in the late 1980s. Nandy writes that the 'modern' Indian reaction to the horrific incident completely sidelined the issue of the latter's own part in Roop Kanwar's death; and that, in effect, the reality of her death was a 'joint communiqué' (*ibid.*: 97) – to quote him from another context – between several sectors of society. This reaction – the branding of the *sati* supporters as barbaric – Nandy further suggests, has more to do with a time of rapid change in which 'the only way *modern* Indians can retain their social and political dominance is by setting themselves up as the final bastion of rationality and as the vanguard of social change in India' (Nandy 1988b: 20, emphasis added).

The responsibility for this contemporary tragedy, he goes on to argue, 'should be shared by social forces to which . . . urban Indians have contributed handsomely' (*ibid.*: 23). These 'social forces' include the rationality of the market place which has benefited a narrow stratum of Indian society and which, in turn, nurtures the 'business culture of religious spectacles, *melas, yatras* and family inheritances' (*ibid.*: 21) of which Roop Kanwar's *sati* was a part. So Nandy does not seek to defend the widow's death in an indigenist vein. Rather, he is concerned to bring into analytical play those social forces which produce spectacles of barbarity – spectacles which allow the modern Indian to say: 'barbarity exists elsewhere', and 'they are to be blamed'. His analysis allows us to interrupt the strategy of the real, to say that there do not exist discrete realms of the (liberal) good and the (fundamentalist) bad and that savagery is not elsewhere.

Now, following from this, I want to suggest that the deployment of a strategy of the real in the Babri Masjid case was occasioned by the necessity to make impervious certain 'conditions of possibility' to which the urban, post-colonised intelligentsia has contributed 'handsomely'. The demolition of the mosque – sponsored by several politico-religious organisations – was carried out by provincial youth who were not only exhibiting animosity towards the Muslim minority; their act, unjustifiable as it was, was also an expression of antipathy towards the metropolitan 'secular' intelligentsia.[17] However, I think the rage had not so much to do with the latter's secular inclinations as with its position in a system of governance – the nation state – where the cultural and political capital of metropolitan life has privileged it materially at the expense of other populations. The foot-soldiers of the army which demolished the mosque are also the products of a process of grossly uneven development which has seen a privileged few prosper through their participation in and control of metropolitan cultural and economic life; the differential educational system of the provincial and metropolitan cities is an important manifestation of this.[18]

It is precisely the non-secular nature of the every-day functioning of the institutions of civil society, as I have suggested is the case with Doon, which makes a strategy of the real, in this case the claim of its 'secular values', imperative. The 'secular values of India' to which the letter above refers is a constitutionally derived notion which does indefatigable duty in the speeches and homilies at countless public occasions concerned with the 'welfare' of the state and civil society. However, the 'real system' – one supposedly informed by the noble sentiments of constitutional dictates, and which may be 'rescued' by lancing the 'fundamentalist' boil upon its body – does not itself exist anywhere. The events at Ayodhya are not *aberrant* acts of 'backward' populations, they are part of the functioning of a larger system where, as in the case of Doon, 'secularism' operates as policy rather than practice, a system in which institutions such as the Doon School have played an important role in elaborating a 'Hindu equals secular' post-coloniality. Hence, the acts of 'the fascists' and the 'devious Kar sevaks' (as public pronouncements branded the Hindu agitators at Ayodhya) are only extreme, and highly visible, manifestations of the overall milieu; we should, as Uberoi puts it in another context, 'resist the intellectual terror that would have us find separate and different causes for the good and the bad sides of . . . modernity' (Uberoi 1978: 84).

Dissent and the post-colonised real

The 'reality' of the real has not, however, always gone unquestioned, nor have its claims been left uncontested. Its critics have attempted to provide alternatives to the version of modernity propagated therein. The School and its proponents have, in turn, engaged with their interrogators in the manner of a competitive joust for the prize of the entire intellectual and cultural territory of the nation state.

Opposition to the School and the system of values it represents, though fragmentary, has come from notable quarters. In 1937, two years after Doon's establishment, Gandhi put forward his scheme of 'Basic Education', a pedagogical project of great ambition. For it constituted a holistic treatment of the self, through incorporating the immediate reality of social existence including manual work into the sphere of education. Learning, Gandhi could be said to be suggesting, consists not in the phenomenological surrender to the (all-) knowing subject – the *guru* – but, rather, must be constituted as an entirely decentred activity; here, there are no comforts of a 'truth' which is the 'reward' of sublimation, but only a complex learning and unlearning which mimics the warps and woofs of the products of the *charkha* (Gandhi 1951). The response to his ideas was as swift as it was unequivocal. The novelist Mulk Raj Anand considered that if Gandhi's scheme became reality, schools would come to be populated by pupils of limited capability who would 'vegetate within the limits of their self-sufficient communities'(Kumar 1989: 2473).

One of the participants in discussions against the Basic Education scheme was the then Joint Secretary in the education department, Girja Shankar Bajpai. Around the time it was publicly mooted, two of Bajpai's sons were students at the Doon School and he had been, it will be remembered, part of the group which had gone to Dehra Dun in 1933 to choose the campus for the new school. So Bajpai's participation in the debate had a wider context than that connected with his official position as an education bureaucrat. In May 1938, an agitated Bajpai addressed the issue of 'Gandhian' education in a letter to an acquaintance, the missive belonging to that private circuit of opinions through which sections of the Indian metropolitan intelligentsia often engaged with Gandhi's ideas. 'I am', he wrote, 'no lover of the Wardha stunt as you call it. One object we had in persuading the Central Advisory Board of Education to appoint a committee to go into the Wardha scheme was to provide an opportunity for authoritative exposure of its crudities and absurdities' (*ibid.*).

Some months after the above correspondence, Gandhi himself was to outline his position on schools such as Doon with engaging directness. In August 1939 T.L.H. Smith-Pearse, then Principal of the Rajkumar College at Raipur and one of the founders of the Indian Public Schools Conference (IPSC), wrote to Gandhi seeking to enlist his support in the cause of public school education (*Handbook on the Indian Public School* 1964: 16). Gandhi responded that he remained unconvinced by the arguments put forward by the IPSC and that in time 'the Basic Education experiment' would 'provide ample data for the school of your dream' (*ibid.*).

Other prominent critics of the School included K.R. Kriplani, Rector of the school at Tagore's Shantiniketan, and Morarji Desai, veteran Congress politician and Janata party Prime Minister in the post-Emergency years. Kriplani declined an invitation to associate his institution with the IPSC on the grounds of 'a fundamental difference' between their outlook on education; and further, on the grounds that his institution did not aim to produce 'leaders', but, rather, 'self-respecting, harmoniously developed human beings' (*ibid.*: 22) who could challenge colonial rule.

But perhaps the most vociferous criticism came from Morarji Desai, doubly remarkable for the fact that he voiced it at the School's annual Founders Day in 1976. Breaking with tradition, Desai spoke to the School in Hindustani and, in a speech of unrelenting admonition, warned that the audience must expect to hear some 'harsh truths'. Rebuking the School for maintaining a system of entrenched privileges for a minority, he warned that if it were up to him he 'would not allow even a single public school to exist' (*DSW*, 11 Nov. 1976). It is some measure of the School's confidence in its own place in the world that it invited Desai, a prominent and long-standing critic of the public school system, to be the chief guest on its Founders Day. It was no doubt emboldened by the knowledge that Desai's opinions could easily be counterbalanced by equally vociferous support from several of the state's other crucial functionaries and intellectuals.[19]

Dissent to the School's vision of modernity from within the School is rare,[20] and in this context it is important to keep in mind the specific circumstances of a post-colonised society. It is true, of course, that a generalised (or 'joyful', to use During's term) understanding of the 'post-colonial' space appears to lead some to expect an all-pervasive insurrectionary milieu against universalising discourses (of modernity, whatever), and an eruption of fragments and little histories. However, the comprehension of post-colonised complexities ought to stem such romanticisation. This is not to suggest that Doon's version of modernity meets no resistance from within the post-colonised space but, rather, that we ought to recognise the differential history of institutional forms within post-colonised and other societies. Hence, while we need to pay heed to the contradictions to the dominant ideology that Connell *et al.* (1982) discovered in their study of Australian schools, we need also to think about how such contradictions might be dissipated in post-colonised societies where the commitment to, say, instrumental rationalism has a very different history.

So, while ex-students such as B.M. (1950–6), who was also a master there for five years during the 1960s, spoke critically of the School's philosophy of modernity, these opinions are neither treated with any seriousness nor given coverage; one of B.M.'s newspaper articles critical of the School was returned to him with a note from the editor, a former Doon student, stating that it would not be published since it dealt with 'internal' matters of the School. Another article by him was published in a special supplement of a national newspaper to commemorate the Golden Jubilee of the School in 1985. In it he remembers his former English Housemaster at Doon who 'inspite of his love for nurturing sweetpeas and strawberries . . . bristled with violence and aggression' and who regularly defied 'the school's ban on corporal punishment with impunity'; and with regard to whom, given the prevailing environment of the School, 'there was no question of any further court of appeal beyond his domain. He was English, white and sacrosanct in Free India!' (Malik 1985).

Women associated with the School – as wives and mothers – are expected to behave according to informal rules of association. In general, the School requires that 'its' women bask in the reflected glories of the males they are attached to, those with direct connections with the School. The following comment in a School magazine from one woman, married to a 'Dosco' and the mother of another, is a fair indication of the roles many like her adopt. She noted how, thanks to the varied extra-curricular activities the School arranges for its students, 'one can quite literally see the child evolving into a fine man' (Aiyer 1985: 158); and after expressing some 'disenchantment' with the Dosco 'personality' ('self-centred', 'clannish', 'childish' tendencies), she concluded in a reconciliatory tone 'but the School remains one, from which I as a mother have always received much warmth' (*ibid.*). For others who choose to express opinions critical of the School, retribution is swift and voluminous. R.S., whose husband was at Doon in the 1950s, described the reaction to a newspaper article about Doon she wrote in 1973 as 'unexpectedly vicious'. And in an article she recounted that 'they [the Old Boys] reacted with a volley of abuse . . . with expressions that ranged from sarcasm to invective and vituperation' (Sahai 1985: 121–2).

The perception on the part of Doon's associates is that the School no longer needs to respond to any criticism levelled at its system of education, for threats to its existence, if ever there were any, have long been effaced through a 'natural' process of the development of a 'rational' attitude towards its value to society. This opinion was unambiguously conveyed by several of Doon's associates. The School's staunchest ally has, in fact, been the nation state, and the state and the School have charted post-coloniality in a warm embrace of mutual benefit. Whereas the former has provided sustained moral and (indirect) financial support, the latter reciprocates through a cadre of the intelligentsia of liberal nationhood which, in turn, supplies the philosophical sophistry to cover its (the state's) contradictions through a science of personality centred on the division between the 'progressive' and the 'backward' sections of the population; it repays the generosity of the state through participation in the strategy of the real.

The lie of the land: the state and the School

The event that provides the most graphic summary of the silent contract between the state and the School is the Golden Jubilee celebrations of 1985. The private commemoration of adolescent memory and institutional nostalgia found a generous patron in the various organs of the state. The cornucopian delights of the four-day event, stretching from 31 October to 3 November, when Old Boys, their wives, and others, frolicked in the warmth of reminiscence, also owed a considerable debt to the inertia of public opinion: the manner in which public funds were commandeered for the cause of the Jubilee elicited negligible reaction from the normally vociferous liberal intelligentsia devoted to the cause of exposing political chicanery corrosive of the 'democratic process'. Of course, several members of the same intelligentsia were bound to a compact of silence through their own, varied, affiliations to the School – an allegiance which, in 1985, carried considerable politico-cultural currency given that the chief guest at the Jubilee was none other than Prime Minister Rajiv Gandhi.

Preparations for the Jubilee celebration had begun several years in advance: fund-raising activities had a target of one crore Rupees and a considerable sum was realised through a one-day India–Australia cricket match specially organised for the purpose. Describing the arrangements, *The Statesman* newspaper (1 Nov. 1985) reported that 'power generating sets mounted on trucks have been supplied by the Army', and that 'several scores of jawans [soldiers], were to clear spaces for Old Boys to park their cars. Officers and men can be seen on the school campus long beyond they normally would be at their places of work.' And, in a timely move 'for the invitees of the Doon School event, the Central Command Tattoo has been fixed for Friday and Saturday. . . . And while the Army may maintain that it is only coincidental that the tattoo is timed with the Golden Jubilee, the school, on its part, makes no secret, in its printed program of the fact that it is part of the Jubilee' (*ibid.*).

The Army also provided additional accommodation for the crush of visitors, and many were billeted at the premises of the Indian Military Academy and other Army establishments located in Dehra Dun. The facilities of the local military hospital, along with an ambulance, were also made available to the School to cater for medical emergencies. The civil authorities were, however, no less forthcoming: 'Guest houses of the Survey of India, Income Tax, Bharat Heavy Electricals, Oil and Natural Gas Commission and some other undertakings are also being used' (*ibid.*). In nearby Mussorie, rooms were made available at the National Academy of Administration, the training institute for civil servants.

There was some consternation, however, over whether the Chief Minister of Uttar Pradesh ought to be invited to the function or not, since 'he is neither an Old Boy [nor] a parent, and so cannot qualify . . .' (*ibid.*). However, his assistance had been invaluable and he had personally 'visited this town ten days ago to see if the district administration had things under control' (*ibid.*). It was thought that the Headmaster 'would have to demand his absence from the Jubilee function'. This was a delicate issue indeed since not only had the state government 'granted excise exemption on liquor to be consumed' by the visitors but had also made available the services of a team of engineers from the State Electricity Board. The engineers, led by the Chief Engineer of the Board, 'went around checking all the electrical fittings on the school grounds' (*ibid.*).

However, the intimacy between the state and the School is not always so graphic, nor its mechanism so patent, in other areas of their liaison. This is especially true of those fraternal acts from which the School draws moral succour. The Merit Scholarship scheme of the central government, discussed in Chapter 6, was one such instance of quiet connubiality. It functioned as the practical elaboration of the legal fiction of 'equality of opportunity': 'there can never be equality of talent', Minister of Education, M.C. Chagla, informed a School gathering in 1965, 'and the duty of the State is to find people who have got very fine talent and give them the opportunity to make best use of their talents . . . and that is why the Ministry of Education gives merit scholarships to the public schools' (Singh 1985: 109). Here the state not only shoulders the financial responsibility for providing for a limited number of 'underprivileged' students from finite funds for *all* educational activity, but also pays homage to that educational system. The function of the public schools, Chagla was to add in his speech, is to 'find the most gifted boys in our country and give them the best education that is possible and feasible . . . to give our country the leaders of our country [*sic*]' (*ibid.*).

But perhaps the finest eulogy composed by the state to the Doon system of education has come in the form of the recent scheme of government-run Navodaya Vidyalayas, schools established on the Doon model. Doon now functions as the imago of the government scheme initiated 'to provide good quality modern education . . . to the talented children [*sic*] predominantly from the rural areas' (*Navodaya Vidyalaya Annual Report* 1989). Under the

1986 National Policy of Education it was 'decided to set up residential schools ... on an average one in each district during the Seventh Five Year Plan' (*ibid.*). Between 1986 and 1989, 256 such schools had been established and admission to the co-educational Vidyalayas is, as at Doon School, on the basis of tests, with all educational expenses being borne by the central government.

It is the corporeal reproduction of public school life at these government schools which constitutes the implicit recognition of the former's prototypic significance: the liberal discourse of the metropolis now casts its ideological gaze upon the fractal tendencies of the province, seeking to bind it to the uniform geometry of 'national integration'; and it is through the agency of the state that sectoral ideology is converted into a national enterprise through an obeisant concert of mimicry moving from district to district. So, at the Vidyalayas 'co-curricular activities and games and sports form an integral part of the curriculum ...[and]... national integration, international under-standing, inculcation of proper values, spirit of healthy competition are essential features of all these activities' (*ibid.*). Some of the other objectives of the schools, the Annual Report says, are 'to develop esprit-de-corps' and 'to develop sportsmanship and leadership qualities'. In this indirect manner, through a verbatim reproduction of the public school manifesto, the state acknowledges their 'importance' – an aspect not lost on those at Doon; 'our scheme of education is officially approved' was a constant refrain during my stay at the School.

The Navodaya scheme is, however, only the latest in a long history of cultural and economic collaboration between the state and the School. Around 1927, for example, an appeal of support for the School was issued in the name of many of the state's most significant servants: 'among whom were the Vice Chancellors of Delhi University, Madras University, Aligarh Muslim University (Aligarh), Lucknow University, Patna University and Mysore University' (Singh 1985: 14). The rapport between the Vice-chancellors and the School established at that time has continued: one of the positions on the Board of Governors of the School is reserved for a 'leading educationist' in the person of a university Vice-chancellor. And, upon the death in 1984 of ex-Headmaster John Martyn (awarded the national hon-our of *Padma Shri*, during his life time) an eponymous educational trust was established with 'personal contribution' from, among others, Prime Minister Indira Gandhi (*ibid.*: 27). The trust lists among its *ex-officio* trustees the Secretary to the Ministry of Education, thus continuing the School's rela-tionship with the most crucial levels of state administration.[21]

Commedia dell'arte: the theatre of domesticated difference

In Chapter 3 I discussed a strike at the School by members of the subordinate staff through which the former revealed the 'childishness' of the latter. The strike also provides an insight into the nature of the School's connections with the grid of power – both centralised and diffuse – that it can call upon and which attend it with alacrity. During November 1986, the Headmaster informed the School's Board of Governors of an 'illegal strike' by the subordinate staff consequent to his refusal to meet their demand regarding work conditions. He noted that the strikers were being 'tutored daily by an outside labour leader . . . keen to establish his presence in the Doon School'.[22] Thereafter commenced a series of acts in a drama where the actors occupying the different roles – policemen, district magistrates, labour commissioners, politicians – all seem to be assigned the same dialogue, suitably improvised to suit the peculiarities of the scene.

On the first day of the strike a group of sloganeering workers were, on a complaint by the Headmaster, arrested and removed to a police lock-up. 'The Deputy Labour Commissioner, the Superintendent of Police, and the District Magistrate', the Headmaster further informed his Board, 'have been fully kept in the picture on a day to day basis.' At several stages, the strikers appealed to various sources for support but received none. The School, however, received support from quarters that might have been expected to provide succour to the strikers. In a personal letter to the Headmaster, the Uttar Pradesh Commissioner and Director of Industries referred him to 'our discussion in your office . . . regarding the strike', explaining that the Labour Commissioner had assured him 'that the matters relating to Doon School will be looked into by him with proper perspective'. Speaking of the labour union under whose banner the Doon employees had struck, he wrote that there was no such body 'registered with the Labour Department'.

Finally, the workers, sensing the weakness of their position, ended the strike and asked to be 'taken back'. One of their leaders wrote to say that 'as per the talk held with the District Magistrate . . . we are all coming back to work'. The Headmaster was ruthless in victory. 'The District Magistrate', he replied, 'had not given you any assurance and had not reached any understanding with you. Your statement that there will be no cut in your salaries for the period of the strike is completely baseless. . . . your strike was illegal.' The dispute was resolved in favour of the School and the strike leaders were removed from School positions, the rest being required to sign a 'Memorandum of Agreement' with the School strictly guiding their conduct on campus. There was no investigation of the matter by any officials or government bodies. Before acquiescing, however, the strikers had turned to what they considered the final court of appeal and wrote to the Prime Minister. In a personal letter to the Headmaster, the private secretary to Old Boy Prime Minister Rajiv Gandhi suggested that the School handle the matter in whichever manner it saw fit.

The skein of public rhetoric and private commitment which surrounds the Doon School, and others like it, is one whose yarn is spun from the strategy of the real and the flush of domesticated difference. In the wider arena of capital which requires the liberal discourse on 'nation-building' for the play of its forces, the School's role is indispensable: it is both the manoeuvre and the consequence of the storm which Benjamin's angel of history watched with helpless silence. The march of post-coloniality – through its accoutrements of a nation state of finite interests and a 'modern' pedagogy obeisant to it – has given us the new colonised and the new primitives. And there is some promise that this will continue. For there are plans afoot for a second Doon School – support for which has also come from the coffers of private interests and the treasury of state generosity. Hence, a group of old boys from Orissa informed the School that the state government was willing to provide whatever assistance was required to establish the second Doon there: that politicians and administrators would be generous with the state's resources, and land and infrastructural facilities would be provided free or at nominal cost (*DSW*, 13 Sep. 1986). The offer of such largesse from the public funds of the state of Orissa, one of the poorest in the Indian Union, is both remarkable and some indication of the politico-cultural webs which bind the School and the nation state in a relationship of mutual munificence.

In Chapter 5 I suggested that the history of the emergence of a North Indian intelligentsia is intimately connected with the history of the Doon School itself, whereby the School acted as the dispensary of metropolitan cultural capital to a provincial intelligentsia. We should see the current enthusiasm and ready offers of help for 'another Doon School' from both private and public sources as part of a contemporary dynamic of capitalism which includes globalisation as one of its contexts. Increasingly, the Doon model of schooling is seen to be necessary for acquiring the cultural capital required for success in the 'world culture' Hannerz (1993) speaks of.

Nevertheless, it seems important also to problematise the 'global' framework which has found such wide applicability in contemporary social science analysis. This is crucial towards an understanding of a complex interconnected world that nevertheless unfolds through engagements with specific cultural and social environments, and through specific grids of power. For, as Das notes, the 'international traveller' is only one kind of subjectivity of our time and to privilege it over all others gives us no purchase, for example, on the consequences of globalisation connected to the 'shattered' subjectivity of the Bhopal slum dwellers in the wake of the 1984 Union Carbide (UCC) disaster (Das 1996: 5). Das's essay on 'suffering, legitimacy, and healing' in this context is a powerful argument for continuing the focus on local experiences and practices as constitutive of contemporary human existence in non-metropolitan – post-colonised – societies. Specifically, through paying meticulous attention to a series of positions of power, Das uncovers that conjunctional space where these positions combined to efface the subjectivity of the victim and the legitimacy of her or his suffering through representing it as simulation, deceit, confusion, and ignorance. Contesting a popular anthropological position, she notes that 'pain and suffering . . . are not simply *individual* experiences' and that 'we need to examine the social mechanisms by which the manufacture of pain on the one hand, and the theologies of suffering on the other, become the means of legitimating the social order rather than being threats to this order' (Das 1996: 138).

In Das's rendering of the UCC disaster and its aftermath, 'theories of theodicy' are wrenched from the religious context and come to be located 'also in other domains, such as those of bureaucracy, law, and medicine' (*ibid.*); they resonate, in other words, with the manoeuvres and strategies of late twentieth-century capitalism and its knowledge regimes. The tragedy of Bhopal, she suggests, lies in the silencing of its victims through the assertion of discourses which, in turn, legitimated the medical system, the judicial system, the bureaucratic apparatus, the nation state, and the global corporate regime, while denying legitimacy to any other perspective; the 'authoritative voice' (*ibid.*: 155) of the 'expert' was used to characterise other positions as frivolous and lacking credibility. So at various times, Indian Government and UCC sponsored medical teams denied that the leaked chemical methyl iso-cyanate (MIC) was as dangerous as claimed, suggested that its long-term effects were minimal, and implied that 'the suffering of the victims was highly exaggerated' (*ibid.*); at other places it was claimed that 'most of the victims were suffering from malnutrition or a previous disease' (*ibid.*), that medical surveys could not be released for public scrutiny, and that since MIC poisoning was inadequately understood by existing medical and scientific knowledge, the protestations of those exposed to it could not be taken seriously.

Judicial input came in the form of the Supreme Court judgment upholding the validity of the state's appropriation of all rights of negotiation on behalf of the victims for compensation with UCC. The judges justified the hasty and paltry settlement negotiated between the Indian Government and UCC on the grounds that the suffering of the victims needed to be addressed swiftly, and that the compensation would allow for the establishment of rehabilita-tion schemes for survivors. And yet, Das says, at no point were the victims ever consulted, the government asked to provide evidence of relief work, or any responsibility fixed for the accident itself; the victims were converted through this process into objects of 'multinational charity' (*ibid.*: 163).

For the sufferers of the tragedy, the consequences of the complex of the strategies, discourses, and practices which made 'victim' itself an abstract category were catastrophic. And the catastrophe visited upon them was doubly heinous in that they were denied the possibility of articulating their pain, since now all but 'legal, technical and scientific forms' (*ibid.*: 156) of discourse were denied any legitimacy.

We find in Das's powerful account of the constitution of 'Bhopal' as a public event, an important example of the complex interweaving of the dif-ferent levels of discourses – personal, bureaucratic, judicial, scientific, statist, corporate, etc. – which made claims over the representation of human sub-jectivity. Late twentieth-century subjectivity, in this tale of the recolonisation of the post-colonised subject, lies suspended – though not always passively – in a mire of forces which seek to define the voice it can have. And, as Das amply illustrates, though a globalisation approach provides a context for the Bhopal tragedy, it is but one of the several contexts, and to give it primacy as the definitive structure of contemporary experience is merely to participate in the silencing of suffering and pain, which are always localised and immediate rather than general and abstract. To regard globalisation as the representative experience of our time and the primary analytical framework (in the sense that Appadurai speaks of it) is, then, to gloss over the intricate connections between different levels of discourses and different positions of power which go towards constituting post-colonised existence; and it is not that Appadurai's work is naive in this regard, but rather that it seems to pay insufficient heed to the location of theory itself.

I want to conclude with an illustration of the rather paradoxical parochialism which underlies (and, I think, undermines) Appadurai's discussion on 'patriotism and its futures'. 'It may be time', he suggests, 'to rethink mono-patriotism, patriotism directed exclusively to the hyphen between the nation and the state' (Appadurai 1993: 427). A worthwhile invitation indeed. However, in the comments which follow this initial inducement to thought, it turns out that the invitation is of a rather exclusive sort, and the collective 'we' Appadurai seeks to address is disappointingly similar to the 'my fellow Americans' category American presidents are so fond of addressing. With respect to the new forms of patriotism, Appadurai says, 'we' should 'allow the material problems we face – the deficit, the environment, abortion, race, drugs, and jobs – to define those social groups and ideas for which we are willing to live – and to die' (*ibid.*).

At a time when the benefits of the latest round of GATT negotiations seem to have mainly accrued to citizens of certain nation states and not some 'post-national' population in general, and with the background of the forced flooding of hundreds of villages in India in the name of development, Appadurai's inventory of 'our' concerns is a cruel parody of the arena of shared human interests. For in the context of a global condition which is as much about the exercise of power as it is about functioning of 'scapes' (Appadurai 1992), it seems more important than ever that we continue to focus our attention on different levels of functioning of the nation state. That is, on the asymmetries *between* nation states, on those which affect the lives of powerless groups *within* nation states, and on those cultural strategies of 'post-coloniality' which declare too stridently their break from the past.

Appendix 1
Donors to the IPSS prior to June 1936

PRINCES

Maharaja of Jammu and Kashmir	Rs	200,000
Nizam of Hyderabad	Rs	200,000
Maharaja of Jaipur	Rs	100,000
Nawab of Junagadh	Rs	50,000
Maharaja of Bhavnagar	Rs	50,000
Nawab of Rampur	Rs	15,000
Maharaja of Orcha	Rs	10,000
Sardar C.S. Angria of Gwalior	Rs	10,000
Raja of Khetri	Rs	5000
Nawab of Bhawalpur	Rs	5000
Maharaja of Datia	Rs	3000

BRITISH INDIA

Ajam's Trust, Bombay	Rs	200,000
Rai Bahadur B.R. Nathany	Rs	100,000
Raja Sir Annamalai Chettiar	Rs	50,000
Sir Dorabjee Tata	Rs	50,000
Sir Rattan Tata Trust	Rs	25,000
Zemindars of Jeypore	Rs	25,000
Raja of Bobbili	Rs	12,000
Raja of Parlakimedi	Rs	10,000
N.W. Wadia Trust	Rs	10,000
Nawab of Chhatari	Rs	7000
Adhinakartha of Tiruvaduthirai Mutt, Tanjore	Rs	6000
Mr J.K. Dubash	Rs	5000
Sir Byramjee Jeejeebhoy	Rs	5000
Mr Ambalal Sarabhai	Rs	5000
Jains of Bengal	Rs	5000
Nawab Sir Muzamilullah Khan	Rs	5000
Nawab Sir Umar H. Khan Tiwana	Rs	250

Source: Singh 1985

Appendix 2

Foundation members of the IPSS, 1936

His Highness the Maharajah of Jammu and Kashmir
His Highness the Maharajadhiraja of Bikaner
His Highness the Nawab of Bhawalpur
His Highness the Nawab of Rampur
His Highness the Maharajah of Datia
His Highness the Maharajah of Orcha
His Highness the Maharajah Jam Sahib of Nawanagar
His Highness the Maharajah of Kapurthala
His Highness the Nawab of Jaora
His Highness the Raja of Rajgarh
His Highness the Maharajah of Bijawar
His Highness the Raja of Sitamau
The Raja of Bansda
The Raja of Maihar

DELHI

Hon. Sir Mohammed Habiullah Sahib, KCSI, KCIE
Hon. Mr S.R. Das
Rai Bahadur L. Moti Sagar (Vice-chancellor, Delhi University)
Lala Raghubir Singh
Mr B. Rama Rau, ICS
Mr G.S. Bajpai, OBE

MADRAS

Maharaja Surya Rao of Pithapuram
Raja Sir P. Ramarayaningar, KCIE, Raja of Panagal
Hon. Sir C.P. Ramaswamier, KCIE
Dewan Bahadur T. Rangachariar, CIE
Hon. Mr Justice C. Madhavan Nair
Hon. Dr P. Subbarayan, Zamindar of Kumaramangalam
Raja of Bobbili
Mr Triuvengadathan Chettiar
Mr Jamal Mohammed Sahib

Hon. Sir Annamalai Chettiyar Kt.
Sir M.Ct. Muthiah Chettyar, Kt.
Mr R.K. Shanmukham Chetty, MLA

BOMBAY

Hon. Sir Cowasji Jehangir (Junior) KCIE, OBE
Mr M.R. Jayakar, MLA
Mr H.J. Bhabha
Mr Ambalal Sarabhai
Sir Jamsetjee Jeejeebhoy, Bart.
Sir Jamsedji K. Dubash
Mr F.E. Dinshaw
Mr Kikabhai Premchand, MLA
Mr D.F. Mulla, CIE
Mr Manecksha Pochkhanawala
Sir Dorabjee Tata, Kt.
Sir Byramjee Jeejeebhoy, Kt.
Mr Lalji Narainji
Sir Nusserwanji Wadia, Kt.
Mr C.N. Wadia
Mr R.S. Pawvala
Sir Monmohandas Ramji, Kt.
Mr D.H. Bhiwandiwala
H.H. The Agha Khan
Mr A.R. Dalal, ICS
Mr J.B. Kanga

BENGAL

Sir R.N. Mukerjee, KCIE, KCVO
Mr T.C. Goswami, MLA
Mr S.C. Mullick, ICS

UNITED PROVINCES

Hon. Maharaja of Mahmudabad, KCSI, KCIE
Hon. Nawab Mohammad Yusuf
Hon. Nawab of Chhatari, CIE, MBE
Nawab Sir Muzammilullah Khan of Bhikampur, KCIE
Dr Zia-ud-Din Ahmed, CIE
Dr L.K. Hyder, MLA
Hon. Justice Nath Misra

PUNJAB

Hon. S. Jogendra Singh
Sir Sundar Singh Majithia, Kt.
Hon. Col. Nawab Sir Umar Hyat Khan Tiwana, KCIE
Nawab Muhammad Mehr Shah
Raja Sir Daljit Singh, KBE
Mr A. Latifi, OBE, ICS
Mr M.V. Bhide, ICS
Hon. Malik Feroz Khan Noon
Hon. Mr Manohar Lal
Lt. Sardar Raghubir Singh of Raja Sansi
Rai Bahadur Lala Ramsaran Das, CIE
Lala Kedar Nath of Gujrat
Rai Bahadur Sewak Ram
Lala Balak Ram
Lala Hari Ram
Lala Ram Jawaya Kapur
Guru Sardool Singh
Lala Sant Ram
Lala Sohan Lal

CENTRAL PROVINCES

Sir S.M. Chitnavis, Kt.
Sir Moropant Joshi, KCIE
Sir Hari Singh Gour, Kt.
Mr B. De, CIE, ICS

BIHAR AND ORISSA

Sir Sultan Ahmed, Kt.
Raja Harihar Parsad Singh of Amawan, OBE

NWF PROVINCE

Hon. Major Nawab Mohammed Akbar Khan
Rai Bahadur Dewan Chand Obhrai

INDIAN STATES

Colonel K.N. Haksar, CIE
Mirza M. Ismail, CIE
Nawab Maula Buksh, CIE
Khan Bahadur Kazi Azizuddin Ahmed, CIE, OBE
Mr Amar Nath Atal

Sheikh Mohamedbhoy, Dewan of Junagadh
Dewan Abdul Hamid, CIE, OBE
Rai Bahadur Pt. Sital Prasad Bajpai

Source: Singh 1985

Notes

Introduction: the seductions of capital

1 There have been several attempts at defining 'intelligentsia' for the Indian context and though I do not share all the assumptions underlying the following, I reproduce it as some indication of thinking on the matter. The intelligentsia, for Rudra, includes:

 1 All white-collar workers in the organised private sector, from managers and top executives down to clerical workers (manual workers ... however, are excluded).
 2 All office workers in administrative services ... (excluding ... maintenance workers, technicians, security officers, etc.).
 3 Teachers ... doctors and nurses, lawyers and judges, engineers and architects, etc.
 4 Writers, journalists, artists ...
 5 Professionals, politicians, trade union leaders, etc.

 (Rudra 1989: 144)

2 From an information pamphlet published on the occasion of the School's Golden Jubilee in 1985.
3 These are Jaipur House, Hyderabad House, Kashmir House, Tata House, and Oberoi House.
4 'An Account of the Origins and Growth of the Indian Public School Conference', in *A Handbook on the Indian Public School* (1964. Publisher and author/s not traceable). This was given to me by Jack Gibson, formerly master at the Doon School and Principal of the Mayo College, Ajmer. Hereafter, 'Handbook 1964'.
5 The cultural significance of the Mayo College for the overall discussion of the book is outlined in Chapter 2.
6 It may be argued that since Krishnamurty later severed his connections with the Theosophists, 'their' history cannot be linked with that of the School; Thapan's book provides ample evidence, notwithstanding her curiously ingenuous statement that 'Krishnamurty is not addressing himself to a particular set of people', that the School's clientele is no different from Besant's supporters in the early part of the century.
7 It should, however, be made clear that I am not making a case here for a grand-narrative type analysis. I only wish to argue against the old anthropological custom of treating the village as an entity by itself, comprehensible 'on its own terms', and its activities unfolding according to the dictates of functionalist anthropology.
8 I discuss the 'staff–inmate' situation at the Doon School in the context of the political and cultural economy of the Indian modernity in Chapter 6, and the

general discussion of the book should make clear that I do not find 'imperme-ability' a particularly useful term, at least not in the sense in which Goffman uses it.

1 Practical minds, solid builders, and sane opinions

1 In the spectacle of the Doon assembly only the Headmaster occupies a position, at the front of the hall and upon a stage, which unambiguously identifies him as 'superior' with respect to the rest of the gathering; but this is hardly a contradic-tion in the story of the nation: there is always a place in this story for the 'leaders' of the national community.

2 I am not suggesting, however, that there are cultural forms which have an objective, 'un-arbitrary' existence; rather, that different political positions lead to different arbitraries.

3 This account was written by a former student, and published on the occasion of Doon's Golden Jubilee celebrations in 1985.

4 From *The Doon School Book*, p. 1 (hereafter, *DSB*).

5 Comment in another obituary in a newspaper of the time.

6 From S.R. Das's obituary in the *Rangoon Gazette* (c. 1928).

7 In a letter to one of his sons written in 1927, he speaks with confidence of the 'success of my proposed school . . .[where]. . . you will yet be able to send your sons' (letter dated 20 Jan. 1927). This prophecy was fulfilled within the first decade of the School's existence.

8 I was kindly given access to the diaries and letters of S.R. Das by Mr Shomie Das.

9 'Vincent [Sir William Vincent] told me that he would like me to save money so as to be able to take up one of the memberships of the Imperial Council which will be open after the Reform Scheme. He said he would do his best to get me appointed. It was very good of him' (diary entry dated 25 Jan. 1920).

10 This information is derived from various entries in Das's diary for 1920.

11 1 lakh = 100,000 rupees.

12 From Willingdon's inaugural address at Doon School opening ceremony, 27 Oct. 1935, quoted in Singh (1985: 9).

13 A hymn from the novel *Anandamath* by Bankimchandra Chatterjee, published in 1882. During the anti-Bengal partition upsurge, '*Bande Mataram* became the slo-gan of Indian nationalism and *Anandamath* the bible of armed revolutionaries' (Raychaudhury 1988:134).

14 It is important to note, however, that unlike Rudra's group in 1989 (see note 1 to the Introduction) the section of the population in the opening decades of this century which could be labelled the metropolitan intelligentsia was a microscopic minority. Also, a very substantial portion of the middle class had some form of connection with landed wealth.

15 I provide an extended discussion in Chapter 4 on the Lawrence School and colo-nial cultural and racial politics.

16 The earliest of the four so-called Chief's Colleges, established in 1870.

17 It may not be out of place here to note that when this interview took place, Rajiv Gandhi, a relative of K.G.M., was the Prime Minister.

18 I discuss the idea of secularism as an official creed – the Indian constitution opens with the words 'a Sovereign, Secular, Socialist Republic' – and as a part of the ethos of the Doon School in Chapter 4.

19 And, as recently pointed out (e.g. Nandy 1988a; Chatterjee 1993b), the discourse of secularism has also impoverished understanding of an important aspect of human existence, that pertaining to religion.

20 Referring to fifteenth-century Aztec priests who chose death in the face of missionary attacks on their beliefs, Nandy suggests, tongue in cheek, that under similar circumstances Brahmin priests 'might have embraced Christianity and

some of them would have even co-authored an elegant *prasasti* to praise the alien rulers and their gods ... [this is] *apadharma*, or the way of life under perilous conditions' (Nandy 1983: 107).

21 '[T]he school estate ... is called Chand Bagh, a corruption, it is believed, of an earlier name "Char Bagh" of a part of the grounds. Here in 1844 the Government had started one of its earliest experimental Tea Gardens' (*DSB*: 8).

22 Several options had been explored before settling on Dehra Dun. The Headmaster of a residential European school in Simla had suggested that the IPSS build its school on land adjoining his school; later, 'Sir Frank Noyce ... with the approval of the Viceroy, initiated an exploration into the feasibility of the Society taking over Mayo College, Ajmer, and converting it from a Chiefs' College to a public school' (Singh 1985: 17).

23 'Viceroy opens India's first Public School', *The Times of India*, 28 Oct. 1935 (hereafter TOI).

24 In his speech at the official opening of the School in October 1935, Viceroy Willingdon was quite forthcoming on the role of his government in the establishment of the School: 'May I add', he was to say, 'that I am glad to know that the Government of India have been able to be of some assistance ... by handing over this fine property as the permanent home for the new Doon School?' (*TOI*).

25 'Public schools, and the Doon School in particular, have frequently been accused of being the exclusive preserve of the rich and the privileged. They have been labelled anti-national and indeed former Prime Minister Morarji declared that they should be closed down' (Singh 1985: 101).

26 Which, notwithstanding its modernist rhetoric, led in many cases to the consolidation of feudal relations of property (Guha 1982).

27 'There can be little doubt that much of what Doon School is today is because of its first Headmaster. . . . His weekly talks to the boys laid out a philosophy which is valid even today' (Singh 1985: 20).

28 'If the system of education evolved at the Doon School is to be extended to a larger number of children, it will have to be accomplished by opening new schools at other locations. Attempts in this direction also have been made since the 1930s, but none of the proposals for a new school has yet borne fruit' (Singh 1985: 95). In recent years, however, renewed efforts have been made to establish other Doon Schools and one of Doon's former Headmasters has been instrumental in the planning and establishment of a public school in Assam, sponsored by a private corporation involved in the tea trade.

29 Who, after fifteen years as a master at Doon, took over the principalship of Mayo College in 1953.

30 A former Doon teacher was Headmaster of Scindia at the time of P.L.'s visit.

2 The marble mirage: constructing the Orient

1 'Subject: Establishment of a College at Ajmere for the education of the sons of the Rulers and Nobles of Rajputana. In paras 121–4 of Bhurtpore Agency Report for 1868–69, Captain Walter, in forcible words urged this necessity: He advocated the establishment of an Eton in India on an extensive scale with a complete staff of thoroughly educated Englishmen' (Foreign/Political A. Dec. 1870/608–9: National Archives of India, New Delhi, hereafter NAI). See also Sherring 1897: 34.

2 Foreign/Political A. Dec. 1870/608–9.

3 Throughout its history, this view was also echoed by many of the princes associated with it: 'Sindhia says "Boarding houses should be in charge of resident European Masters, who should exercise supervision over the boy in points of morality"' (Home/Education Jan. 1903/27–9); whether such sentiments had their origin in genuine conviction or political necessity, one cannot say.

4 Foreign/Political A./37, Indore Residency, dated 5 Aug. 1870, 162. From Maj. Gen. H.D. Daly Officiating AGG, Central India to C.U. Aitchison, Sec. to the Govt of India, for Dept with the Governor General.

5 An earlier version of this chapter was written before I came across T.R. Metcalf's (1989) work on colonial architecture. I have, since then, incorporated his many insights in the revised version, and though there are various points of agreement between our analyses, I hope the differences will be seen as an effort to continue and add to the discussion.

6 Of course, in a very real sense, the industrial revolution also provided, to use the expression of Daniel Headrick's book title, many of the 'tools of empire' (Headrick 1981; see also Pratt 1993).

7 '[T]he major effect of the Panopticon: to induce in the innate a state of conscious and permanent visibility that assure the automatic functioning of power' (Foucault 1979: 201).

8 The Spartan ideal was a common point of reference in Victorian discourses of Britishness. See, e.g. Richards 1987.

9 This is, of course, a well-mined area of contemporary scholarship. European opinions on the nature of the differences between Oriental and Occidental societies were too numerous and varied to allow a representative sample here. They ranged, however, from the observations of the Marquess of Hastings, likening the intellectual and manual attainments of 'natives' to those achievable by a trained animal, to the more sophisticated, though scarcely less damning, opinion of Thomas Macaulay who suggested that Oriental institutions 'taught astronomy which would move laughter in girls at an English boarding school' (Majumdar 1960: 12). In the Mayo College museum one can still see an old chart depicting the 'Races of Mankind', on which are depicted twelve different (male) faces, beginning with the 'Caucasian' and ending with the 'Kafir', the 'Hottentot, and the 'Papuan'.

10 For a parallel discussion of British notions of 'traditional' Indian clothing, see Cohn 1983.

11 For an attempt to apply Gramscian ideas to the Indian context that does seem worth pursuing, see Torri 1990.

12 I owe this reference to Sinha 1995. A further point I wish to make here is that although many of the 'martial' races were regarded by the British as brave but stupid (Omissi 1991: 17), an exception had to be made in the case of Rajputs of the princely classes. See also Cohn 1983; Das 1996 (especially Chapter 5) for relevant discussion.

13 See also O'Hanlon 1997, especially p.16.

14 Sometimes, the native manly races would slip up and have to be reminded of their own traditions: 'The other day during the riding school when a boy fell from his horse, it appears that all the other boys immediately dismounted and let go of their horses. Such behaviour . . . shows not only fear but absolute cowardice which is hardly in the old tradition of Rajputs who were famous for their prowess and bravery on horseback. The principal trusts that such behaviour may never occur again' (Mayo College Orders Book 1885–9, College archives.)

15 And, as in other regards, the princes came to accept that the College had come about as a result of their own perceptions of their needs. Before the establishment of the College, the Maharaja of Jodhpur noted in 1930, 'the ways of the Rajputana were exceedingly wild, and placed innumerable difficulties in the path of any educational system' (*Mayo College Jubilee Souvenir* 1930: 40).

16 Foreign/Political A. Dec. 1870/608–9. KW note of C.U. Aitchison dated 23 Aug. 1870. Almost all the 'native' designs furnished by the princes for residential accommodation had, in fact, been drawn up by British architects and engineers (information from various volumes of the *Mayo College Magazine*).

17 Curzon favoured a 'practical' course of study: 'Given that these Chiefs are not

going to be University students', he observed, 'and cannot reasonably be expected to find their main interest in after life in English literature, their education seems to me to offer scope for the construction of a special curriculum, of the most unscholastic and unpedantic kind . . .' (Note of Lord Curzon. Home/Education A. Jan. 1903/27–9). In the opening decades of the twentieth century, the curriculum was specially redesigned to suit the perceived needs and abilities of the princes.

18 Speech of Lord Curzon at the Chiefs' College Conference, Calcutta (Home/Education, A. Jan. 1903/ 27–9).

19 Orders Book 1881–84, and 1885–89. Mayo College archives.

20 Address of the principal at the Prize Giving Ceremony, *Mayo College Magazine*, Sept. 1924.

21 The following gives some idea of the often less than luxurious living conditions at English public schools around the turn of the twentieth century:

> And the always damp towels with their cheesy smell: and, on occasional visits in the winter, the murky sea-water of the local baths, which came straight in from the beach and on which I once saw floating a human turd. And the sweaty smell of the changing room with its greasy basins, and, giving on this, the row of filthy, dilapidated lavatories which had no fastenings of any kind on the doors, so that whenever you were sitting there someone was sure to come crashing in. . . . forks with old food in between the prongs, neck-of-mutton stew, and the banging doors of the lavatories and the echoing dormitories.
>
> (George Orwell quoted in Gathorne-Hardy 1978: 182)

22 Proceedings of the Calcutta Conference. Home/Education, Jan. 1903/27–9.

23 The temple still exists and is in active use; the mosque, however, is no longer there.

24 The young prince of Alwar, who came riding on an elephant, surrounded by a retinue of 200 servants, and who was received by the entire staff which had lined up at the gate; the event was commemorated by the construction of an archway, the Alwar gate.

25 Secretary P.W.D. to Mant, 7 Oct. 1876, quoted in Metcalf 1989: 78.

26 Metcalf makes a similar point and suggests that clock-towers aimed to remind passers-by ('natives' in particular) of both the 'supremacy of the Raj', and the 'virtues of punctuality'. He also points to another important aspect of the 'new era' perspective: that the crown surmounting the tower 'was made of iron, [and] forged in a British foundry' (p. 80); the Oriental design was, then, also circumscribed by the 'latest advances in European structural engineering' (*ibid.*). I am grateful to David MacDougall (personal correspondence) for some suggestions in this context.

27 In 1902, Curzon pointed out that whereas the total number of students in the four major English public schools was 2,500, 'the four Chiefs' Colleges in India only contain between them from 180 to 190 students' (inaugural speech of the Viceroy, Chiefs' College Conference, Calcutta 1902–3. NAI). However, the situation, with regard to numbers at least, appears to have improved in subsequent years so that in 1930 Viceroy Irwin could observe that 'the youth of no less than twelve . . . of the present Ruling Princes of Rajputana was spent within these grounds' (*Mayo College Jubilee Souvenir* 1930: 36).

3 The garden of rational delights

1 My reference is to the roles played by such 1950s and 1960s film stars as Raj Kapur, Sunil Dutt, and Balraj Sahni. There were, of course, several filmic variations on the theme of the city-educated engineer who goes to the countryside to,

say, help in the construction of a dam. The exception to this scenario was, perhaps, the hero-as-sensitive-artist space occupied by the film-maker and actor Guru Dutt. Filmic representations of Indian modernity are explored in some detail in Chapters 4 and 5.

2 Though, of course, the novel's denouement is not one of hopelessness in the face of dominant ideologies but, rather, asks the reader to reflect upon the possibilities of political alternatives.

3 The 'Conference' takes its inspiration from the educational philosophy of Kurt Hahn and draws its membership from private schools across several continents. A Jewish refugee from Nazi Germany, Hahn established the Gordonstoun School in Scotland. His educational philosophy, described by one observer as 'reactionary and ludicrous' (Gathorne-Hardy 1978: 91), placed great emphasis on the control of adolescent male sexuality. The Round Square International Service (RSIS) 'was started in 1981. . . . [It is] fundamentally an international association of schools having a common objective of character development through the medium of service and adventurous activity. It was originally formed in response to an invitation received by the Headmaster of Lawrence School, Sanawar [who went on to be the Headmaster of the Doon School], to do social service and get [*sic*] relief to the villages of India. Students and teachers from all over the world: from Switzerland, England, Canada, West Germany and India come to take part and work for this humane motion [*sic*]' (*Chandbagh IV* 1985: 174).

4 In 1955, Radhakrishnan, then president of the republic, visited the School as chief guest on its Founders Day. He was also, for the term of his presidency, the ex-officio head of the Board of Governors of the School.

5 For an exploration of 'somatic masculinity' in a different cultural context in India, see Alter 1994.

6 It has been suggested, however, that by the turn of the century, the fixation with 'physical culture' had begun to wane in the Indian nationalist context (Rosselli 1980), and had come in for considerable criticism in England (Vance 1985). Interestingly, an earlier instance of dissent to the 'muscular Christianity' model by an Indian who was not necessarily against all things western came from Keshabchandra Sen (1838–84), one of the leading lights of the Brahmo Samaj. In an 1866 lecture, he noted of the British and their religion that 'their muscular Christianity has led many a Native to identify the religion of Jesus with the power and privilege of inflicting blows and kicks with impunity' (original source David C. Scott (ed.) *Keshab Chunder Sen* (1979), quoted in Chatterjee 1993: 390).

7 For an interesting discussion in this context, see Nandy 1980.

8 The most outstanding examples of this were, of course, Rammohun Roy and the Tagores who 'combined zamindari [revenue farming] with money-lending and business enterprise' (Sarkar 1985: 11). Rabindranath Tagore was, as Kopf puts it, 'the privileged and poetically gifted son of a prominent Brahmo zamindar, who [liked to] drift along the rivers of up-country Bengal in a houseboat, cursing "the organised selfishness of Calcutta city life"' (1979: 196).

9 Herbert Spencer should, of course, be given chronological priority in any such discussion, having been both a part of and an influential contributor to 'a specific moment in the history of natural science and of the ideology of science; and . . . a specific moment in the technology and organisation of an industrial society' (Spencer (1969), from the Introduction by Donald Macrae). Indeed, Marshall himself formally acknowledged Spencer's influence upon his work. However, for my purposes here, it is Alfred Marshall who provided the most directed exegesis on the rationality of the 'business-like' classes.

10 Indian Industrial Commission, *Minutes of Evidence. 1916–17. Vol.1. Delhi, United Provinces and Bihar and Orissa. 1917*, Calcutta: Superintendent Government Printing India.

11 Behdad's comments, made in a different context, are also relevant for the present discussion on the scientific gaze. The nineteenth-century European tourist guidebooks, he says, often provided 'details concerning the agricultural and geographical state of [villages described, as well as listing] such seemingly unimportant data as the number of households and taxpayers' (Behdad 1994: 45). 'Such specifications', he says, 'are not so much an acknowledgment of the tourist's need for a detailed description of what he or she may want to see . . . as they are a sign of an obsession with absolute completeness' (*ibid.*: 45–6).

12 Tunwala is a Harijan village near Dehra Dun 'adopted' by the Doon School in 1938, and where, for several years, through a School society called the *Dehat Sabha*, Doon students carried out 'rural development' work.

13 *The Cassell Concise English Dictionary* (1989).

14 The Judaeo-Christian vocabulary may owe something to the fact that the writer, Arthur Foot, was himself a product of the English public school system. Images from that religious tradition can also be found in other places in the same account: 'If a boy has neglected to do his homework he will be given a green slip of paper simply bearing his name, his lapse and what he must do to make up for it' (*ibid.*: 15).

15 Similar comments were also made on several occasions by many of the School's senior students.

16 The report cards concerned with academic progress contain 'three columns under each subject, one for industry, one for achievement, and one for efficiency' (*DSB*: 27).

17 '[F]rom 1935 onwards there was a very definite rule that if a teacher hits a student and the student reports the matter to the Headmaster, the teacher is asked to leave. . . . [Once] a boy was hit by a Housemaster who was, consequently, asked to leave the school' (interview with S.S., student at the Doon School 1963–8).

18 The staff body is not a homogeneous one and there exists an implicit hierarchy within it that does not always have to do with seniority. Some members of the staff may enjoy a more privileged position due to 'cultural' reasons: they have themselves studied in a public school (Doon has several Old Boys on its staff), and constitute the pool from which Headmasters of other public schools are drawn. During my stay at the School one of the Housemasters, formerly a Rhodes scholar, was selected as Headmaster of the well-known Lawrence School, Lovedale, in the state of Tamil Nadu. I discuss the differences between the teachers at Doon School in Chapter 6.

19 'Mr Foot's letters to his mother – Chandbagh II: Moneylenders', in *The Doon School Weekly* 6 Oct. 1968, Foot Commemoration Number.

20 The original letter is in Hindi and is contained in a file concerned with the strike. I discuss the strike itself in Chapter 7.

21 I discuss the Indian family in the context of colonial and post-colonial gender and cultural politics in the next chapter.

4 Secularism, the citizen, and Hindu contextualism

1 This new memory sought to 'recapture' the likeness of the nation as it existed before the advent of British rule, when, it was asserted, it was a united, clearly recognisable entity. The unity of the nation, 'that was not adequately realised through political struggle in the present . . . was to be realised in the past, through a judicious reconstruction of Indian history' (Pandey 1994: 247). So, whereas Sister Nivedita (1923) spoke of the unchanging essence of the Indian mind since time immemorial, Swami Dayanand referred to the 'primary authority' (Pandit 1974: 67) of the Vedas as the unifying force of Indian society.

2 Tagore's hymn combines a series of striking images of the nation as constituted by

the communities which have surrendered their 'parochial' identities, of its delineation through its embeddedness in nature, and the invocation to a divinity defined as the 'Dispenser' of [the nation's] destiny. Further, its topographical imagery is redolent of a Hindu world – the 'holy' river Ganges, and the abode of the gods, the Himalayas; its appeal to non-Hindus remains unanalysed.

3 'Memorandum of Association of the Indian Public Schools' Society', in *Constitution of the Indian Public Schools Society*, The Doon School.

4 Apparently, this sentiment was in contrast to that prevalent among the mid-twentieth-century Sri Lankan metropolitan intelligentsia. There the spread of the English language was considered a sign of 'denationalisation' (Michael Roberts, personal communication). This chapter has benefited considerably from a close reading by Michael Roberts.

5 The author of this article was to achieve considerable fame in later life as the editor of a prominent national newspaper.

6 So, Nehru noted that, compared with India, the 'profit motive' was much more deeply ingrained in the West (Nehru 1960: 396).

7 S.R. Das in a letter to his son, 20 Nov. 1924.

8 It is some indication of his perception of the School's emphasis on a consciously areligious atmosphere that immediately after this comment he felt constrained to ask that the conversation be treated as confidential.

9 It is possible to suggest that in as much as this 'secular' formulation relies on the notion of an encompassing transcendental form, it is already Hinduised. I owe this point to Michael Roberts (personal communication).

10 In the same vein, the 1928 Royal Commission on Agriculture noted that 'good communications also react upon every aspect of the cultivator's life for the closer connection they create between the villages and the towns must stimulate the more backward rural community to demand a higher general standard of living. They also induce an interchange of ideas and so broaden the cultivator's outlook on life' (Verghese 1976: 107).

11 Home/Sanitary A. Dec. 1909, 24–7: National Archives of India, New Delhi, hereafter NAI.

12 This is a common enough theme during the colonial period: in 1889 the British Political Agent in Kotah state deployed an entire garrison in order to remove a young prince from the wardenship of the women of the *zenana* in order to send him to the Mayo College (Foreign, Dec. 1889/377–9: NAI).

13 *Some Account of the Lawrence Military Asylum* (c. 1850). Document courtesy Manju Khan and K.J. Parel.

14 The curriculum was largely organised around instruction in vocational activities: girls learnt to be good wives and adept domestics, boys were trained to be absorbed in colonial working professions in the railways etc. (from documents provided by Manju Khan and K.J. Parel).

15 I do not mean to downgrade the importance of the vernacular intelligentsia, rather I wish to suggest that the 'public voice' which tends to be heard most clearly in India has tended to be articulated in the English language. Hence it is not at all surprising that, despite the existence of a wide variety of radical positions within vernacular Indian literature, claims of the emergence of an 'authentic' Indian voice are usually linked to Indian writing in English. This is, of course, part of the politics of 'post-coloniality', global marketing, and departments of literature at metropolitan universities.

16 My gesture here is to van der Veer's (1994) critical evaluation of the 'syncretic' and 'tolerant' characterisations of Indian society; however, the inadequacy – and Orientalist legacy – of these terms need not imply the existence of (more or less) the same pattern of Hindu–Muslim relationship before and after colonialism, and a convergence between statist and non-governmental discourses of intimacy and

neighbourliness in the post-colonised era. It could be that we have yet adequately to capture the 'every day' in the Indian context that, as van der Veer recognises, can offer complex forms of resistance to discourses from 'above'.

17 'Hybridity' doesn't quite seem the right term in this context, as Bacchhan also has a clear idea of himself as a Hindu, but he is open to the possibilities of contiguous, though different, life ways.

18 See Chapter 1.

19 Its long association with the School is indefatigably pointed out by Doon's associates.

20 Bergson's conception of 'pure perception as an ideal limit . . . something that exists only in theory rather than in fact . . . since it involves no duration and is instantaneous' (Lacey 1989: 114).

21 I had used this term earlier in my discussion with him.

22 An idea also present in the work of twentieth-century historians such as Eric Hobsbawm (1994).

23 Western Uttar Pradesh, where Dehra Dun is situated, has a substantial Muslim population, and the nearby city of Saharanpur is named after the Sufi mystic Shah Haran Chisti.

24 There is now an aging and well-placed group of pre-Partition Old Boys in Pakistan, many of whom visited the School on the occasion of its Golden Jubilee in 1985 (*DSW*, 25 May 1985).

25 Those, as Radhakrishnan might have said, 'professing crude thoughts and sub-merged thoughts civilization has not had time to eradicate' (Radhakrishnan 1975: 40).

26 Students only had access to television reporting of the event through the state-owned Doordarshan channel. Uncensored (though often sensationalised) cover-age was available to the general population through the so-called video magazines produced by private companies. Some of the most graphic images of the occur-rence came from the Newstrack video magazine, owned by the publishers of India's most successful English-language news magazine, *India Today*.

   Contemporary developments in the subcontinent with respect to cable and satellite technology have, of course, considerably changed this scenario.

27 The School had, in fact, already been functioning for one and a half months, receiving the first group of students on 10 Sept.

28 My reference is to Bakhtin's idea of 'chronotopic motifs': 'A particular sort of event, or a particular sort of place that usually serves as the locale for such an event, acquires a certain chronotopic aura, which is in fact the "echo of the generic whole" in which the given event typically occurs. . . . A chronotopic motif is . . . a sort of "congealed event," and a chronotopic place is a sort of condensed reminder of the kind of time and place that typically functions there' (Morson and Emerson 1990: 374).

29 'Doon' means valley, and here it refers to the place where the School is situated rather than the School itself. Dehra Dun is the anglicised form of Dehra Doon which means '"the shrine in the land lying at the foot of the hills" and the "dehra", temple or shrine, from which the city and district take their name is that of Guru Ram Rai who settled there in 1676' (*DSB*: 5).

30 For the purposes of this discussion I have included references to Buddhist images and symbols as part of the cultural 'heritage' of the Hindus since this is a common perception among (upper caste) Indian Hindus and one which is only sporadically unsettled by the awareness of *Dalit* conversions to Buddhism as a protest against Hinduism.

31 The words finally chosen were 'Knowledge Our Light'.

32 His virtues as a philosopher-statesman are currently on display on his own home page on the World Wide Web.

33 Radhakrishnan, in many of his photographs, projects a similar image: a man of this world, but, somewhat enigmatically, in tune with a 'greater' spirituality.

34 These comments are of some significance coming as they do from a member of the staff who is considered to have a 'cultural' awareness, having been educated at Shantiniketan, the university founded by Tagore.

35 A fuller analysis would have to address the issue of the response of the non-Hindu students to Hindu contextualism. I can only add that though I met some Muslim and Christian students (both past and present), none remarked on the subject, and if anything, spoke of the School as secular in its approach.

36 Though the exploration of the contradictoriness of early nationalist discourse constitutes the central task of Sudhir Chandra's analysis, Pandey also speaks of the 'contradictions, inconsistencies, [and] ambiguities' (1994: 254) which marked second phase nationalist thinking.

37 My formulation of the problems with the realist epistemology in the Indian borrows, of course (if somewhat tangentially), from Michel Foucault's investigations into the functioning of power in western societies and from his insistence that 'the analysis, made in terms of power, must not assume that the sovereignty of the state, the form of the law, or the over-all unity of a domination are given at the outset; rather, these are only the terminal forms power takes' (Foucault 1990: 92).

38 Peter van der Veer (1994) appears to make a similar point in noting that the 'modern Hindu' in taking on western notions of 'tolerance' has led 'in a universalist version, to an inclusion of all religions in the Vedanta, the "spiritual" essence of Hinduism in its philosophical form, as in the philosopher-president Sarvepalli Radhakrishnan's famous formula: "The Vedanta is not a religion, but religion itself in its universal and deepest significance" ' (1994: 68).

5 The management of water: capitalism, class, and science

1 I will elaborate later upon my use of the terms 'metropolitan' and 'provincial' in this context. These are, of course, broad generalisations, and I do not mean to imply that the different categories of intelligentsia can be seen as completely homogeneous in terms of their thinking; the idea, here, is to suggest that there is a case for differentiating the 'national' intelligentsia into the metropolitan and the provincial, and that it possesses considerable analytical value.

2 The term 'provincial-metropolitan' designates that section of the national intelligentsia which, provincial in origin, aspired to the intellectual and material life style of its metropolitan counterpart; it fulfilled these aspirations through the establishment of metropolitan-inspired 'training' institutions, such as Doon School, in the provinces. I hope that the specific meaning of this term will become clearer as the chapter progresses.

3 From 'Note to the Second Edition' of the Autobiography.

4 The autobiography, first published in 1961, is, predictably, a paean to the benefits of modernity, the 'progressive' attitudes of the English, and the 'moderating' influences of tradition; nevertheless it is also an interesting exercise in the writing of a personalised social history of Punjab as seen through the eyes of five successive generations of one family.

5 'Having dug the canals, the task before the Government was to people this land. They raised a cadre of energetic men called Land Settlement Officers, who set about attracting people from the populated Punjab to this land of opportunity' (Tandon 1968: 157). 'Land Settlement Officer' and 'Colonising Officer' were used interchangeably, and the latter term is used in the early records of the School to describe the professional background of parents.

6 '[My father] had to ensure its flow with the minimum of losses. From the main canal smaller channels, and from them still smaller channels took the water into the

fields [and] at distribution points men were posted to let out water at fixed intervals' (Tandon 1968: 43–4).

7 *Gazetteer of the Chenab Colony 1904*, Lahore: The Civil and Military Gazette Press (reprinted 1985, Delhi: BR Publishing Corporation). Patwaris, Zilladars, and Munshis were the various (Indian) revenue and administrative officials who proliferated with the incursion of the Raj into the agricultural sector.

8 Economic capital '. . . is immediately and directly convertible into money and may be institutionalised in the form of property rights'; social capital is 'made up of social obligations ("connections"), which is convertible, in certain conditions, into economic capital and may be institutionalised in the form of a title of nobility' (Bourdieu 1986: 243).

9 Over the years, the situation regarding admissions changed drastically and demand for places at the School increased exponentially. At the Silver Jubilee celebrations of the School in 1960, the Headmaster made the following comments on the School's 'waiting list' for admissions:

> We have 131 children on the list for January 1971, sixty for August 1971, and ten for January 1972. The total number on the list is about 2800. Of these about 600 will eventually get admission and the rest will be disappointed. About 1000 parents a year accept our assurance that there is no point in them registering their sons.
>
> (*DSW*, 19 Dec. 1960)

10 The Tandons had moved to Sargodha from the town of Gujarat in West Punjab, now in Pakistan.

11 I have used the 1987 edition of the Record. And though another School document (Singh 1985) notes that seventy-two boys moved to the school premises on 10 September 1935, the very first list of students in *The Dosco Record* contains a smaller number of names. This may be because some of the 'first' boys left very soon after joining: 'The Doon School was something of an experiment when it started and many boys did not stay very long. These boys have been omitted' (*The Dosco Record*, Foreword to the 1st edn).

12 I was not able to determine the professions of the remaining ten.

13 In the year-wise lists, it is not possible to identify the region of origin of every student and I have confined my focus to those cases where the information is relatively unambiguous.

14 Gramsci defined 'organic intellectuals' as follows:

> . . . every 'essential' social group which emerges into history out of the preceding economic structure, and as an expression of the development of this structure, has found . . . categories of intellectuals already in existence and which seemed indeed to represent a historical continuity uninterrupted even by the most complicated and radical changes in political and social reform.
>
> (Forgacs 1988: 302)

In the present context, the 'essential' social group is one whose character is defined by its commitment to specific forms of post-colonised modernity (see also Torri 1990).

15 For those who did not belong to it, an old Kishor Kumar song provides an apt ode: 'permit *ke bina mermit*' ('life is hell without a permit').

16 In Nagarjun's Hindi novel *Baba Batesarnath* (1961), a villager reflects on political independence and its 'benefits' for the rural poor: '. . . who's benefited from independence? . . . our ministers have achieved a high level of independence. And, of course, the senior officers of the secretariat have profited from it' (Nagarjun 1961/1990: 127).

17 This decline should also be seen against the background of the information that each year approximately 50 per cent of the admissions are 'reserved' for sons and brothers of ex-students. The Headmaster told me in 1990 that he had recently increased the number of places at the School reserved for sons and brothers of ex-students to this figure. Expressing concern for what he saw as a *recent* trend – the 'North Indianisation' of the School in terms of its students – he saw this move as one way of broadening the regional composition of its clientele. Implicit here is the suggestion that in its early years the School had a much more 'cosmopolitan' character and drew its students from all parts of the country; and that, in this sense, its mission and objectives were part of a pan-Indian enterprise.

18 100 lakhs = 1 crore.

19 This term has, in recent years, come to denote rural or semi-rural property, usually in the vicinity of an urban settlement, purchased by prosperous city-dwellers as a holiday retreat. These 'farms', whose proliferation is most obvious on the outskirts of Delhi, usually have a dwelling on the site and are increasingly becoming places of regular residence.

20 '. . . boys prepared cosmetics, toilet materials, pharmaceutical products, various polishes, creams, inks and phenyl. For some years all the phenyl and ink used in the school were prepared by members of the Society' (*DSB*: 54).

21 At the time of my meeting with A.K.B., his son, who had been a student at the Doon School, was also present. He had a somewhat different opinion on his father's move to the School: 'Frankly', he said, 'an important reason for my father taking up a position at the School was for my education; there is no way someone like him could have sent me to Doon on his own income.'

22 *Sudhir Ranjan Khastgir* (n.d.) The State Lalit Kala Akademi, Uttar Pradesh.

23 Martyn's views on the insertion of the scientific method in the midst of the chaos of culture finds echoes in times much closer to the present. Hence, according to Kopf, H.T. Colebrook's *The Translation of Two Treatises on the Hindu Law of Inheritance* (1810), 'was important because it demonstrated how Europeans were able to pull together the fragments of a chaotic and contradictory Hindu legal system and reconstruct it along modern lines' (Kopf 1969: 88–9).

   In the same book we also find an Indian historian's verdict – presented by Kopf to support his own discussion of the work of the nineteenth-century British Orientalists – on the efforts of the linguist William Carey in producing a text-book on Bengali grammar. The historian S.K. De concluded that Carey had transformed 'the chaotic and dialectal variety of the vernacular into definite forms' (*ibid.*).

24 See also Gathorne-Hardy (1978), and T.W. Bamford's *The Rise of the Public Schools* (1967).

6 The order of men: sentiments of the metropolis, settlements of civil society

1 There is ample evidence of this sensibility in the planning process of New Delhi, and the files of the Public Works Department at the New Delhi National Archives – such as the 'Final Report on the Town Planning of the New Imperial Capital' (June 1913) – make for fascinating reading.

2 This is part of Lefebvre's critique of the treatment of issues of spatiality by writers such as Julia Kristeva, Jacques Derrida, and Roland Barthes – that school 'whose growing renown may have something to do with its growing dogmatism' (Lefebvre 1991: 5). In as much as these comments point to the disappearance of the concrete subject, they are also applicable to discourses on the metropolis.

3 I use 'Gandhi' merely as a convenient shorthand to indicate an attitude that was also shared by many others.

4 I have used the somewhat clumsy term 'non-metropolis' in preference to something more clear-cut as 'rural' or 'provincial' in order to reflect the complexity of
   the Other of the metropolis in the post-colonised context. In many ways the
   culture and 'ethos' of the provincial town in India cannot be sharply differentiated
   from 'rural ways'. The cultural continuity between the provincial city and the
   surrounding rural milieu, at least for North India, is an observable fact of provincial urban existence. It seems best, therefore, to express the opposition as that
   between the metropolitan milieu and that of the non-metropolis.
5 'De-propertied' in the Indian context should be seen to imply a larger process
   than that connected with material possessions: it is the process of the cultural and
   economic disenfranchisement of sections of the population that is at stake here.
6 The sense of national destiny as one bound up with metropolitan spaces was, of
   course, most clearly articulated in the *tabula rasa* discourse around the construction of the city of Chandigarh. It was well captured in the following observations
   of an Old Boy and architect in a 1954 School publication. The planners, he noted,
   are 'starting with virgin soil', and 'the atmosphere of [Le Corbusier's] Chandigarh
   will be that of a well ordered society that still preserves some of its more traditional and indigenous atmosphere' (Mody 1954: 62).
7 It is entirely appropriate then, that Baudelaire' s 'hero of modernity' (Tester 1994:
   7) is the anonymous but all-seeing *flâneur*.
8 It could be argued that this is a misreading of Pal's discussion of city life and that
   his 'little republic' derives from the 'village republic' idea popularised by, among
   others, Sir Charles Metcalfe (Inden 1990). However, though Pal uses similar terminology, his *intent*, as this discussion suggests, was quite different, and he quite
   clearly meant to convey the image of a metropolitan rather than a rural community. He had, after all, explicitly severed links with the province. I am grateful to
   Jim Masselos for raising this issue.
9 My debt here to what Anderson calls the 'secular counterparts' (Anderson 1986:
   56) of religious pilgrimages should be obvious.
10 *Innovative Leadership Provided by the Doon School* (n.d.).
11 This sorry state of affairs was also reiterated by the Report of the Education
   Commission of 1966. See also Anand 1945.
12 One position on the School's Governing Council is reserved for an 'educator',
   usually the Vice-chancellor of a prominent university.
13 There were several others of a similar background and 'prospects' to D.L. at the
   School during my stay there and I use his case as shorthand for all such teachers.
14 The politics of 'authenticity' is not an issue here; what is of importance is the
   cultural politics of *identities* in the post-colonised context.
15 Following the establishment by the government of its own schools – Navodaya
   Vidyalayas – based on the Doon model, this scheme has recently been discontinued. The significance of Navodaya Vidyalayas is discussed in Chapter 7.
16 *National Policy on Education 1986. Programme of Action 1992* Ministry of Human
   Resource Development, Government of India.
17 Foreign/Internal A., Dec. 1907, 28–38. From E. Giles, Director-General of Education in India to E.H.S. Clarke, Deputy Secretary to the Government of India in
   the Foreign Department (National Archives of India). Sherring was, of course, the
   author of an early account of Mayo College (see Chapter 2).
18 See Naik and Nurullah (1974) for a more complex discussion of pre-colonial
   indigenous education systems.
19 Of course, I don't mean to suggest that a large city may not provide more 'freedoms' for women in practice; my intention is to explore the philosophical moorings of the metropolis as an idea.

7 Conclusion: 'post-coloniality', national identity, globalisation, and the simulacra of the real

1 Sunder Rajan also takes up this position through outlining the specificities of 'developing' societies and of 'uneven development' (1993: 6), and the consequences of this for non-metropolitan feminism.

2 Hence, David Harvey's call (1989) for a rejection of a politics of difference and 'a return to some form of international working class movement' (Morris 1992b: 473) to counter the global power of the new forms of capitalist formations is, Morris says, of extremely limited applicability. Harvey's 'logic', she says

> can't make sense of the terms of struggle in Australia around Aboriginal Land Rights, and it can't explain how a hundred thousand Kooris have managed to make those struggles unignorable now by anyone dealing at the level of national economic policy, with the mining and tourist industries, along with its 'global' implications, like environmental policy, and how they have done this by mixing and inventing new traditions as well as preserving old ones.
>
> (Morris 1992b: 474)

3 Notwithstanding the objection one might have to the somewhat uncritical abandon with which terms such as 'diaspora' and 'exile' are used in discussions by and about (in particular) Indian intellectuals.

4 However, whether this transnational mnemonics will be as much a part of the lives of their children and grand-children is highly debatable.

5 Though, one suspects, a very particular kind of migrant life, that of the migrant intellectual.

6 As indeed is that of others such as the contributors to the Featherstone edited volume on 'Globalization and Culture'. Featherstone's own introductory piece is particularly insightful, concluding, as it does, with the *caveat* that 'it is all too evident that discussion of a global culture is generated from within a particular time and place and practice. This one within a Western European academic setting in English' (Featherstone 1992: 11).

7 There are some other highly questionable observations in Appadurai's article. In the search for material to fill out his crucial category of 'postnational formations', the 'radical Hindu group known as Ananda Marga' (1993b: 420) is presented as a likely candidate. The movement, Appadurai says, is one of many around the world 'aggressively opposed to specific nation-states' (*ibid.*). This would seem to be a somewhat simplistic view of the Ananda Marga. My own childhood memory of the movement's membership in a North Indian town during the late 1960s is one of male doctors, lawyers, and engineers, groups which are not particularly known for anti-state sentiments or activities. At the present time, a relative of mine resident in the United States is an active Ananda Margi; he is also an MBA, is anti-union, and works as a senior executive in the corporate sector.

8 I don't have the space here to elaborate on this point but can point to Ashcroft *et al.*'s (1989) work as representative of post-coloniality-as-style school.

9 The English-language news magazine *India Today* is one of the forums for this.

10 Given that a lack of such knowledge only condemns the already marginalised to an even more oppressive existence, I do not question the importance of this work; my primary intent is to point to the complex nature of so-called 'post-national social forms'.

11 'It [habitus] does not designate ... metaphysical habitudes, [or a] mysterious "memory". ... These "habits" do not just vary with individuals and their

imitations, they vary specially within societies, educations, proprieties and fashions, prestiges' (Mauss 1973: 73).

12 Of course, as this report also points out, the qualifications attached to the Court's assent had effectively diluted the original intent of the recommendations.

13 Incidentally, the managing editor of *India Today* is himself a former student of the Doon School and the magazine had, during the Mandal controversy, been persistently outspoken in its opposition to the reservations system.

14 '... funeral flames leapt upwards searing into the nation's memory the beginning of the end of another cycle in India's timelessly churning wheel of vicissitude' (Baweja and Viswanathan, 'Darkness at Midlife', *India Today*, 15 June 1991).

15 A random sample of some of the visitors: President Rajendra Prasad (1950); Jayprakash Narayan, veteran socialist and associate of M.K. Gandhi (1951); A.C. Bannerjee, Vice-chancellor of Allahabad University (1952); S. Radhakrishnan, sometime Vice-chancellor of Andhra and the Banaras Hindu Universities and President of the Republic (1955); M.C. Chagla, Minister for Education (1965); Nurul Hasan, Minister for Education (1974); M. Hidyatullah, jurist and Indian Vice-president (1982); Rajiv Gandhi, Prime Minister (1985); Professor M.G. Menon, Minister for Science and Technology (1990).

16 I am mindful that Giri's later life as a Congress politician and Indian President should make for circumspection in evaluating the 'radicalness' of his political position. However, what is important here is that Giri's public reputation relied heavily on his career as a prominent trade unionist and yet he saw no contradiction in his association with a School whose ideals and objectives fall squarely in the midst of the life of capital.

17 I wish here to point to the complex set of factors – 'the conditions of possibility' – which attach to the Babri episode, rather than to make a case for the unimportance of the anti-Muslim sentiment as an explanatory factor or provide a variant of the false consciousness argument where all actions mask a fundamental set of political-economic motivations.

18 It is thus not entirely coincidental that Delhi University is now host to large numbers of students from the provinces, those who have come to comprehend the importance of metropolitan cultural capital in the post-colonised condition.

19 So it was gleefully reported that Desai's position on public schools faced sustained opposition from a member of his own party, Doon ex-student Piloo Mody (Singh 1985).

20 I am grateful to Bob Connell for raising this issue (personal communication).

21 Vijaya Lakshmi Pandit, Jawaharlal Nehru's sister, was also one of the trustees.

22 Information from the 'Strike File', held at the Doon School.

Bibliography

School documents, government reports, and archival sources

Handbook on the Indian Public School (1964). Author/s and publisher not known.

The Doon School Book (*DSB*). A collection of articles on various aspects of School life, mainly authored by Headmaster Arthur Foot, and published in 1948 by the Old Boys' Society.

The Doon School Weekly (*DSW*). Various issues from 1936 onwards.

Chandbagh I. A Doon School Miscellany (1954). Published by the Doon School.

Chandbagh IV. A Doon School Miscellany (1985). Published by the Doon School.

Constitution of the Indian Public Schools Society (1936/1986). Published by the Indian Public Schools Society, Dehradun.

The Dosco Record (1987). An annual register of Doon School alumni initially compiled by its second Headmaster John Martyn and first published in 1979 by the Doon School Old Boys' Society.

Innovative Leadership Provided by the Doon School. A general-purpose information pamphlet published by the School, c. 1989.

Some Account of the Lawrence Military Asylum (c. 1850). Publisher/s and author/s not traceable.

Mayo College Magazine (*MCM*), various issues.

Mayo College Silver Jubilee Souvenir (1930). Mayo College archives.

Mayo College Orders Book 1881–84 and 1885–89.

Report of the Education Commission (1964–66). Education and National Development (1966). New Delhi, Ministry of Education, Government of India.

Annual Report 1988–89 (1989). The Navodaya Vidyalaya Samiti, New Delhi.

Annual Report 1989–90, Part I (1990). Department of Education, Government of India. Ministry of Human Resource Development, New Delhi.

Foreign/Political Files of the Government of India (1870–1947) relating to the Mayo College stored at the National Archives of India, New Delhi.

Home Department Files (1870–1947).

Gazetteer of the Chenab Colony 1904. Lahore, The Civil and Military Gazette Press (reprinted 1985, Delhi, BR Publishing Corporation).

Indian Industrial Commission (1917) *Minutes of Evidence 1916–17 Vol. 1. Delhi, United Provinces and Bihar and Orissa*. Calcutta, Superintendent Government Printing India.

Books and articles

Ahmad, A. (1994) *In Theory: Classes, Nations, Literatures*, London: Verso.

Aiyer, G. (1985) 'Impressions', in *Chandbagh IV. A Doon School Miscellany*, Dehra Dun: The Doon School Old Boys' Society.

Ali, I. (1988) *The Punjab Under Imperialism 1885–1947*, New Jersey: Princeton University Press.

Alter, J.S. (1994) 'Celibacy, sexuality, and the transformation of gender into nationalism in North India', *Journal of Asian Studies* 53 (1): 45–66.

Anand, S.P. (1985) 'Satisfaction and dissatisfaction in the school teaching profession', *Indian Educational Review* 20 (1): 55–64.

Anderson, B.R.O'G. (1986) *Imagined Communities: Reflections on the Origin and Spread of Nationalism*, London: Verso.

Appadurai, A. (1990) 'Disjunction and difference in the global cultural economy', *Public Culture* 2: 1–24.

—— (1993a) 'Number in the colonial imagination', in C.A. Breckenridge and P. van der Veer (eds) *Orientalism and the Postcolonial Predicament*, Philadelphia: University of Pennsylvania Press.

—— (1993b) 'Patriotism and its futures', *Public Culture* 11: 411–29.

Ariès, P. (1973) *Centuries of Childhood*, London: Jonathan Cape.

Arnold, D. (1993) *Colonising the Body: State, Medicine and the Epidemic Disease in Nineteenth Century India*, Berkeley: University of California Press.

Ashcroft, B., Griffith, G., and Tiffin, H. (1989) *The Empire Strikes Back: Theory and Practice in Post-Colonial Literatures*, London: Routledge.

Bacchhan, H. (1969/1993) *Kya Bhooloon Kya Yaad Karoon* (autobiography in Hindi), Delhi: Rajpal and Sons.

Badiuzzaman (1975/1985) *Chanko Ki Wapasi* (in Hindi), New Delhi: Rajkamal Paperbacks.

Bajaj, J.K. (1988) 'Francis Bacon, the first philosopher of modern science. A non-western view', in Nandy (ed.) *Science, Hegemony and Violence. A Requiem for Modernity*, Delhi: Oxford University Press.

Bakhtin, M.M. (1990) 'Forms of time and of the chronotope in the novel. Notes towards a historical poetics', in M. Holquist (ed.) *The Dialogical Imagination. Four Essays by M.M. Bakhtin*, Austin: University of Austin Press.

Bamford, T.W. (1967) *Rise of the Public Schools: A Study of Boys' Public Boarding Schools in England and Wales from 1837 to the Present Day*, London: Nelson.

Bardhan, P. (1984) *The Political Economy of Development in India*, New York: Basil Blackwell.

Basu, T., Datta, P., Sarkar, S., Sarkar, T., and Sen, S. (1993) *Khaki Shorts and Saffron Flags: A Critique of the Hindu Right*, New Delhi: Orient Longman.

Baudrillard, J. (1988) 'Simulacra and simulations', in M. Poster (ed.) *Selected Writings*, Stanford: Stanford University Press.

Bayly, C.A. (1975) *The Local Roots of Indian Politics. Allahabad 1881–1920*, Oxford: Oxford University Press.

Behdad, A. (1994) *Belated Travelers. Orientalism in the Age of Colonial Dissolution*, Durham: Duke University Press.

Benjamin, W. (1985a) 'On some motifs in Baudelaire', in H. Arendt (ed.) *Illuminations*, New York: Schocken Books.

—— (1985b) 'Thesis on the philosophy of history', in H. Arendt (ed.) *Illuminations*, New York: Schocken Books.

Benson, E.F. (1987) *Queen Victoria. An Illustrated Biography*, London: Chatto and Windus.

Berger, J. (1965) *The Success and Failure of Picasso*, Harmondsworth: Penguin Books.

Berger, J. and Mohr, J. (1975) *A Seventh Man: Migrant Workers in Europe*, New York: Viking Press.

Berman, M. (1988) *All That is Solid Melts into Air: The Experience of Modernity*, New York: Viking, Penguin.

Béteille, A. (1981) *The Backward Classes and the New Social Order* (The Ambedkar Memorial Lectures Delivered Under the Auspices of Bombay University), Delhi: Oxford University Press.

Bhabha, H.K. (1984) 'Of mimicry and man: the ambivalence of colonial discourse', *October* 28: 125–33.

—— (1990) 'Introduction: narrating the nation', in H.K. Bhabha (ed.) *Nations and Narration*, London: Routledge.

Bhattacharjee, A. (1975) *Jayaprakash Narayan. A Political Biography*, Delhi: Vikas Publication House.

Bhattacharya, S. (1974) 'Positivism in nineteenth century Bengal: diffusion of European intellectual influence in India', in R.S. Sharma (ed.) *Indian Society: Historical Moorings*, New Delhi: People's Publishing House.

Bourdieu, P. (1977) *Outline of a Theory of Practice*, Cambridge: Cambridge University Press.

—— (1986) 'The forms of capital', in J.G. Richardson (ed.) *Handbook of Theory and Research in the Sociology of Education*, New York: Greenwood Press.

Bourdieu, P. and Passeron, J-C. (1977) *Reproduction in Education. Society and Culture* (trans. R. Nice), London: Sage.

Breckenridge, C.A. and van der Veer, P. (eds) (1993) *Orientalism and the Postcolonial Predicament*, Philadelphia: University of Pennsylvania Press.

Brown, E.C. (1976) *Har Dayal. Hindu Revolutionary and Rationalist*, Delhi: Manohar Books.

Bulsara, J.F. (1948) *Bombay. A City in the Making*, Bombay: National Information and Publications Ltd.

Casey, E.S. (1987) *Remembering. A Phenomenological Study*, Bloomington and Indianapolis: Indiana University Press.

Chakrabarty, D. (1992) 'Postcoloniality and the artifice of history: who speaks for "Indian" pasts?', *Representations* 37: 1–26.

—— (1993a) 'Marx after Marxism: history, subalternity and difference', *Meanjin* 52 (3): 421–34.

—— (1993b) 'Modernity and ethnicity in India, *Communal/Plural* 1: 1–16.

—— (1995) 'Radical histories and the question of enlightenment rationalism. Some recent critiques of *Subaltern Studies*', Economic and Political Weekly XXX (14): 751–9.

Chakravorty-Spivak, G.C. (1989) 'Who claims alterity?', in B. Ruger and P. Mariani (eds) *Remaking History*, Seattle: Dia Art Foundation.

Chandoke, N. (1991) 'The post-colonial city', *Economic and Political Weekly* XXVI (50): 2868–73.

Chandra, S. (1994) *The Oppressive Parent. Literature and Social Consciousness in Colonial India*, Delhi: Oxford University Press.

Chatterjee, P. (1986) *Nationalist Thought and the Colonial World. A Derivative Discourse?*, Tokyo: Zed Books.

—— (1993a) 'The nationalist resolution of the women's question', in K. Sangari and S. Vaid (eds) *Recasting Women. Essays in Colonial History*, New Delhi: Kali for Women.

—— (1993b) *The Nation and its Fragments: Colonial and Postcolonial Histories*, Princeton: Princeton University Press.

Clifford, J. (1992) 'Travelling cultures', in L. Grossberg *et al.* (eds) *Cultural Studies*, London, New York: Routledge.

—— (1993) 'On collecting art and culture', in S. During (ed.) *The Cultural Studies Reader*, London: Routledge.

Clifford, J. and Marcus, G.E. (1986) *Writing Culture. The Politics and Poetics of Ethnography*, Berkeley: University of California Press.

Cohn, B. (1983) 'Cloth, Clothes and Colonialism', paper prepared in advance for participants in symposium No. 93 'Cloth and the organisation of human experience' held at Troutbeck, Amenia, New York, 28 Sept.–5 Oct. 1983. The Wenner-Gren Foundation for Anthropological Research.

—— (1988) *An Anthropologist among the Historians and Other Essays*, Delhi: Oxford University Press.

Connell, R.W. (1980) 'On the wings of history', *Arena* 55: 32–55

—— (1995) *Gender and Power*, Oxford: Polity Press.

Connell, R.W., Ashenden, D.J., Kessler, S., and Dowsett, G.W. (1982) *Making the Difference: School, Families and Social Division*, Sydney: George Allen and Unwin.

Coomaraswamy, A.K. (1964) *The Arts and Crafts of India and Ceylon*, New York: Farrar, Strauss.

Das, V. (ed.) (1990) *Mirrors of Violence*, Delhi: Oxford University Press.

—— (1996) *Critical Events. An Anthropological Perspective on Contemporary India*, Delhi: Oxford University Press.

de Souza, A. (1974) *Indian Public Schools. A Sociological Study*, New Delhi: Sterling Publishers.

Deleuze, G. and Guattari, F. (1986) *Nomodology: The War Machine* (trans. B. Massumi), Minneapolis: University of Minnesota Press.

Douglas, M. (1970) *Purity and Danger. An Analysis of the Concepts of Pollution and Taboo*, London: Routledge & Kegan Paul.

During, S. (1987) 'Postmodernism or postcolonialism today', *Textual Practice* 1(1): 32–47.

—— (1992) 'Postcolonialism and globalization', *Meanjin* 51(2): 339–53.

—— (ed.) (1993) *The Cultural Studies Reader*, London: Routledge

Embree, A.T. (1989) *Imagining India: Essays on Indian History*, Delhi: Oxford University Press.

Featherstone, M. (1993) 'Global culture: an introduction', in M. Featherstone (ed.) *Global Culture: Nationalism, Globalization and Modernity*, London: Sage.

—— (ed.) (1993) *Global Culture: Nationalism, Globalization and Modernity*, London: Sage.

Forgacs, D. (ed.) (1988) *A Gramsci Reader. Selected Writings 1916–1935*, London: Lawrence and Wishart.

Foucault, M. (1979) *Discipline and Punish. The Birth of the Prison*, New York: Vintage Books.

—— (1980) *Power/Knowledge: Selected Interviews and Other Writings 1972–77*, New York: Pantheon Books.

—— (1982) *The Archaeology of Knowledge and the Discourse on Language*, New York: Pantheon Books.

—— (1990) *The History of Sexuality Volume 1. An Introduction*, London: Penguin Books.

Fox, R.G. (1985) *Lions of Punjab. Culture in the Making*, Berkeley: University of California Press.

Frankel, B. (1983) *Beyond the State? Dominant Theories and Socialist Strategies*, London: Macmillan Press.

Gaeffke, P. (1978) *Hindi Literature in the Twentieth Century*, Wiesbaden: Harrasowitz.

Gandhi, M.K. (1927a) 'Wanted workers', *Young India*, 10 March, pp. 108–09.

—— (1927b) 'Three speeches', *Young India*, 2 Sept., pp. 369–70.

—— (1928) 'True and false industrialisation', *Young India*, 24 May, pp. 756–7.

—— (1951) *Basic Education*, Ahmedabad: Navjivan Publishing House.

—— (1990) *An Autobiography. Or the Story of My Experiments with Truth*, Ahmedabad: Navjivan Publishing House.

Gathorne-Hardy, J. (1978) *The Old School Tie. The Phenomenon of the English Public School*, New York: Viking Press.

Geetha, V. and Rajadurai, S.V. (1995) 'One hundred years of Brahminitude. Arrival of Annie Besant', *Economic and Political Weekly* XXX (28): 768–1773.

Ghose, A. (1924) *A System of National Education for India. Some Introductory Essays*, Calcutta: Arya Publishing House.

Goffman, E. (1976) *Asylums*, Chicago: Alldine Publishing Company.

Grossberg, L., Nelson, C., and Treichler, P.A. (eds) (1992) *Cultural Studies*, New York: Routledge.

Guha, R. (1982) *A Rule of Property for Bengal: An Essay on the Idea of Permanent Settlement*, New Delhi: Orient Longman.

Gupta, A. and Ferguson, J. (1992) 'Beyond "culture": space, identity and the politics of difference', *Cultural Anthropology* 7 (1): 6–23.

Hall, S. (1992) 'Cultural studies and its theoretical legacies', in L. Grossberg *et al.* (eds) *Cultural Studies*, New York: Routledge.

Hannerz, U. (1993) 'Cosmopolitans and locals in world culture', in M. Featherstone (ed.) *Global Culture: Nationalism, Globalization and Modernity*, London: Sage.

Harvey, D. (1989a) *The Urban Experience*, Oxford: Basil Blackwell.

—— (1989b) *The Condition of Postmodernity: An Enquiry in to the Origins of Cultural Change*, Oxford: Blackwell.

Headrick, D.R. (1981) *Tools of Empire: Technology and European Imperialism in the Nineteenth Century*, New York: Oxford University Press.

Hobsbawm, E.J. (1994) *Age of Extremes: the Short Twentieth Century 1914–1991*, London: Michael Joseph.

Hughes, A. (n.d.) *A Glimpse into the Early History of Mayo College*, (n.k.)

Hussain, Z. (1965) *The Dynamic University*, London: Asia Publishing House.

Inden, R. (1992) *Imagining India*, Oxford: Blackwell Publishers.

Iyer, R. (1987) *The Moral and Political Writings of Mahatma Gandhi, Vol. III*, Oxford: Oxford University Press.

Jaywardena, K. (1995) *The White Woman's Other Burden: Western Women and South Asia*, New York: Routledge.

Jha, P. (1992) 'Does Narsimha Rao have a moral right to continue?', *The Pioneer* 12 Dec.

Jordanova, L. (1989) *Sexual Visions. Images of Gender in Science and Medicine Between the Eighteenth and Twentieth Centuries*, London: Harvester Wheatsheaf.

Kapferer, B. (1979/1984) 'Introduction. Ritual process and the transformation of context', *Social Analysis* (Special Issue Series).1: 3–19.

—— (1988) *Legends of People, Myths of State: Violence, Intolerance, and Political Culture in Sri Lanka and Australia*, Washington: Smithsonian Institution Press.

Kishwar, M. (1986) 'The daughters of Aryavarta', *Indian Economic and Social History Review* XXIII (2): 151–8.

Kochar, R.K. (1991) 'Science as a tool in British India', *Economic and Political Weekly* XXVI (33): 1927–33.

Kopf, D. (1969) *British Orientalism and the Bengal Renaissance. The Dynamics of Indian Modernization 1773–1835*, Berkeley: University of California Press.

—— (1979) *The Brahmo Samaj and the Shaping of the Modern Indian Mind*, Princeton: Princeton University Press.

Kumar, K. (1989) 'Secularism: its politics and pedagogy', *Economic and Political Weekly* XXIV (44–5): 2473–6.

—— (1991) *Political Agenda of Education*, Delhi: Sage Publications.

Kumar, R. (1985) 'All king's men dance to Doon's tune', *The Statesman*, 1 Nov.

Lacey, A.R. (1989) *Bergson*, London: Routledge.

Lefebvre, H. (1994) *The Production of Space* (trans. D. Nicholson-Smith), Oxford: Blackwell.

Lelyveld, D. (1978) *Aligarh's First Generation: Muslim Solidarity in British India*, Princeton: Princeton University Press.

Levinas, E. (1989) 'Reality and its shadow' in S. Hand (ed.) *The Levinas Reader*, Oxford, Basil Blackwell.

Ludden, D. (1993) 'Oriental empiricism: transformations of colonial knowledge', in C.A. Breckenridge and P. van der Veer (eds) *Orientalism and the Postcolonial Predicament*, Philadelphia: University of Pennsylvania Press.

Majumdar, R.C. (1960) *Glimpses of Bengal in the Nineteenth Century*, Calcutta: Firma K.L. Mukhopadhyaya.

Malik, B. (1985) 'With remorse, regret and a peg of gratitude', *The Times of India*, Oct., Doon School Golden Jubilee supplement.

Mangan, J.A. (1986a) *Athleticism in the Victorian and Edwardian Public School*, London: The Falmer Press.

—— (1986b) *Games Ethic and Imperialism: Aspects of Diffusion of an Ideal*, Hammondsworth: Viking Press.

—— (1987) 'Social Darwinism and upper-class education in late-Victorian and Edwardian England', in J.A. Mangan and J. Walvin (eds) *Manliness and Morality. Middle-class Masculinity in Britain and America 1800–1940*, New York: St Martin's Press.

Mangan, J.A. and Walvin, J.A. (eds) (1987) *Manliness and Morality. Middle-class Masculinity in Britain and America 1800–1940*, New York: St Martin's Press.

Manin, L. (1993) 'Contentious traditions; the debate on *sati* in colonial India', in K. Sangari and S. Vaid (eds) *Recasting Women. Essays in Colonial History*, New Delhi: Kali for Women.

Marshall, A. (1938) *Principles of Economics*, London: Macmillan.

Marx, K. (1978) *Capital Vol. I*, Moscow: Progress Publishers.

Mauss, M. (1937/1973) 'Techniques of the body', *Economy and Society* (2): 71–88.

Metcalfe, A. (1988) *For Freedom and Dignity. Historical Agency and Class Structure in the Coalfields of New South Wales*, Sydney: Allen and Unwin.

Metcalf, T.R. (1989) *An Imperial Vision: Indian Architecture and Britain's Raj*, London: Faber and Faber.

Mill, J.S. (1991) *On Liberty and Other Essays*, Oxford: Oxford University Press.

Mithileshwar (1993) *Pratinidhi Kahaniyan* (in Hindi), Delhi: Rajkamal.

Mody, P.H. (1954) 'Chandbagh to Chandigarh', in *Chandbagh I. A Doon School Miscellany* (see documents).

Morris, M. (1992a) Intervention made at a conference paper, in L. Grossberg *et al.* (eds) *Cultural Studies*, New York: Routledge.

—— (1992b) 'On the beach', in L. Grossberg *et al.* (eds) *Cultural Studies*, New York: Routledge.

Morson, G.S. and Emerson, C. (1990) *Mikhail Bakhtin. Creation of a Prosaics*, Stanford: Stanford University Press.

Mukherjee, H. and Mukherjee, U. (1957) *The Origins of the National Education Movement (1905–1910)*, Calcutta: Jadavpur University Press.

Nagarjun (1961/1990) *Baba Batesarnath* (in Hindi), Delhi: Rajkamal Paperbacks.

Naik, J.P. and Nurullah, S. (1974) *A Students' History of Education in India (1800–1947)*, Delhi: Macmillan.

Nairn, T. (1982) 'Antonu Su gobbu', in A.S. Sassoon (ed.) *Approaches to Gramsci*, London: Writers and Readers.

Nandy, A. (1980) *Alternative Sciences: Creativity and Authenticity in Two Indian Scientists*, New Delhi: Allied Publishers

—— (1983) *The Intimate Enemy. Loss and Recovery of the Self under Colonialism*, Delhi: Oxford University Press.

—— (ed.) (1988a) *Science, Hegemony and Violence. A Requiem for Modernity*, Delhi: Oxford University Press.

—— (1988b) 'The human factor', *The Illustrated Weekly of India*, 17 Jan.

—— (1990) 'Final encounter: the politics of the assassination of Gandhi', in R. Jeffrey *et al.* (eds) *India, Rebellion to Republic*, New Delhi: Sterling Press.

Nehru, J. (1960) *The Discovery of India*, New York: Anchor Books.

Nietzshe, F. (1983) 'On the uses and disadvantages of history for life', in *Untimely Meditations* (trans. R.J. Hollingdale), Cambridge: Cambridge University Press.

O'Hanlon, R. (1997) 'Issues of masculinity in North Indian history: the Bangash Nawabs of Farrukhabad', *Indian Journal of Gender Studies* 4(1): 1–19.

Omissi, D. (1991) '"Martial Races": ethnicity and security in colonial India 1858–1939', *War and Society* 9(1): 1–27.

Orwell, G. (1978) *Selected Writings* (ed. G. Bott), London: Heinemann.

Pal, B.C. (1973) *Memories of My Life and Times*, Calcutta: Bipinchandra Pal Institute.

Pandey, G. (1991) 'In defence of the fragment. Writing about Hindu–Muslim riots in India', *Economic and Political Weekly* XXVI (11, 12): 559–72.

—— (1994) *The Construction of Communalism in Colonial North India*, Delhi: Oxford University Press.

Pandit, S.S. (1974) *A Critical Study of the Contribution of the Arya Samaj to Indian Education*, New Delhi: Sarvadeshik Arya Pratinidhi Sabha.

Parekh, B. (1989) *Colonialism. Tradition and Reform. An Analysis of Gandhi's Political Discourse*, New Delhi: Sage Publications.

Pateman, C. (1989) *The Disorder of Women. Democracy. Feminism and Political Theory*, Cambridge: Polity Press.

Pathak, R. (1992) 'What the verdict means', *India Today*, 15 Dec., pp. 56–8.

Pratt, M.L. (1993) *Imperial Eyes: Travel Writing and Transculturation*, New York: Routledge.

Puri, N. (1985) *Political Elite and Society in the Punjab*, New Delhi: Vikas Publishing House.

Radhakrishnan, S. (1975) *The Hindu View of Life*, New York: Macmillan Publishing Company.

Rajadhyaksha, A. and Willemen, P. (1994) *Encyclopaedia of Indian Cinema*, New Delhi: Oxford University Press.

Raychaudhuri, T. (1988) *Europe Reconsidered. Perceptions of the West in Nineteenth Century Bengal*, Delhi: Oxford University Press.

Renu, F. (1954/1984) *Maila Anchal* (in Hindi), New Delhi: Rajkamal.

Richards, J. (1987) ' "Passing the love of women": manly love and Victorian society', in J.A. Mangan and J. Walvin (eds) *Manliness and Morality. Middle-class Masculinity in Britain and America 1800–1940*, New York: St Martin's Press.

Roberts, M. (1990) 'Noise as cultural struggle', in V. Das (ed.) *Mirrors of Violence*, Delhi: Oxford University Press.

Rosselli, J. (1980) 'The self-image of effeteness: physical education and nationalism in nineteenth-century Bengal', *Past and Present* 86: 121–48.

Rudolph, S.H. and Rudolph, L.I. (1984) *Essays on Rajputana: Reflections on History, Culture, and Administration*, New Delhi: Concept.

Rudra, A. (1989) 'Emergence of the intelligentsia as a ruling class', *Economic and Political Weekly* XXIV (3): 142–50.

Rushdie, S. (1988) *The Satanic Verses*, New York: Viking.

Sahai, R. (1985) 'The Doon School revisited', in *Chandbagh IV. A Doon School Miscellany*, Dehra Dun: The Doon School Old Boys' Society.

Said, E. (1978) *Orientalism*, New York: Pantheon Books.

Sangari, K. and Vaid, S. (eds) (1993) *Recasting Women. Essays in Colonial History*, New Delhi: Kali for Women.

Sankrityayan, R. (1948/1994) *Ghummakkad Shashtra* (in Hindi), Delhi: Kitab Mahal.

Sargent, J. (1968) *Society, Schools and Progress in India*, Oxford: Pergamon Press.

Sarkar, S. (1983) *Modern India*, Delhi: Macmillan.

—— (1985) *A Critique of Colonial India*, Calcutta: Papyrus.

Sarkar, S.C. (1961) *Tagore's Educational Philosophy and Experiment*, Santiniketan: Visva-Bharati.

Sartre, J-P. (1966) *Being and Nothingness. A Phenomenological Essay on Ontology* (trans. with Intro. by Hazel E. Barnes), New York: Washington Square Press.

Sassoon, A.S. (1982) 'Hegemony, war of position and political intervention', in A.S. Sassoon (ed.) *Approaches to Gramsci*, London: Writers and Readers.

Scrase, T.J. (1993) *Image, Ideology and Inequality: Cultural Domination. Hegemony, and Schooling in India*, New Delhi: Sage.

Seidler, V.J. (1994) *Unreasonable Men. Masculinity and Social Theory*, London: Routledge.

Sherring, H. (1897) *The Mayo College. 'The Eton of India'. A Record of Twenty Years 1875–1895*, Calcutta: Thacker, Spink and Company.

Simmel, G. (1971) 'The metropolis and mental life', in D. Levine (ed.) *On Individuality and Social Forms. Selected Writings*, Chicago: University of Chicago Press.

Singer, M. (1972) *When a Great Tradition Modernizes. An Anthropological Approach to India*, New York: Praegar Publishers.

Singh, A. (1991) 'Ramamurthy Report on education in retrospect', *Economic and Political Weekly* XXVI (26): 1605–13.

Singh, K. (1982) *Heir Apparent. An Autobiography*, Delhi: Oxford University Press.

Singh, S. (1985) *Doon. The Story of a School*, Dehra Dun: Indian Public Schools Society.

Sinha, M. (1995) *Colonial Masculinity. The 'Manly Englishman' and the 'Effeminate Bengali' in the Nineteenth Century*, Manchester: Manchester University Press.

Sister Nivedita (1923) *Hints on National Education in India*, Calcutta: Ubodhan.

Sobti, K. (1991) *Daar Se Bichudi* (in Hindi), New Delhi: Rajkamal Paperbacks.

Spencer, H. (1969) *Man Versus the State. With Four Essays in Politics and Society*, Harmondsworth: Penguin Books.

Srivastava, S. (1993) 'The management of water: modernity, technocracy and the citizen at the Doon School', *South Asia* XVI (2): 57–88.

—— (1996) 'Editor's Introduction', *The Australian Journal of Anthropology* (special issue: 'The National Artifice') 7: 91–103.

Sunder Rajan, R. (1993) *Real and Imagined Women. Gender, Culture and Post-colonialism*, London: Routledge.

Tandon, P. (1968) *Punjabi Century 1857–1947*, Berkeley: University of California Press.

—— (1980) *Return to Punjab 1961–1975*, New Delhi: Vikas Publishing House.

Tester, K. (ed.) (1994) *The Flâneur*, London: Routledge.

Thapan, M. (1991) *Life at School: An Ethnographic Study*, Delhi: Oxford University Press.

Torri, M. (1990) '"Westernised middle class", intellectuals and society in late colonial India', *Economic and Political Weekly* XXV (4): PE2–PE11.

Turner, B.S. (1996) *The Body and Society. Explorations in Social Theory*, London: Sage Publications.

Turner, G. (1994) *Making it National: Nationalism and Australian Popular Culture*, St Leonard's: Allen and Unwin.

Turner, V. (1967) *The Forest of Symbols: Aspects of Ndembu Ritual*, Ithaca, NY: Cornell University Press.

Uberoi, J.P.S. (1978) *Science and Culture*, Delhi: Oxford University Press.

Uberoi, P. (1995) 'Imagining the Family: An Ethnography of Viewing "Hum Aapke Hain koun. . .!', paper presented in the seminar on 'The consumption of popular culture in India', School of Oriental and African Studies, London, 19–21 June.

Vance, N. (1985) *The Sinews of the Spirit. The Ideal of Manliness in Victorian Literature and Religious Thought*, Cambridge: Cambridge University Press.

Vasudevan, R.S. (1995) 'Addressing the spectator of a "third world" national cinema: the Bombay "social" film of the 1940s and 1950s', *Screen* 36 (4): 305–24.

Veer, van der P. (1994) *Religious Nationalism: Hindus and Muslims in India*, Berkeley: University of California Press.

Verghese, B.G. (1965) *Design for Tomorrow. Emerging Contours of Indian Development*, Delhi: Sterling Publishers.

Verghese, K.E. (1976) *The Development and Significance of Transport in India*, New Delhi: NV Publications.

Verma, M. (1992) *Sansmaran* (Memoirs; in Hindi), New Delhi: Rajpal and Sons.

Vidyarthi, L.P. (1961) *The Sacred Complex in Hindu Gaya*, London: Asia Publishing House.

Virilio, P. (1986) *Speed and Politics: An Essay on Dromology*, New York: Columbia University Press.

Viswanathan, G. (1989) *Masks of Conquest: Literary Study and British Rule in India*, New York: Columbia University Press.

Viswanathan, S. (1988) 'On the annals of the laboratory state', in Nandy (ed.) *Science, Hegemony and Violence: A Requiem for Modernity*, Delhi: Oxford University Press.

White, H. (1992) *Tropics of Discourse: Essays in Cultural Criticism*, Baltimore: Johns Hopkins University Press.

Williams, R. (1975) *The Country and the City*, St Albans: Paladin.

Willis, P.E. (1977) *Learning to Labour. How Working Class Kids Get Working Class Jobs*, Westmead: Saxon House.

Yayawar, B. (1991) *Phanishwarnath Renu Arthat Mridangye Ka Marm* (*Memoirs and Critical Analysis of Renu*) (in Hindi), New Delhi: Wani Prakashan.

Young, M.F.D. (ed.) (1971) *Knowledge and Control: New Directions for the Sociology of Education*, London: Collier-Macmillan.

Index